GETTING BY IN HARD TIMES: GENDERED LABOUR AT HOME AND ON THE JOB

Getting By in Hard Times describes the experiences of working-class women and men during the period of 'economic restructuring' that began in the 1980s. Meg Luxton and June Corman examine the shift from a pattern where women were full-time housewives and men were income earners to one where women are increasingly income earners as well.

Based on a case study conducted from 1983 to 1996 of households where one person was employed at Stelco's manufacturing plant in Hamilton, Ontario, the book shows how working-class families make a living by combining paid employment and unpaid domestic labour. Four surveys and in-depth interviews were conducted in 1984, with follow-up interviews in 1994 and 1996. During this period of government cutbacks and increasing participation in the labour force by women, there was a loss of secure employment for men, as the steel plant cut its labour force by about two-thirds. Standards of living went down because of reduced incomes and the imposition of more unpaid work on the family household.

Getting By in Hard Times shows how growing insecurities undermined class politics while heating up gender, racial, and ethnic tensions. At the same time, people struggled to find ways of making their lives better. By focusing on the daily coping strategies of working-class women and men, this book gives a human face to Canada's changing gender, race, and class politics.

MEG LUXTON is Professor of Social Science and Women's Studies at Atkinson College, York University.

JUNE CORMAN is Professor of Sociology at Brock University.

Getting By in Hard Times

Gendered Labour at Home and on the Job

MEG LUXTON and JUNE CORMAN

UNIVERSITY OF TORONTO PRESS
Toronto Buffalo London

© University of Toronto Press Incorporated 2001
Toronto Buffalo London ·
Printed in Canada

ISBN: 0-8020-0783-X (cloth)
ISBN: 0-8020-7147-3 (paper)

Printed on acid-free paper

National Library of Canada Cataloguing in Publication Data

Luxton, Meg
    Getting by in hard times : gendered labour at home and on the job

    Includes bibliographical references and index.
    ISBN 0-8020-0783-X (bound)   ISBN 0-8020-7147-3 (pbk.)

    1. Iron and steel workers – Ontario – Hamilton – Attitudes.
    2. Working class – Ontario – Hamilton – Case studies.   3. Class
    consciousness – Ontario – Hamilton – Case studies.   4. Sex role –
    Ontario – Hamilton – Case studies.   I. Corman, June Shirley, 1952–
    II. Title.

    HD8039.I52C36 2001   305.5′62′0971352   C2001-900866-X

This book has been published with the help of a grant from the Humanities
and Social Sciences Federation of Canada, using funds provided by the Social
Sciences and Humanities Research Council of Canada.

The University of Toronto Press acknowledges the financial assistance to its
publishing program of the Canada Council for the Arts and the Ontario Arts
Council.

University of Toronto Press acknowledges the financial support for its publishing activities of the Government of Canada through the Book Publishing
Industry Development Program (BPIDP).

Contents

[handwritten annotation:] → Broad overview of ppl talking (and of fam but

Tables

Acknowledgments

This book is one result of a collaborative research project on two related studies – the Steelworkers Families Project and the Hamilton Families Project – both supported by research grants from the Social Sciences and Humanities Research Council of Canada. We appreciate their funding, which made our research possible. For over a decade we worked together with our co-investigators Wally Seccombe and David Livingstone on this project. We met regularly to develop the surveys and interviews, analyse the data, and develop our arguments. Their work has significantly shaped this book.

We also acknowledge the support and cooperation of United Steelworkers of America Local 1005 at Stelco's Hilton Works, in Hamilton, Ontario. The survey of Local 1005 members was approved by the union's executive, the steward's committee, and a general membership meeting in 1982. Various union members have been very helpful throughout this research project, explaining the operations of Hilton Works and discussing the experiences of workers employed there. We thank them all for their help, especially Alex Auchinvole and Chuck Emberson. Many members of Local 1005 and their spouses, as well as many members of the Hamilton general public, participated in our surveys, in-depth interviews, and numerous other discussions. Our deepest thanks go to the people who shared their insights and experiences in the course of the research. We regret that they must remain anonymous for reasons of confidentiality.

The sample surveys were administered by Social Data Research in Hamilton and the Institute for Social Research at York University in Toronto. Marshall Mangan, now at the Faculty of Education of the University of Western Ontario, performed Herculean feats of computer manipulation to produce the data files used in this project. The research by Anne Boyd in an unpublished paper on the Women Back Into Stelco campaign at McMaster University, and that by Denyse Rodrigues, 'The Relationship between Women's Employment Status and their Participation in Local Neighbourhoods: The Case of Hamilton Steelworker Households,' her Master's thesis in geography at York University, were very helpful.

Laszlo Gyongossy, Ester Reiter, and Rhona Shaw assisted in the first round of in-depth interviews. Elizabeth Asner conducted the first round of supplementary in-depth interviews in 1989 with middle-class women. Belinda Leach did follow-up interviews in 1994 as part of her own research and generously allowed us to use her material as part of this book.

Important technical and research assistance was also provided by Maggie Breau, Andrew Clement, Ann Gatensby, Joyce Hanley, Doug Hart, Naimh Hennessy, Clinton Kewley, Ellen Long, Jane Robinson, Matt Sanger, and other students from Brock, McMaster, OISE / University of Toronto, Trent, and York Universities including: Jan Campbell-Luxton, Janne Cleveland, Fataneh Farahani, Gail McCabe, Kim McIntyre, Erin Miller, Amrita Persaud, Michelle Webber, and Jen Woodill.

Numerous colleagues have commented either on the background work that lead up to this book or on this manuscript, including especially Joan Acker, Pat Armstrong, Doug Baer, John Bearn, Kate Bezanson, Marian Binkley, Judith Blackwell, Robert Brym, Val Burris, Paul Campbell, Bob Connell, Mike Donaldson, Wenona Giles, Alan Jeffrey, Jennifer Keck, Linzi Manicom, Heather Jon Maroney, Thelma McCormack, Haideh Moghissi, Mary O'Brien, Susan Prentice, Norene Pupo, Dorothy Smith, George Smith, Murray Smith, Pam Sugiman, Julian Tanner, and Eric Olin Wright.

The Feminism and Political Economy Network met over several years and read a draft of the manuscript at a crucial point; their comments were invaluable. Thank you, Sisters in Struggle: Sedef Arat-Koc, Kate Bezanson, Barbara Cameron, Alice de Wolff, Bonnie Fox, Marnina Gonick, Haideh Moghissi, Ester Reiter, Katherine Side, Pam Sugiman, and Leah Vosko.

Jane Springer, writer and editor extraordinaire, wrestled a difficult first draft into submission and helped us rework it into a viable manuscript. Mary Newberry did the index quickly and with impressive care. We also acknowledge the assistance of two anonymous reviewers.

Several colleagues and friends provided us with invaluable personal and intellectual support: Paul Campbell, Jan Campbell-Luxton, Michelle Campbell-Luxton, Anne Corman, Bobby Corman, Norma Corman, Alice de Wolff, Chris Duffy, Wenona Giles, Christine Ensslen, Daniel Ensslen, Harald Ensslen, Heather Jon Maroney, Patricia McDermott, Dennis Miner, Maureen Miner, Jim Petersen, Kathryn Petersen, Ester Reiter, Linnea Wehrstein Seccombe, Jane Springer, and Helena Wehrstein.

Some of the material in this book has been published in other forms, and we thank the following publishers and journals for granting permission to include it here: Fernwood, *Studies in Political Economy*, *Labour/Le Travail*, and Garamond. Elsevier Science granted permission to publish excerpts from Meg Luxton, 'The UN, Women, and Household Labour: Measuring and Valuing Unpaid Work,' *Women's Studies International Forum*, vol. 20, no. 3, 1997, pp. 431–9.

GETTING BY IN HARD TIMES: GENDERED LABOUR AT HOME AND ON THE JOB

1

A World Turned Upside Down: Working-Class Lives in Hamilton, 1980–1996

On a chilly Saturday in February 1996 over a hundred thousand people from across Ontario gathered in Hamilton in one of the largest protests ever held against a provincial government.[1] As they marched through the city streets past the convention centre where, the ruling Conservative party was holding a policy conference, their picket signs, buttons, and chants affirmed widespread opposition to government cutbacks to health care, education, welfare, and other social services.[2] The protesters attacked support for business and profits at the expense of commitments to equity: 'No to greed! Yes to sharing! Cut back profits, not the caring!' some of them shouted.

One of the marchers in the Hamilton Day of Action, a part-time shoe clerk, was trying to support her three children and her laid-off steelworker husband on her minimum wage job. She explained why for the first time ever she was marching in a political demonstration: 'I've never been political. I've never done anything like this before, but this government is going way too far. They are destroying our lives! My husband's always worked hard, and he's on lay-off. My brother-in-law died so my sister and her kids had to go on welfare and now it's been cut and they can't live on it. Her kids – my nieces and nephews – they're not getting enough food to eat! And I had to get a job and there's no decent child care for my kids and I don't know from one week to the next what hours I'll get or even how many. This government is turning perfectly ordinary people like me into protesters!' (303 F 1996)[3] Her husband, who was carrying a picket sign that called for 'Jobs and Justice,' added: 'I started at Stelco in 1978, before our oldest was born. In those days you knew that if you worked steady, you'd have a job and good wages and you could look after your family. If anyone had told me then I'd be laid off at 45 and depending on my wife to support our family, I'd have laughed in his face. But here I am. I feel like my world's turned upside down' (303 M 1996).

Elsewhere in the crowd, four women marched arm in arm, chanting enthusiastically:

> What do we want? Day Care! When do we want it? Now!
> What do we want? Equal Pay! When do we want it? Now!

Each had a sign pinned to her back that declared: 'I was part of the Women Back Into Stelco campaign. I was a steelworker and I got laid off. Jobs for all. Equal access and equal pay for women!' One of them explained: 'We were all part of the Women Back into Stelco campaign in the late 1970s. When we won, we were all hired on at Stelco, but when the lay-offs happened, well, you know what happens to women – last hired, first fired. We've all lost our jobs there. But, well, I guess one of the things I learned in the women's liberation movement was that if you get together and organize and protest, sometimes you can make things change. So it's hard times right now, but we're here and we are fighting back' (221 F 1996).

Another marcher, carrying a Steelworkers Local 1005 sign, explained that although he still had his job at Stelco, the changes of the previous decade had made his life difficult: 'Twenty-seven years I've put in there and I'm a good worker. But what used to be a good job has gone bad. And with all the changes this government's making, it's hard times now for people like me' (304 M 1996). Most of the people marching on the Hamilton streets that day were hoping for an end to the hard times. The shoe clerk captured the sentiment of many: 'I don't want to be a protester. I just want to have an ordinary life' (303 F 1996).

The Issues at Stake

As participants in the Days of Action, we share the concerns of our co-marchers regarding the dramatic political and economic changes of the 1980s and 1990s – forces known as 'economic restructuring,' 'globalization,' and 'the neo-liberal agenda,' or more colloquially, as lay-offs, cutbacks, and hard times (Cohen 1994; Bakker 1996).[4] Through widespread unemployment, wage cuts, reorganization of work, and an erosion of the social security system, these socioeconomic changes have reduced standards of living for many people.

To investigate the impact of these changes on working-class women and men, we interviewed people whose livelihoods depended on employment at Hilton Works, a steel-manufacturing plant owned by Stelco – the Steel Company of Canada – whose workers were members of the United Steelworkers of America (USWA), Local 1005. Our initial interviews took place in 1984, during a period of government restructuring, following several years of dramatic lay-offs at Stelco. We interviewed men who were hourly employees at Hilton Works, and their wives or partners, focusing on the daily lives of 'perfectly ordinary,' predominantly white, Anglo-Celtic, working-class women and men. We also interviewed women employed at Hilton Works, who had got their jobs as a result of the Women Back Into Stelco campaign, which in 1980 had reversed Stelco's male-biased hiring practices. Ten years later, in 1994, and again in 1996, we did follow-up interviews. The book studies white heterosexual working-class families and white women whose employment in 'men's jobs' challenged the gender divide basic to that family form.

This book addresses a series of questions about the connections among class and gender relations, family forms, labour markets, and the process of capital accumulation: between 1980 and 1996 these relationships were reconfigured in ways that threatened to turn working-class worlds upside down. Our first question is: What happened to these women and men, whose lives spanned four generations, in the period of restructuring? We argue that economic restructuring made it difficult to get by in hard times, even for those workers who had managed to hold on to well-paid industrial jobs, and for their families.

Second, what has happened to women's efforts to challenge their subordination by renegotiating divisions of labour and by gaining greater recognition of the worth of their labour, both in paid employment and in unpaid domestic labour? Although young women and men setting up new households are more likely than those of previous generations to insist that they will both do domestic labour (see Fox 1997), our study shows that women of all ages still do more domestic labour than their male partners. We argue that material conditions continue to make equitable sharing difficult, undermining the efforts of those who aspire to gender equity in the home. Despite important changes, labour force segregation and pay inequalities remain, and women retain primary responsibility for caregiving – for children, and for people who are ill, elderly or in other ways in need of special care. We show that women are bearing a disproportionate share of the cuts, and are working longer and for inadequate compensation, both at home and in the paid labour force. Women act as 'a reserve army' of unpaid labour, expanding and reducing their domestic labour in reaction to changing state and business practices.[5] Their work remains oppressive and undervalued (Elson 1992; Fraser 1997).

Third, how have these white working-class women and men, who were actively engaged in renegotiating gender relations and identities, tried to defend their class and race positions and their standards of living? We argue that neo-liberal restructuring has increased gender, race, and class inequalities and intensified the pressures on working-class people and their communities, leaving them more vulnerable both materially and politically. As they work longer hours at less secure jobs, their orientation to work and family increases, often at the expense of their involvement in, and orientation to, larger communities. As they defend their own standards of living, many of these white Anglo-Celtic people become more hostile to equity struggles by women, people of colour, immigrants, and other minorities. In defending their own privileges, they undercut the possibilities of alliances with others.

Like the shoe clerk and her husband, who were surprised to find themselves at a political demonstration, the majority of the people we interviewed considered themselves 'perfectly ordinary' and part of a Canadian cultural mainstream. We argue that for the most part, those workers who considered themselves as 'ordinary' citizens were not aware that being 'ordinary' and not 'the other' is a point of privilege.[6] That privilege is underscored by their sense that, until the mid-1990s, they had few reasons to publicly protest government policies. Being 'ordinary' obscured their particular racialized, ethnic, and class locations and the way their specific gender relations and family forms shaped their lives.

The Context of the Case Study

Our interest in this case study was sparked by the fact that in 1981 Hilton Works, one of the largest steel employers in Canada, had begun a drastic downsizing of its workforce and a major restructuring of work in its plant. Steelworkers, through their struggles over union recognition, pay, working conditions, and gender equity, have played an important role in the development of contemporary Canadian working-class culture. Their experiences reflect historic changes in family forms, divisions of labour, and gender relations, all of which have significantly shaped Canadian society.

The Development of a Contemporary Working Class in Hamilton

Hamilton with a population of about 300,000, is located at the western tip of Lake Ontario, on the Niagara escarpment. Part of the regional municipality of Hamilton-Wentworth, it forms the hub of an area that stretches southeast along the lake to Niagara Falls and northeast around the lake towards Toronto.[7] Stelco's thousand-acre plant dominates the Hamilton waterfront.

Originally Aboriginal land, in the early 1800s Hamilton developed as a major point of entry for settlers moving into southwestern Ontario and as a commercial and manufacturing centre. Founded by United Empire Loyalists, it was settled largely by people from the British Isles, and thus developed a predominantly Anglo-Celtic Canadian culture. During the first two decades of the twentieth century, Hamilton became one of Canada's major industrial cities – based on steel manufacturing at the Steel Company of Canada (Stelco), which was formed in 1910, and Dominion Foundries and Steel Corporation (Dofasco), which was founded in 1912 (Weaver 1982; Anderson 1987: 215–16).[8]

Class inequalities in Hamilton were sharp in this period. The financiers, merchants, and industrialists created spacious neighbourhoods on the edges of the Niagara escarpment, while crowded working-class communities grew up around the port and industrial areas. Workers protested low wages and poor working conditions early on, fostering a tradition of working-class militancy. At the same time, the city's spatial class divisions, created strong working-class communities and cultures (Heron 1988; Storey and Petersen 1987; Storey 1994).

Throughout the 1910s and 1920s, Hamilton's economy grew. As the heart of the Canadian steel industry, it came to be known as 'Steel City' (Dear, Drake, and Reeds 1987). Propelled by steel-based manufacturing such as farm machinery, elevators, and parts for automobiles and bridges, it developed a diverse economy with a university, medical centres, a range of commercial and service enterprises, and a textile and clothing industry that in 1931 provided 24 per cent of Hamilton's manufacturing jobs, many of them held by women.

Hamilton was particularly hard hit by the depression in the 1930s.[9] Many small industries went bankrupt; even Dofasco was threatened. In 1933 over 22 per cent of all families were on relief, and the city's population declined (Wood 1987: 130–1). The war years (1939–45), however, generated massive demands for steel products. By 1941, 74 per cent of all employed people in the city, were in the manufacturing sector, more than half of them in metalworking (Wood 1987: 132). In 1943 Stelco built a new blast furnace that was one of the largest in the world. With the high demand for labour, workers came to Hamilton from other parts of Canada, and the steel plants hired women to replace male workers who had joined the war effort. After the war almost all of these women were laid off, even though the steel plants were still expanding.

The long economic depression, and the subsequent sudden boom in the context of wartime restrictions, exacerbated existing class inequalities (Badcock 1984). Wealthier residents moved away from the deteriorating inner city to the older upper-class neighbourhoods at the base of the escarpment or to attractive new residential developments in the west end. In contrast, by 1945 most of the working class lived in districts that were classified as 'blighted' or, slums. A number of areas lacked running water and sewage, and many families shared housing in the centre and the north end. In 1950 many working-class people were still living in 'temporary' wartime housing, either barracks or small cottages (Wood 1987: 133–4). These class-based residential separations made visible the class differences between the financiers, merchants, and factory owners and the people who worked for them.

At the end of the war, the Canadian economy was still booming, while most working-class people lived in relative poverty. A wave of working-class struggles across the country demanded that capitalist employers and governments redistribute some of the country's wealth to working people. One result of these struggles was the development of the postwar welfare state, often called the Keynesian welfare state after its principal architect, economist John Maynard Keynes. As Linda McQuaig (1998: 256) notes: 'Out of the experience of the Depression and the Second World War emerged a radically different approach. Under the influence of John Maynard Keynes and others, the top priority of government was to be full employment and the betterment of living conditions for the population at large. These goals were to take precedence over the rights of finance capital. This priority given to the economic rights of the general population was to be protected through a new international financial system, worked out at Bretton Woods, which placed limits on the mobility of capital.'

The Canadian government, like many governments in advanced capitalist countries, responded to workers' demands by imposing certain investment restraints on capitalists and corporations. The limited postwar welfare state that developed in Canada compensated working people, in part, for the inadequacies of the private wage system by intro-

ducing programs such as unemployment insurance and family allow-
ances. It also subsidized employers' labour costs, by funding the long-
term reproduction of the labour force through, for example, education
and training. The increased development of state-funded infrastruc-
tures such as roads and transportation systems encouraged industrial
development and also improved living conditions generally.

At the heart of postwar state policies was an affirmation that the state
was both 'fundamentally necessary for ensuring the economic security
and internal stability of the Canadian family' and committed to promoting heterosexual nuclear families where men were income earners and
women were homemakers (Golz 1993: 12). Much of this government
support for working-class families was intended both to produce growing markets for consumer goods, by increasing working-class buying
power, and to reduce labour militancy and working-class protest movements. However, even these minimal concessions did improve the living
standards of many working people (Ursel 1992).

Labour–management relations in Hamilton's steel companies shaped
class politics throughout the city, and played an important part in developing Canada's welfare state policies. The early labour policies and
practices of the two big steel companies, Stelco and Dofasco, were generally paternalistic but Stelco's harsher version led to the emergence of
a militant union at Hilton Works (Storey 1981a, 1981b; Roberts 1981;
Freeman 1982; Kervin et al. 1984). Workers' struggles at Hilton Works
to form a union and curb management domination, culminating in a
bitter strike in 1946, were of pivotal importance in consolidating industrial unionism in Canada (Heron 1988) and led to the formation of
Local 1005 of the United Steelworkers of America (Kilbourn 1960).[10]

During the postwar boom, USWA Local 1005 at Hilton Works, one of
the biggest union locals in Canada, was a national leader in winning better wages and working conditions. Its successes laid a basis for the
demands of other unionized industrial workers and were instrumental
in 'setting industrial relations in Canada on a completely new footing'
(Heron and Storey 1986: 231). Hilton Works was a classic case of the
capital–labour accord: workers accepted managerial prerogatives and
productivity norms in exchange for increasing wages and job security.[11]
Still, struggles between Stelco management and union activists over specific wage and working conditions were often contentious, for example,
sparking a wildcat strike in 1966 and another strike in 1969 (Livingstone
1996). Thus, Local 1005 gained its reputation as one of the most militant union locals in the country.

In contrast, Dofasco managed to avoid unionization and to maintain a 'family image.' The Sherman family, which founded Dofasco, remained active in the company and used a management approach that stressed employee participation, including, for example a profit-sharing program, what is claimed to be the world's largest annual Christmas party, and financial support for extensive community recreational facilities. More importantly, Dofasco management matched every wage settlement at Stelco (Storey 1981a, 1994). By setting standards of living for a significant layer of the Hamilton working class, the contracts negotiated by Local 1005 and Stelco management made Hamilton a fairly prosperous city. With the two big steel firms dominating the economy, and limiting civic politics, Hamilton was dubbed 'Canada's largest company town' (Weaver 1982: 161, 166; Freeman and Hewitt 1979). What happened in the steel mills affected the whole city and reverberated throughout the country.

In this postwar period (1945–80), as southern Ontario's economy expanded and changed, Hamilton grew rapidly, from having a population of 196,000 in 1950 to 297,000 in 1970 – an increase of 51 per cent in twenty years. However, textile and clothing industries, which earlier had employed many women, declined in the postwar period; by 1961 they provided only 3 per cent of all Hamilton's manufacturing jobs. In their place, the heavy industries expanded. Steel manufacturing boomed during the postwar period. Between 1945 and 1960 Dofasco quadrupled its output. Stelco doubled its output between 1950 and 1962. Dominated by the two major steel companies, Hamilton was the undisputed capital of the Canadian steel industry, producing over half of the country's postwar steel.[12]

These conditions attracted many new European immigrants. Between 1951 and 1971 people from Italy, Germany, the Netherlands, and Poland increased the ethnic diversity of the city (Badenhorst 1987: 18). The various ethnic groups tended not to mix. As Harold Wood observes (1987: 134): 'The growing residential separation of different income groups was accompanied to some extent by a segregation based on country of origin as migrants from places other than the United Kingdom tended to form their own neighbourhoods. Thus the working-class parts of town began to be divided by language, and to some extent by religion, into a number of fairly distinct and visibly identifiable ethnic districts.'

Stelco management's hiring practices over the years were systemically racist and sexist. The Brantford Six Nations Reserve is nearby and there has been a black population in Hamilton since the early twentieth century, yet very few Aboriginals, Blacks, other visible minorities, or francophones were hired on.[13] Some European immigrants were hired, and at least during their first years, were considered by their co-workers to be 'foreigners' or 'others;' but their numbers remained relatively small, overwhelmed by the mass of workers of British and Irish descent. Stelco had hired women in response to the labour shortages of the war, and it continued to hire a few women until 1961, although by then any women in the plant were employed in one particular worksite, the tin mill. Between 1961 and 1978 Stelco hired no women at all, even though during those seventeen years about 30,000 of the applications for jobs at Stelco were from women (Luxton and Corman 1991).[14]

This selective hiring created a very specific layer of the working class – typically English-speaking, racially and ethnically white, Anglo-Celtic Canadian men, whose union militancy and willingness to tolerate the working conditions at Stelco ensured them a comparatively high wage and good benefits.

Hamilton's economy continued to expand into the early 1970s when over 600 industries operated in the city. The steel industry represented more than 60 per cent of Canada's steel production (City of Hamilton 1970). The growing economy facilitated the increased participation of women in the paid labour force, although not in heavy industry and especially not in the steel plants. The various small manufacturing plants and commercial and service enterprises hired women, so that Hamilton's overall female labour force participation rates were slightly higher than those for most of the rest of Canada. However, the major manufacturing industries in Hamilton, such as the large steel plants, tended to hire men over women more often than comparable plants in other parts of Canada (Pollard 1989: 379). As a result, although women's overall labour force rates in Hamilton were higher than the national average, their participation in manufacturing was disproportionately lower.

The types of jobs available to women and the practice of paying women less than men meant that few women in Hamilton earned enough to support themselves and children and/or a spouse. In contrast, men working in Hamilton's manufacturing plants earned comparatively high wages. Both the organization of work in heavy industry, and the welfare state policies that complemented it, were based on a specific gender order that assumed that men as income earners should make a 'family wage' – enough to support a wife and children, and women would remain out of the labour force to provide unpaid domestic labour for their husbands and children (Evans 1997). The Hamilton economy created an auspicious climate for the formation of families based on a gendered division of labour, where men were income earners and women were primarily responsible for domestic labour.

Fuelled by the postwar boom, new housing developments were built 'on the mountain' (the top of the escarpment) and, with new and improved roads, in the smaller nearby communities such as Grimsby, Stoney Creek, and Flamborough. Far away from the steel plants and the run-down, crowded conditions of the centre of the city, these districts offered postwar working-class families new, single-family dwellings on suburban lots. Large shopping centres and local services spread across the city, generating more employment, especially for women in clerical, sales, and service jobs.

In the 1970s Hamilton's growth slowed, expanding at only two-thirds the rate of Ontario and half that of Canada. The growth rate of Hamilton's labour force was less than half that of the province. Rather than developing a more diversified economy, Hamilton became even more dependent on steel, because the steel industry remained strong and hiring continued at Stelco, Dofasco, and other steel plants in the city. Primary metals was the fastest growing employment sector, increasing by over 20 per cent to constitute more than 40 per cent of manufacturing employment and about 20 per cent of total employment. By 1980 primary metals production increased to nearly half of the total value of shipments and value added in the Hamilton region (Webber 1986: 204–12).

Hamilton's labour market by 1980 was still heavily weighted towards manufacturing and was unique in the province. A far smaller proportion of manufacturing employees were women than in the province overall (14.6 per cent of Hamilton's production workers and 25.1 per cent of its administrative workers, compared with 23.3 per cent and 29.9 per cent for Ontario). Manufacturing employees were 80 per cent production workers, compared with 72 per cent for Ontario as a whole. Hamilton workers were relatively well paid as production workers; on average they earned nearly 90 cents per hour more than the average provincial worker (Webber and Fincher 1987: 240). Prospects for Hamilton steel and for the city's economy were generally seen to be rosy. In this context, a group of women, with the support of Local 1005, launched a campaign which, by 1980, forced Stelco to hire women. Pointing to Stelco's growing profits, Local 1005 went on strike in 1981 demanding pay increases.

By the early 1980s the City of Hamilton had a population of 306,000, while the population of the region of Hamilton-Wentworth was 410,000 (City of Hamilton 1980: 5; Statistics Canada 1985). The municipal government boasted about a range of new government, commercial, and service enterprises, as well as new amenities such as a farmers' market, a library, a coliseum, as well as theatres and parks. It also stressed that 'Hamilton's economy is solidly based on the steel industry. Over 60% of Canada's steel output is produced by Stelco and Dofasco, which have their home in Hamilton and which employ over 28,000 people ... Secondary manufacturing in Hamilton benefits from the stability and continued growth in the steel industry and promises faster growth in terms of employment and sales' (City of Hamilton 1980: 15).

Thus, in the period between the late 1940s and 1980, the development of the major manufacturing industries in Hamilton, and particularly their hiring and employment practices, combined with the organizing initiatives of their workforces, produced a very distinctive working-class population. The long postwar economic boom and union struggles had enabled steelworkers at Hilton Works, like other unionized industrial workers, to win a standard of living higher than that accessible to previous generations of workers and their families. Their specific work and family arrangements were widely accepted as a cultural ideal, confirming their sense of themselves as part of a cultural mainstream. Analysing Canadian society in this period, John Porter (1961) observed that as the sharp, visible distinctions of class blurred most people in Canada came to see themselves as middle class. Class divisions were reconceived as rankings in social status based primarily on wealth (Livingstone and Mangan 1996a: 1; Leach 1997). Referring to steelworkers at Hilton Works, Belinda Leach argues: 'These particular workers were among the very few in Canada, who have, more or less, lived out the promise of the Keynesian welfare state ... the hegemonic strategies of the state were most effective in this kind of community, constituting reliable workers with steady jobs, law abiding subjects and good consumers' (1998: 192).

A Period of Restructuring, 1980–1996

The period beginning in the early 1980s and continuing through to 1996 was one of dramatic change in Canada, as patterns of international capital investment and government policies of globalization and economic restructuring significantly altered the social and economic terrain. In the early 1980s, governments and business interests began a process of restructuring that radically transformed the way of life that had developed for working people in the previous period (from the late 1940s to the late 1970s). Between 1980 and 1996 the political elites, wealthy capitalists, and their associates, such as chief executive officers (CEOs) and bond raters, orchestrated an attack on the system of social welfare that had developed since the 1950s and which was based on regulating the capitalist market and taxing capital. Marjorie Cohen describes the shift as one from a period in which 'the deep contradictions in capitalism were modified by a system of social welfare based on the assumption that the well-being of the economy depended on the well-being of the people in it' to a situation in which 'social and economic well-being for people is subordinate to the well-being of the corporate sector' (1997: 5).

Governments pursued neo-liberal economic policies involving three related strategies, all of which favoured capitalist elites at the expense of the majority of people. As part of trade liberalization, through measures such as the North American Free Trade Agreement (NAFTA), governments eroded the controls on private corporations that regulated labour relations, working conditions, and environmental protections, thereby increasingly freeing capitalist enterprises from responsibilities for the local economy or society (Boyer and Drache 1996). They implemented monetarist policies, targeting inflation rather than unemployment, ensuring an advantageous economic climate for investors in pursuit of capital accumulation or profits while unemployment increased. In so doing, they created a growing national debt (Cohen 1997). Using the debt as justification, they cut social programs, including health care, education, unemployment insurance, family allowance, and pensions, all of which provide people with a basic standard of living regardless of their individual wealth (McQuaig 1995).

Dramatic changes in the labour force demonstrated the impact of these changes on working people. The most serious recession in Canada since the depression of the 1930s began in 1981–2: between 1981 and 1984 approximately one million workers lost full-time jobs and were not recalled (Picot and Wannell 1987: 90). By 1986 these people had an unemployment rate of about 25 per cent, more than twice the national average. Those who did get new jobs took an average of about six months to find them, and 45 per cent of these people suffered 'pay cuts which left them earning an average of 28 percent less than they did in their old jobs' (Picot and Wannell 1987: 124).

The goods-producing sector was severely hit. Between 1981 and 1982 employment in this sector decreased by 9 per cent. In Canada 141,000 manufacturing jobs disappeared between 1981 and 1985, and employment in primary industries and construction also declined. In contrast, employment in the service sector continued to increase and by 1985 accounted for 70.4 per cent of total employment (Moloney 1986: 92).

Fewer people were able to support themselves and their families with 'good' jobs in primary industries such as manufacturing and construction that were typically full-time and full-year, paid living wages and benefits, and were often unionized, giving workers certain protections. Instead, more people had to rely on service sector jobs, which were often part-time, low paid, and with few benefits; many of them were not unionized (Akyeampong 1986: 148).

The attack on welfare state provisions had a disproportionate impact on women. As Shelagh Day and Gwen Brodsky (1998: 1) point out 'For women, who are poorer than men, more vulnerable to domestic violence, and more likely to be caregivers for children and older people, the diminished commitment to social programs and services, and to national standards, has significant immediate and long-term consequences. For single mothers, elderly women, Aboriginal women, immigrant women, women of colour and women with disabilities – who are among the very poorest Canadians – the impact is more drastic.' These changes placed enormous pressure on public and private sector enterprises to restructure. In the public sector, hospitals, schools, and social service agencies cut staff, increased workloads for the remaining employees, and in some places, closed facilities or eliminated services altogether. Between the late 1980s and mid-1996, about 470,000 federal and provincial government jobs were eliminated (Breaton 1998: 15). In the private sector, firms replaced older, less-efficient plant and production technologies to shorten production cycles and lower per-unit costs. They did so in two ways: by renovating existing facilities, replacing outmoded machinery with newer technologies, reorganizing production, and downsizing existing workforces in the process; and by circumventing or bypassing older plants (shutting them down, or leaving them to wither and die) and setting up new, state-of-the-art facilities at 'green-field' sites.[15]

Steel companies internationally had been exercising both options since the 1970s, when the steel industry entered the recession. To remain profitable, steelmakers in advanced capitalist countries with older steel plants resorted to 'mothballing,' closures, and mergers of plants. They also developed many lighter, stronger, and more durable products, both to retain traditional markets, such as the automobile market, and to enter new markets, such as residential housing. Companies also implemented a variety of technologies, many computer-based, aimed at increasing efficiency and steel quality, including continuous casting, and mini-mills.[16] These changes led to dramatic increases in productivity and reductions in operating costs. The number of worker hours needed to produce a ton of steel in the United States was cut from eleven in 1982 to six in 1988 and fewer than three in the mid-1990s, with labour costs coming down to about 20 per cent of the sales dollar (Hicks 1985; McManus 1988: 52). Steelworkers around the world became vulnerable to global restructuring.

Hamilton went through major changes, driven primarily by massive restructuring in the international steel industry that reverberated through the local region (Corman et al. 1993). The region lost 17,060 high-paid manufacturing jobs betwen 1981 and 1991 (SPRC 1993). In 1995 the Economic Development Department of the City of Hamilton reported:

> Over a period of ten years, the economy of Hamilton-Wentworth has undergone considerable restructuring through downsizing, expansion and diversification of various business sectors. Traditionally known as a steel centre, the Region has changed considerably. Today, over 50% of the employment base is engaged in health care industries, environmental services and education. Steel and steel related industries account for 24.1% of the Region's employed. As well, significant contributions have been made in the areas of printing and publishing, food and beverage processing, transportation equipment, environmental research and technologies, textile and electrical machinery. (Desoer 1995: n.p.)

Typical of, and central, to this restructuring was what happened at Stelco. Its postwar history of continual growth of capital, steel production, and employment came to an abrupt end in 1981. The beginning of a recession reduced domestic demand for steel at the same time as Stelco's markets were being seriously threatened, especially by underpriced European and low-cost Third World steel. Just prior to the downward spiral in demand for steel, Local 1005 went on strike demanding pay increases. The 1981 strike at Hilton Works and the economic recession of 1982 marked a turning point in both the history of the Hamilton steel industry and its centrality in the local economy, as Canadian steelmakers incurred their first major aggregate financial loss.[17] Production fell to only 55 per cent of its capacity (Verma, Frost, and Warrian 1995). Canadian steel executives started to talk about restructuring: 'Everything we are doing is directed toward reducing costs. Unless you can really slash costs, you aren't going to be in business one of these days. You must find ways to make more efficient use of energy, more efficient use of materials, more efficient use of labour and facilities. Nobody is talking about building more facilities or more capacity these days ... The ultimate challenge is greater productivity and higher quality at lower cost.'[18] Between 1980 and 1996 the Canadian steel industry eliminated about 29,000 jobs (Statistics Canada 1996a: 46).

From 1981 to 1983 Stelco's net worth dropped steadily, and Stelco management responded with new capital investment, labour restructuring, and by repositioning itself in the steel market. At the heart of this was a massive job reduction.[19] Local 1005 lost over 60 per cent of its 1980 membership by 1993. By 1996 Hilton Works had eliminated about 8,000 jobs; Local 1005 membership stabilized at 5,000 members (Livingstone 1996).

While the cutbacks at Stelco were the most dramatic, they were part of a larger pattern in Hamilton. Between May 1981 and January 1983 the city lost a quarter of its manufacturing jobs (Webber and Fincher 1987). By 1983 the pre-strike steel labour force in Hamilton had been reduced by about 30 per cent (from 29,000 to 21,000). Thousands of workers lost their jobs as numerous companies closed down (Houser 1988: 5). Thousands more retained their jobs but endured pay cuts, more unpredictable schedules, and greater insecurity. The crisis of the 1980s made employment prospects disproportionately worse for women and wiped out the gains they had made getting hired in heavy industry. Employment levels between 1981 and 1983 for women in industry dropped by 9,100 jobs, a decrease of 25 per cent in two years, compared with a loss of 8,400 jobs for men, a decrease of 9 per cent (Csiernik and Cain 1985). Between 1980 and 1996 unemployment rates in Hamilton, like in Ontario, were 6–7 per cent, except in 1981–5 and 1991–3, when in Hamilton they rose to over 10 per cent (Badenhorst 1987: 58; Human Resources Development Canada 1998a: 1).

By 1996, reflecting patterns typical across North America, Stelco and other manufacturers were doing very well once again, but the labour market in the Hamilton area had changed significantly. Hamilton still produced 40 per cent of Canada's steel, but the industry had reduced its labour force by 50 per cent since 1980.[20] Stelco and Dofasco continued to be the largest single employers, but together both steel companies employed only about 14,000 people in Hamilton in 1995, about 7 per cent of the regional workforce (Macrury 1996). The high rates of unemployment of previous years had declined, but the types of jobs available were less in manufacturing and more in health care, environmental services, and education. For example, the percentage of the labour force in manufacturing and construction dropped steadily from a high of 58 per cent in 1951 to a low of 31 per cent in 1995 (Badenhorst 1987: 61; Desoer 1995). The available jobs were far less likely to offer the relatively high wages, benefits, and protections that unions had won for workers in heavy manufacturing. Unemployment and insecurity haunted the steel-making workforce. Hamilton's working people faced more precarious employment, with less predictable schedules, lower pay, and fewer benefits.

In contrast, the top six Canadian banks made their highest profits ever.[21] CEO pay rates skyrocketed; the salary of Stelco's chief executive James Alfano increased by 254 per cent from 1996 to 1997![22] A steelworker presented his view of this trend: 'The free capitalist system is extremely popular right now. But to me it is extremely unfair because I think that over a period of years that we are producing a complete society of haves and have-nots. That's what I believe we are beginning to see now because of the "free market"' (075 M 1994).

By the mid-1990s Hamilton's 'steelworkers and their families [were] facing unprecedented change in major areas of their lives and social identities' (Leach 1998: 182). It was in this context that in 1996 thousands of people in Hamilton took to the streets in the February Day of Action, protesting the impact of economic restructuring, the increase in inequalities between working people and the wealthy financiers, merchants, and industrialists, the harsh cuts to social services, and rollbacks of government regulations protecting working people. The day itself was one moment in a larger effort to defend the working conditions and living standards of working-class women and men. For those who remembered the appalling conditions working-class people suffered in the early part of the twentieth century, the fight had a particular poignancy. For those who had come of age in the period of postwar prosperity, the changing economic and political climate threatened to turn their world upside down. And so 'perfectly ordinary' people took to the streets.

The Study

This book is part of a larger study of the impact of restructuring on gender, class, work, and family life in Hamilton, Ontario, conducted between 1980 and 1996 (details of the study are included in Appendix A). Because we wanted to study nuclear family dynamics, the first stage of the study involved a 1984 survey of 187 cohabiting couples. One person in each couple was an hourly worker at Stelco's Hilton Works plant (185 men and two women and their partners). These people were randomly selected from the membership list of the United Steelworkers of America, Local 1005, the union at Hilton Works. Interviewing each person individually, we asked extensive questions about their paid work, domestic labour, and community experiences, as well as their responses to a wide array of social issues. Over the next year, we did in-depth open-ended interviews with individuals from forty-four of those households, exploring their responses to the survey questions in more detail. Specific people were selected to represent variations in women's and men's work status, family phase, and positions on social issues. The people who participated in the in-depth interviews were also asked to complete a time diary. This asked them to record everything they did, how long it took, and whom they were with when they did it, in one twenty-four-hour period. Ten years later, in 1994, in collaboration with Dr Belinda Leach, we did further in-depth interviews with thirty people (Leach 1997, 1998).

In 1984 we interviewed a total of twenty-six women steelworkers to explore the ramifications of the 1979–80 Women Back Into Stelco campaign (Luxton and Corman 1991; Livingstone and Luxton 1989). We also wanted to investigate their experiences of paid work, domestic labour, and community participation and their attitudes about social issues. In 1996 we interviewed five of them again, asking them what had happened to them in the intervening years and inviting them to reassess their experiences with the hindsight of more than a decade.

The majority of the steelworkers we interviewed in 1984 had survived the initial cuts although almost half (47 per cent) had received at least one lay-off notice. Most were either retired or still employed by Stelco in the 1990s. To investigate the impact of unemployment on daily life, we interviewed 234 laid-off steelworkers in 1984 (Corman 1993).

The United Steelworkers of America Local 1005 gave us access to their members and supported the project from the outset. Several members of the union worked with us throughout the study, helping us understand their industry, the massive changes it underwent, and its impact on the lives of its workers. They gave us formal interviews several times throughout the study and offered innumerable informal assessments. Finally, in 1996 we interviewed a number of former steelworkers

and several of their partners who were participating in the Hamilton
Days of Action.

When we refer directly to any of the in-depth interviews in this text,
we follow the quotation with an identification number. Where we interviewed two people from the same household, they have the same identification number. We indicate whether the speaker was a woman (F,
female) or a man (M, male) and the year of the interview.[23]

The People in the Study

One focus of the book is on the 185 male steelworkers and their wives or
partners. All of the statistical analyses refer to the 1984 interviews with
these couples. For this part of the study, we selected people who lived
together as couples. Almost all of them had children (85 per cent);
73 per cent had children living at home, and most lived as nuclear families; just a few lived with other people as well. The men ranged in age
from twenty-two to sixty-five years; the median age was thirty-seven.
Women were on average about two years younger than their partners.
They ranged in age from nineteen to sixty-four; the median age was
thirty-five. While their educational levels varied, the majority had
attended or completed high school.[24]

These people had a lot in common. Most belonged to the white majority common to both Hilton Works and the city of Hamilton. Forty-five per
cent of men and 44 per cent of women described themselves as 'just
Canadian.' A further 29 per cent of men and 25 per cent of women identified closely with the United Kingdom. There were two people who
called themselves 'Aboriginal,' and four people who were 'Asian.' The
majority of both men and women were born in Canada. English was the
first language for three-quarters of them. There was considerable intra-
ethnic marriage: 54 per cent of people born in countries other than Canada or the United States were married to someone born in the same
country as they were. Among Canadian-born men, 87 per cent were married to women born in Canada; 91 per cent of Canadian-born women
were married to Canadian-born men. This marriage pattern reinforced
ethnic homogeneity. Almost all of them also identified themselves as
Christians, and a majority reported attending church. Table 1.1 shows
their educational attainment, country of birth, and religious affiliation.

We also focus on twenty-six women steelworkers, who provide an illu-
minating contrast to the nuclear families where the men were Stelco
workers. Only seven were married or living with common-law partners;

TABLE 1.1
Educational attainment, country of birth, religion, and church
attendance for women and men

	Women (%)	Men (%)
Educational attainment		
Elementary	17	18
Some high school	30	31
Completed high school	32	35
Community college	15	13
Some university	5	3
Country of birth		
Canada	66	69
Britain and Ireland	14	8
Mediterranean	7	8
Eastern Europe	5	8
Northern Europe	5	4
United States	0	1
Asia	1	1
Latin America	1	0
Religion		
None	7	10
Protestant	59	55
Catholic	31	30
Other	4	5
Church attendance		
Never	26	33
Few times a year	32	34
Regularly	42	35

three were divorced; sixteen were single. Ten were sole-support parents of young children. Five were living with their parents and other siblings; three were living in collective households with several adults and children. One identified herself as a lesbian. They ranged in age from twenty-two to sixty-two; the median age was thirty-two. Their educational levels ranged from Grade 8 to Bachelor's degrees. All were white. All but two were born in Canada, and all but four identified themselves as Canadians; the others were Québécoise, Irish/Scottish, Italian, and Yugoslav. Religion was not relevant for any but one practising Roman Catholic.

Eight of these women had been activists in the Women Back Into Stelco campaign, four of them motivated by their prior political commitment to socialism and women's liberation. As members of the Marxist organization, the Revolutionary Workers' League, these four shared a radical left-wing political analysis that advocated political and economic organizing by working-class women and men to overthrow the power of private capital, in order to establish a society based on collective ownership of all resources.[25] They were also activists in the women's liberation movement, a radical grassroots current within the larger feminist movement.[26] This political perspective informed the strategy of these four activists and their analysis of what happened to them.

The majority of the people we interviewed had lived in Hamilton for most of their adult lives; many had grown up there. Over years of growing up and going to school in local neighbourhoods, and working and living in the city as adults, they had ties with kin and friends throughout the area. Although their households were scattered throughout the Hamilton region, from Grimsby and Stoney Creek to Burlington, most were clustered in several distinctly working-class neighbourhoods. A woman steelworker whose father was a steelworker described growing up in the 1970s in the east end: 'I didn't live on the mountain. I came from a house with three bedrooms, ten kids, four beds, six girls in a bed. So you didn't grow up with a lot of lavish. Your biggest luxury was an apple' (213 F 1984). The majority lived near other steelworkers; more than half of the women steelworkers had close relatives who worked at Stelco.

Many of the couples had lived in their neighbourhood for lengthy periods – the mean was eight years – and they knew many of their neighbours. Half of them reported knowing at least nine of their neighbours by name, and more than half said that they felt part of their neighbourhood.

Our Theoretical Framework

Deconstructing Ordinary: Race, Class, and Gender

Most of the people we interviewed, except those who were part of a visible minority, considered themselves part of the cultural mainstream. A white Canadian man viewed issues of ethnic conflict in Canada as irrelevant to his own experiences: 'If I ever read of areas of conflict, I don't think it would ever have anything to do with me. I read all that [about ethnic conflict]. But I don't see any connection with my life' (015 M 1994).

In contrast, a white woman steelworker described how a talk with one of the few black men in the plant led to a moment of realization about the links between racism and sexism: 'This black guy came in and says "I want to talk to you." He says, "You may not know this, but me and you have a lot in common." I look at this Black guy, this burly guy. How the hell do we have anything in common? And he says, "Prejudice will follow you everywhere you go. I have been battling prejudice for twenty-five years. The only way you beat them, is you've got to be smarter"' (213 F 1984). She reflected on the difficulties of being a member of a minority in the workplace: 'For a coloured man to start at Stelco, it was almost as bad as if you were Italian. My dad went through that and I guess I understood what he meant. They probably didn't get it as much, because they were Italian, as being Black. The Italians, we were just like the crud of the earth compared to, with, you know. They all thought that Polish were downgraded too' (213 F 1984).

Part of the dynamic of racism is that the dominant group escapes being identified as racialized by appearing as 'the norm'; its identity is unproblematic (Frankenberg 1993). Race and racialization are usually associated with the subordinate groups who experience discrimination and oppression. As a result, studies of racism in Canada have, for the most part, focused on those groups that are not 'white' – Aboriginal peoples, Blacks, people of colour, and members of visible minorities. White people are also racialized, but in ways that give them privileges.

Historically founded through imperialist conquest, Canada developed, as a colonial settler society, a white mainstream Anglo-Celtic Canadian culture.[27] 'White' refers to the European immigrants who settled in Canada, where eventually their distinct ethnic heritages were assimilated and blended (without ever entirely disappearing) into a cultural mainstream. This white identity was constructed as a collectivity by differentiating such people from those identified as non-white – Aboriginal, African, or Asian peoples, for example. Stuart Hall (1980: 338) describes processes of racialization, starting with:

> the concrete historical 'work' which racism accomplishes under specific historical conditions – as a set of economic, political and ideological practices, of a distinctive kind, concretely articulated with other practices in a social formation. These practices ascribe the positioning of different social groups in relation to one another with respect to the elementary structures of society; they fix and ascribe those positionings in on-going social practices; they legitimate the positions as ascribed. In short, they are

practices which secure the hegemony of a dominant group over a series of subordinate ones, in such a way as to dominate the whole social formation in a form favourable to the long-term development of the economic productive base.

In this book, 'Anglo-Celtic Canadian' refers to an ethnicity based on a national origin, a shared cultural heritage, and usually a common language, English, from Britain (England, Scotland, Wales) and Ireland, which is differentiated from Aboriginal peoples, francophones, and non-anglophone immigrants.[28] Only the minority who did not share this background articulated a clear sense of themselves as people with racialized, ethnic or linguistic identities as, for example, Black, Asian, Italian, or francophone. For the majority, because their racialized, linguistic, and ethnic identity was emblematic of the cultural mainstream and therefore unproblematic for them, it was largely invisible and rarely an issue in their daily lives.

In the interviews, we asked people to identify what social classes existed and then to locate themselves in that scheme. Over 90 per cent of them said that social classes existed in Canada. The majority, drawing on dominant liberal discourses of social status, identified a three-part system, and located themselves in the middle. A steelworker elaborated: 'I think the majority of people are middle class. There are poor people – some by choice, some because they don't have any choice. Then there's upper class, quite a few rich people. They are different people, people with money' (151 M 1984).

Dominant liberal discourses in Canada describe a society divided into three classes based on socioeconomic status differentiated by degrees of wealth and access to standards of living. 'Upper class' refers to the very wealthy, and 'lower class' refers to those who are poor or dependent on state welfare payments. In contrast, the vast majority who have to work for a living are considered 'middle class.' In this model there are no inherent conflicts of interests or class antagonisms. Instead, there is simply a continuum from poor to rich and differences among people are readily explained by their individual initiative – the harder you work the better off you will be.

A majority of those interviewed shared this perspective, which combined a recognition that they worked for their living with an appreciation that their standard of living was comfortable. Another male steelworker explained: 'I would say most of us working at Stelco are middle class, simply because we're making a decent wage down there now.

We got a little bit of security and pretty near everybody down there is either involved in a mortgage or owning their own home, stuff like that. So I would say it's middle class' (029 M 1994).

This discourse articulated very real experiences for most people, yet it was challenged by the experiences of wage labour. Drawing on the long history of Marxist, socialist, and trade union political discourses, many people also identified themselves as working class. Marxist theories see class in political and economic terms. Where people are located in the property relations affects all aspects of their lives and the way they understand their experiences. Erik Olin Wright (1997: 30) elaborates this perspective: 'Ownership of the means of production and ownership of one's own labor power are explanatory of social action because these property rights shape the strategic alternatives people face in pursuing their material well-being. What people have imposes constraints on what they can do to get what they want.' Marxist theories argue that the extent to which people own and control both the means of production and their own labour power locates them in a class structure. Those who own and control the means of production form the capitalist class. Those who do not own any means of production must sell their labour power to others for a wage. They form the working class. These relations are inherently conflictual; owners want to ensure maximum profits, while workers want to earn as much as possible.

A former steelworker expressed this perspective looking at Hilton Works at night – a thousand acres of buildings with sparkling windows, where red and gold flames cut through the darkness and smoke plumes fly skyward: 'From here it looks so beautiful, almost like a jewelry box. But I know those fires are deadly and the smoke is pollution. It's a bit like what working there was like. Really enticing – the pay and benefits and that great feeling of being important – I'm a steelworker. But beneath all that dazzle, it was just bloody hard work so I could make what was considered to be a "decent living" so other people, who sure don't have to work here, can get rich' (223 F 1996).

The class structure of any advanced capitalist society is, of course, more complicated. It includes not only the bourgeoisie or corporate capitalists, but also small-scale employers and landlord or rentier capitalists, as well as managers and a petty bourgeoisie of self-employed people (Livingstone and Mangan 1996b; Clement and Myles 1994). It includes both workers employed by private enterprises and those working for the state sector. It includes not only the traditional proletariat of manual workers, but also service workers. There are intermediate strata of salaried employees, such as managers, supervisors, and professional employees, who have substantial authority over other workers or the design of their own work. Many others are outside the employed work-force for periods of time – homemakers, students, and pensioners, and those who are unemployed and looking for jobs. There are also the peo-ple who support themselves by more marginal or illicit forms of subsis-tence such as prostitution, panhandling, or crime.

When we asked people to locate themselves in a predetermined selec-tion of class categories; lower class, working class, middle class, upper middle class or upper class, 46 per cent of women and 44 per cent of men chose working class. 'We have got to get one thing straight. Is the working class middle class or not? We will keep it to people who are working, who are making a wage, not a salary, somebody who has to go to work for a wage. Blue collar, I guess that's what I am. I'm not a salary man, not working in the office, so I guess you can put me in the working class' (126 M 1984).

A woman with experience working with the union, the women's movement, and left-wing groups said of herself, 'I no longer look at an employer as – he does you a favour, he hired you. So what if you are doing an unsafe job? He is giving you a job. I no longer look at a fore-man or management as someone who is your friend because they are nice to you. You make a profit for them. Like I know that one third of your day, you have already done enough work to pay your way in the world and the rest is all profit for them' (213 F 1984). This designation captured the fact that all of them depended for their living on at least one family member selling her or his capacity to work – their labour power – for wages.

> I think that there's the very, very rich, the very wealthy. Within the upper class, there's sort of a structure of people who have enough money to buy and sell you and me. Then you get your doctors and lawyers and everything else who make a fair bit of money. Then there's the working class. There's nothing special about what we do for a living – anyone could do it with the right training. And then unfortunately below that is anyone of a number of people that through bad luck or their own doing are not very well off one way or another. (049 M 1984)

A feminist corrective to Marxist class analyses insists on integrating gender. It argues that the class location of married women is related to the type of work they perform – paid or unpaid – that it is not merely the same as their husbands' (Phillips 1987). David Livingstone and Marshall Mangan (1993) have developed this position further, arguing for the concept of household class. Based on their work, we argue that working-class households are those dependent on both the wages earned by one or more household members and the domestic labour that converts the wages into usable goods and services for household subsistence. Where families are pooling and sharing units, their class positions are comprised of the combinations of the class locations of their members (Livingstone and Asner 1996). For example, when a working-class female nurse lives with a male steelworker, the household is working class; if she leaves him for a physician, her household class changes.

One of the women steelworkers offered an explicitly socialist interpretation of capitalist social relations: 'I am working class. I don't have any property. I can't work for myself. I can just go to work and get paid. But without people like me – working-class people – the bosses and capitalists wouldn't make any profit, and then, instead of being the upper class, they'd become just ordinary folks like us, wouldn't they!' (221 F 1996).

Although few people shared her socialist politics, many drew on both discourses to explain their appreciation of their social location. Like other middle-class people, they earned a living by working, and their income secured them a modest version of middle-class living standards. But the conditions under which they sold their labour power located them as workers in the relations of production. They recognized that the extent to which people have access to wealth, the degree to which they can actually control what happens to them and to which they have control over others or are controlled by others, deeply affect their experience of daily life. They captured this complexity with the concept of 'working middle class': 'I would put myself in the working middle class. We're not rich, we're not poor. I work regularly, but we're not going to be millionaires' (186 M 1984).

The sense of being part of a cultural mainstream was reinforced for the couples because their households' divisions of labour and sources of employment were conventional. The work they did was quite gender-specific. In 1984 the men had anywhere from one to thirty-eight years seniority at Stelco; the median was sixteen and a half years. The women's work varied: 43 per cent were homemakers; 57 per cent combined home-making and paid employment (28 per cent part-time, 29 per cent full-time). Most of the women with paid employment were in clerical, sales, and services. Just a few earned an income through small-scale commission sales of, for example, household wares or make-up.

Our 1984 survey caught a working-class population in the middle of the transition from a single-wage to a dual-earner family economy. For most strata of the Hamilton population, the shift occurred fairly gradually over several decades; for the households of steelworkers the changeover was more abrupt. Younger steelworkers, hired on in the 1970s, tended to have partners who, like other women of their generation, were more likely than older women to assume that they would have paid employment for much of their lives. For the families of most Stelco employees, the male income earner / female housewife arrangement remained possible through the 1970s, but then disintegrated with the long strike of 1981.

The 1981 strike, followed by extensive plant restructuring and massive lay-offs, disrupted well-established family subsistence strategies, not only for those who lost their jobs permanently, but also for those who were laid off for months and were subsequently recalled, and even for workers who managed to remain employed throughout. In 1984 almost half of the steelworkers we interviewed had been laid off for some time during 1982–3; 6 per cent were no longer at Hilton Works at all. With the earning capacity of this overwhelmingly male labour force curtailed or in jeopardy, an increasing proportion of their partners sought employment or increased their hours of paid work to compensate. At the time of our interviews in 1984, wives were employed in 57 per cent of households. During part of the 1982–3 period, 24 per cent of the wives had been unemployed and looking for paid work. By 1996, 80 per cent of the wives of men at Stelco were employed.

The women steelworkers challenged the conventional divisions of labour. Two of them, in their sixties, had been hired at Stelco in 1949 and had worked in the tin mill ever since. The rest were hired after the launching of the Women Back Into Stelco campaign. Eight of them had been active in the campaign. Before working at Stelco they had held a range of jobs, mostly so-called traditional women's jobs. When the lay-offs began, with the exception of the two long-term tin mill workers, they had so little seniority that all but one were part of the first round of lay-offs. By the time of the interviews, they had had anywhere from four to thirty-two months of unemployment. In 1996 only a few women were still working at the plant.

Theorizing Social Reproduction

In this book we start from the premise that, in Canada, as in other developed capitalist societies, the great majority of people subsist by combining paid employment and unpaid domestic labour to maintain themselves and their households. Looking at the economic aspects of this work, we see that it does a number of things. These two labours are key aspects of social reproduction – the activities required to ensure day-to-day and generational survival of the population. They are interdependent processes of production and consumption that combine to generate the household's livelihood. In the labour market, people sell their capacity to work, or their labour power, to an employer.[29] In the work process, that capacity or labour power is consumed and generates its monetary recompense, a wage or salary.[30] In their homes and in consumer markets, people use those earnings and their unpaid labour to produce the means of subsistence for themselves and their family members. Each day the means of subsistence are prepared and consumed and the capacity to work again is produced.

From this perspective, women's unpaid labour in the home is not a private service for their families, but an important and socially indispensable labour that contributes to the production of the labouring population and its labour power – that is, workers who are ready and willing to sell their capacities to work in the labour market (Seccombe 1974; Luxton 1980; Hamilton and Barrett 1986). Domestic labour involves the production of labour power as a commodity to be sold in the labour market, while wage work presupposes the exchange of labour power (Seccombe 1992). Because the demands of these two labour processes generate a specific range of constraints and possibilities that shape daily life, they are key processes that constitute and reproduce class, gender, and race relations in a context that is already constituted by state, law, and ideology (Maroney and Luxton 1997).

Antonella Picchio (1992) argues that there is a fundamental conflict in capitalist economies between the process of capital accumulation, or profit-making, and the process of social reproduction of the labouring population.[31] She argues that the state and the family are two key sites where the conflicts between the needs of capitalists for profit-making and for a labouring population are negotiated. The state also partially regulates the conflict between these two spheres (for example, through immigration, minimum wage laws, provision of education and health care, or welfare and pro- and anti-natalist policies). For Picchio, 'the insecurity of reproduction, inherent in the wage system, has induced the state to assume certain direct responsibilities for social groups such as low-waged workers, the unemployed, the wageless and people with no waged person to depend on. The state, however, has never been a neutral institution with regard to social classes; still less has it been so with regard to the gender division of labour in the process of reproduction. Control over women's work leads to control over the whole reproduction of the population' (1992: 112).

Families, through domestic labour, produce, sustain, and restore their members, trying to ensure as high a standard of living as possible within the constraints of also producing their labour power. Families, and particularly women's unpaid domestic labour, act as alternators in much the same way as a car alternator recharges the battery: 'The family, however defined and composed, functions as an alternator; in the outside world the direction of energy is from the reproduction of persons to production of commodities (capital accumulation), while in the family this direction has to be reversed – at least apparently – in favour of a more human process whereby the reproduction of persons is the goal and commodity production is the means' (1992: 98).

When we talk about the way daily life is constituted through the conflict between capital accumulation and social reproduction, we begin with the Marxist assumption that human action or praxis is central to the production and reproduction of social life. We assume that social life is produced through people's actions as they negotiate relationships in the material world, develop ways of thinking about and acting in their world, and attempt to influence its direction through political activities.

People are situated in particular material circumstances, such as specific periods of economic expansion or recession, types of labour markets or prevailing demographic patterns (such as typical birth rates), or standards of living and the cultural practices associated with them. Those circumstances shape their experiences. Either it is easy to get paid work or jobs are scarce; either it is impossible to raise a child outside of marriage or single parenting is acceptable. Based on their experiences, people make sense of their lives. They explain their experiences in terms of the various discourses, or ways of thinking, available to them.[32]

There are many discourses, some of them competing. For example, in early twentieth-century Canada, dominant discourses held that women should not get pregnant unless they were married. By the late twentieth century, those discourses had been seriously challenged by alternative perspectives that promoted increasing legitimacy for single mothers, lesbian mothers and mothers in common-law partnerships. We call particular systems of explanation ideological when they are implicated in the construction and maintenance of systems of domination.[33]

Some discourses or ideologies become hegemonic, that is, they become all-pervasive in ways that appear to be common sense (Williams 1983: 145). Prevailing discourses in contemporary Canada put a high value on working for a living, in striking contrast, for example, to ancient Greece where 'working for the necessities of life was seen as the distinguishing feature of slaves' (Arendt 1958: 61, cited in Picchio 1992: 12). Similarly, the assertion that individuals have the right to own private property (a concept incomprehensible to seventeenth-century Huron) is hegemonic in Canada today.[34] The logic of the market reproduces a division of assets which leaves many people relying on wage labour to survive. The inevitability of this division of property in capitalist economies is often seen as natural and normal despite the precarious consequences for wage earners. In the period of the study a previously hegemonic discourse that linked prosperity, full employment, and high wages was replaced by a newly hegemonic discourse that insists that 'the reality of global competition' means that workers must become 'more productive' – work harder for less pay – and that the state must reduce payments to the social wage, that is, government provisions funded by general revenues from taxes that redistribute wealth and resources, such as health and education, subsidized transportation, electricity, and water, and welfare.

Discourses help to shape the ways people are able to think about their lives, rendering some things so taken for granted that they seem natural, making it possible to imagine some alternatives while leaving other things unthinkable, and imposing limits on the imagination. These understandings allow people to act and reflect on the discourses available, assessing and re-evaluating them. In this process people develop their own sense of identity. To the extent that they are in similar situations to others, they are part of a group and their individual identity shares characteristics of the group. When they explicitly see themselves as part of a group, they begin to develop a sense of collectivity.

The most immediate group available to everyone is formed by their close social ties: family, neighbours, co-workers, and friends. The various loose networks of association to which people feel they belong form their communities. These are normally open-ended, non-exclusive, and reciprocally constituted. Communities are often based on common interests and activities and include both formal organizations (a union or a church) and informal ties (the casual congregation of dog walkers in the park).

People living in families whose livelihoods depend on wage and domestic labour are subject to pressures that strengthen nuclear family ties and subordinate their ties to friends and communities. These tendencies are reinforced by the way markets influence social life. Competing for jobs in the labour market and private consumerism require individuals to attempt to get the 'best deal' possible for themselves, undermining tendencies to subordinate their own immediate pursuits in support of more collective interests. As capitalist market relations penetrate more and more areas of social life, the competitive individualism they foster becomes increasingly prevalent.

The extent to which people consider themselves part of other groups often depends on their understandings of their particular circumstances. For example, even in a period of massive lay-offs, a steelworker may experience his unemployment as a personal problem; if he sees himself as one of thousands hit by restructuring, he recognizes that his personal troubles are part of a larger social issue (Mills 1961). When people assess their collective experiences together, they move from the personal to the social and even to politics; they develop new ideas and are able to transform personal complaints into political demands. For example, a woman whose boss or fellow worker makes unwanted sexual advances may hate his suggestion or touching and wish he would stop. When she and other women compare their experiences, they can recognize a social problem and come up with strategies to deal with it. Strategies might include direct action such as dropping a hammer on his toes and apologizing or using existing discourses and power relations, for example, going to his boss and complaining that he has been embarrassing her. If they give the problem a different name with new political and moral meanings, such as sexual harassment, the focus shifts from something embarrassing to women to something shameful for men to do. A new way of thinking makes political organizing possible – educating fellow workers, negotiating new contract language, or lobbying for protective legislation. By developing alternative or contestative discourses, people struggle to change the existing power relations in order to improve their lives.

Key!

Conclusion

Bracketed by two moments – 1980 just before Stelco began its massive restructuring initiatives, and 1996 when Stelco declared itself profitable again – this book presents a case study illustrating the way working-class people make a living. Chapter 2 begins with an overview of families at work. As individuals and members of families, women and men develop a variety of coping strategies for managing the demands imposed by both wage and domestic labour in the context of heterosexual nuclear family forms and sex/gender divisions of labour.[35]

Sex/gender divisions of labour in the labour force and the household reflect and reinforce familial gender practices and discourses. The prevailing practices that made steelmaking 'men's work' have at the same time generated a specific form of working-class masculinity – steelworker – and protected jobs in steel for men. Conversely, the practices that have made domestic labour 'women's work' and created the gender-specific occupation of housewife or homemaker made it harder for women to enter the paid labour force and difficult for men to take on domestic labour full-time. The awkward terms 'woman steelworker' and 'househusband' reveal the gender specificity of the normative division of labour.

Chapters 3, 4, and 5 focus on paid employment, examining the different ways women and men are located in relation to family responsibilities and participation in the labour market. Chapter 3 looks at life on the job for hourly workers at Hilton Works. The wage-labour contract, where employees exchange their capacities to work for a payment, gives management considerable authority over the way labour power is consumed in the labour process, but within those constraints, workers develop a workplace culture that makes day-to-day life on the job more amenable and lays a basis for working-class solidarity and union militancy. Local 1005, with its links to the larger international steelworkers' union, and the municipal, provincial, and federal union federations, provided workers at Hilton Works with the benefits that large, well-organized, industrial unions typically provide their members (Heron 1986).

The day-to-day experiences of individual workers on the job were significantly determined by the way their union defended workers' interests. The union was also instrumental in the employment equity struggle to force Stelco to hire women.

Chapter 4 documents the difficult period of Stelco's restructuring. Committed to ensuring and increasing profitability, Stelco management employed a number of strategies to cut labour costs by reducing the actual number of workers required and expecting the remaining workers to relinquish previous job protections and accept reduced pay increases. As union membership was reduced by about 62 per cent, the union's effectiveness was challenged, and individual workers confronted repeated threats of unemployment. Caught between pressures to cooperate with management to protect jobs and the necessity of defending existing contract protections, Local 1005 and its rank-and-file membership struggled to modify the worst effects of restructuring.

Chapter 5 examines the ways in which women make their decisions about whether or not to combine paid employment with their responsibilities for family caregiving. The systemic discrimination inherent in the labour market reinforces women's economic subordination and undermines the efforts of those women and men who are struggling to create more equitable relationships in their own families. The chapter also illustrates some of the ways that women reproduce their own subordination by participating in discourses and practices that subordinate them. The difficulties confronting the women who worked at Stelco further illustrate the strength of existing gender ideologies and divisions of labour.

Chapters 6 and 7 analyse domestic labour, showing how profoundly the demands of paid labour affect it, while the way domestic labour is organized, in turn, shapes the capacities of people to take on paid employment. As a labour of social reproduction, domestic labour mediates the contradictions inherent in making as good a life as possible for family members while producing and restoring labour power.

Building on this understanding, Chapter 8 argues that the tensions between the demands of paid employment and domestic responsibilities impose significant constraints on people's lives. The competing demands complicate efforts to create and maintain friendships, community, or other relationships and make it harder to participate in other activities. In this sense, nuclear family forms are anti-social; their organization sets up dynamics where family relationships tend to compete with, rather than complement, other relationships. While paid employment and domestic labour require a certain commitment of regular time and energy, what people do with the rest of their time is largely discretionary, bounded mainly by the available time, money, and regional resources, as well as by the cultural norms and social networks they are involved with. Decisions about discretionary time are made in a context where the constraints and possibilities shaping their lives are significantly determined by forces that are not readily visible and seem to be beyond their immediate control.

We conclude with Chapter 9, where we argue that the various dynamics of social relations based on gender, class, race, and ethnicity generate widespread social patterns or trends that play out in particular ways in each historic period and in different regions or places. The changes in economic and social policies between 1980 and 1996, such as capitalist globalization and restructuring, have turned upside down the worlds of the women and men whose livelihoods depended on employment at Hilton Works, unsettling previous securities and making it harder for them to get by, while posing important political challenges to the ways they understand their world and intervene to shape its course.

The struggles of these people to secure a comfortable standard of living in the face of neo-liberal restructuring, however, were exacerbated by dynamics that make individuals responsible for their own families with little support from the larger society and little impetus or ability to take responsibility for others beyond the boundaries of immediate household or kin and friendship networks. Despite such obstacles, they worked hard to create strong families, friendship ties, and communities to provide sources of intimacy, solace in an insecure world, and to secure the best life possible for themselves and those they cared about.

2

Families at Work: The Dynamics of Paid Employment and Unpaid Domestic Labour

In 1984 a homemaker with three children commented on changing patterns of work and family over three generations. At seventeen she had married a nineteen-year-old Stelco worker. Describing herself as 'kind of in the middle,' she compared herself with her mother and her daughter: 'My mother married young, had kids, stayed home all her life, and is still married to my father. He's a trucker. He's always worked hard, never earned much, but he's the breadwinner. She'll never work. Like her, I married young, had my kids – the youngest is just four. That's just what women did. You got married, he worked, you stayed home with the kids. My daughter, now, she's only twelve, but she's sure she won't get married. She's planning to be a vet' (180 F 1984). The woman went on to speculate about possible changes in her own work: 'I've stayed home with the kids so far, but I think I may go to work when the youngest starts school. He's got a good job, but things just cost a lot. Money doesn't go so far these days' (180 F 1984).

When interviewed ten years later, she had been employed full time for over seven years. Her daughter, by then twenty-two years old, was at university, beginning to study veterinary sciences: 'It's a big change, eh, from the way things used to be. I'm working and my husband, well, when I was at home, he never did anything around the house except bill paying. He still doesn't do much, but some. And my daughter, she's at school. She's sure she'll have a job, a career, for all her life. She won't be home like I was, but I hope she'll marry, have kids' (180 F 1994).

Her description captures some of the changes in the way white, working-class families have organized paid and domestic work for women and men while underscoring the widespread commitment to marriage and the heterosexual nuclear family. Typically, men have been income earners and women have had the main responsibility for domestic labour, although women were often income earners as well, through either formal paid employment or a variety of informal activities. Increasingly, women have taken on regular employment, in part because smaller families make it more possible; often because their families need additional income; sometimes because the women enjoy paid work or aspire to careers. When women are employed, men are under more pressure to help out with domestic labour. Such changes in sex/gender divisions of labour have important implications for gender and family relationships.

Other changes in gender and family relations were identified by another woman: 'As a lesbian I think things are changing. Lesbians in the 1950s had to be in the closet. Even in the early 1980s I wasn't out at work. I was scared how people would react. Now I'm out and it's okay. People can see I'm not so different from them – I go to work, come home, look after my kids. Some people still go crazy at the idea of gay marriage but really, except for I love a woman, I live the same as most people' (226 F 1996). Implicit in her discussion is the recognition that while sexual orientation continues to be a contentious political issue, lesbian and gay struggles have posed significant challenges to prevailing norms about heterosexuality, marriage and family forms, and sex/gender divisions of labour. At the same time, they have not disrupted the basic organization of working-class life based in private households dependent on unpaid domestic labour and income from paid employment.

Some women and men have attempted to renegotiate divisions of labour. Others have challenged prevailing marriage and family forms, and through such struggles have modified their understandings about gender identities. Yet, the competing demands of paid and domestic labour impose constraints that cannot be solved at the level of the individual household. Women and men, as individuals, develop their own strategies for coping. They make choices about how to ensure their livelihood, setting up and adapting their routines of daily life. They do so according to their own personal, biographically developed, and culturally shaped tendencies and preferences – a combination of deeply ingrained outlooks, habits, and predispositions. They do so in negotiation with those around them, as family members, as friends, neighbours, co-workers, and community participants. But they do so in circumstances they have little control over – particularly prevailing gender and race relations and the tensions between capital accumulation and social reproduction that working-class families have to mediate.

Nuclear Families and Companionate Marriage

All of the couples we interviewed took for granted a commitment to heterosexual companionate marriage or common-law relations, and for the most part accepted prevailing gender differences, including divisions of labour and distinctions between masculinity and femininity. As one woman insisted: 'Men and women are different. Men are not women; women are not men' (188 F 1994).

The overwhelming majority (over 90 per cent) asserted that the nuclear family was the ideal arrangement for raising children. For them, marriage and parenting were natural parts of adult life and among the most important activities of their lives. As couples, they had lived together anywhere from a few months to forty-one years; the mean was 15.5 years. They assumed they would have children, and when they did, they organized much of their lives around providing for, caring for, and raising those children: 'It's just the way things are, eh? You get married, you have kids, you work, you look after your family. That's life' (010 F 1984). Seventy-three per cent of the couples had children living with them, usually one or two, occasionally three; 12 per cent had adult children who lived elsewhere.

Even when their experience of the nuclear family was negative, it was hard for them to envision alternatives. A few of the people we interviewed held strong convictions about the importance of marriage as a lifelong commitment. For them, this meant sticking it out even when things got difficult. For example, one woman, whose husband was domineering and abusive, insisted that she was going to stay with him because she wanted her marriage to work: 'I just really want it to work out. Right now it's bad. We don't talk much and when he's mad, sometimes he really hurts me, like, really bad. That's not what a marriage should be, but I think I have to just hang in 'til we make it work' (181 F 1984). Even when she had enough money to live independently, she stayed, and ten years later, was still affirming her belief in marriage for life: 'I thought about leaving, but I really think marriage is about commitment' (181 F 1994).

Even those who did not share this marriage-for-life philosophy had difficulty imagining other ways of organizing their intimate life. A woman whose husband was rarely at home qualified her insistence that the nuclear family was the ideal by noting that it did not always work in practice: 'But we have a nuclear family and a father who isn't here most of the time. We're closer to a single-parent family. [The children] see the man spending more time in the community than with his family' (105 F 1994). She concluded that there is 'a lot to be said for extended families' (105 F 1994), but her extended kin lived far away, her single-family house was not designed to accommodate other residents, and nothing in her experience encouraged her to live collectively. Such structural and ideological constraints meant she had no way of reorganizing her situation to be part of an extended family. Nor was she able to envision the community as anything but competition with familial relations.

In fact, the sense that nuclear families and friendship and community ties are in competition, that commitment to the one implies rejection of the other, was widespread. Some people saw friendship and community ties as something young people are part of; the process of maturation involves relinquishing adolescent friends for a commitment to a spouse and children. A woman contrasted her husband's behaviour and their consequent marital stability to that of some of his friends: 'He's not like a lot of the fellows we know. Most of the guys we used to chum around with have split up. I think it's because the fellows are immature. They just want to go right on partying even when they have kids and a wife' (069 F 1984). The willingness of men to put their families first was a measure of a good husband for many women, especially those who worked at home and relied on their partners for their main adult companionship: 'I'll say this, he comes straight home after work. He doesn't go out with the guys after work. He says "I'm more interested in getting home to see my kids and my wife"' (188 F 1984).

For most of the people we interviewed, a good relationship also included a sense of intimacy and companionship: 'And we just have a good relationship. We're happy. We always sit down together, before dinner, when the kids are outside and have a coffee. And he'll tell me about his day and I'll tell him about mine. And then we'll have supper. And if we miss that, we both miss it' (176 F 1984). Such intimacy and companionship reinforced people's commitments to their families, confirming their sense of the importance of family life. In affirming their strong orientation to heterosexual nuclear families, the majority of people we interviewed were conforming to prevailing Canadian trends, thus strengthening their sense of being 'ordinary.'

Throughout most of the twentieth century, prevailing ideologies maintained that adult men and women should marry and cooperate to make a livelihood and raise children. This nuclear family – a married couple and their children – came to be idealized as the preferred family form (Adams 1997). It was complemented by an ideal of companionate marriage where wife and husband are companions, best friends who cooperate to their mutual benefit. As this ideal became widespread, it provided a framework that masked the basic inequalities between wives and husbands. Complementary theories about child-rearing insisted that parents, and particularly mothers, were best suited to raise children; the widespread acceptance of these ideas created difficulties for those engaged in any other child-rearing practices.

These assumptions about marriage, family, and child-rearing rested on and reinforced a sex/gender division of labour that confirmed gender differences while obscuring class and race or ethnic differences. A similarity in family forms across classes reinforced liberal discourses of socioeconomic status where only access to wealth differentiates people (Mandell 1995). Differences in family form among subordinated, racialized and ethnic populations were readily attributed to the supposed inferior status of such groups (Das Gupta 1995).

Masculinity and femininity constituted the two normative contrasting identities. A housewife explained how she thought about gender: 'I know that some people don't marry – there's single parents or homosexuals, eh? But really, I think men and women are different. They do different things and they should. And it's best if people marry and have kids. You know, there are just some things that are for men. Women are different' (108 F 1984). Ten years later, in the context of a continued increase in women's labour force participation, she had modified her position: 'Men and women can do the same work ... for most things' (108 F 1994). But she retained a strong conviction that 'the nuclear family should be encouraged. It's the best way for families' (108 F 1994).

In the early part of the twentieth century, some writers offered powerful critiques of the nuclear family (Gilman [1898] 1966), and activists in different parts of the world tried to organize alternative sexual, domestic, and child-rearing arrangements (Hayden 1981; Rowbotham 1992: 87–94). In Canada such alternatives were limited to easily ignored tiny enclaves.[1] The dominant ideology prevailed, and while it became increasingly acceptable for adults to remain single, the belief that the heterosexual married couple was the only appropriate family form in which to have children retained strong support.

Challenges to the idealization of this family form have come in a variety of ways. Common-law relationships have become widespread – by 1996 of all families 11.7 per cent were common law and almost half had children (Statistics Canada 1997a). Single parents (chiefly mothers, but some fathers) have won some recognition of their legitimacy. Single-parent families constituted 14.5 per cent of all families by 1996, and one in every five children was living with a single parent (Mitchell 1997). Aboriginal communities have asserted the importance of collective, community child care, especially in the face of genocidal government policies that threaten to remove children from their homes (Monture-Angus 1995: 192). Immigrants have challenged federal government definitions of family, calling for family reunification that recognizes extended kin ties (Hathaway 1994a, 1994b). Lesbian and gay activists have fought for adoption and custody rights and spousal benefits (Arnup 1997).[2] The growing recognition of widespread violence against women who are abused, beaten, and even killed by their male partners has increased the recognition that not all marriages are ideal, tempering romantic notions of companionate marriage with a more sober appreciation of the unequal power relations between women and men.[3]

Other modifications of the importance of the heterosexual nuclear family form are indicated by demographic changes. People are living longer, marrying, if they do, at a later age, and having fewer children. These changing patterns of longevity, marriage, and childbearing mean that there is an increasing diversity in the way people form families, and marriage and child-rearing take up a decreasing proportion of adult life (Statistics Canada 1997a). For example, by the 1990s, rates of first marriage were the lowest they had ever been in Canada, while the numbers of adults not living with a spouse or partner had steadily increased. According to the 1996 census, one-third of adults had never married and 15 per cent were no longer married (Statistics Canada 1997a). Some women complete childbearing in their twenties, which means they finish active parenting in their forties; others begin in their late thirties or early forties, so they do not finish active parenting until they are in their sixties. In the first half of the twentieth century, most women spent ten to fifteen years bearing children, compared with five years or less in the 1990s. The average number of years parents spend actually living with at least one child has decreased from over thirty to under twenty. Women who have children spend less than half of their adult lives actively parenting (30 per cent by 1981 compared with 50 per cent in 1921).[4]

Despite these challenges, the only widely recognized alternatives to heterosexual couples are single parents, or, increasingly, lesbian and homosexual couples: the nuclear family form remains dominant; 85 per cent of households in Canada in 1996 were reported to be based on nuclear families (Carey 1997).

While day care and other forms of early childhood education are widely considered to be good for children, as well as providing support for parents, especially when they are at their paid work, there are no broadly accepted alternatives to nuclear or single-parent family child-rearing. Many types of reconstituted families formed by divorce and remarriage have proved that children can be well cared for by a variety of adults. Like violence against women, evidence of child abuse and incest have modified romantic idealizations of parent–child relation-ships with popular conceptions that 'some people do it wrong' (Carey 1997: A28). However, such changes have not led to widespread question-ing of nuclear family structures. The parent-child family form remains the norm. Developing other alternative family forms – such as extended families, communal households, or collective communities like a kib-butz – is not on the social agenda at this time (Gavigan 1997). For exam-ple, one of the activists in the Women Back Into Stelco campaign had lived in a communal house with six adults and three children in the 1980s. She believed that her co-workers did not take issue with her domestic arrangements because her high profile in the campaign and her explicit socialist feminist politics had already marked her as differ-ent or 'other': 'Well, when they found out I lived communally and looked after kids who weren't mine and all, they just shrugged and rolled their eyes. I was just too different, so they could ignore me' (223 F 1996).

Because heterosexual nuclear marriage is normalized, all other social forms are discriminated against, and people who live in ways that differ from the ideal are penalized, with increasing severity the more they dif-fer.[5] Gays, bisexuals, lesbians, and transgendered people have to 'come out'; heterosexuals do not. People who live alone may be gossiped about and excluded from couple-based social occasions, but otherwise suffer little discrimination. Some municipalities have by-laws to prohibit peo-ple from living in alternative domestic sexual and family arrangements.[6] Gays and lesbians are overtly discriminated against in the law and through violence on the street.[7] In 1984 one of the women steelworkers was a lesbian who was known or 'out' in the lesbian and gay community in Hamilton, but not identified as a lesbian, remaining 'closeted,' at work. She described her fears of what the reaction of her co-workers' would be: 'I hope they don't find out. There's lots of homophobia at work – "dyke" or "lessy" or "fag" are favourite swear words. If they thought women at work was weird, a dyke would make them crazy' (226 F 1984). Two gay men, a couple who were both steelworkers, refused to be interviewed because they preferred anonymity for similar reasons.

Nuclear Families and Divisions of Labour

Both paid employment and domestic labour are necessary for household survival, but the organization of capitalist employment, on the one hand, and of domestic labour, especially child care, on the other, has resulted in a situation where the demands of one are contradictory to the demands of the other. People try to manage these competing demands by attempting to ensure that the demands of domestic labour, especially caregiving, are met while supplying enough labour power to employers to cover their subsistence costs. These include, where possible, enough to raise their immediate living standards and to provide children with more years of education than their parents had.

In the early twentieth century, the tension between the two labour processes was mediated by the predominant sex/gender division of labour. Referring to working-class households in Ontario at the turn of the twentieth century, Bettina Bradbury (1995: 427) notes: 'Women's work in the home was crucial. Whether a family could muster one or several wage earners, most wives had to work hard at making the money earned go as far as possible.' Bradbury goes on to show that while this work was 'crucial to the survival and reproduction of the working class' (460), it kept most women tied to the home, 'dependent on the wages of others to perform their daily tasks, which society was less and less likely to view as work' (461).

Men as husbands and fathers were obligated to be income providers; women were expected to put their responsibilities as wives and mothers first (Strong-Boag 1986).[8] The higher the man's wage rate and the steadier his employment, the less income other family members were compelled to provide. Conversely, when men's wages fell or their employment was disrupted or curtailed, families were forced to increase the involvement of other earners, who took whatever paid work they could get. While children were the main source of supplementary family income in the nineteenth and early twentieth centuries, women were in the mid- to late-twentieth and early twenty-first centuries (Bradbury 1993: 14).

The expectation that men were income earners meant their primary orientation was to paid work, and masculinity – what it means to be a man – was closely associated with competence at paid employment. The assumption that men have wives to do domestic labour, especially child care, reinforced employers' assumptions that male workers could work eight-hour shifts or longer, could be counted on to do overtime, and would not need time off for the arrival of a new child or to care for sick children or the elderly. Many men might be able to refuse 'overtime'; relatively few had employers who would permit them to work 'under-time,' except under exceptional and temporary circumstances. For many men, this responsibility as income earners justified their reluc-tance to do domestic labour and reinforced their assumption that it was women's work.

Since the late nineteenth century, organized male workers have fought for a 'family wage' – an income sufficient to support a man, his wife, and their children (Land 1980; Barrett and McIntosh 1982). The close association of masculinity with 'breadwinning' meant that men who were unable to make enough money to support their families were considered to have failed to live up to one of the most important tests of adult masculinity.[9] A man's ability to support a wife and children sym-bolized both his successful conformity to masculinity and represented the ideal of the good life. Such ideas were prevalent among the male steelworkers. As one of them explained: 'Everybody has a different idea of where easy street is. Mine is working full-time, and the wife is home and taking care of the kids' (089 M 1984). Although the actual numbers of men who succeeded in winning such wages is unclear, especially among the working class (May 1982), the most successful sectors of the labour force were those in large, well-organized industrial unions, such as Stelco workers.[10]

If young male workers could tolerate the working conditions of the standard entry-level jobs at Hilton Works – the searing heat, fumes, and dangers of the coke ovens and blast furnace – and if they did what they were told by supervisors, they could make a career of steelmaking, enabling them to continue living in Hamilton. This well-paid, long-term job stability provided a relatively secure economic basis for family forma-tion. Many of these men 'settled down' – found partners in and around Hamilton, got married and lived together, and bought homes with hefty mortgages (a deterrent to quitting the job). Most were their fami-lies' main money-makers, particularly once they had children. A man described what this meant to him: 'It's dark when I get up and so quiet. In a way I sort of like it. It's peaceful. But it's real lonely. I wander through the house real quiet so as not to wake anyone. They're all sleeping. I feel so responsible. It makes me realize I work to support my family. There I am at 5 in the morning tiptoeing around, going off to work, all alone so that they can have a decent life' (061 M 1984). Because such well-paid secure employment was rarely available to women, most women needed a relationship with a man to ensure their own and their children's economic security. A secure job made family life more possible; commitment to family life made the job more necessary.

Ideologies of appropriate masculine behaviour were complemented by ideologies that associated femininity with motherhood and asserted that all mothers, regardless of class, race, or ethnicity, ideally working full-time in their own homes, provided the best and most appropriate child care (Arnup 1994). In her 1993 study of professional-class women in Hamilton, Elizabeth Asner quotes a woman born in the 1920s who described how she understood the social convention: 'When we were young a man didn't want his wife working. It was a matter of pride. And that's what women did then. We wanted to be with our babies. Very few women worked if there were children. I suppose there were some who had to – and then you heard occasionally about a woman doctor. But that wasn't the norm' (1993: 143).

This powerful discourse of motherhood tended to collapse all women together, obscuring the significant differences among women, masking upper-class privilege, and describing as less fit mothers the women who were unable or unwilling to conform. Such views typically ignored the fact that few upper-class women did their own child care because they were able to hire live-in nannies and that many working-class women had no choice but to work for pay.[11] They also ignored the ordeals of many Aboriginal parents whose children were forcibly removed from them and sent to foster homes or residential schools (Campbell 1973; Joe 1996), and those of Black women who tended to have higher than average rates of paid employment and thus were unable to conform to this notion of 'good mothers.'[12] Women who chose not to have children and those who could not were typically considered selfish or worthy of pity. Lesbians were rendered invisible and assumed to be incapable of parenting. It was an ideology that assumed prevailing white, heterosexual, middle-class ideals were appropriate for everyone.

When the majority of mothers worked at home – as they did until the early 1970s – the assumption that women were primarily responsible for domestic labour appeared logical and even 'natural.' Indeed, there was such a close association between women and domestic labour that there were widespread assumptions that it was 'women's work.' Equated with

TABLE 2.1
Canadian labour force participation rates of all men, all women, and married women
1901–96[a]

Year	All men	All women	Married women	Women as a % of the total labour force
1901	78.3	14.4	n.a.	13.3
1911	82.0	16.6	n.a.	13.3
1921	80.3	17.7	2.16	15.4
1931	78.4	19.4	3.45	16.9
1941	85.6[b]	22.9[b]	3.74	24.8
1951	84.4	24.4	9.56	22.0
1961	81.1	29.3	20.7	29.6
1971	77.3	39.4	33.0	34.4
1981	78.7	52.3	51.4	40.8
1991	75.1	58.5	61.7	45.4
1996	72.4	57.6	61.6	45.2

n.a. = not available.
[a]Population 15 years of age and over.
[b]Inclues those on active service in the Armed Forces.
Sources: F.H. Leacy, (ed.), 2nd ed. of M.C. Urquhart (ed.), *Historical Statistics of Canada* (Toronto: Macmillan, 1965: 107–23). Statistics Canada: *Historical Labour Force Statistics* (1995a), cat. no. 71-201; *Labour Force Annual Averages*, cat. no. 71-529; *Women in Canada* (1995b), cat. no. 89503E p. 78; 1961 *Census*, cat. no. 94-536; *Labour Force Annual Averages* (1996), cat. no. 71-220-XPB, p. B-8.

'natural' feminine behaviour, it was often described as 'a labour of love.' The assumption that women would be homemakers permeated social-ization practices and educational systems, with the consequence that women were discouraged from obtaining the educational or training credentials that would enable them to qualify for many jobs (Gaskell and McLaren 1987; Gaskell, McLaren, and Novogrodsky 1989). In Asner's study, a professional-class woman, born in the 1930s, recalled her parents' reaction when her teachers suggested that she go to teach-ers' college: 'It was a waste of money and it wasn't suitable for a young woman to go away to school' (1993: 152).

Table 2.1 shows how these various trends have translated into labour force participation rates for men, all women, and married women. Only 2.2 per cent of married women participated in the labour force in 1921, as compared with 61.6 per cent in 1996. Throughout the twentieth cen-tury, as more and more married women took on paid employment, and as the spread of feminist ideas undermined beliefs in fixed sex/gender divisions of labour, the easy association of domestic labour and women became more problematic.[13] Increasingly, the division of labour between women and men living together has become a point of contention. 'When the children were small I was home with them so I did the housework because I was home more. But when the kids were in school and I went back to work part-time, of course, you're home part-time, so it seemed like I did more. When I went back to work full-time, I said he should do more around the house. It's only fair, the sharing. He does some of the housework. I usually do the laundry. I'd like it if he'd do more' (080 F 1994).

Considerable political dissension developed between those who support employment for mothers of young children and those who argue that mothers should be at home. Debates intensified about what child care arrangements were best for the child, and what work strategy was 'the best' for married women, especially mothers (Teghtsoonian 1993). Comparisons were made between women who worked at home full-time and women who combined paid employment and domestic labour, investigating their marriages, their children, their personal health, and their happiness.[14] While empirical studies have concluded that mothers' employment has no negative impact on their children and may have positive benefits (Hayes and Kamerman 1983; Chess and Thomas 1984; Allessandri 1992), in the mid-1980s many people were still opposed to married women with young children taking a job outside the home (Boyd 1984; Reid 1987). 'I think when the kids are young, the wife, you know, that she should be home with the kids' (089 M 1984).

Although more and more mothers with ever younger children remained in the labour force, as neo-conservative views gained prominence, this belief was reinforced:[15] 'When I worked at Stelco in the early 1980s, my kids were in day care and most people took it in their stride. Now, my youngest is in day care and I think some people are even more shocked than they used to be. They tell me I should be careful and ask if I really think day care is okay! I think there is a reaction happening' (224 F 1996). This debate is linked to larger sociopolitical discourses about who is or should be responsible for caring for children and elderly people. While some argue that children are the private responsibility of their parents, most people believe that child care is at least in part a social responsibility, where the society as a whole should bear some or all of the costs (Doherty 1995).

Unions and women's groups have had to fight for workplace and government policies that help individuals and families cope. They have demanded paid maternity and parental leaves (for both mothers and fathers), and unpaid leaves for all workers for personal and family responsibilities, arguing that social reproduction is a collective responsibility and that employers and governments have obligations to ensure that workers are not penalized for having personal and family commitments (White 1993).

When governments wanted married women in the paid labour force, during the 1939–1945 war, they provided child care services and produced propaganda insisting that such care was good for children. In an effort to get married women out of the labour force, in the postwar period, they closed the nurseries and produced propaganda claiming maternal care was the most appropriate care for children (Prentice et al. 1988: 298–9, 305–6). In the 1970s, as more women with young children entered the labour force, demand for publicly funded child care services increased. Throughout the 1980s successive federal governments promised to implement a national child care policy to provide quality child care. However, with the growth of neo-liberal economic policies in the mid-1990s, the government abandoned such plans and there was growing insistence that home-based maternal care was best (Friendly 1997).[16] A mother articulated her contradictory thoughts about who should bear responsibility for child care: 'I've had sitters for my kids and day care. They loved the day care. I think government should provide day care, like school, for everyone. But then, shouldn't parents be responsible for their own kids?' (105 F 1994). This debate is further complicated when the mothers are married to men who apparently earn enough to support a dependent wife and children. Even the staunchest opponents of mothers' employment will concede that single parents or very poor women may be forced to work at paid employment, but object when it appears that the woman has economic 'choice.'

These contradictory orientations to women's work were intensified in the mid-1990s, for example, by policies introduced by the Conservative government of Ontario as part of its attack on the welfare state. Welfare state policies typically assumed mothers should be at home with their children and so provided some meagre social assistance designed to enable women to do so (Little 1998). The Tories cut welfare payments by 21.6 per cent (Scott 1998: 122). Then, in legislating 'workfare,' the requirement that recipients of social assistance work for their money, the government began to argue that even mothers of young children should work outside the home for their welfare payments (Bezanson 1996). However, their fiscal constraints policies meant that they resisted providing child care. While the resulting dilemma posed terrible hardships for the women caught by it, it illustrates the way neo-liberal values assert child care as a private parental responsibility.

Despite the discursive shifts about mothers' employment, such debates reinforce the belief that the nuclear family is the appropriate form for raising children. The only question they pose is how satisfactory any kind of 'substitute' child care – for example, a father, a sitter, or a day care centre – could be. Rarely do they acknowledge that the fundamental problem lies in the way the nuclear family and domestic labour, on the one hand, and paid labour, on the other, are organized to be mutually incompatible (Luxton 1993).

Although child care is the most obvious, other aspects of domestic labour have also been part of a struggle between those who insist that they are a private family responsibility, those calling for collective, not-for-profit services, and those advocating private, for-profit provision of care. Health care and related caregiving for dependents offer good examples (Armstrong and Armstrong 1996). A steelworker described her experience when her mother was about to be released from hospital: 'The doctors said she was to leave the hospital, but she needed full-time care. I realized they were assuming that I would take care of her – just because I was the daughter, I guess' (208 F 1996). When she explained that she couldn't do so, hospital personnel suggested she apply for leave from work, and when that too proved impossible, recommended that she pay for private care: '"Well," I said. "Just a minute here. I have two young kids and a full-time job." One of them asked me if I couldn't get time off work. And just who did he think would pay me to stay home? You think Stelco would pay me? They don't even want to pay me if I'm sick – so to look after my mother – what a joke! So then they told me about a nursing home, but do you know, it cost more than I was even earning a month!' (208 F 1996). Only after a lengthy struggle involving a lot of work was she able to get the social services to arrange adequate care: 'Finally what we got was fine. It was great and they took real good care of my mother. But what a fight it was to get it' (208 F 1996).

The lack of collective support for caregiving and women's responsibility for family members means that women's participation in the labour force has continued to be constrained in ways that men's is not, while men's participation in domestic labour is still limited in ways not experienced by women. For most men, still typically the higher income earners, the demands of paid work are paramount, and the home is primarily a place of rest and relaxation. Women, especially those with children, are primarily responsible for caring for their families; the home remains a daily worksite. Women's capacity to take on paid work depends on their ability to make care arrangements for their children and accommodate the demands of their husbands' work.

Women with major familial duties often forego job opportunities that require commuting long distances or shift times that conflict with the domestic schedules of other family members. Women with young children tend to seek employment closer to home than men do, with more flexible working hours and employers who are willing to accommodate their family responsibilities: 'It's part-time. I'd like more hours but it's close to home, so I can be here when the kids come home from school. It's easier to get my housework done too when I'm not scrambling to get to work. But I'm not making very much' (089 F 1984).

These constraints typically force women to take jobs with fewer hours, less security, and smaller pay cheques (Duffy and Pupo 1989). When, women make substantially less income than their partners in two-earner households, the household as a unit has a strong incentive to maintain the priority of his employment over hers, which in turn secures his position as the head of the household. In this way, market forces, operating anonymously, reinforce the male income earner's advantage.

Desires to offset men's power and foster their own economic independence have contributed to women's increasing participation in paid employment. But this stops well short of equality on both fronts. If a couple decides to challenge existing sex/gender divisions of labour by sharing more equitably the twin responsibilities of making money and familial duties, the inequalities inherent in the labour market work against them. Very few women have jobs that pay enough to support a dependent spouse and children; few even earn enough to support themselves and a child. In fact, many working-class women earn so little that paying for child care while they are at work eats up most of their earnings, so that it makes economic sense for them to stay at home: 'The one year I worked, I said "I don't even know why I work." I didn't even make any money. It wasn't really worth it. And still to this day, it's not really worth me working' (021 F 1994).

Very few working-class men have jobs that readily accommodate the demands of child care or other caregiving. A woman described the way Stelco policies precluded her husband's involvement in even emergency child care: 'Once I was in hospital and both our kids got sick. He tried to get time off work to stay with them, but his foreman said he had no time coming so if he didn't come in, he would be suspended or fired' (301 F 1994).

Any man who found a job more suited to the demands of child care would likely end up working fewer hours, with less security, and a smaller pay cheque. His family would suffer a loss of income, unless his partner could either earn as much as or more than he had or make up the difference by working more hours.[17] Most women are in no position to do this. Given the way paid and unpaid work are organized and rewarded, few couples can afford to share paid and unpaid work more equally between them.

Domestic sex/gender divisions of labour and unequal pay and employment opportunities for women that support men's power in families are reinforced by state welfare provisions (Chunn 1995). Family-based programs forged in the interwar (1920–39) and postwar (1945–80) periods, when the income-earner husband / dependent wife family economy was at its peak, were designed to buttress this family form and counteract any initiatives to socialize domestic labour (Bakker and Scott 1997: 289). With the retrenchment of the welfare state, social policies have retained the gender inequalities of the income-earner husband / dependent wife family form, while cuts have intensified the orientation to private rather than collective responsibility for caregiving (Brodie 1996).

A woman described her sister's experience of this aspect of gendered welfare. Since the death of her husband the sister had relied on social assistance for herself and four children. Although she had established a relationship with a man who provided love and emotional support to her and the children, she was unwilling to risk further involvement with him for fear of losing her income: 'This new guy, he's really great. He makes my sister really happy and the kids adore him. But she doesn't want to see him because her worker said she would get cut off. It seems like they think if a woman sees a guy, he is supposed to support her' (303 F 1996).

If the economic deck is still stacked against an egalitarian redistribution of responsibilities within families and among the larger community, so are the prevailing cultural forces. The pervasive ideal that families should be self-reliant and that husbands ought to be their families' primary income earners also assumes that women should be available to provide unpaid caregiving whenever it is needed. Thus, in a myriad of subtle ways, gender inequalities give advantages to men, regardless of whether they exercise them with selfishness or consideration.[18]

Household Subsistence and the Individual Wage[19]

For individuals and their families, the social organization of paid employment and domestic labour imposes constraints within which they negotiate their daily lives. People living in families are under pressure to make the best of these circumstances by reconciling their individual interests with the collective obligations of family life and by pooling and sharing various resources. A man described what this meant in his case: 'Before I had kids, when I got sick of my job, I'd quit and take off for a few months. Well, I can't do that anymore' (002 M 1994).

Although the whole household depends on the income from paid employment, nothing in the wage form takes account of that fact. The wage is a payment made to an individual – who is hired and fired as an individual. The fact that the wage paid to one employee is spent supporting a family while another employee lives alone and supports only himself or herself is beyond the scope of the employer's active concern. Firms reap no advantage from their workers' children; their upbringing makes no contribution to the accumulation of the shareholders' capital. Consequently, most employers have little incentive to make special provisions for employees who are pregnant or breastfeeding, nursing the sick or elderly, or in any way involved with family caregiving.[20]

Since it is the worker who earns the wage, it is his or hers to spend as he or she sees fit. This market-driven individualism means that any responsibility that a worker may have to provide for a family is an additional obligation, not particular to wage earners, and in no sense intrinsic to the wage form. The wage's variable price fails to recognize or reward childbearing, builds in no means of recouping the costs of child care, and does not induce adult children to support their elderly parents.[21] It offers no incentives to provide support to larger networks of kin, friends, or community. Workers are free, if they wish, to live alone or with friends without marrying or having children; they can work for companies such as Stelco until they retire and die without ever living, as adults, in family households.

When wage earners do form families, the pressure mounts to find work and to keep a paid job. For them, toiling to 'put food on the table' is not simply a matter of personal subsistence; income earning becomes a family obligation. 'I worked real hard for my pay cheque. And I saved. Real slowly. I saved to get married and have a kid. I worked to buy a house. In 1978 I had a mortgage of $51,000. I never thought I'd pay it off. I still haven't. We had another kid – more expenses. So I have to work' (010 M 1984).

This collective responsibility binds workers to the productive requirements and financial viability of the firms that employ them. As employers have often noted, when male workers marry and begin to have kids, they 'settle down,' and are much less likely than single men to quit their jobs or take risks that jeopardize their employment. Conversely, the loss of employment and the inability to find a job is profoundly disruptive to families. In a 1994 interview, a man attributed the breakdown of his marriage, in part, to employment disruptions: 'You know, I was continuously getting laid off all the time. I found jobs here and there, but it was difficult to get a start. Sure you get your unemployment, but by the time that comes in, you use up all the money that you made and then it's like starting all over again. It was difficult. That was one of the reasons [for the marriage breakdown]' (140 M 1994).

Just as workers are legally free to quit work, regardless of their family status, employers are legally permitted to lay them off, regardless of their family status. But while workers with family responsibilities are much less likely to quit their jobs, it is not true that employers are more likely to keep them; employers, generally take no account of their workers' family status when they make lay-off decisions. The fact that private employers have no long-term responsibilities to their employees allows them to move their capital about at will, take risks, and accumulate more wealth. As the downsizing of the 1980s and 1990s showed, getting rid of workers can be very profitable for corporations, at least in the short term.

While individual employers have little direct interest in their workers' family attachments, it is in the long-term interests of the capitalist class that there be a ready supply of workers on a day-to-day and generational basis, and business interests share with the rest of society a desire for stable and peaceful social relations. Such contradictory interests mean that, while on the one hand, the dynamics of a capitalist economy foster individualism, there continues to be widespread pressure to maintain both family forms that assure low-cost social reproduction and class relations based on working-class acceptance of existing or even reduced standards of living.

Both the freedom of employers' to dispense with workers and the individual character of the wage form have been limited by modern industrial relations. In regulated industries, employers must show just cause and go through the proper procedures to fire individuals; to lay off large numbers of workers, especially under union contracts, advance notice and pay settlements are generally required. In many workplaces, workers have won benefits (e.g., life and health insurance) that recognize their family obligations. These costs to employers, while not inconsiderable, are held in check by the provision of the social wage, especially publicly funded schooling and health care.

Wage rates and benefits vary enormously by occupation, by the gender, race, and ethnicity of typical workers, by region, from nation to nation, and from period to period. At any particular time or place they are products of contention, negotiation, and compromise (Lebowitz 1991). Wage increases are more likely when workers' bargaining power is strengthened by strong labour unions, when the employer has made substantial, capital investments and has a major stake in the training and skills of the current labour force, as well as when there are strong government social services and welfare provisions. In that case workers can accumulate savings which they can use to support their children for a longer time and buffer the insecurity of the private wage system. These conditions were met for Stelco's Hamilton workforce in the postwar period.

Wages tend to sink towards the floor of daily maintenance when unemployed workers are plentiful, workers are unorganized and forced to compete with each other for jobs, the costs of capital mobility and labour replacement are low, and minimum wage regulations and pension-fund provisions are weak or absent.[22] In Hamilton after 1980, labour's relatively strong position was eroded on all fronts.

In any specific context, each working-class household has to determine how much labour power to offer for sale in order to make enough money for its members to live 'decently.' Will one person working full-time suffice, or are additional wage earners necessary? Do wages cover just the workers' personal maintenance (i.e., the present labour force), or do they fund, in addition, their spouses and children (i.e., costs of its eventual replacement by the next generation)? Nothing in the private wage system resolves these issues.

Between the late 1940s and the late 1980s, the labour movement, the feminist movement, and other social reformers modified the deficiencies of the private wage system by fighting for a social wage. The social wage includes all government provisions funded by general revenues from taxes that redistribute wealth and resources, such as health and education, subsidized transportation, electricity and water, and welfare.

In the countries that belong to the Organization for Economic Cooperation and Development (OECD), public expenditure rose from 29 per cent of the gross domestion product (GDP) in 1960 to 39 per cent in 1990.[23] Taxes rose concomitantly to pay for these programs, and the extremes of wealth inequality were modified. A study of the distribution of wealth in Canada in 1989, for example, before the major cuts to social security, shows both the way in which a private market economy produces inequalities and the impact of social security programs on redistributing wealth. According to Statistics Canada data, before social security payments, the poorest 20 per cent of Canadian families received only 1.2 per cent of all income; with social security payments, they received 4.8 per cent of total income. The people in the middle stayed about the same; the next 20 per cent received a slightly smaller share, while the top 20 per cent – the richest families in the country – had a smaller share of the national income after income redistribution, going from 47.2 per cent to 43.2 per cent. What this meant for individual families was that, based on the operations of the private market, the two million households of the poorest Canadians had an average annual income in 1989 of just $2,189. With social security payments, their income rose by $7,671 to a total of $9,860, an increase of 350 per cent. In contrast, the wealthiest 20 per cent of households had their annual income reduced by only $2,650 (McQuaig 1993: 41–2).

Even after governments eliminated or cut a range of social security programs through the 1980s and 1990s, government income supports continued to make a significant difference. Between 1980 and 1996, 60 per cent of Canadian families with dependent children experienced a decline in their average earnings from employment. In 1980 the poorest 20 per cent of the population earned about $12,000 (expressed in 1996 dollars). Government income transfer programs raised this to $18,500. By 1996 the average earnings for this group were just under $6,000 (Yalnizyan 1998: 53). Income transfers from government programs resulted in average incomes of $17,000 (Yalnizyan 1998: 54). However, while income transfers in the 1990s reduced the poverty of the poorest families, they did nothing to reduce the growing inequality between rich and poor in Canada. For example, in 1996 in Hamilton-Wentworth, 24 per cent of households had an annual family income of under $20,000, in comparison with 8 per cent of households whose income was over $100,000. In addition, 54 per cent of one-person households had an income of less that $20,000 (Brown 1999).

Household Coping Strategies

To secure a livelihood, working-class families, but particularly women, have developed a variety of strategies in an effort to manage the competing demands of earning an income and providing domestic labour. Each approach creates problems. One solution is to pay for domestic labour, either by hiring replacement labourers such as babysitters, cleaners, or housekeepers, or by purchasing services such as restaurant meals, nursery schools, and dry cleaning. Hiring domestic help or purchasing such services is expensive, and well beyond the means of most households. Few working-class households can even afford to pay the full costs of unsubsidized child care.[24] The strategy where women are homemakers while men earn the income makes the household division of labour clearcut. However, it depends on the man's ability to earn a family wage, puts pressure on him as the sole income earner, renders the woman economically dependent, and reinforces her subordination. This strategy falls apart if any of the conditions that make it possible are undermined, often by circumstances beyond the control of any or all members of the household. For example, as Stelco's restructuring laid off more and more workers through the early 1980s, reliance on the man's family wage eroded. A woman recalled how her husband's secure employment influenced her decision to stay home and how the loss of income affected them:

> When we started living together I had a crummy job I hated, so when the baby came, I was happy to quit and we had enough money to get by, so I stayed home. We had three kids under ten at the '81 strike. That was so hard – six months without an income. Christmas was awful. I cried all day. I tried hard to find work, but there was nothing to be had. By the end of the strike, we had used up all our savings. And then he was laid off. We rented our house to make enough money to pay the mortgage, and we moved into a friend's basement flat – five of us in two rooms. It was hell. (301 F 1996)

The homemaker wife / income earner husband strategy also depends on the long-term survival of the personal relationship. Women who have paid employment are less financially vulnerable to the vagaries of marriage. As an ex-wife, the same woman described what that vulnerability could look like: 'I did everything perfectly – just like you should. I was the ideal wife and mother. And where did it get me? One day, he announced he was leaving and that was it. At least when he was laid off, he got notice ahead of time and UI for a year. I didn't. Me and the kids were left high and dry – no notice and no money. Suddenly we were alone and poor' (301 F 1996).

Another woman described the consequences for her and her children when her marriage ended: 'I married young. I was nineteen, just out of school. He had a good job, making good money – so we were set. We had two kids and I was at home. When they were four and five, the marriage fell apart. I found myself with two kids, no money, no job, no education' (208 F 1996). After several difficult years on welfare, she was accepted into a training program that included day care for her children. After a lengthy search for work, she got involved in the Women Back Into Stelco campaign and eventually got a job at Stelco. Two years later she was laid off. Just before her unemployment insurance ran out, she got a job at another steel plant in Hamilton. She described the daily coping strategies she used to make a living for herself and her children: 'It's tough. Like you have to keep the job. I don't want to be unemployed ever again. It's too hard. So, I have to do what's necessary to keep the job. But I work so we can live. So the job can't take over. I have to do my housework and take care of my kids. And I need time just to be with them' (208 F 1996). While her experience shows how vulnerable people are when the male income-earner strategy fails, it also shows how difficult it is for a woman without a male partner to have children and to manage both paid and domestic work. Government provision of services such as welfare, training, day care, unemployment insurance, and affirmative action and employment equity legislation are important in enabling people to manage their livelihoods.

The strategy based on both partners taking paid employment means that the responsibility for generating income is shared, thereby providing the household with some protection from the vagaries of the labour market: 'She brings home a pretty good wage. It takes the burden off the groceries and any other small things. Before, I was the sole earner' (152 M 1994). It also reduces women's subordination and dependence on their husbands. However, with no one available to do domestic labour full-time, it is harder to get it done, and there are additional expenses as well as complications arising from scheduling, coordinating, and planning. In such situations women remain largely responsible not only for most of the domestic labour, but also for arranging child care and juggling the competing demands of both partners' paid and unpaid work. A nurse with a small daughter described the constantly shifting patterns she juggled as her husband worked three rotating shifts, and she worked alternating twelve-hour days and nights:

What typical day? If I work day shift, I'm up at 5:30 a.m. I have something to eat or not, it just depends. If I'm driving with [a friend], I'll get [my husband] to drop [the baby] off. If not, I'll drop her off at about 10 after 6, go pick up [my friend], go to work. I'm home between 7:30 and 8:00 at night. And I just have to make lunches.

If he's working nights, he gets home around 7:00 a.m. He gets his best sleep if I'm working days and [the baby] is at the sitters. If we both work nights, if it's only one, she can stay at the sitter or if it's a long stretch – for two or three – I'll take her out to my mum's. When [my husband's] on afternoons and I'm on nights, I take her over at 6 p.m. and then he'll pick her up at 11 p.m. (042 F 1984)

In most households where both partners are employed, it is likely that the woman's paid time is worth substantially less than her husband's; consequently, it makes sense financially for her to quit work in order to care for a newborn while her spouse retains his job. This 'sensible' coping strategy widens the pay gap between them because her earning potential is diminished by moving in and out of the labour force. The more continuous employment record of her husband is rewarded with promotions, seniority (meaning he is less likely to be laid off), training opportunities, and so on. This strategy also reproduces gender differences, because it reinforces women's involvement in caregiving while undermining men's possibilities of increasing theirs.

Challenging Sex/Gender Divisions of Labour

The most effective strategies are those that move beyond private initiatives by individuals or couples to public efforts to actually change the social and economic organization of work and family life. Women have challenged the inequalities they face in the paid labour force by unionizing, so they too can win greater job protection and better remuneration, by demanding increased pay in so-called women's jobs through pay equity initiatives and by fighting for employment equity – access to all jobs. In the late 1970s groups of women actively challenged existing patterns of labour force segregation by demanding women's access to so-called men's jobs. The 1979–80 Women Back Into Stelco campaign was one of the best examples of such an organizing effort (Luxton and Corman 1991).

The campaign was sparked when Stelco management hired a woman doctor, and some male workers protested at having to report to her. The union executive, however, complimented Stelco for its non-sexist action and then attacked it for not hiring women in production and trades. Union president Cec Taylor stated publicly that he 'wished Stelco would take a more enlightened approach to employing women production workers.' He went on to declare that the union would support women's efforts to get hired: 'Stelco does not hire women production workers in Hamilton, but female applicants have never complained. We can't fight their cause for them if they don't complain and come and see us' (Van Harten 1979b).

Eight women responded, met with the executive, and at the 10 October 1979 general membership meeting, Local 1005 members voted 197 to 3 in favour of launching a campaign in support of forcing Stelco to hire women. As a first step, the union laid charges with the Human Rights Commission on behalf of five women. The women formed a Women Back Into Stelco Committee, stressing the 'back' to signify that Stelco had previously hired women, during the war and continuing until 1961. Their key argument was that in the eighteen years since then, Stelco had received approximately 300,000 job applications and had hired about 33,000 men. Of the applications, about 10 per cent, or 30,000, were from women, and not one had been hired. This practice, they argued, proved systemic discrimination. Stelco never refuted the figures.

In an effort to defuse the issue, Stelco hired two women in November 1979, although a company official insisted: 'The hirings were not tied to the complaints. The women had been hired because they brought with them the qualifications needed for the jobs' (Van Harten 1979a). Neither the union nor the committee were impressed. The union continued to provide support, allowing the committee to use union facilities and raising the issue in the labour movement. Taylor brought a motion to the Ontario Federation of Labour (OFL) convention in November 1979 that passed after some discussion: 'Whereas Stelco in Hamilton has hired 33,000 men since 1961 and not one woman, therefore be it resolved that ... the OFL support Steelworker Local 1005's efforts to compel Stelco to hire a minimum of 10 percent of women in the Stelco workforce' (Ontario Federation of Labour 1979).

The committee engaged in a wide variety of activities, all intended to keep the issue alive and part of public debate. They organized demonstrations, contacted Hamilton area parliamentarians, federal and provincial government labour departments, and held press conferences and rallies. At the 1980 celebrations for 8 March, International Women's Day, the main slogan was 'We need jobs, decent wages too!

Stelco hire 10 percent women!' The poster promoting the event featured a 1943 photograph of women welders with a caption that demanded: 'You hired us during the war, why not now?' A week later the Human Rights Commission arranged a meeting between the committee and Stelco. Almost immediately Stelco began to hire women.

The five committee members who had filed complaints with the commission demanded: (1) a job in production at Stelco; (2) retroactive pay and seniority effective from the first hiring period after the application; (3) personal and moral damages of $3,000 each; (4) assurance of affirmative action practices according to section 6A of the Human Rights Code; (5) that Stelco include a minimum of 10 percent women in future hirings (Women Back Into Stelco Committee Press Release, 26 March, 1980). At the first meeting, four of the five women were offered jobs to start within the month and retroactive pay settlements in excess of $7,000. All four accepted the jobs, but only one accepted the back-pay settlement. The others held out for a better settlement, including seniority. By the end of March 1980, Stelco had hired all five complainants and about thirty other women; by summer, Stelco claimed to be hiring about 13 per cent women.

The Women Back Into Stelco campaign was significant for several reasons. It challenged the practices of a major capitalist employer and the profoundly masculine organization of steelmaking. It ensured that some women got access to the well-paid industrial jobs they had been barred from. Their hiring taught them and the men they worked with that women can work in heavy industry. It underscored the potential usefulness of anti-discrimination legislation and showed that working collectively, especially with the support of the feminist and labour movements, makes it possible for women to improve their employment situation. Reflecting back on the campaign nearly twenty years later, one of the activists assessed its importance: 'It gave me a real sense that it is possible for people to change their lives for the better. Getting that job made it possible for the first time for me to support myself and my kids adequately. But fighting that fight – that taught me to stand up for myself' (221 F 1996). However, the victory and subsequent hiring of about 200 women occurred just at the moment when Stelco began its massive lay-offs. As the last hired, the women had no seniority and so were among the first to be laid off. By the mid-1980s there were only a dozen women in the plant. By 1996 there were just a few. Women's efforts to challenge their subordinate place in the labour force were effectively wiped out by Stelco's restructuring initiatives.

Choices and Constraints in the Shaping of Daily Life

The difficulties inherent in the various strategies available reveal some of the ways in which the demands of household subsistence impose constraints on daily life. While the most immediate and obvious constraints are those of paid and domestic labour, other, often less visible, forces are also at play. How people live is partly determined by the type of housing in their area, the consumer goods available, the social services to which they have access, and state legal structures and practices. It is shaped by their consciousness and by dominant ideologies of gender, class, race, family, and work. It is also shaped by the logic of 'the market,' the way the labour and consumer goods markets make certain choices appear inevitable and render others almost unthinkable.

For most of the people we interviewed, the external circumstances shaping their daily lives, especially the complex demands of paid and unpaid work, were usually taken for granted. While the ways they intrude in people's lives, especially the hectic pace and conflicting demands of daily life may be irritating and the focus of frequent grumbling and complaining, the patterns underlying them usually go unexamined. A man articulated a widespread sense that such routines were natural and inevitable: 'You know, I go to work, I come home – that's what I do. That's just the way life is. Sure it would be nice if it was different, but it isn't' (069 M 1984). A woman described how deeply internalized her routines were: 'I have been getting up at the same time to go to work for so long that I never need an alarm. I just know that it's time to wake up, and so I do' (010 F 1984).

When it seems unlikely that prevailing circumstances can be significantly changed, most people take a position of pragmatic acceptance: 'It would be nice to have the same day off as my wife so we could spend time together. I try to swing it but it doesn't happen. So I can't spend my time with her – I do other things instead' (021 M 1984). The demands of getting by each day, the investments people have in doing so, and the repertoires of understanding they have to draw on rarely allow them the chance to envision a genuinely alternative society: 'Well, I don't really think it could be any different. It's just what goes on each day. You go to work, you look after your family. I can't imagine doing anything else' (010 F 1984).

The typical acceptance that the demands of daily life are 'just the way life is' is complicated by the widespread belief in choice – the idea that because they decide which of various possibilities to select, decision-makers are responsible for the outcome. A mother struggling to cope with the conflicting·demands of paid employment and domestic labour articulated the dilemma posed by the dialectics of choice and constraint. First, she dismissed her own concerns with a resigned sense of inevitability: 'It drives me crazy. But there's nothing I can do about it. That's just how things are' (069 F 1984). She went on to attribute the problem to her own decision-making: 'Well, it's my choice. I guess I could quit work and stay home. It's just that seems impossible, too' (069 F 1984). Her dilemma reflected the fact that while people do make choices, and so in a sense make their own lives, they do so in circumstances not of their own choosing and often not under their control.[25]

Conclusion

The work people do to sustain themselves and their families – paid employment and domestic labour – generates a cycle of production and consumption. In their household and in the shops, their domestic labour combines the money earned with unpaid subsistence labour to produce the means of subsistence, such as meals, clean clothes, and the social relations of home and family. In their day-to-day lives, people consume or use these products of domestic labour to ensure their own livelihood and provide for their children. By doing so they are also making possible the production of labour power, people's capacity to work.

As household subsistence requires a monetary source, some household members must sell their labour power to an employer, that is, attach themselves to the labour market. In the process of their day-to-day employment, they exert their labour power; it gets used up or exhausted in exchange for a wage or salary. And so they return home, where they use the income generated to supply their household subsistence. As they eat and sleep and relax, they are simultaneously living their lives and reproducing their capacities to work again.

In this way, while people do unpaid domestic labour primarily to make their own and their families' lives better, they are also subsidizing employers, ensuring that workers are available and able, on a daily and generational basis, to do the work employers want done. Because existing divisions of labour mean that women are more responsible for domestic labour, women provide a disproportionate amount of the socially necessary, but unpaid and undervalued, labour that sustains working-class life and assures the labour force that produces the profits and provides the services for employers in both the private and the public sectors. And because women do most of the domestic labour, men are relatively freed from those obligations. As a result, employers have been able to expect men to make paid employment their major orientation, and for the most part, have been able to organize paid employment to maximize its efficiency with little regard for the rest of workers' lives.

3

Working for Stelco

A man who had worked at Stelco since he left school at sixteen described his experience of the job: 'I've been there since I was a kid. I've seen lots of changes. But I was always glad to have a job there, though I didn't always like the job. Good pay, good benefits, a strong union which meant management couldn't just walk all over you. I'm proud of being a steelworker. We're men who know how to do a tough job and do it well. It's just about the best job a guy like me could get' (061 M 1984). His pride in his ability to do a difficult job well and in being part of a unionized skilled workforce was typical. So was his careful distinction between his appreciation of having a good job and the extent to which he actually liked it. Typical, too, was his assumption that steelmaking is a man's job.

In a workplace as large as Hilton Works, with so many distinct worksites and labour processes, each subject to change, workers found it hard to describe what working there was like: 'There's no "typical" to be found. Like me, a few years ago I was monitoring stuff where I had to make quick decisions about adjustments. Now I monitor a computer. I know what the guys I work with do, but there's thousands of guys doing who knows what' (010 M 1984). Most rank-and-file workers would agree with the crane operator who said: 'You show up for work. Maybe they leave you alone to get on with it – that's the best. Maybe they tell you to do this or that, and you know, sometimes that's okay. The company is making changes and some are fine. Mostly they're not, because management doesn't have a clue what really goes on. So you do your job. On good days, you get to see guys you can talk to. On bad days, you hope you'll make it to the end of the shift. And then you go home' (002 M 1984).

These comments capture a number of key elements in the way workers approached the day-to-day routines of life on the job at Stelco. Like
most workers, this man had a strong sense of his ability to do the job, 'to
get on with it.' He expressed a typical frustration with management's
interventions which he was forced to attend to but for which he had little respect. He recognized the unequal power relations between workers
who sell their ability to work for a wage and employers who control the
labour process and so can tell workers 'to do this or that.' He had a
sense of scorn and close-to-the surface anger towards management for
its lack of knowledge and its practice of imposing changes without con-
sulting the people who knew the labour processes most directly.

Periodically, that pride and anger were mobilized to fuel strikes and
other serious struggles to defend workers from management policies
and practices, but generally it was expressed only as frustrated grumbling. Few workers ever articulated an explicit acknowledgment of the
class conflict inherent in the capital–labour relationship, in which
employers strive to make profits by increasing productivity while keeping wages as low as possible, and workers try to improve their working
conditions while winning the highest pay rates possible.

The crane operator's appreciation of his social relations with 'guys
you can talk to' and his matter-of-fact approach to his job ('You show up
for work ... do your job ... and then you go home') were also typical.
Male steelworkers valued their jobs while taking for granted their attachment to the labour force. They also understood the importance of their
pay cheques and had a deep appreciation of many of the ways in which
the job had an impact on their daily lives off the job. However, available
discourses discouraged workers from recognizing that management's
capacity to organize steelmaking as it does, both depended on, and
enforced, Stelco workers' ability to leave the rest of their lives at the
plant gate.

Hilton Works

The physical location of the plant, in an industrial area away from residential neighbourhoods, its massive size, and industrial architecture –
dozens of large interlocking buildings spread over a thousand acres –
and its security – high fences and monitored gates, powerfully convey
the message that Stelco as a workplace is a separate world from the rest
of the city. A steelworker described his experience of that separation:
'When you go through the gate, you enter a different world. You just

TABLE 3.1
Number of employees by division at Hilton Works, 1972–1996

Division	1972	1981	1983	1989	1991	1996	1981–1996 (change)
Steelmaking	2,650 (24)	2,865 (24)	2,517 (27)	2,036 (28)	1,862 (29)	1,997 (37)	−868 (−30)
Finishing mills	4,755 (43)	5,234 (43)	2,674 (29)	2,850 (40)	2,583 (40)	2,367 (44)	−2,867 (−55)
Maintainence and Services	3,775 (34)	4,048 (33)	3,187 (34)	2,265 (32)	1,940 (30)	1,052 (19)	−2,996 (−74)
Bumped/ uncertain	–	–	982 (10)	–	–	–	
Plant total	11,180	12,147	9,360	7,151	6,385	5,416	−6,731 (−55)

Source: Livingstone (1996) based on USWA Local 1005 membership records.

have to leave the rest of your life behind because when you are at work, that's all that counts' (061 M 1984).

Hilton Works, like all 'integrated' steel plants, was a noisy, dirty, big, and physically challenging workplace.[1] One labourer described it: 'It was such a big place. The equipment is so large. It was gloomy and kind of depressing, too. It seemed like there was no sun. It's dull, like it's a misty place. Where I was there was lots of noise. We had to wear earmuffs' (204 F 1984).

The job structure of an integrated steel plant includes production workers in both front-end units that prepare the ingredients and make molten steel and finishing units where the steel is treated and rolled into specific forms; tradespeople such as electricians, machinists, or welders, staff service units that maintain, repair, and modify the plant (for details see Appendix B). It is very expensive to stop and start steelmaking furnaces and machinery, so integrated plants work on a continuous production process and require many production workers and some service maintenance staff to work shifts. The around-the-clock operations of Hilton Works' coke ovens, blast furnaces, and processing mills generated a wide range of jobs and working conditions that imposed very different demands on the workers. Table 3.1 gives an overview of the main divisions of labour at Hilton Works, showing the changes from 1972 to 1996.[2]

A typical shift began when workers arrived at one of the plant gates, went to their assigned change room, got dressed, and reported for work at one of the hundreds of different jobs. Each job brought a specific physical and social environment and demanded particular physical activities, levels of knowledge, expertise, and skill. An open hearth worker described the steelmaking department: 'It's where you have the big open hearths that produce 500 tonnes of steel in a couple of hours. Steelmaking also has the basic oxygen furnaces which, although they don't produce 500 tonnes, will produce 100 tonnes of steel in half an hour. So you've got this constant power thing there, just the machinery and what you're doing because it's a powerful situation to be in' (221 F 1984).

An industrial mechanic in the continuous caster described his work after the introduction of new computer technologies.

We're working to finer tolerances now. The job is more mental now; it's got a lot more finesse in it. The computers changed it a lot. Everything from the cooling of the steel right through is all controlled by the computer. But there is still alot of manual labour around. There's lubricators, there's guys up above at chains and ladles. And they have one monitor guy. He monitors all the computers, four computers at control. The computer runs the show, but the monitor guy has to look after cooling water from the heat exchangers because, if we get a real increase in the temperature of the cooling water, then it becomes dangerous for the guys that are pouring steel around a mould, and then they have to be told to shut down. (011 M 1994)

At some point during the shift, workers were entitled to a thirty-minute lunch break. Although there was a cafeteria, most workers ate in lunchrooms near their worksite. Some brought packed meals, others used the cooking facilities in their lunchrooms. Other breaks, for coffee or bathroom use, were less predictable and subject to endless negotiations. These breaks not only provided relief from the rigours of work and a chance to eat, they also created moments when workers could socialize with each other. What was possible during these breaks varied from place to place and depended on the attitude of the local supervisor: 'In our department they didn't want you to have any friends, not like the 1210 Mill. In the 1210 Mill, you worked with the same crew and had a fixed schedule. As long as you were there, those were the guys. Here, I don't know what I'm working next week. Here the foreman won't let us play cards on our lunch break' (090 M 1984).

The demands of working at Hilton Works obviously varied considerably, but one pattern was widespread: ultimately, individual workers had limited control over what happened to them. The employer set the shift schedules, dictated the work process and the job each worker was assigned, and determined how many people had jobs. However, collectively both through their union and through their day-to-day activities, workers played important roles in shaping the organization of the labour process and plant practices. Part of the daily routine for each worker involved negotiating the various and often competing demands of co-workers and supervisors, the actual production process, the regulations of the workplace and of the collective agreement, and the history and cultural practices of the particular worksite. Each in their own way accommodated themselves to the requirements of the workplace while striving to make it as tolerable or even enjoyable as possible. An electrician described his struggles with his supervisors who wanted him to take inappropriate responsibility for approving work: 'They tried to give us more responsibility as far as giving clearances, but that's not our job. See, our construction foreman used to do that. Now the maintenance foremen don't know anything about it, they're trying to get us to do it. But there's no way I'll sign a sheet saying I give a clearance for this' (152 M 1994).

At the end of a shift, workers returned to their change rooms, showered, and dressed to leave. Exchanging their labour power for wages was demanding: 'I earn every cent of it. This is tough work. It's relentless. When I come out of that place at the end of a day, I'm in rough shape' (069 M 1984).

In 1981, prior to the strike, Hilton Works had a generally stable and experienced workforce; the average seniority in the plant was over thirteen years and the average age was thirty-seven. Nearly 30 per cent were under thirty years of age, as Stelco continued to hire young workers who would ensure the generational reproduction of their workforce. Majorities in all age groups had spent most of their working lives at Hilton Works (see Table 3.2).

The 1980s brought fewer chances to leave for other jobs, mass layoffs of those with low seniority, the closure of the open hearth, and generally cleaner and safer working conditions. By 1984 there were very few workers under the age of twenty-five in the plant, and by 1996 virtually no one was under thirty-four. The Stelco wage lure and the promise of a good pension became even more compelling for those who remained.

TABLE 3.2
Age and seniority profile, Hilton Works Bargaining Unit, 1981–1996

Age group (years)	Percentage of total workers				
	1981	1982	1984	1989	1996
<25	12	11	2	–	–
25–9	17	12	16	4	0.03
30–4	13	12	17	19	0.46
35–9	11	12	19	17	18
40–4	9	9	13	16	24
45–9	9	11	5	13	22
50–4	10	13	13	12	18
55–9	11	13	8	12	12
60–4	7	7	6	7	5
≥ 65	1	1	1	1	0.66
Average age (years)	37	41	42	44	47
Average seniority (years)	13	17	18	21	24
Total workers (n)	12,576	9,338	9,731	7,325	5,145

Sources: Livingstone (1996) based on: for 1981 – *Actuarial Report on Stelco Inc. Bargaining Unit Pension Plan as at December 31, 1981*, prepared by William M. Mercer Ltd., April 1982, Appendix III, p. 14; for 1982 – USWA 1005 Computer Records (May 1982); for 1984 – Steelworker Families Project Sample Survey estimates (Nov. 1983 to Feb. 1984); for 1989 – Stelco Active Employees Report (Feb. 1989); for 1996 – Stelco Active Employees Report (Nov. 1996).

Job Attractions

Most steelworkers (over 80 per cent) expressed general satisfaction with their job. Many of them got satisfaction from both doing their jobs well and meeting productivity goals: 'At night I would see the beauty of the plant, the power of it. There was only me between a mistake and a clean job' (224 F 1984). They enjoyed the challenges of their work, learning the skills, and developing extensive knowledge about the operations: 'I've got to admit that when you put on your equipment and work at the back of the furnace, you feel powerful' (221 F 1984).

They also enjoyed the camaraderie and friendships with workmates, both on the job and after work. Some retired men missed this socializing so much that they attempted to recreate their networks through a breakfast club: 'The first five of us met by accident. I went for breakfast and in the restaurant were two other retirees, who were waiting for two others. We met once every three months for breakfast, and the last time it was forty. And they were all people similar to us who have parted company with or been kicked out of the steel company' (075 M 1994).

Most appreciated the advantages of working in a unionized plant. While individual workers have all sorts of ways of responding to management's efforts to control them and the organization of the workplace, from setting up informal work practices to quitting, workers have also fought to form and maintain their collective effectiveness through their union. An older worker explained why a union was necessary: 'I am not a radical union man, but I've always belonged to a union. I was a union steward for a while. I don't think I could work in Stelco without a union, because I worked there in 1945–46 when they were organizing the union. Stelco was a hell of a place to work for without a union' (112 M 1984). The union's struggles to improve the workplace and working conditions secured not only their pay rates and benefits but also the respectability and pride that went with steelmaking. As a crane operator explained: 'Anything that we have down there at Stelco, we fought for. I have great respect for the union. They're there to help the working man' (029 M 1984).

Union membership was automatic with employment at Stelco; beyond that, members varied in the extent to which they participated in union life. The 1984 survey found that a very large proportion of the rank-and-file membership, over two-thirds, had actively participated in some union-sponsored industrial or political actions, and about 40 per cent had filed a grievance against Stelco (Livingstone 1993: 47). Some got active on principle; some got pulled in by friends. Some gained the respect of their co-workers, who persuaded them to take on a union position; a few refused to have anything at all to do with the union.

An older man told a story about how he got involved as a union activist. He quit school at fifteen and lived on the streets for a few years. Then he got a job in a small steel plant:

> I was a hoodlum. I was angry and I was out for myself. But I wanted to keep my job, so even when management fucked me over, I didn't lose it, though it came close. Then there was a strike. I didn't know nothing about the union, about contract negotiations. I had to picket to get strike pay and I was pissed off. But on the line, you start talking. I started to really like the guys I met on the line. Then I started to hear them saying they were mad too, and for lots of the same reasons I was. Well, one thing led to another. I was tough on the line, but kept cool so they said I'd be good in

TABLE 3.3
Support for trade unions (%)

Union support needed	Male steelworkers (N = 177)	Spouses (N = 104)
Absolutely	31	22
Usually	32	37
Sometimes	31	35
Usually not	3	4
Never	3	3

negotiations and asked me to be on the committee. And I was good. And then I started to feel good, instead of fighting everyone, I was fighting for everyone. And I've been a union man ever since. (310 M 1984)

When he moved to Hilton Works, he continued to be active in the union. He described the importance of Local 1005: 'The union looks out for the workers and stops management from its drive for profit at all costs. They don't care who gets killed as long as they make their profits. They don't want workers to make enough to support themselves and their families if it means a lower profit margin. The union reminds management that workers are people and have the right to be treated well' (310 M 1984). The majority of male steelworkers and their partners agreed that trade unions were important (see Table 3.3).

While the union protected workers and ensured better pay and working conditions, it also drew people together, encouraging them to work for their collective interests, and it created policies and practices that helped them see beyond their individual concerns. One of the women explained:

I wasn't into any union or women's thing. I heard there were jobs, I went, I got one. A few people came round, tried to get me to come to the union meeting. One of the girls wanted me to come to this women's committee. No way, not for me. This is just a job, union, women – that's politics, no thanks. But [after conflict with a foreman] the union helped me file my grievance, and they were really helpful. So I went to the next union meeting. Now I think people have to help each other. You can't do it alone. And at the union I have learned about discrimination and I've made friends. (201 F 1984)

   The union gave workers a collective way of responding to the collective power of management. The negotiated collective agreements and the union structures and procedures provided workers with basic protections that made their job more tolerable and even comparatively desirable. At a time when Local 1005 was struggling with internal divisions and the external challenges of the lay-offs, one man stressed the importance of (male) union solidarity: 'I'd like to see the union get back to a brotherhood' (108 M 1984).[3]

   Stelco jobs were among the best available for people with their levels of education and formal training. The working knowledge of steelworkers has traditionally comprised quite specialized skills grounded in localized apprenticeship and on-the-job training practices (Bowen 1976). Little formal schooling was needed to do the job. About half of the steelworkers at Hilton Works had not finished high school and less than 20 per cent had any post-secondary education. In response to a general increase in the educational attainments of new entrants into the labour force, Stelco had used a Grade 12 diploma as a hiring screen since the late 1960s. But according to our survey findings, the company continued to hire workers without school diplomas for skilled jobs during the 1970s. There was an increasing tendency for younger workers to have higher levels of schooling and trades certification. However, many older workers with little formal schooling had trades certification and there was little correlation between the amount of schooling, and the amount of on-the-job training required to do most jobs in the plant.

   Whatever the officially recognized training requirements of their jobs, virtually all Hilton workers benefited from an extensive and often subtle informal learning culture in the plant. A veteran machine operator's account was indicative: 'As far as learning to operate this machine, you can't really put a date as to when you actually learn how to operate it. It's something that over the years you just acquire a feel for, and then one night the operator doesn't show up and they'll say okay, you're it now, and that's when you start' (075 M 1984). Similarly, experienced tradespeople stressed the importance of other workers' tacit knowledge. A repair electrician observed: 'We fix anything that's electrical. We've learned from experience that if you want to find out what's wrong with a machine, you listen to the operator. It's like your wife looking at you. She sees you everyday; if something changes, she notices. The operators know the sounds' (108 M 1984).

   The attraction of a job at Stelco was so strong that Stelco had to do hardly any external advertising to find willing workers. Most of the male

TABLE 3.4
Job search strategies of male Hilton Works steelworkers and
their spouses, 1984 (%)

Strategy	USWA Local 1005 Workers (N = 172)	Spouses (N = 89)
Cold application (chance)[a]	57	27
Friends in company	19	24
Relatives in company	16	11
Employment agency	3	6
Advertisement	2	27
Other	3	3

[a]The respondent took a chance and made an unsolicited
application for a job and was hired.

steelworkers employed in 1984 had simply applied in the hope that
Stelco might be hiring (see Table 3.4). About a third heard about the
job through relatives or friends working there. In contrast, the
employed wives of Hilton workers, like the Canadian labour force in
general, were much more likely to have found their jobs through advertisements and much less likely to have applied to their employer on
chance.

For most Hilton workers the biggest attractions of the job were the
basic wages, benefits packages, pensions, job security, and health and
safety provisions. As one young coke oven labourer put it: 'It's the
money. A lot of people go in with the impression that they are only
going to work here until they get their feet on the ground, a little bit of
money and then they are going to go. But once you get in and you get a
taste of the money, forget it. It's almost like you can't go because the
money is so good' (015 M 1984).

The importance of the compensation package was confirmed by the
collective bargaining priorities (Livingstone 1993). As Table 3.5 shows,
the top priorities for the 1984 round of collective bargaining were the
more extrinsic ones – better pensions, more job security, better benefits,
basic wage increases, and longer vacations. Shift scheduling, better
health and safety, as well as retraining and other issues related to
improving intrinsic work qualities were given lower priority. In 1984
younger Hilton workers with little seniority were primarily concerned

TABLE 3.5
Top bargaining priorities, Hilton workers, 1984 (%)

Bargaining item	Top bargaining priority[a] (N = 172)
Better pensions	48
More job security	46
Better benefits	34
Basic wages	34
Longer vacations	34
Shift scheduling	20
Better health and safety	18
More retraining programs	16
Concessions	16
Shorter hours	15
Reduced overtime	7
Equal pay for women	2
Paid maternity leave	1

[a]Percentage of individual union members who picked these items as among the three that were most important to them.

about whether they were going to be laid off: job security was the key priority for a majority of those with under twenty years' seniority. Older workers were much more interested in getting better pension benefits: two-thirds of those with more than twenty years were preoccupied with pension issues.

Job security and a steady, relatively high income compensated workers for the consumption of their labour power under often arduous conditions. These jobs made it possible for men to fulfil one of the main requirements of adult masculinity – the capacity to support a family, and for women to earn a living wage. But the trade-off exacted a high price.

The Consumption of Labour Power

The way their labour power was consumed on the job – ranging from the way shifts determined their routines to the fatigue or stress they took home with them – affected the life Stelco workers led off the job. Yet Stelco's organization of work was only possible because, on the whole, workers were free of most of the responsibilities for domestic labour.

TABLE 3.6
Paid work schedules of male Hilton workers and their spouses, 1984 ($N = 172$[a])

Hilton worker's schedule	Hilton worker's spouse's schedule (%)					Hilton worker's schedule (%)
	Home-maker	Chooses hours	Regular days	2 shifts, no nights	3 shifts	
Regular days	57	2	24	5	12	26
2 shifts, no nights	42	0	42	8	8	7
3 alternating shifts	42	4	34	6	11	67
Her schedule	48	3	32	6	11	100

[a]Includes only those still employed at Stelco in 1984.

Employment at Stelco also forced workers to accommodate its demands, subordinating their lives to Stelco's routines. Parenting was particularly incompatible with this job, a situation most pronounced for single parents. A woman steelworker explained: 'There is no twenty-four hour day care. I ended up hiring a young woman to come and live with us which was fine for a while. But she also wanted a better job than taking care of a couple of kids at odd hours. If you are a male with an established and stable family situation, I am sure it is much easier to handle' (221 F 1984).

Shift Work

Determined largely by Stelco management in the interests of maximizing production, and based on the assumption that workers could prioritize paid employment, shift schedules imposed on all aspects of the lives of Stelco workers, their families, friends, and communities. The 1984 work schedules of Hilton workers and their spouses are summarized in Table 3.6. About one-quarter of the workforce, mostly tradespeople, were on regular steady days, as maintenance work is more efficient and less costly in daylight hours. About three-quarters of Hilton's unionized workers were on shift work, the vast majority of them on three alternating days (7:00 a.m. to 3:00 p.m. or 8:00 a.m. to 4:00 p.m.), afternoons (3:00 p.m. to 11:00 p.m. or 4:00 p.m. to midnight), and nights (11:00 p.m. to 7:00 a.m. or midnight to 8:00 a.m.).

While few people liked shift work at all, only about a third of Hilton workers (33 per cent) expressed a preference for the established pattern of five eight-hour shifts a week. Most workers wanted to move to a smaller number of longer shifts, assuming that compressing work into fewer days would give them more free time. A small majority (51 per cent) wanted ten-hour shifts, while 16 per cent said they would prefer twelve-hour shifts.

With the massive downsizing in the 1980s, Stelco increasingly tried to move to twelve-hour shifts, presumably because that schedule made it easier to run continuous twenty-four-hour production with fewer workers.[4] Twelve-hour schedules involve working for a few days from 8 a.m. to 8 p.m., having a few days off, and then working for a few nights from 8 p.m. to 8 a.m. In 1996, 25 per cent were still working regular steady days; about 35 per cent were working twelve-hour shifts; about 40 per cent had three rotating eight-hour shifts (Livingstone 1996).

Everyone agreed that rotating shift schedules, whether eight or twelve hours, created all kinds of problems. Many regretted the impact of shift work on their health. A tradesperson described his experience: '[Night shift] was just a nightmare for me. I couldn't eat properly on night shift. No matter how much sleep I had, I'd still be tired because something in my body said, "It's nighttime. It's dark. You should be sleeping. What are you doing up?"' (002 M 1994). His experience was typical. Medical research suggests that shift work 'can push you into an early grave, and make your working life less productive while it lasts' (Miller 1984: C20). A labourer compared shift work to jet lag: 'My body feels like it's always in some other time zone and I never get caught up. So I am always tired, run down, and vulnerable to getting sick' (204 F 1984).

Everyone complained about the impact of rotating shifts on social life. Their time off rarely coincided with anyone else's. Most shift workers with low seniority had only six free weekends a year, and some had even fewer: 'I get one weekend every twenty weeks. I had it last week' (090 M 1984). They also complained vehemently about the negative impact shifts had on their families: 'You try not to take your work home with you, but it's impossible. The job just pollutes your whole life. Shifts just mean your whole family is always bouncing around. Shift work destroys family life' (069 M 1984).

It is difficult enough to run a household, have a life together as a family, see friends, or engage in community activities when one person works shifts. If both have paid work, it becomes even harder, and if both work shifts, the complications are endless. As Table 3.6 indicates, in the mid-1980s women were homemakers in about half of these households, a much higher proportion than in Canadian households in general. Those women who took paid jobs tended to get part-time work and, as Table 3.6 further suggests, to avoid shiftwork themselves if at all possible. However, in households where the men were on alternating shifts, about 10 per cent of the women had jobs with alternating shifts themselves.

Through the 1980s the constraints imposed by shift schedules increased, as more and more women took paid jobs. By the time of the 1990 strike at Hilton Works, the vast majority of Local 1005 members had a spouse pulling in a pay cheque, a big contrast with the situation in 1981. As one striker was quoted at the time: 'This strike is different because we all have our wives at work. I would say 75 to 80 per cent have wives who work. No one is getting skinny' (Peters 1990). Coordinating two different work schedules made life even more difficult, creating more tensions and providing fewer opportunities for the couple to be together.

Each of the shifts imposed a different rhythm. Day shift was the most compatible with other routines in the city. What many people liked about afternoons was that they had some day time free and their sleep was not unduly disrupted. But those whose children were in school complained that they didn't get time with their children for the entire week. Women with young children described endless lonely evenings, two out of every three weeks, at home alone with the children. Everyone complained about night shift: 'Nights are terrible, just terrible. I just hate night shift so much. He only gets about four hours sleep on nights. Well, he can manage on that but it's rough. He finds it hard to sleep. Our bedroom is right off the living room and with three kids (on weekends), well, you just can't keep them quiet. I try but you just can't' (029 F 1984).

However, what people complained about most was the disruption caused by unpredictable scheduling. Older workers recalled an earlier period when scheduling was predictable: 'At one time I could tell you in June what shift I would be working in September' (217 F 1984). But after the 1981 strike it got worse. Over a quarter of steelworkers received less notice in 1984 than they got in 1981; only about 5 per cent received more. Over half of alternating shift workers were receiving notice of less than a month, and more than a third got less than a week's notice. Some identified oppressive shift scheduling as evidence of Stelco's indifference to workers: 'The shifts are the worst shifts in the world, and it doesn't have to be that way' (223 F 1984).

The constant changes meant they could never do anything outside of work on a regular basis: 'You can't plan ahead three weeks to go somewhere because it never works out. They always change your shifts around on you' (089 M 1984).

When Stelco management instituted twelve-hour shifts, many hoped the change would be an improvement for workers, too. This schedule gave more of them more consecutive time off, especially on weekends. But it also increased the proportion of the workforce who had to work night shift, and did little to diminish the pull of shift work on other spheres of life, particularly its disruptive effects on household relations.

An industrial mechanic explained how his shift work made it hard for him to keep up with domestic chores: 'On day shift, we get up around quarter to six and I try to do some chores outside before I go to work. It's the only way to keep up because I'm working twelve-hour shifts' (011 M 1994). He described the way shift work reduced his social life and created tensions with his family: 'But twelve-hour shifts is not the greatest for social life. Put it this way, I don't have many friends because of that. I'm off every other weekend; I'm working every other weekend. One week, the nights; one week, the days. If you want to know, there's a lot of stress when I'm on nights around here, too. Like [my wife] is stressed out by the time I'm finished my stint of nights and she tries to keep [the children] quiet and she can feel that, you know?' (011 M 1994). His partner concurred: 'There's just a different feeling in the house when he's on nights. Just try and be careful. His tolerance is low, understandably, but it's just that it's low, you know. So stuff that he can normally take, he can't take it – not in night shift' (011 F 1994).

Older workers, whose children were grown and whose mortgages were paid off, could afford to trade a wage cut for more regular hours. They were quick to seize the opportunity if it arose, and their comments in praise of steady days shed light on the devastating impact of shifts on people's lives: 'Life is much better. You are fresh. You can take more, you can handle more. You can take a little more pressure. You can take it because you are fresh minded. You think a little better' (031 M 1984). Their partners also reported dramatic changes: 'It's a lot better now. He's just a labourer who pushes a broom [with lower pay]. But to heck with it. With both of us working we can manage. I'm much happier since he went on days, much more content. I don't have those awful nights. We have time to get a hold of our lives. He's a lot better, nice and personable since he stopped working shifts' (097 F 1984).

What happened to these steelworkers and their partners was typical of national trends. By the mid-1990s shift work had generally become much more common, particularly for the growing proportion of married women in the active labour force. A 1995 national survey found that only about 39 per cent of employed Canadians had regular day work schedules (*Toronto Star*, 30 August 1996: E3). The disruptions imposed by paid work were growing.

From People to Labour

On a day-to-day basis, and over a lifetime, working at Hilton Works was demanding. An industrial mechanic described how he felt at the end of a shift: 'By the time I get home in the evening and have supper with the family, it's too late to do anything. You pretty well just want to flop down on the couch. You're tired. You don't feel like doing any more' (011 M 1994).

Many jobs exposed workers to physical dangers, health hazards, high levels of stress, or exhausting labour.[5] In the 1984 survey, over 70 per cent indicated that they were exposed to physically dangerous or unhealthy working conditions, especially air pollution problems and toxic chemicals. As a finishing-mill labourer commented: 'This is a dangerous job. You run a bar 200 feet long and it is red hot and it goes at a fast speed. They pay you good money, but ...' (109 M 1984). Many workers talked about the risks and dangers they faced as a matter of course: 'Over the years we have had a few killed and a few maimed. Most of it is not through our own neglect' (112 M 1984).

Such health and safety issues were a point of contention between workers and management, and the union worked hard to reduce management's capacity to take risks with workers' well-being. In 1985 workers charged Stelco doctors with covering up medical evidence of job-linked illnesses over ten years. They identified a fibre-induced lung condition – pneumoconiosis – hearing loss, eye, skin, and respiratory problems as serious recurring health issues (Deverell 1985a, 1985b). Other workers were identified as having high levels of PCBs in their systems; health and safety representatives expressed concern about the high numbers of deaths among the recently retired (Palmer 1986).

Throughout the 1990s the union executive and health and safety representatives maintained a sustained critique of health and safety standards. They noted higher production records while management ignored safety inspections, complained about growing forms of job stress and management's indifference, and argued that 'The resources

are for improving production first and safety comes in second'
(McNight 1999: 9). They also complained that job amalgamation often
put workers at risk. An electrician gave an example: 'They are putting
more and more pressure on. I was injured because I was doing a
labourer's job. I had to do drilling through a concrete floor because the
labour department wouldn't do it, but we had to get the job done, so we
had to do it' (152 M 1994).

Many workers expressed a deep sense of alienation from the work. In
the words of an experienced finishing-mill labourer: 'You punch in and
then hate it for the next eight hours. You never know where you are
working when you go in. Let's face it, you can spend thirty years working
for them. And if they can eliminate your job, you're nothing. You're just
a piece of meat. They couldn't care less' (090 M 1984).

Traditionally, one of the most important antidotes to such alienation
was offered by the skilled trades. By the mid-1980s, even this option was
under attack. Dennis O'Brien, the grievance chairperson of a finishing
division explained: 'The company clearly wants the skilled jobs to
become as much like production jobs as possible. In our industry, one
of the main hopes for a young worker for job security and a decent work
life is to get into a skilled trade. Every skilled trade job lost is one less
opportunity for a quality job' (1989).

An older worker who had recently retired described the consequences of a life at Hilton Works: 'It's like you are just worn away. The
day-to-day work leaves you tired each day, but you rest and then you're
fine for the next days. But year after year, it kind of builds up and gets
harder. And everyone has an accident that leaves them just a bit not so
great. Most of us have had lots of small things over the years and they
add up. After a lifetime at Hilton Works, most of the life in you has been
sucked dry' (217 F 1984).

Although many workers complained readily about specific aggrava-
tions and used the grievance process regularly to defend themselves, few
challenged the basic terms of the exchange of labour power for wages.
They grumbled about the way shift work disrupts their lives and were
quick to complain about health and safety concerns, yet they accepted
the fact that to make the money they needed to live on, they had to put
up with a lot. The basic capital–labour exchange of wages for labour
power was taken for granted and naturalized: another day, another dollar. The liberal claim that labour market exchanges between employers
and employees is fair for the most part obscures the class exploitation
inherent in the consumption of labour power. One steelworker articu-

lated a sense of this perspective when he described his work: 'You know, management used to call us "labour," then we became "human resources," you know, a bit like raw materials or electricity only more troublesome and more expensive. When you walk in that gate it's like magic. You get changed from being "people" to "labour" or "resources"' (304 M 1996).

Workplace Culture[6]

Despite the organization of the work that used workers' skills and energies to maximize production and therefore profit without much care for its impact on the people involved, workers created a workplace culture or way of life out of the routines at the plant. Whether it was card games in the lunchroom or animated conversations about sports, cars, supervisors, or union issues, workers created friendship networks and communities in the workplace. The pleasure created by these activities made the job more attractive. As they shared both a sense of pride in their skill and competence on the job, and a critique of Stelco's mismanagement, they developed bonds that helped to keep the union strong. But membership in that culture was ultimately determined by Stelco management's hiring practices. While shared experiences drew people together, the competition for jobs combined with serious political and social differences also created conflicts among them.

Workers, Blacks, and Ethnics: Racism at Work

All workers struggled against management's tendencies to treat them as commodities, but some also had to struggle against their co-workers' tendencies to treat them as 'ethnics,' 'Blacks,' or 'Indians' rather than as co-workers. Because management's hiring practices resulted in a predominantly white, Anglo-Celtic labour force, most steelworkers said nothing about race or ethnic relationships on the job. However, a few people who were members of minority, racialized, or ethnic groups did. Like the Black man who told a white woman steelworker that he had been battling racist prejudice at Stelco for twenty-five years, racial minorities and immigrants from Eastern and Southern Europe confronted at Stelco a version of the racism prevalent in Canadian society. Most telling was the way people from minority groups were identified by their white, Anglo-Celtic co-workers as 'Blacks' or 'ethnics' long before they were recognized as workers. A man described his experience: 'For years I had was just called "Injun." They'd say "hey! Injun, do this!"' (199 M 1984).[7] Another man's comment gives a hint of the pain caused by such racism: 'I get called "the Eyetalian." I don't mind. It's true. But I think some of them don't even know my name' (108 M 1984).

A woman whose Italian father had worked at Stelco since the 1960s said that Italians and Poles were 'just like the crud of the earth' and 'downgraded' (213 F 1984). A man who had worked at Stelco for decades and spoke with a strong accent said: 'I talk okay but lots of guys, they make fun of how I talk' (004 M 1984).

A union executive, who was white and British, commented on racism at work: 'The labour movement has just begun to talk about racism in unions. Our local hasn't touched it. I guess until recently I would have said it wasn't an issue for 1005 because we're all white. But I know that isn't really so. There's not a lot of minorities, so they haven't been complaining' (310 M 1984).

Because about 80 per cent of the workers were white, English-speaking, and of British background, the small numbers of workers from other backgrounds were themselves divided and scattered throughout the plant. There was little opportunity for them to organize on the job or in the union to try to challenge the endemic racism they encountered. As a result, it was left to individuals to decide, on a case-by-case basis, whether or not they would challenge the racism they encountered. Such individualized efforts had no impact on Stelco's hiring practices, union policies, or the prevailing workplace culture.

Masculine Workplace Culture: Sexism at Work

Because large-scale industrial settings such as Hilton Works have often been considered 'men's work,' one of the ways men make sense of these environments is by equating their ability to tolerate noisy, dirty, and noxious work with notions of masculinity. These are tough jobs and it takes a 'real man' to do them; as real men they have the capacities to handle anything the job can 'throw at them.' As Claire Williams (1993: 66–7) has argued: 'A class imperative to take risks is fundamentally built into certain men's jobs. The result may be that the risk taking, over time, comes to be part of the masculine self-identity of the man.' An electrician described this process: 'At one time you were looked upon as being a wimp if you used earmuffs or other safety equipment on the job – you weren't considered a man' (Palmer 1986).

The steelworker identity and workplace culture that develop in such situations are typically masculine (Stewart 1981). The shared experience of work and co-worker camaraderie is shaped by their shared masculinity, which is defined in opposition both to women and to men of other classes (Willis 1979). An appreciation of their capacity for physical endurance distinguishes these men from the more effete executives in their clean white shirts and spotless suits. A male steelworker described the qualities needed to work at Stelco: 'You got to be tough and you got to be willing to take risks. You got to be strong. It takes a real man to work here' (199 M 1984).

Masculine shop-floor culture is one of the ways that men extract meaning and pleasure in the midst of alienating work situations. The unpleasantness and the danger of the working situation sometimes have been reinterpreted into a heroic exercise of manly confrontation with the task. A male steelworker noted: 'The coke oven, where I am, is really rough. The men who work there, they got to be really tough you know, just to keep at it, day after day' (197 M 1984).

The notion of steelmaking as men's work is not merely a simplistic assertion of male chauvinism, but is bound to men's sense of responsibility as income earners. Both their wages and the sacrifice and strength required to do the work provided basic self-esteem and self-worth. The wage packet conferred 'breadwinner power' and status: 'Like I believe a man is the breadwinner, you know. He supports his wife and kids. That's just the way it is. And that's the way it should be. Men earn the money' (198 M 1984). At the same time, the organization of work as a sphere separate and distinct from the rest of daily life is reflected in the way masculine workplace culture is unlike, and in some cases, opposed to, domestic life.

Workers at Hilton Works, like others in male-dominated heavy industrial or resource extraction environments, expressed their discontent with work, but rarely in explicit criticisms of class relations or of the alienated labour processes. Instead, they mediated their discontent through forms of language and interplay that expressed sexual competition and antagonism (Gray 1984; Meissner 1986). Sexually antagonistic language pervaded the steel plant. The employees characterized work itself – especially difficult work – as feminine and to be conquered: 'It's a real bitch' or 'Give her hell.' They often described their exploitation by management by using terms for submissive sexual intercourse – 'We're getting fucked' or 'We're getting screwed around.'

Gender was central to how male workers approached other aspects of their work.[8] One of the few ways in which workers can influence the design of their worksites is in their choice of pictures on the walls. Locker and lunchroom walls were often papered with pin-ups of apparently sexually available women – imagery that both continued the theme of sexual antagonism and suggested an activity that sharply contrasted with the workplace. This involved not only fantasized sexual activity deemed to be pleasureable in ways that work is not, but sexual domination in which the male (as viewer) is in a position of power over (the image of) women in ways that the worker never has power at work.

Even when workers expressed discontent on the job as direct political opposition to management, they often filtered this opposition through a language of masculinity. Male workers described standing up to management in masculine terms. One male Stelco worker described another approvingly: 'He never takes any shit from the foreman, and when they give him a hard time he fights back hard – he's a real man' (199 M 1984).

The masculinist worker consciousness is usually taken for granted as a normal part of how work is understood. Even men who do not like it tend merely to distance themselves from particular manifestations of it – objecting to swearing or to food throwing, for example – rather than developing a critique or opposition to the total culture. Only when challenged explicitly does this deep misogynist form of gender consciousness become visible. The Women Back Into Stelco campaign posed such a challenge.

The Challenge from Women Steelworkers

Before the Women Back into Stelco campaign won in 1980, and forced Stelco to begin fair hiring, there were over 12,000 men and just 28 women – all stationed in the tin mill.[9] These women were hired on in the 1940s and 1950s. Most of the tin-mill women were close to retirement – by 1984 there were ten left – and their isolation in the one worksite meant, as one of them said, that 'Most men didn't even know there were any women' (217 F 1984). Their years of experience had given them an appreciation of the sexism that shaped their working lives. A woman who had retired in the early 1980s after over thirty years said she and the other women like her had faced discrimination all the years they were there. She complained that both management and the union had negotiated regulations that prevented women from working nights and meant women were unable to apply for other, easier jobs outside the tin mill. She described years of being told by co-workers that she didn't really need the job: 'That used to make me so angry. The men seemed to think, you are single, you've got no dependents, you must be rich. I said my single status does not help me one bit when I go to the grocery store. I still pay the same as you do for my groceries, my phone bill, hydro, and rent. Because I'm not married doesn't mean they are going to give me a discount' (217 F 1984).

Another tin-mill worker who retired after more than thirty years said: 'We started at the bottom and I was still at the bottom when I left. I did my work and every penny I brought out of Stelco I earned' (218 F 1984).

The several hundred women hired between November 1979 and the start of the strike in August 1981 were always a tiny minority, and most were there for only a short period. At their peak, they were less than 1 per cent of the total workforce, and they were scattered throughout the plant. Women worked in just over half of all the work areas. About a third worked in the plate and strip mill; about a quarter in the coke ovens, the blast furnaces, and the steelmaking department (Boyd 1982: 51). In many of the other areas, women worked in groups of two or three; it was not uncommon for there to be only one woman in an area. There were huge sections of the place never touched by their presence. However, the high-profile public campaign and its politically charged focus on gender politics and women's oppression created intense reactions from management, the union, and many male workers.

These women included a few activists with well-developed political analyses of class and gender, who considered their efforts to get women hired as part of a larger struggle to strengthen socialist politics in the unions and build union support for women's liberation: 'I'm a socialist and in women's liberation. I think change comes from working-class people uniting to fight the ruling class, to get power away from bosses, and make the government ours. And I think women's liberation depends on unity between working-class women and men, which will only happen if women get men on side. And a precondition for that is that women have the same kind of power as men. So getting these jobs is a start' (221 F 1984). Most of the women, however, applied for ordinary reasons – the good pay and presumed job security. But as Jennifer Keck (1998) has argued, in crossing the gender divide, women workers in male-dominated industries became 'extraordinary.'

Stelco management was forced to hire women. There was little in their response that indicated significant support for the women, and much suggested active hostility. They treated the women as if they were male workers, ignoring the gendered and sexist organization of the workplace and its ingrained masculine culture. Some of the women were convinced this was a deliberate strategy intended to drive the women out: 'Stelco's tactic is to hire us and then hope that we would quit' (223 F 1984).

A male co-worker offered supporting evidence: 'They gave me one woman that gave the company trouble. They were looking for ways to fire her. We trained her, and the foreman used to come out every day hollering, "Where the hell is she?" I said to the foreman, "She is not giving me any trouble. She is doing one hell of a job." And then they gave her a lay-off paper. The day that she went, I said, "You know, you have been one of the best skillmen, ever." She just looked at me' (074 M 1984).

Management made no provisions for the specific needs of women workers, and their everyday experiences demonstrated that they were not welcome. When they showed up to get their safety equipment, many could not get the right size: 'They didn't have a pair of boots that were small enough, same thing with the hard hat' (208 F 1984). Job titles either explicitly assumed men – serviceman or foreman – or implied negative meanings when associated with women. One woman became a hot-bed hooker: 'My kids get a bang out of that. They tell all their friends, "My mother's a hooker at Stelco"' (205 F 1984). On the job they confronted a lack of appropriate facilities. All workers agreed that many lunchrooms, change rooms, and washrooms were inadequate and run-down. In addition, most of the women either had to walk excessive distances or share the men's facilities. There were numerous reports about embarrassments and tensions over shared washrooms. One woman was sure the company used this as a deliberate tactic to divide the workforce. She wrote in the union paper: 'Facilities are inadequate ... Many areas have one washroom for men and women with a partition around the urinal. It's not fair to the men or the women ... I believe that Stelco welcomes these tensions' (Field 1980).

Management's intransigence was most clearly revealed when a blast furnace worker who learned she was five weeks pregnant applied for a transfer on the grounds that the carbon monoxide levels would harm her fetus. She reported the decision of the head of Stelco's medical department: 'He told me he could not recommend that I be transferred out of the blast furnace area because that would be admitting that there is a health problem not only for pregnant women working there but for all employees' (Boyd 1982: 61). She booked off sick while waiting for a response to her transfer request, which never came through. The strike and her subsequent lay-off diverted the issue. Management's consistent refusal to acknowledge the problems women faced provided a legitimacy to the indifference or opposition of many workers to efforts to make the plant more accommodating for women.

The union gave active support to the campaign, and formal but cautious support to integrating women into both the union and the plant once they were hired.[10] The union supported women's efforts to improve facilities and approved the formation of a women's committee. During the 1981 negotiations they tabled six proposals, drawn from other union contracts, related to women: the elimination of sex-biased language from the contract, the establishment of an equal opportunities committee, a non-discrimination clause, procedures for sexual harassment complaints, child care subsidies, and provisions for maternity and paternity leave. They won new non-sexist contract language such as serviceperson or repairperson; the rest of the demands were dropped.

More radical efforts to undermine the legacy of years of systemic discrimination against women were never on the agenda for Local 1005 or Stelco. The women's committee unsuccessfully urged Local 1005 to arrange education sessions on sexual harassment. They also suggested various tactics to try to strengthen women's position, such as dual seniority lists so that women would not automatically have the lowest seniority. Few of these suggestions were taken up by Local 1005.

Neither management nor the union provided any workshops for supervisors or workers on ways to reduce gender tensions and smooth the integration of women. There was no anti-sexual harassment policy. However, even small gestures on the part of the union made the women feel more connected: 'At the last union meeting some of the older guys were saying brothers and sisters in the union. Well, that's really great because when I first started none of the guys would mention sisters in the union' (207 F 1984). The failure of either management or Local 1005 to take anti-sexist initiatives against the masculine organization of the plant, the union, and the workplace culture left a vacuum easily filled by gender tensions and hostility.

Inevitably, when women entered the plant, they posed a challenge to the established masculine culture. Since there were so few women, it was impossible for the women to simply be workers. They were always women first: 'A lot of men are still shocked when a woman walks by, and they make a big deal about it. And I wish that it wasn't like that, that I could just go to work, get my work done, and not be hassled by anyone.

I always wish that as soon as I punch in, poof – I was a guy – and as soon as I punched out, I was back to my old self' (203 F 1984).

Gender dynamics played out differently in each worksite and on each shift depending on the particular combination of the traditions of the site, the reactions of the men, and the responses of the women. A single woman in her mid-twenties with a six-year-old daughter described the range of reactions: 'There are the men who think it's great that women are getting into Stelco and doing that type of work. There are men who feel I'm taking another man's job who might be raising a family. There are men who feel I should be at home with my daughter and not working in a place like that. And then there are the men who are just there to bug you because you are a woman. So there is a mixture, but most of them are easy to get along with' (203 F 1984). Her sense that the majority were accommodating was widely shared by the other women. But as one said: 'It's maybe a minority who hate women and were mean and sexist, but the whole culture, that whole male thing, was intrinsically hostile to women. And that overshadowed the decent guys' (222 F 1984).

When a group of women showed up at one location for their first day of work, they were met by cheering men who clapped them in under a huge welcoming banner. Some of the older men who had worked with women in the tin mill, or during the war, easily adjusted to the reappearance of women. Some men supported employment equity: 'They have as much right to work as anybody else' (029 M 1984).

That support in principle was strengthened by those who worked beside women and observed their proficiency: 'I think if she can do the job, she's entitled to be there. We've a couple of women at work out there with us and they do a fine job – like no problems whatsoever. And there's no hard feelings or anything at all. If she can do the work just as well as so-and-so can and probably better so ...' (140 M 1994). That recognition encouraged some male steelworkers, particularly those with more secure jobs and employed wives to express explicit support for the principle of gender equality at Stelco: 'My wife works in a factory ... I had a woman on my crew. I don't think she made any difference. I think it's natural. I think what we've done in the last forty years is unnatural, in the fact that it was an all-male environment' (074 M 1984).

In many places men tended to be resistant to the abstract idea of women, but receptive to particular individuals. They worried that the presence of women would disrupt their routines and their ways of making the place their own. A former steelworker recalled: 'Several guys told me they didn't want women. I remember one young guy, he said, "I got women bugging me all the time – my mother, my girlfriend. I don't need no more women bugging me and now there's going to be women bugging me here. This has been my one place free of women, and now they're here!" But then he said, "But I don't mind you. You're like one of the guys"' (221 F 1996).

Some of the men's resistance related directly to their efforts to limit competition for jobs. The assertion of masculinity was partially a defence, a way of insisting on the exclusion of women to protect specific jobs and more general job skills from increased competition (Cockburn 1983): 'I do not like to have a woman at Stelco. It is a male preserve, and let us have it that way. I see working at Stelco as a male thing to do. I can see women going into the post office. That is a more female-type job' (015 M 1984).

It was also a defence, a way of avoiding conscious attention to their working conditions. When the newly arrived women expressed horror at the working conditions, raised questions about health and safety, or queried long-accepted shift patterns, they forced the men to examine them, too: 'It was just the job. I never thought about it. I'm a guy, that's what I do. But when the women came, they were new. They asked questions. And they were workers, too. Suddenly I had to think about it' (010 M 1984).

Men's anxiety was most frequently expressed as concern about appearance, behaviours, and language. Some worried that they would have to wash and shave more often and dress better: 'They said to me "Damn, women are here. We can't wear torn pants anymore"' (207 F 1984). Several complained that even though there were women in the lunchroom, they were not prepared to keep their feet off the table or stop their food fights. Their most frequently expressed concern was that they would have to 'clean up their language'; swearing was a regular practice most men felt was inappropriate in front of women: 'A lot of the fellas cuss at work yet they wouldn't do it at home. And once we started working down there, a lot of them really curtailed themselves' (202 F 1984).

They had a point. Many of the women were disgusted by what they encountered – men pissing against the walls, filth in the toilets and lunchrooms, and graffiti: 'I can't hold my breath long enough or stand on that toilet high enough to go to the washroom. I don't want to read that disgusting filth on the wall' (213 F 1984).

The women tried to clean things up. Some men supported them, scrubbing graffiti about women off the walls, challenging others to remove the pin-ups, and pointing out that writing sexist slogans was like writing racist slogans. In some places, the men appreciated the disruption of the masculine workplace culture, as it made things nicer for them: 'They thought it was great having the women because the language picked up and the place was a lot brighter and cleaner' (204 F 1984). In other places men felt invaded and harassed, embarrassed, and inhibited; the new standards limited their traditional ways of letting off steam and asserting themselves in opposition to women and 'suits': 'Here were these women telling us we were disgusting pigs and slobs. It wasn't a very nice feeling. But I guess they were right' (010 M 1984).

Most of the women described an initial period of testing after which many of them became 'one of the guys': 'At the end of the third day, I walk into the lunchroom. You don't realize when you've got ear plugs in how loud you are talking, and I said, "You fucking son of a bitch," washed my hands, took my ear plugs out, and turned around. There wasn't a sound in the lunchroom. It dawned on me that maybe they had heard what I said. So I just say, "Oh gee, fellas, I'm sorry. I forgot you weren't used to that sort of language!" Well, they just split right up and after that we were the best of friends' (205 F 1984).

Even when female co-workers were accepted by the men, certain gender-based strictures and inhibitions remained, making interactions awkward: 'It was a strange feeling always being watched. I was afraid I was doing something wrong' (211 F 1984). Gender politics were all-pervasive and interfered with growing friendships and socializing: 'One time I went to the tavern with them, and they all automatically walked in the men's side and I sort of stood there and said, "Hey guys!" "Ah, come on, you're one of the guys, too." So I walked in there and nobody seemed to notice there was this silly woman sitting there' (208 F 1984).

Not all women fared so well. In some sections a few men were overtly hostile (Hossie 1985). A woman from the hot-strip mill described the dangerous hostility some women faced. Her relief foreman was vicious: 'He had to prove that women couldn't do the work. He constantly picked on me' (204 F 1984). He made her do a variety of unsafe things. He was reported to management by other men on several occasions, but only after he instigated a life-threatening incident that happened to be witnessed by a supervisor was he removed from his position as supervisor: 'I passed out and the next thing I knew I was throwing up from the fumes and gases. They said I could have died from the fumes' (204 F 1984).

Men opposed to women at Stelco justified their position by defending men's employment rights or by insisting women steelworkers were violating feminine sexual propriety: 'Either you shouldn't be here because you're taking a man's job or you shouldn't be here, you're a slut' (212 F 1984). The women were frequently accused of taking the job because they wanted sex: 'I was getting up to leave the lunchroom [after resting in the dark] and one guy says, "Well, did you get it today?" And everyone is looking – you just got to deal with it' (212 F 1984). The older tin-mill women said that attitude had been around for decades: 'They all thought we must be riff-raff. They cast us in the same category as prostitutes' (217 F 1984).

Pornography and sexist graffiti provoked some of the most heated and public contentions as women had to figure out what to do about it. Some decided to ignore it: 'After all, they were there first. You can't turn around and make a big stink over something that has nothing to do with you. If you don't like it turn the other way' (202 F 1984). Some insisted on removing it, despite antagonizing some of the men. Others subverted it. In one lunchroom, women put up several sexually explicit pictures of men. In another, a woman added tiny bikini underpants and a bra to the pin-up. Another woman walked up and looked closely at a picture in her lunchroom: 'They all knew I was looking at it. And I went, "Gee, isn't she kind of pretty?" and I walked out' (213 F 1984). Those particular pictures disappeared quickly.

In some parts of the plant, women's presence and particularly their complaints about the pin-ups resulted in vicious graffiti attacks that threatened women with sexual assault and even death. Some women were physically attacked: 'This guy who'd been getting madder and madder every day, one day, he just grabbed me by the neck, pulled me behind the shed and was choking me, swearing and threatening to rape me, beat me up. He kept saying, "That's what you want, you bitch! I'm going to give it to you good." When the guys pulled him off me he was screaming, "I'm going to kill you!" The bruises lasted for weeks' (221 F 1984).

The family-based sex/gender division of labour and the male breadwinner ideology were clearly the root of much of the anxiety and anger. Several women offered analyses of the links between this ideology and men's resistance to women: 'Every morning you say to yourself, "I can't stand this job but I gotta go in, cause I gotta support the wife and kids." Well, if the wife can work, then it destroys the whole argument. So we are a tremendous threat to that' (Easson, Field, and Santucci 1983: 217).

Almost all the women were grilled about their marital status, and whether the men in their lives approved of their employment. They were also interrogated about whether their employment denied a family man what was more rightfully his. Some women suspected this concern masked a deeper fear that if some women could be self-supporting, maybe their own wives could be: 'I think they are threatened that this woman could leave in a year or two and raise her own family. She got out. She's free' (Easson, Field, and Santucci 1983: 217).

Even more profoundly, the lives of women steelworkers challenged the basic premises of gender and family divisions of labour: 'The man goes out and does the job. It doesn't matter how he does it, he's got to make a lot of money, and the women stay home and take care of the children, can fruit in the summer, and bake cakes in the winter. It's a very nice well-ordered life. And we were changing that order. Not only were we working with them, many of us were also going home and doing what their wives were doing as well. And it was very difficult for some of them to get through that' (221 F 1984). When the women were associated with men who also earned Stelco wages, many expressed discomfort about there being two high-income earners in one household. An open-hearth worker described questions she heard repeatedly: '"What does your boyfriend or your husband think of you working here? I wouldn't let my wife work here." When they found out my boyfriend was working at Stelco, "Boy you two must bring in a lot of money"' (212 F 1984).

In a similar vein, women found that their male co-workers were often loath to admit to their wives or girlfriends that they worked with women: 'There's guys down there who won't tell their wives they work with me. Their wives don't know I exist' (206 F 1984). The men claimed wives would disapprove and make trouble: 'One of the guys was saying his wife doesn't like the idea of him spending eight hours at work with a female' (203 F 1984).

A number of women described their delight at the friendships they developed at work and their shock and hurt at meeting co-workers off the job who cut them dead. A woman described another woman co-worker who went over to say 'hello' to a male co-worker at a party: 'She saw him at work every day and talked every day. But for the sake of the girlfriend, he pretended he didn't know her' (212 F 1984).

The reactions of steelworkers' wives towards women working in the plant were just as varied as their husbands.' Some were fully supportive, others objected on the grounds that steelmaking was too demanding and that men supporting families should have preferred treatment: 'I do not think that women should work at Stelco. It is a man's world traditionally and they are the breadwinners' (078 F 1984).

As the insecurity provoked by lay-offs and restructuring meant workers were more on the defensive, the assertion of the importance of men's jobs increased: 'And I think because of more women working now, there are probably more problems because a lot of men have lost their jobs, and I think probably the relationships are strained a bit between men and women in the workplace because of competition with women for jobs, for promotion' (011 M 1994).

Two contradictory trends reshaped gender politics at Hilton Works. As a local of the United Steelworkers of America, 1005 was linked to the labour movement. Through the 1980s and 1990s the labour movement across Canada began to take up women's issues, holding conferences, educationals, and training programs, and developing new structures and positions (White 1993). Steelworkers developed a Women of Steel course which sought 'to raise the consciousness of women and empower them to mobilize the union to support issues of concern to women' (Fonow 1998: 118). They held their first national women's conference in December 1996 (Fonow 1998). The Local 1005 executive and many union members came to understand women's issues and sexism in new ways. At the same time, the lay-offs and lack of new hirings meant there were so few women that Local 1005 as a union or in negotiations had little cause to take gender more seriously.

Years later, looking back at the experience of women at Hilton Works, a former steelworker commented on the gender and class politics of that period:

> What happened to our attempts to get women hired on is sort of like what happens whenever workers try to improve their situation against bosses. If it doesn't threaten their profits, bosses can be indifferent. And as for other workers, some are part of the fight, some are supportive from the sidelines, and some are hostile if they think their own interests are threatened. There was a moment in the late 1970s when it looked like there might be a chance for working women to get what men have. But then profits fell, and to please their shareholders, bosses will screw workers as much as possible. (221 F 1996)

She concluded with a description of working at Hilton Works that echoed what many of her male coworkers had said: 'It was the best job I ever had, the best job I could imagine having. I would have given up a lot to keep it. The best was the pay, of course. But it was also a job where I could be a skilled worker and a workplace where, sometimes, I had a chance to affect the way that work was organized. I was proud to be a steelworker' (221 F 1996). Pride, and the skilled work and decent pay that produce it, continues to be one of the most important legacies of working at Stelco.

Conclusion

For people who worked for Stelco, the routines of daily life were sharply divided between time on the job and time off. Once they were at work, they were expected to concentrate on the job, undistracted by whatever else might be going on in their lives. Day-to-day life on the job at Hilton Works was determined in the first instance by Stelco's hiring practices and ways of organizing work. But as individuals, and collectively through their union, workers reconfigured their jobs and helped to shape the labour processes in the plant. Their pride in their ability to do the job off-set the alienation generated by the way their labour power was consumed. Their income-earning capacities gave most of these workers a sense of satisfaction that enabled them to leave work each day ready to return the next: 'I leave at the end of a shift real tired and glad to go home. But you know, it's a good feeling too, to know that you did a good day's work and earned every penny you take home with you' (061 M 1984).

For the thousands of men and women who worked there over the years, Hilton Works was not just a way to make good money by producing steel. Brought together initially by their shared experience as workers, their relationships often reflected, and reproduced, the prevailing individualism, competition, racism, and sexism of Canadian society. But through their day-to-day efforts on the job, in the lunchrooms, and in the union offices, with co-workers, the union, and management, they produced a workplace culture that made the job more tolerable, offered personal friendships, and linked them into larger communities, while giving meaning to their labour. Their shared culture gave most of them a sense of solidarity and the fortitude to cope with the changes that so severely transformed their working lives during the period of Stelco's restructuring.

4

Restructuring Hilton Works

A union activist who had served several times on both the union executive and the negotiating team described his impression of the relationship between workers and management at Hilton Works: 'It's so contradictory. The company needs workers. It can't work without labour. And lord knows, people need jobs. So they need each other. They're essential for each other. That makes it sound sort of equal or balanced, but it isn't at all. Because the company makes the jobs and gets to decide who gets one' (310 M 1984).

In a capitalist economy, the livelihood of workers is tied to the investment decisions of companies whose priority is maximizing returns for owners or shareholders, not the standard of living of employees. Underlying the organization of labour processes and plant practices that shape the day-to-day experiences of workers are management's profit-making strategies. These are typically determined by forces far removed from the concerns of the workers on the plant floor and often unknown to them. They are even more remote for workers' families despite their significant impact on household livelihoods.

The same union activist reflected on the relationship between the day-to-day experiences of workers on the shop floor and the activities of management: 'What's clear is [management] haven't a clue who their workers are or what workers know about the job, and they don't care. And we don't know who they are either. The only time you really see it is during negotiations. Then sometimes you get a glimpse of what drives management, and you realize it has nothing to do with making it possible for workers to do the job well. It's about what's happening in Japan or Korea or U.S. interest rates. Or it's about some new theory of management dreamed up by some hot shot business school professor' (310

M 1984). He went on to describe union–management negotiations: 'Stelco management, to my way of thinking, is so locked into seeing its workforce as a problem to be controlled. If the company would just treat workers with respect, recognize that most workers know more about making the plant work than they do, and pay people decent wages, a fair share of their profits, Hilton Works would run more smoothly. But they want superprofits and it's almost like a game to them. There's no cooperation; they have to beat us' (310 M 1984).

Such dynamics had been part of Hilton Works for decades, but in the context of years of growth and expansion, these management practices were offset by regular hirings and secure employment. When Stelco restructured in the 1980s and 1990s, the deep inequalities of the capital–labour relationship were revealed more starkly. In its effort to regain profits, Stelco got rid of workers. The more workers it laid off, the better it did. But the more workers it laid off, the more vulnerable were those who remained, as management increased its control over their working conditions.

A steelworker, reeling under the impact of the first few years of lay-offs, expressed the sense of shock many felt when the jobs they had assumed were secure, suddenly became precarious: 'It was like the world falling off from under your damn feet. You don't know what you are going to do' (074 M 1984). By the mid-1990s the insecurity of restructuring had become the norm. Workers understood the links between their own employment and the profitability of the company: 'I try not to think about my job security because it's a manufacturing plant. They need sales and they're trying to do all the sales they can. There's no guarantees. I think we're all running on a very fine line. If we don't get the orders, there's going to be big problems, you know' (011 M 1994).

By 1994 steelworkers were all too familiar with the 'big problems.' Younger workers had lived through repeated lay-offs and recalls. The resulting wage losses meant they were, as the same man put it, 'struggling to stay alive' (011 M 1994). He elaborated: 'I got 20 years, you know, and there's not too many guys below me. The junior guy in our shift has got fourteen or fifteen years. And he's just been able to qualify for a mortgage. Up to that point he couldn't even qualify because he was getting laid off. He was working six months, laid off six months. And there's still guys in that position there' (011 M 1994). Older workers typically did not experience as much financial hardship but had to adjust to new working conditions; as their job categories were collapsed, they were bumped around the plant and shift scheduling became more erratic. A veteran construction electrician explained:

> I've worked steady days with every weekend off, except for a while in the early 1980s. But now they are changing their schedules, so who knows what will change. You could be put on shift anytime, because you're multicrafting. I would definitely say multicrafting has increased conflict. The feeling of most of the guys – they don't like it. They are not happy with their work. It's hard to be happy with the work anyway, but now they're not happy because they are getting basically pushed around and you can't do the things you have actually been trained to do. Like for years we were trained to be construction electricians, and now we can't do that. (152 M 1994)

After years of lay-offs, all the remaining workers were concerned about their jobs: 'As for Hamilton and the steel industry, I guess, well, nothing's for sure anymore, and you can have the greatest job, but no matter where you live, nothing's for sure. And I think everyone knows that now' (152 M 1994). And most shared the concern of another worker who described the toll such insecurities imposed on him and his family: 'You don't know if tomorrow you are going to have a job. You don't know if your family is all of a sudden just going to pack and leave on you because they are fed up with it' (090 M 1994). But while they offered very clear descriptions of the impact of restructuring on their lives, the separation of workplace and home meant that workers' struggles focused specifically on the workplace.

Management Strategies[1]

Prior to 1981 Hilton Works was one of the most profitable and efficient integrated steel mills in North America, and in the three preceding years it had made record profits. Local 1005 went into contract negotiations in 1981 determined to win a share of those profits for its members. In the face of company resistance, the union went on strike for 125 days – the longest shutdown in Stelco's history – and won a settlement of more than 50 per cent over three years (Kervin et al. 1984). However, the beginning of a recession in 1981 reduced domestic demands for steel just as Stelco's markets were threatened by competition from Europe and Asia and its steelmaking capacities were increased by the newly opened Lake Erie Works. Stelco's postwar history of continual growth of capital, steel production and employment came to an abrupt end (Livingstone 1993: 27).

In response, Stelco management instituted a dramatic restructuring intended, as the chair of the board declared: 'to regain market share lost during the strike, improve cost competitiveness, and restore profit and working capital positions to allow for planned expansion' (Gordon 1981: 3). Their goal was to reorganize the work process to produce steel, especially high-quality automotive specialty steels, using fewer person-hours per ton (Baker 1982). Management's strategy involved a massive capital investment in new technologies, including extensive computer-ization and new waste management systems combined with major reduc-tions in labour costs. Hilton workers bore the brunt of these changes, as the new technologies enabled management to reduce the labour force, reorganize divisions of labour, and 'restructure' the remaining workers.

Management's central prerogative is its control over hiring and firing, over how many jobs there are, and who gets them. During this restruc-turing period, management drew on previous practices in its effort to ensure its labour needs were met while keeping its labour costs as low as possible. Its capital investments and reorganization of the operations of the plant were designed to reduce the number of workers, as Stelco strove to produce what was called a more 'flexible' workforce. It regu-lated major fluctuations in its labour force requirements by using a lay-off–recall system. To cope with short-term or specific demands such as increased sales, major service projects, or absenteeism, management combined callbacks with other strategies such as the use of increased overtime and contracting out (Corman 1990). Many workers who con-tinued to be employed at Hilton Works were bumped to different jobs around the plant. Many had to retrain, obtaining formal certification for knowledge often previously learned on the job (Sanger 1988). Stelco's capacity to implement such changes depended on its ability to ensure that both individuals in the plant and Local 1005 ceded to them.

Capital Investments

Although there was widespread speculation in the early 1980s that Stelco might consider closing its Hilton Works operation and concen-trate on its newer Lake Erie Works, Hilton Works remained central to Stelco's operations. As Lake Erie developed its capacity to produce con-tinuously cast raw steel, it took over from Hilton Works' old coke ovens and more labour-intensive open-hearth furnaces. But Hilton Works' three basic oxygen furnaces and its various plating, rolling, and bar mills comprised the bulk of Stelco's steelmaking and finishing capacities. As CEO Peter Gordon insisted, in an effort to quash the rumours of a shutdown: 'Hilton Works, the cornerstone of the industry, will never face the wrecking ball ... Stelco planners see no end to Hilton's future. An updated plant there can continue in operation forever' (quoted in Mitchell and Wickers' 1982: 19).

By 1984 Stelco had begun to upgrade Hilton Works. It made changes to the basic oxygen furnaces and finishing mills to allow for more specialized flexible production. It installed a continuous casting system that cost $270 million (Mitchell 1984). Over the next five or six years it made major investments, including installing various remote-control computer systems and galvanizing and bar-mill lines to produce high-quality specialty steels for the automotive industry. The 1986 revamping of the no. 1 bar mill cost $100 million.

During the 1990s Stelco tried to increase efficiency by reducing the diversity of its product lines and lengthening its production runs of high-value products such as galvanized steel. It installed a $172 million galvanizing 'Z' line in 1991, and a pulverized coal injection facility in 1995. By 1996 Stelco management anticipated that before the decade ended it would have spent, since 1990, more than $1 billion in improvements to Hilton Works. Newspaper coverage of this investment noted: 'Stelco's capital improvements are not designed to increase the payroll – in 1996, Stelco's labour costs clocked in at over $880 million – but it will help the company dramatically lower its costs' (Akin 1998).

Management succeeded in cutting costs and increasing production. The amount of steel shipped per employee went from 180 tons in 1980 to 383 tons in 1995 (Stelco Annual Reports 1989, 1995), and Stelco achieved massive profits in the mid-1990s (Verma, Frost, and Warrian 1995).

Lay-offs and the Making of a Contingent Labour Force

Between 1981 and 1992 management issued over 8,000 lay-off notices (Corman 1993: 57). It was not in Stelco's interest to lose its investment in a well-trained and experienced workforce during a short-term recession, so management used lay-offs and recalls to accommodate its fluctuating labour force requirements. By laying workers off, while promising them possible recalls if they were needed later, management created a reserve of experienced unemployed steelworkers.[2]

Although management had the unlimited right to impose lay-offs, the union had negotiated various provisions in the contract that required management to respect seniority when laying workers off and to give workers advance notice of thirteen weeks. It also specified that when Stelco was ready to rehire, laid-off workers had priority according to their seniority and the length of time they had been on recall lists. The maximum time workers could remain on the recall list was three years. When labour requirements were uncertain, management issued indefinite notices. At any time in the thirteen-week notice period, they could withdraw the lay-off. In practice, many workers received several notices which were withdrawn at the last minute. Many more were actually laid-off and then recalled. Laid-off workers had to strategize about whether to look for other employment, often at much lower wages, or remain on the recall list, hoping for another chance to work at Stelco.[3]

Stelco's vague promises of re-employment kept many workers waiting in the hopes of permanent recall to Hilton Works (Corman 1993). A woman steelworker explained: 'If I were fortunate to gain some seniority I don't know if I would want to give it up. It would be a hard thing to do. Once you have worked at Stelco, it's hard to work elsewhere' (207 F 1984). But even lengthy seniority actually offered little security to laid-off workers. A young male labourer summed up the 1984 situation well: 'Anyone with less than ten years seniority is gone if there is a cutback. To me it's almost like working seasonal work at Stelco. You are there for a couple of months, and then when winter comes, and things slow down, you are out' (015 M 1984).

As Hilton Works downsizing continued, and the slim chances of permanent recall became more evident, the reserve labour pool shrank accordingly. This same labourer explained why in 1994 he finally decided to reject yet another recall: 'I kept on getting laid off, called back, laid off, called back. So finally, when they called me back for summer relief, I signed a waiver that I didn't want summer relief' (015 M 1994). He and his family couldn't afford to wait any longer: 'I was working at a part-time job, and I took further training in industrial maintenance. We weren't getting anywhere. When I was working during the summer I would save up, and then when I got laid off we would end up spending all our savings. So it was time to move on' (015 M 1994). However, he noted: 'There's the odd one that kept going back, hoping to be the one that doesn't get laid off anymore' (015 M 1994).

The continuing lure of Stelco was confirmed by the fact that hundreds of those who were laid off in the early 1980s continued to accept recalls and further lay-offs right up to 1996; some seventeen-year Stelco workers were on cyclical lay-off for over fifteen years (Prokaska, 25 April 1996: B1). A finishing-mill labourer who hung in for that long described the layoff–recall system in 1994: 'You get laid off a lot now over what I did ten years ago. Since the strike in [August–November] 1990 they never called us back until May of '91. You work twenty weeks, you get laid off. April, the following year, you get called back. You work twenty weeks, you get laid off. Now, I just got recalled again. In October I'm out again. So for four years they have just been playing stupid games with you. It makes it hard' (090 M 1994).

This layoff–recall cycle not only undercut workers' annual earnings each year, it also disrupted their seniority, which meant they had to put in more years before they could retire: 'I've worked at Stelco fifteen years. I've only got eleven years' service, because you lose every time that they lay you off, or every time that you go on strike, they don't count that as time served, so at the end of the year, like, at the end of thirty years' employment they come to me and say, there, now you have to make up four years. So you've got to work thirty-four years' (090 M 1994). This strategy gave maximum flexibility to management but resulted in maximum insecurity for workers. Table 4.1 records the declining employment levels for salaried and hourly workers at Hilton Works as a proportion of total Stelco employees from 1980 to 1996.

Overtime

From Stelco's perspective it was cheaper to pay overtime than to recall workers and pay their benefits. Stelco's official position was that it asked for voluntary overtime only to fill rush orders and replace absent co-workers. But while hundreds of workers were still on active lay-off in 1985, Hilton Works clocked 26,244 hours (or 656 weeks) of overtime (Wardoch 1986)!

With a reduced workforce and restrictions on hiring new workers, plant-level superintendents were often left with little choice but to entice and intimidate many workers into doing excessive overtime. The enticement was simple – overtime rates of one-and-a-half times the regular amount of pay. The intimidations were more insidious, often compelling workers to sacrifice personal plans with family or friends and pitting co-workers against each other. For example, if a worker did not report to work, the foreperson pressured a worker from the previous shift to work overtime by threatening to send the current crew home if

TABLE 4.1

Hilton Works employment levels, 1980–1996, including percentage of Hilton employees on salary and Hilton employees as a percentage of all Stelco employees

Year	USWA 1005 Bargaining Unit	Salaried employees	Total	Salaried/ Hilton employment (%)	Hilton/ Stelco employment (%)
1980	13,025	2,051	15,076	13.6	59.1
1981	12,576	2,019	14,595	13.8	53.8
1982	11,196	2,037	13,233	15.4	54.5
1983	7,975	1,737	9,712	17.9	55.2
1984	9,731	1,640	11,371	14.4	53.6
1985	9,972	1,635	10,717	15.3	55.5
1986	8,556	1,599	10,155	15.7	56.2
1987	8,129	1,694	9,823	17.2	57
1988	7,850	1,658	9,508	17.4	57.2
1989	7,390	1,632	9,022	18.1	55.8
1990	7,291	1,590[a]	8,881[a]	17.9[a]	57.2[a]
1991	6,607	1,518	8,125	18.7	63
1992	5,690	1,566	7,256	21.6	56.9
1993	5,170	1,548	6,718	23.0	56.2
1994	5,463	1,454	6,937	21.0	58.8
1995	5,317	1,409	6,796	21.0	58.8
1996	5,195	1,412	6,607	21.4	59.5

Source: Livingstone (1996) based on *Stelco Hilton Works Personnel Reports* (Oct. 1989 and Nov. 1996), and *Stelco Annual Reports* (1989–95).
[a]February 1990 pre-strike estimates based on Local 1005 records.

he or she did not agree to work. If the worker refused, the foreperson then explained to the incoming crew that they were being sent home because an inconsiderate worker would not work a few more hours. The blame was put on the worker, not on the company's policy of operating shorthanded (McCreadie 1988).

Reducing Jobs by Contracting Out

Stelco increasingly contracted out work to small companies instead of using permanent employees. Non-unionized service contractors hired laid-off trades workers at a fraction of the wage they earned at Stelco. The union resisted these initiatives and warned workers to monitor the practice: 'Contracting out of our jobs is also a major concern; our work-force is slowly being disintegrated while it is obvious that the contractors' workforce is increasing. When you see contractors doing jobs that our workers could be doing, inform your steward' (Balloch 1988). In spite of tighter bargaining agreement language on the issue, the company continued to use contractors extensively, both for modernization projects and for standard plant maintenance work that Local 1005 members were quite capable of performing.[4] While a few individuals were able to get work either as or from subcontractors, the majority did not. Those who did, lost their union protection, worked for lower pay with few or no benefits, and forfeited the legal protections that regulated larger employers. The women who had forced Stelco to reverse sexist hiring practices were unable to ensure fair hiring from small contractors; none of them secured such jobs.

Bumping

The dramatic changes imposed by management sent reverberations through the plant that affected the people left on the job. The most obvious changes involved departmental and divisional restructuring, as a number of plant departments were closed and others created. A large number of departments were amalgamated in the 1987 contract. At the same time, Hilton's traditional four divisional structures – (1) steelmaking, (2) hot rolling mills, (3) cold mills, and (4) maintenance and services – were officially replaced by the six divisions that had effectively been in operation since 1984: (1) ironmaking, (2) steelmaking, (3) plate and strip, (4) cold rolling and coating, (5) rod and bar, and (6) maintenance and services.[5] Management was able to erode protective departmental seniority criteria, imposing plant-wide seniority for job openings posted in an entire division.

With the mass cutbacks, management was able to use seniority provisions selectively. They ignored seniority to get rid of 'troublesome' workers and to retain highly skilled younger workers. Workers with relatively high seniority in older departments were 'bumped' into other jobs, while some with less seniority in newer departments remained there. As Stelco eliminated certain positions, the workers in those jobs were temporarily assigned or 'bumped' to other positions, while the workers with the lowest seniority were laid off. Each temporary assignment required them to learn a new job, in new surroundings, with new co-workers. As the restructuring continued for several years, many people on temporary assignment never returned to their original departments. They lost their departmental seniority entitlements to days off and promotions, and they had their participation in apprenticeship programs suspended. Many had to give up more favourable shift schedules such as steady days or regular weekends off, and most lost thousands of dollars because they were no longer eligible for promotion to higher paying positions.

Job Reclassification

Management's strategy for reducing employees involved an attack on the long-established and hard-won job classifications of both production workers and tradespeople. It sought to make workers more 'flexible' by requiring them to do work previously done by others and by expecting them to learn many different jobs.

The major changes in the job structure of Hilton Works after 1981 were the amalgamation of production jobs and the creation of 'super-trades,' or multicrafting, which transformed traditionally certified trades into several generalist trade designations, for example, industrial mechanic, welder fabricator, and several general technician job categories. There were also some efforts to break down the divisions between production and trades with the development of the 'operator mainte-nance' job description, where line workers took on minor maintenance work. A finishing-mill operator described the new job structure: 'The tradespeople are starting to get into production. They're trying to make everybody more knowledgeable in that area. That's why they want to push us into operating maintenance. They want us to fix our own machinery because they're not going to hire anybody' (140 M 1994).

Production job amalgamations generally meant that semi-skilled machine operators had a wider range of monitoring tasks and basic maintenance work and increased responsibility. The following line worker's comments were typical: 'The new line is a lot faster. They seem to be putting more and more on us, but not giving us an increase in money to compensate for the responsibility. At one time in my depart-ment we had over 200 people and now we've got 100' (099 M 1994). Another production worker, assigned to the state-of-the-art Z-line, said: 'They've amalgamated a lot of the jobs. They've cut the workforce at least in half but we still make the same product, maybe even more. I'm more busy but now we're doing it through the computer terminal. There's more responsibility on most of the jobs because there's added work to them' (078 M 1994).

Trades workers expressed more concern with job amalgamation per se, both in terms of multicrafting and crossover into production work.

Many trades workers with multiple basic certifications were permanently assigned to production departments.

Job amalgamation, with its new job requirements and skills, was a mixed blessing for workers. It involved retraining to learn to work with the new production processes, especially the computers, and translated into higher base wage rates, as well as intensified workloads. A former millwright who was reclassified as an industrial mechanic in a finishing mill described the main changes: 'They've taken a blend of millwrights, pipefitters, and machinists and they've kind of amalgamated our jobs together, multicrafting ... Basically it's the same job except I'm working to finer tolerances. Like, the job I was on ten years ago was a lot more physical. Now it's a lot more mental and it's got a lot more finesse in it. The computers changed it a lot' (011 M 1994).

Retraining

Like other Canadian steel companies in the context of computerization and heightened competition, Stelco became much less willing to rely on gradual informal workplace learning. Organized joint management–union training programs increased greatly in the 1990s.[6] Employees of Hilton Works received an average of about four days of training each year (Canadian Steel Trade and Employment Congress [CSTEC] 1993, 1996). Virtually all Local 1005 members participated in an extensive health and safety training program. Training programs for maintenance-operator and operator-maintenance entailed several weeks of formal training. Workers were expected to take multicraft training and other technical skill upgrading programs, as well as computer literacy and quality improvement courses (Warrian 1989).

While many enjoyed the opportunity to learn new skills and relished the new computer competencies they developed, many others found the formal training less than satisfactory. Multicraft training typically involved veteran tradespeople in one area learning the rudiments of another and drawing on the knowledge of experienced workers in these other trades whenever they actually needed to cross over. A certified electrician in the service department said: 'We had some Mohawk College training for a week and we had two days down at the welding services and then we had some in-house training ... The hard part is trying to remember it because you don't use it as often because we're specialized in different areas and you basically stay in your own specialty. You don't cross over too much, but when you do you've got to start thinking'

(137 M 1994). He warned: 'There's still enough guys around in the other trade. You're usually working with them. So it's not too bad ... But there's less and less senior guys to talk to when there's a problem' (137 M 1994). Experienced tradespeople assigned to production departments often had more extensive retraining. A construction mechanic who became an industrial mechanic on the continuous caster described it: 'They gave us extensive training before this place started up. When we came to the caster, it was like going back to school. They made us get our gas tickets and then we had eighty hours in hydraulics upgrading, right? Like forty hours in class and forty hours on the job' (011 M 1994).

For the few younger workers who were able to enter the new combined trades jobs without prior certification, the required training time was broken into small units and reduced to about one-sixth of the prior apprenticeships. This, of course, meant that there were losses in the extent of the tacit knowledge conveyed to trainees (Petersen and Storey 1986; Sanger 1988). The general emphasis was on obtaining generic 'bits and pieces' of basic trades knowledge through short courses. This diversity appealed to some new entrants, including the following industrial mechanic: 'We're in an ongoing training process. You're assuming bits and pieces of different trades. So instead of having four or five separate trades, now they're concentrating on just having one person do the duties of the other five. So that's the ongoing training program. It's more efficient for the company and it's more interesting for us. I mean, you can never learn too much. If they want to send you back to school, I'm all for it' (047 M 1994).

It is debatable whether there was a general upgrading of the skill levels actually needed to perform the work that retained and retrained Hilton steelworkers did.[7] Certainly, workers were increasingly expected to perform a greater variety of tasks and to cooperate among themselves in executing them. But the individual worker's depth of formal and informal knowledge, and job control of work design, were often effectively undermined (Villa 1987). Many Hilton workers recognized that there had been little actual upgrading of the knowledge base of their work. As a younger mill labourer put it: 'There's no future left in the job. You know, like where do you go? If they lay me off this time, I'm just going to go back for retraining somewhere, probably through CSTEC. My options are open really, electronics maybe ... The job hasn't really changed over the past ten years, it's basically the same deal, same job, everything's identical. The skill requirements are just the same as it was when I started here' (090 M 1994). A veteran construction electrician, who became a general industrial technician, offered an account of the gap between the acquisition and application of working knowledge after the construction and maintenance departments merged: 'They figure you can just go in and do the job, be given the job that morning and have it done that day. It doesn't work that way ... All we are is numbers to fill in for maintenance guys, because as far as multicrafting is concerned all we have ever done is maintenance work. I have not done instrumentation, I have not done electronics, etc. So they're giving the good old government a run for their training money' (152 M 1994).

In spite of the pervasive rhetoric about the need for workers to upgrade their skills to respond to global competition and technological change, an increased array of job tasks and work intensification should not be confused with upgrading. The construction electrician turned industrial technician explained further: 'Yes, we should know more about instrumentation. You go to the training at Mohawk, you come back and don't use it, so you lose it. Really, that's it, as far as I'm concerned, the training is a washout. They're training you, but they're not using your knowledge. It's now happening in all departments' (152 M 1994).

In-depth studies of workplaces both in Canada and in other advanced industrialized countries have offered little evidence of significant increases in the cognitive skills and substantive knowledge required to perform the work.[8] These Hilton workers, along with growing numbers of working-class, underclass, and professional and managerial workers, recognized that they were generally well qualified to perform most of the available jobs. They also knew that there was growing under-utilization both of formal credentials and existing workplace knowledge and that the primary problem was not a lack of suitable training but a lack of suitable jobs.[9] The same man said it well: 'If I was laid off, there are skills I could fall back on. I've taken some courses and I have my own computer. I'd have to do something, because your sense of self-worth would really drop off. I would want to support my family, so I would do anything I could to do that. But it's difficult now because there just aren't many jobs out there. The only jobs there are part-time employment, you'd have to take two or three crummy jobs' (152 M 1994).

Indeed, steel employers' discovery of the merits of formal retraining programs may be driven less by a need to enhance workers' knowledge and more by the desire to use 'credentialism' to recreate and streamline job classifications. It is a means to continue to reorganize and control an already highly experienced and practically knowledgeable workforce along more flexible lines (Maurice 1995). In any event, many formal

work skill retraining programs have either ignored or disrupted steelworkers' existing skills and knowledge. In contrast to the old job lad-
ders, the new ones are largely devoid of any sense of 'job ownership.' A
production labourer's complaint about not being able to apply his
increased formal training to a specific job appeared to be widespread in
the plant: 'They don't want us to do the job that we've been trained for.
They want to use us as floaters. You go, wait a minute, I got a letter
signed by everybody that says the job is mine. [The foreman] says, well,
we're not honouring that' (090 M 1994). Both at Hilton Works, and in
labour markets generally, the basic problem is not a lack of skills and
knowledge but a lack of decent jobs in which to apply them. As a service
department tradesperson said: 'We have such a big work area and so few
people. You look around and wonder if anybody's in the shop ... They
aren't hiring anybody at Stelco but you really have to be qualified to get
any job. Actually there are so many people looking for jobs, everybody is
overqualified and it's more or less personality or if they like you or whatever' (163 M 1994).

Management–Union Relations

Individual workers drew on a variety of perspectives and strategies in
their responses to Stelco's restructuring, but as their tenacity in the
1981 and 1990 strikes showed, collectively they had a strong commitment to defending their hard-won working conditions. Local 1005's history as a strong, militant union meant it had negotiated trend-setting
wage agreements and resisted arbitrary authority through both formal
grievance procedures and its active oppositional workplace culture.[10]
Over the years of restructuring, though, Local 1005 took a beating as its
membership (and thus its budget) was cut in half, it went through fac-
tional fights, and it lost important protections as court rulings and legis-
lative changes undermined former legal rights.

Prior to 1981 Stelco management had never relinquished its conservative, authoritarian management style of the old industrial relations
school. Management had no tradition of formal consultation with Local
1005 over products, prices, work organization, or technology (Adams
and Zeytinoglu 1987; Adams 1988). As it implemented its dramatic
restructuring, this management style was gradually modified. There
were substantial changes in both management strategies and union
responses during the fifteen years of restructuring. Throughout the
restructuring process, the balance of power shifted in Stelco's favour, as

the union made pragmatic accommodations in its attempts to defend the rights of its members.

Reorganizing the Plant and Disorganizing Lives[11]

Management's shift from its long-established 'expansion at all costs' to a consolidation of existing resources was signalled by the massive lay-offs of 1981–1982 (Allan 1982). In 1982 the chair announced that management had decided: 'to engage in a systematic cost containment and productivity-oriented evaluation of a wide range of operational procedures' (Baker 1982). In one year management eliminated close to 4,400 jobs or 35 per cent of the hourly rated workforce. Some of this unprecedented job loss was accomplished through attrition – early retirements or quits, but mostly it involved indefinite lay-offs. To facilitate its efforts, management tried to gain control over the right to determine which workers were laid off or recalled. The union fought hard to retain certain protections and defend principles such as seniority entitlement to jobs.

Subsequent lay-offs came in several stages, including a two-week shutdown of the plant in December 1982. Smaller lay-offs continued over the next two years; even the end of the recession in 1984 meant only a temporary reversal of long-term cutbacks in employment. This initial period of major lay-offs effectively eliminated women from Hilton Works. The 1984 survey of unemployed steelworkers located twelve women who ranged in age from twenty-four to fifty-five. Seven had accumulated only one year's seniority, four had two years; only one had three. They had been unemployed anywhere from three to thirty-four months, with an average of twenty-one months. Only six retained recall rights. The rest were either unemployed or had other, lower-paying, mostly non-unionized jobs. These lay-offs also eliminated many of the younger men.

As Stelco made new demands on the workforce, it appealed to workers to forget the strike and work more efficiently to help the company regain lost customers. In response, Local 1005's leadership pointed out that Stelco's authoritarian management was inadequate and stressed the need for greater cooperation. As Local 1005 president Cec Taylor declared, in anticipation of a period of subdued growth through the 1980s:

We acknowledge the challenges presented to companies and workers alike by these economic conditions. But we are not enthusiastic about con-

tributing our effort to Stelco's recovery and renewed profitability on the
older worker-boss basis. We want the respect from the Company, both in
terms of wages and on-the-job working conditions, that is due us
considering our central role in the steelmaking process. We earn Stelco's
profits, surely we deserve management's respect. I hope that from this
strike Stelco has learned that the heavy-handed employee relations of the
past are obsolete and will no longer work effectively. (1982: 1)

The pessimism embedded in this appeal was confirmed in 1983, as
more mass lay-offs were coupled with unilaterally imposed experiments
in reduced work crew levels.

Appealing to 'market realities,' management also tried to reopen the
1981 collective agreement in an effort to target the employment costs
built into it. In the context of mass lay-offs and declining profits, Local
1005 agreed to an early contract settlement in 1984. Many of the
remaining workers, concerned about their security, had increasingly
adopted a conciliatory tone with management: 'There may not be a
strong spirit of unionism in the membership, not right now. Right now,
everyone's out to cover his own ass, basically. And it's only natural. What
do I have to do to survive, myself? And right now that's the way it is, and
you see it over and over again' (029 M 1984). The 1984 contract offered
improved pension eligibility and income security, but no significant
wage increase. And by 1985, the new works manager Robert Milbourne
had carried out a second wave of massive layoffs, relying to some extent
on attrition and early retirement packages.

Throughout the 1980s management tried to develop 'new industrial
relations' to create better cooperation between management, the
union, and the workforce. But despite repeated assertions of its commitment to new, more consultative approaches, management typically fell
back on older, more heavy-handed management styles. Although joint
management and labour committees proliferated, Stelco managers
proved to be ineffective at negotiating changes to traditional workplace
rules and job classifications. A crane operator spoke for many workers
when he described management's relation to the union: '[The union] is
there to help the company too. But the company doesn't realize that.
It's just a continual battle between Stelco and our union' (029 M 1984).

During this period Local 1005 leaders generally took strong positions
defending workers from management's specific restructuring initiatives.
They led demonstrations against lay-offs, contracting out, discriminatory lay-offs of the few women steelworkers, and for unemployed work-

ers' benefits. Local 1005 organized a long boycott of multicrafting or 'supertrades' training programs. It made frequent appeals to workers to report any abuses of the contract. It followed up many previously ignored health and safety complaints and established an independent workers' health centre.

As the impact of lay-offs reverberated through the plant, bumping pitted workers against each other; resentment and frustration grew. Workers were also increasingly under pressure to work overtime, a strategy that divided the workforce by benefiting some at the expense of others. People were tempted by the money, especially as everyone had lost pay during the 1981 strike, many had lost more during periods of lay-off, and most were afraid of future lay-offs. Other workers, though, strongly opposed overtime. As a production worker explained: 'As far as I'm concerned, guys that work overtime should be fined through the union. I disagree with it altogether. There are guys out on the street. I'm working but they're not and they're in the same boat as I am. There are senior guys who should be retired, working overtime like crazy. I don't buy that. We had a guy work twenty-four hours straight the other day. Sick!' (029 M 1984).

In 1985, when union appeals to membership and to management to reduce overtime failed, the union asked the provincial government to enforce the 100-hour limit on overtime contained in the Employment Standards Act. In the interim, overtime continued to be a critical issue. Internal company documents leaked to the media in 1987 indicated that the amount of overtime became so excessive that company officials had cautioned superintendents about 'breaking the law' and instructed them to reduce overtime (Hallman 1987: A1). The government dragged out the investigation until 1990, then ruled in Stelco's favour.

The union and individual workers continued to fight excessive overtime, but there were persistent accusations of workers regularly employed for over sixty hours a week.[12] As laid-off workers' recall rights expired, the remaining workers become more inclined to accept overtime. A decade later, the same production worker remained opposed in principle: 'Guys were laid off. Why should I be doing their jobs? It's just totally outrageous' (029 M 1994). But: 'Now I've finally started working it, after they called everybody back. The union can't control it. Now the general attitude is if I don't do it, then somebody else is going to do it anyways. So why not grab it while I can?' (029 M 1994).

Stelco continued to rely on divisive shop-floor tactics and the threat of lay-offs, especially around contract time, while union leaders focused on maintaining and expanding workers' contract provisions.[13] Early contract negotiations in 1987 resulted in plant-wide seniority rights to retrain for new jobs and some improvements to pensions and vacation benefits, but there was no wage increase beyond a cost-of-living allowance (Estok 1987).

In the 1987 contract the union managed to rectify some of the injustices by getting some control over bumping and improving the language regarding promotions. On Labour Day 1988 a large delegation of steelworkers organized by Local 1005 protested in front of Stelco Tower against the use of contractors, overtime, and multicrafting, and for a solution to group benefit problems (Crone 1988; Martin 1988). Local 1005 joined the company in calling for federal government subsidies to aid workers' early retirements and support in fighting U.S. trade sanctions against Canadian steel companies (Lefaive 1990c).

Although Stelco had made healthy profits in 1988–9, it was still struggling with a high debt burden, and it sustained substantial losses in the first half of 1990. It was strongly committed to cutting its workforce and was intent on splitting the company into a number of discrete businesses with separate union contracts (Lanthier 1990; Godfrey 1990). Stelco built up steel inventories, laid off hundreds of workers, and made separate offers to different locals in attempts to break the long-established pattern of chain bargaining with all Stelco locals together. Coming up to the 1990 negotiations, management initiated a number of efforts intended to persuade the workforce of management's sincerity. It reorganized the labour relations department, orchestrated a community advertising blitz, invited workers to dinner meetings for 'information exchanges,' offered more human relations courses for supervisors, and gave workers tours of customers' facilities' (Christmas 1990). During negotiations, Stelco offered Local 1005 minimal wage and pension increases and proposed eliminating cost-of-living adjustments.

Despite management's efforts, there was a widespread sense of anger and frustration among the workers. Most thought that management treated them badly, in arrogant and heavy-handed ways. After six years of downsizing, with no real wage increases and in light of the healthy profits of the previous year, the union wanted some significant gains for its members. The anger workers felt about the way management had treated them was close to the surface and was articulated explicitly in the militancy leading up to and during the strike. With the contract due to expire on 31 July, 1990, over 90 per cent of the membership supported a strike to back up their demands (Lanthier 1990).

The 1990 strike was long and bitter – 106 days, or three and a half months. A month and a half into the strike, Stelco slashed dividends to shareholders, cut executive salaries, and threatened publicly to close some of its operations – including large parts of Hilton Works (Hallman 1990; Davie 1990). Shortly afterwards, negotiations broke down and picket lines turned violent over independent truckers carrying Stelco's warehoused steel.

The resolution of the strike a month later included a cost-of-living allowance and base rate pay increases amounting to over 5 per cent in each year of the three-year deal, better pension base rates with greater worker control and indexing, stronger limits on contracting out and permanent lay-offs, an income-sharing scheme, and more flexible access to training programs. These gains were substantial over Stelco's pre-strike offers and led Leo Gerrard, USWA district director, to declare the contract 'one of the most socially important collective agreements nego-tiated in the last decade' (Lefaive, 5 November, 1990a: A1).

But Stelco also won its most important objective: effectively breaking chain bargaining (Lefaive and Hughes 1990). As a result, the Lake Erie Steel Company subsequently had a separate contract no longer pat-terned on Hilton Works. This loss allowed for more competition and a downgrading of the collective agreement.

Immediately after the strike, John Martin, president of Local 1005, made another plea for greater cooperation with Stelco management, much as Cec Taylor had a decade earlier: 'We have to stop fighting one another and start making this business work, or eventually it is just going to collapse underneath us. 1005 is prepared to work with the company, not to be taken advantage of by the company, but to honestly work with the company [to negotiate the next contract in 1993] without any of the pain we had to suffer in 1990' (Cited in Lefaive, 5 November 1990: A1).

The immediate aftermath of this strike was essentially a rerun of what had happened in 1982–4, including a very slow recall of workers, large permanent lay-offs, while rumours of closure circulated and both sides pledged greater cooperation. The chair and CEO Fred Telmer placed a renewed public emphasis on improved worker relations: 'The hard-nosed legalistic approach just doesn't work any more. One of the under-lying principles is much more open communication with our employ-ees, to involve them in activities, discussions about what's happening in the plants themselves. Turning around the legalistic approach will take some time, well into the '90s' (cited in Hallman 1990: 19).

A market downturn after the 1990 strike meant that steel prices and

Stelco share values continued to plummet. These events led to larger lay-offs. In 1992 the company announced another lay-off of over 1,000 hourly workers, many with more than fifteen years seniority (Fowlie 1992). For example, in late 1992, the coke ovens were staffed by 308 operators, seventy maintenance workers, and sixty-three tradespeople from the services division. By early 1993 Stelco management had reduced the workforce in the coke ovens to 215 maintenance operators (Frost 1996). To cope with the reduction of workers, management unilaterally announced a new plan to blend largely unrelated operating and maintenance jobs into fewer hybrid positions and to do so in less than two months (Davie 1992a). Local 1005 leadership protested that the time frame was unrealistically short, and the company consented to consult the local about implementation (Davie 1992b).

The cumulative effect of downsizing had a serious impact on the union and its capacities to defend its members in the contract negotiations of 1993 and 1996. By 1993 Local 1005 had lost over 60 per cent of the members it had had in 1980. From 1993 to 1996 active membership remained around 5,000 workers. Salaried employment also declined but more gradually, so that the proportion of salaried employees increased from under 15 per cent in the early 1980s to over 20 per cent in the 1990s.

In 1992–3 Stelco's weakened market condition undercut the union's bargaining position once again. The members gave Local 1005 a strong mandate to take a more cooperative approach to the company in coordinated rather than chain bargaining (Westell 1992), to become involved in the job-cutting and amalgamating process, and to negotiate the contract early to reassure jumpy customers (Davie 1992b). A month later, in the wake of continuing financial losses, Stelco offered its own olive branch by opening its books to Local 1005 for the first time (Morrison 1992). After several months of intense talks, a new three-year contract was approved in May 1993. There was virtually no pay increase, and cost of living became part of regular pay, something Stelco had wanted since 1990 (Papp 1993). Most significantly, both parties agreed to a joint work restructuring committee whose mandate was 'to find mutually acceptable ways and means to deal with the ongoing restructuring of work to ensure their competitive position' (Stelco–Local 1005 Basic Agreement 1993).

Both Stelco executives and Local 1005 leaders generally maintained this consultative mode between 1993 and 1996 in a centralized and limited form (Frost 1996). A union activist described this stance: 'But I honestly believe that the company and the union are working together now to get the job done. And that's what you need' (029 M 1994).

The reaction of workers varied. An industrial mechanic observed that Stelco management had made some specific efforts to involve the remaining workers in company affairs: 'The company cut the whole place to pieces. They cut the workforce in half. [But] they don't want to shut the place down. You still keep your distance with supervisors, but generally the company is treating us pretty well. There are no job security guarantees, but we're given daily briefings. There's a paper circulated across the plant. You know, they don't keep us in the dark any more like they used to. Before, a lot of people used to feel negative about the company. Now it's a little more positive. Stelco, Dofasco, everybody's struggling to stay alive' (011 M 1994).

A steelworker described the effects of low steel prices on workers' expectations of their union: 'Workers now realize in order for the company to survive and them to survive, they've got to get along, which became a necessity for either one to survive. 1005 used to be hard line. In order to survive, we've got to be flexible' (176 M 1994). The combination of job insecurity and instability made many workers take a pragmatic approach to the new constraints they faced: 'I don't see the management–worker thing so much any more. The union and the company are pretty tolerant of each other now, friendlier. Unions like 1005 had a lot of power back in the early '80s. They got a lot of things accomplished. Since then, companies and unions have to work together' (166 M 1994).

This worker's concern for job security in uncertain times was strengthened by his appreciation of the difficulty faced by older workers: 'Besides, I'm around forty and the thought of starting over again in a different line of work is scary' (166 M 1994). For many, the frustration with the deterioration in working conditions was something to be endured in the hopes that they could keep the job for thirty years and so ensure a secure pension: 'I just hope to get my thirty years. Even with the seniority you're still in doubt. The steel industry went for a dive, the economy went, everything else. Of course, the government hasn't helped either' (152 M 1994).

Hilton workers also remained aware of serious limits to more cooperative relations in the face of sometimes uncooperative or misleading supervisors, shoddy treatment of pensioners, subcontracting of departed workers' jobs, and other company claims that did not square with their own experiences. In 1994 a service department tradesperson articulated these concerns: 'A little more cooperation works better than what they did before. But I still think there's a problem. A foreman will tell us something and tell us it's gospel, right. But when you go outside the shop, you find out what's really going on, then you find out he's really lying to you. I think upper management is pretty much the same way. And they'll just keep bringing in more and more contractors and not hire anybody' (163 M 1994).

Rank-and-file militancy on the shop floor showed no signs of diminishing (Frost and Verma 1997). The rate of grievances formally filed in the 1990s was even greater than the rate after the 1981 strike (Livingstone 1996). One young finishing-mill operator expressed ongoing frustration: 'Their industrial relations are terrible. Their employee relations are bloody awful. And then they say, "Well, be happy guys. Get on the team. Help us out here." What the hell for? There's no future down there anymore. Well, to hell with the team' (090 M 1994).

Workers' scepticism appeared to be warranted. Despite the general stability of employment, and Stelco's return to profitability in the mid-1990s, the industrial relations system at Hilton Works remained highly centralized with little real worker involvement. As Frost and Verma (1997: 18) conclude in their assessment of the Hilton Works system: 'For effective employee involvement, power and decision making need to be decentralized from the offices of the Operations Manager and the local union president to include a broader cross section of management especially at the level of the shop floor, in addition to a more diverse group of union leaders and members. The local union is a strong one and therefore has the potential to be an effective voice for its members across a whole range of issues with which it has not traditionally dealt.'

In 1996, however, the balance of power in contract negotiations remained in management's favour. The first contract recommended by the executive in March 1996 included better pensions, improvements to health benefits, and income sharing, and an end to cyclical lay-offs for eligible workers who had been on lay-off–callback for many years (Holt 1996). There was no wage increase beyond the cost of living (Prokaska, 29 March 1996d). This contract offer was narrowly rejected by the membership, at least partly because younger workers were not prepared to accept such a long contract without a wage increase (Prokaska, 4 April 1996a). A month later, a revised six-year contract with a lump-sum payment of $500 up front and wage increases in the last three years was accepted by a two-thirds majority (Stelco–Local 1005 Tentative Agreement April 1996). This six-year contract was the longest ever in the Canadian steel industry. The long-term contract cemented management's restructuring strategy to make Hilton Works one of the more viable and profitable of the old integrated steel plants.

In late 1996 Hilton Works employed about 60 per cent of Stelco's total workforce. It remained the site of most of Stelco's capacity to produce high value-added products and still produced 60 per cent of Stelco steel. In 1997 Stelco reported a profit of $137 million (CBC *Radio, 8 a.m. News,* 28 March, 1998); Stelco management's restructuring of Hilton Works was a resounding success for both management and shareholders.

A Restructured Workforce

After all the retooling and turmoil of the 1980s and 1990s, Hilton Works was a quite different place to work. There were fewer jobs, a more limited range of jobs, and production and maintenance work had become more closely integrated. The occupational structure in the plant changed significantly, as the number of production jobs requiring heavy physical labour decreased and the proportions of managerial, technical, and trades employees increased.[14] Workers at Hilton Works, like many workers in North America and elsewhere, were being turned into general workers who could do whatever tasks management required of them, and who could be terminated by their employer relatively easily.

A tradesperson who had remained in the service department explained the general intensification of trades work and the crossover to production work:

> There's just less guys to do the job faster. We're running with 70 per cent less men and we're still putting out the same amount of product here. So you tell me that's not efficiency! Stelco has become more trades-oriented. Trades have really crossed over and are doing more labour work than the art of the trade, because they can get rid of a janitor and you can sweep your own floor. We keep seeing the shop go down and down and down and we say, 'Where's the bottom?' I think they're going to keep cutting back until they actually get in trouble. (137 M 1994)

What made the cuts even more galling for the remaining workforce was the daily presence of contract labourers and the continuing pressure to do overtime. In 1997 the total value of work contracted out exceeded $100 million, with 200 to 300 contracted employees in the plant every day, and the total overtime in the plant was 906,734 hours or about 435 jobs (Knox 1998: 14). This pattern had become common

across the North American workforce. Some employees worked longer
and longer hours for somewhat higher wages, while growing numbers of
people were forced to do temporary or contract work or were chroni-
cally unemployed and increasingly impoverished (Schor 1991; Donner
et al. 1994; Livingstone 1998a). As a laid-off steelworker noted: 'When I
hear how many workers are doing hours and hours of overtime, getting
richer while I get poorer, and I hear about hundreds of contractors
swarming around Stelco doing my old job for less pay and no benefits,
and then I see that Stelco's profits are up. I wasn't laid off because there
was no work, that's for sure' (221 F 1996).

Although the immediate consequence of restructuring was Stelco's
renewed profitability, the more long-term implications posed serious
questions for management, the union, and the ongoing practices that
shape the day-to-day experiences of workers on the plant floor. In 1984
more than 90 per cent of the unionized male workers we interviewed
had spent most of their working lives at Hilton Works; they had an average age of forty-two and average seniority of more than eighteen years.
By 1996, like workers at most other integrated steel plants in Europe
and North America (Albright 1995), people at Hilton Works were on
average in their late forties with about twenty-five years' seniority; there
was no one under thirty-four. This demographic imbalance meant that,
if Stelco failed to regenerate its workforce, as these remaining workers
retired, there would be no experienced younger workers to fill their
places.[15] Stelco could confront a serious labour crisis if forced to hire
large numbers of new workers who would have to learn on the job without access to the years of accumulated knowledge and expertise held by
older workers.

This looming demographic problem posed serious issues for the
workplace culture and the tradition of union solidarity as well. Prior to
1981 workers' solidarity was promoted by Stelco's practice of hiring new
workers on a regular basis to replace retirees or quits and to incremen-
tally expand the workforce. Because these new workers were typically
from a similar background as those already in the plant, and steady hiring meant new workers were always a minority, they were readily incorporated into the union with its tradition of collective action. The
postwar struggles, and their lessons, were a living legacy passed on to
successive generations of steelworkers who were socialized into both the
workplace culture that made day-to-day experiences more tolerable and
the militant solidarity necessary to threaten strike action in response to
management recalcitrance.

The 5,000 workers remaining at Stelco in the late 1990s who had been hired prior to 1981 were part of that tradition and retained that historic memory. But, by 2002, if people continued to retire after thirty years of service, only 2,500 of these workers will remain in the plant and therefore part of the union. Their average age would be forty-eight (Livingstone 1998a, 1999). Despite the local's long tradition of collective militancy, these aging workers would probably have particular interests related to retiring; their focus in contract negotiations would likely be on early retirement and pensions, and many would probably prefer to serve out their time and leave rather than continue fighting further management initiatives to retrench.

Stelco's future hiring strategies could dramatically alter the union and its politics. Unless it decides to close Hilton Works, management will have to hire a lot of new workers in a short period of time. A rapid influx of new hirees would complicate the ways in which new workers are socialized into the culture of union militancy of Local 1005. These new, younger workers, many of whom could be women, or workers of ethnic, racialized, or other minorities, would dramatically alter the demographic profile of Local 1005, and they could raise very different, and perhaps new, issues at the bargaining table. The future of Local 1005 will depend on how new workers respond as union members and how the union responds to the challenge to build working-class solidarity in the face of profoundly different political traditions and interests.

Conclusion

Workers' experiences of restructuring at Hilton Works illustrates the tenuous hold they have on access to jobs and their inability to guarantee a pay cheque to support themselves and their families. Workers who kept their jobs did so by accommodating themselves to demands they often objected to and, in the process, gave management greater control over the workplace than it had had since the 1946 struggle to form a union. The women and men who lost their jobs through no fault of their own forfeited employment security that offered a decent income and anchored a particular kind of domestic life. A forty-nine-year-old steelworker who had put in twenty-nine years at Hilton Works articulated his profound sense of betrayal when Stelco's restructuring wiped out his secure standard of living: 'They're making so much profit that they're taking money away from us, so that we can't spend it. Our washing machine broke down and even though I'm making good money and my house is paid for, with the kids and the rest of the expenses, I didn't have the $600 to buy a new washing machine. And I should have. For the length of time that I've been working at Stelco, there's no reason why I shouldn't be able to go out and say, "Hey, we've got to get one." I couldn't do it. My wife had to take the clothes to the laundromat. We shouldn't have had to do that' (029 M 1984).

Twelve years later, one of the laid-off women steelworkers summed up what had happened: 'By focusing on profits instead of jobs, they've made it harder for everyone except the very rich who make a living off their shares. Sure there's a few workers still making good money, but most workers now, they work long hours but can't hardly make enough to support their families. Who knows where it will all end?' (223 F 1996).

5

Women's Work: Juggling Job and Family

A woman married to a steelworker reviewed her work history, showing how her decisions about whether or not to take paid employment and the hours she worked were shaped by her husband's projected earnings and shift schedule, her child care responsibilities, and the availability of a job she could do: 'I was working full-time which is like a forty-four-hour week when he was first on strike. And they were really good to me because, when he did finally go back to work, I stayed part-time. I worked around his shifts' (078 F 1984).

She left paid work to be at home full-time with their first baby; then when Stelco announced further lay-offs, her employer called her back to work: 'I remember it was a big shock to almost everybody because Stelco said they were having a massive lay-off and [my husband] would have been in that number. I had quit my job at this point, thinking everything was okay again. And they phoned me and asked if I wanted my job back. And I was just like, "Yes!" From going in the morning, "Oh, what are we going to do this time?" to them calling me at 8 o'clock at night and saying, "Hey, we heard the Stelco news. Do you want your job?" And it was like, "Yes, I do."' (078 F 1984).

Her unusually cooperative employer allowed her to change the hours she worked as her household circumstances changed: 'I worked until I had [the baby] in 1987, and then I went back to work in 1990 during the strike, because we knew with the strike coming, he would get laid off after, because every time there was a strike, this would happen. And at this point, we now had a home, the kids. So I went back to work. I was just really lucky that this company hired me. They sort of knew about me from years ago' (078 F 1994). In face of the unpredictibility of the Stelco lay-off lottery she and her husband did their best to plan:

I went back full-time. We had an agreement because [my husband], at this point, should have been getting laid off, but it never seemed to come. And this started in September or October and we waited, we waited, and people in his job were getting laid off and we were still waiting, so I made a deal with them that if he didn't go back to work, I would work for them full-time 'til December, which is like their busy time will be over. So I end up getting a sitter, and it was lucky that my sister-in-law was out of work at the time and she lived close, so it was real convenient. So we were both working full-time for a little bit. And then, he never did get laid off. (078 F 1994)

Her account demonstrates the complications resulting from women's responsibility for juggling the tensions between paid employment and domestic labour. Conversely, the experiences of the women who applied to Stelco demonstrate the way sexism limited women's employment opportunities. Stelco's management justified its resistance to hiring women by arguing that certain 'men's jobs' were unsuitable for women. They were too physically challenging, too rough and, most importantly, incompatible with domestic labour. A woman described how her application was received when she first applied to Stelco:

They asked me if I really knew what I was getting into; if I had made special arrangements for my two children; did I know the job would involve shift work. They said I wouldn't have much time with my children. So I asked them if they asked male applicants those questions. 'That's different,' they said. Then they said, 'You realize if I hire you, you'll never have another statutory holiday or weekend off.' He said, 'Can you lift fifty pounds?' I said 'Yes, but I understand forty pounds is the legal limit.' It sure didn't feel like he was just making the job clear for me. It sounded like a warning. Like he was thinking 'I don't think a woman can do this job.' (222 F 1984)

The experiences of both the store clerk and the steelworker illustrate the systemic discrimination women face in the paid labour force and the fundamental incompatibilities between paid employment and domestic labour. They show how profoundly women's work is shaped by gender ideologies and practices and how difficult it is to effect changes. They also demonstrate the impact of economic restructuring on women's work as their inability to rely on secure employment, either for themselves or their partners, destabilized their lives. As a former steelworker observed in 1996: 'Stelco was so concerned that we couldn't do the job because our family responsibilities would get in the way. But what got in the way was not having a job' (221 F 1996).

Women and Stelco: Challenging the Dynamics of 'Women's Work'

The activists who initiated the Women Back Into Stelco campaign did so in part to challenge prevailing assumptions about 'women's work.' The feminist movement, and particularly its women's liberation current, developed critiques of sexism, posed challenges to gender stereotypes, and provoked public discussions about whether men are better suited than women for certain jobs (Pierson et al. 1993; Pierson and Cohen 1995). The feminist movement also gave voice to, and legitimated, women's complaints about typical 'women's jobs' and their desires for better jobs and pay. A woman steelworker commented: 'Women are becoming more forward, more pushy. It has taken a lot of years for us to come forward and speak our minds. I think these feelings are there in every woman but they just haven't known what to do. You need help to bring it out' (225 F 1984).

The feminist movement gave increasing numbers of women the confidence that they could do 'men's jobs' and that they had the right to demand equality. It also provided a model of social change based on organizing collective actions. For example, one of the initiators of the campaign had previously worked for a major union as the equal opportunities coordinator. When she resigned to try to get a job at Stelco, she wrote in the union newsletter: 'My time as OPSEU's [Ontario Public Service Employees Union] equal opportunities coordinator has convinced me that women will never achieve equality in the workplace until we break out of the traditional female job ghettos, and are represented in industrial jobs by industrial unions' (*OPSEU News* 1979).

The activists involved in the Women Back Into Stelco campaign argued that opposition to hiring women reflected sexist notions of women's capabilities and was an attempt to hold onto men's privilege. The campaign victory and subsequent hirings showed conclusively that women can do the work and, where necessary, combine it with child care and other caregiving work.

I worked at Stelco for five years from when they had to hire us, because of the court ruling, 'til I finally lost my recall rights. And then I lucked out and got another job at [another steel company]. So I've been a steelworker for fifteen years now, and a single parent. I've raised my two kids who were three and five when I started. And my mother moved in when she got sick so I looked after her for six years too 'til she died. So no one can tell me steelmaking is no job for a woman or that women can't do both – but it sure wasn't easy! It took a hell of a lot of hard work, coping with all those demands. (208 F 1994)

The women who subsequently took advantage of their victory by applying to Stelco did so for the same reasons men did: 'The pay was dramatically higher. I wanted to get an industrial job on account of the money. It was more money than if I was doing women's work' (224 F 1984). Most women who got hired at Stelco doubled their wages from $4 to $5 per hour to $8 to $10 per hour and they presumed their long-term prospects would be better:[1] 'I worked at Burger King. I was making $3.50 an hour and I went to Stelco and I was getting over $10' (204 F 1984).

They noted that employment in 'men's jobs' was significantly better than that in 'women's jobs,' because of membership in a strong union and the resulting higher pay rates, greater security, and stronger health and safety protections. Most were frustrated by the limitations of the 'women's jobs' they had held previously: six had worked as waitresses, five in poorly paying clerical jobs, one had been a gas station attendant, and one had worked in a beauty salon. Nine of the twenty-six had previous work experience in light industry, for example, on the assembly line in a plant manufacturing glass bottles or a paint-canning factory. These were small enterprises with low pay and poor working conditions. Several women pointed out that the physical requirements demanded by so-called men's factory jobs are often no greater than those of 'women's jobs.' Others claimed that working at Stelco required less of them than either their former jobs, such as waitressing, where they regularly moved stock around, or everyday domestic life: '[The personnel man asked] if I could carry around a fifty-pound bag of cement. I said I carry a forty-pound kid around the shopping malls, why couldn't I carry around a bag of cement?' (208 F 1984).

The women noted that workplaces like Stelco, which once relied on physical strength and endurance, have become increasingly mechanized. As a result, large size or physical strength are no longer as critical. By 1984 a male steelworker reported: 'Steelmaking doesn't require a great amount of brawn. It's pretty well a push-button business now' (075 M 1984). Furthermore, some women were willing to challenge the notion that physical strength was limited to men: 'I've never seen a job I couldn't do or any other woman couldn't do' (207 F 1984).

Many of the women had personal ties with Stelco workers. Nine had fathers at Hilton Works, five had other close male relatives employed there. One had an aunt who had worked there during the war: 'My dad is down there. All my brothers worked there' (213 F 1984). Such contacts gave them confidence that they could do the work: 'I was daddy's little girl growing up, and daddy was a steamfitter pipefitter in steam generation. And I knew almost everybody in the department. My father would come home and he loved his work, and he really liked to talk to somebody about it. So ever since I was a little kid who hung on Daddy's every word, he could talk to me about it. By the time I was old enough I knew different things' (208 F 1984).

Once they were at Hilton Works, most women agreed that while the money was the most important, other aspects of the work appealed to them, too: 'It is good money, but still when your kids start going to school all day and you're at home all the time you get fed up' (202 F 1984). Some found the challenge of heavy industrial work more interesting than 'women's work': 'Office work never appealed to me. I don't know, it just didn't seem interesting. It wasn't for me' (211 F 1984). Even where jobs actually required strength, or were assumed to require it, some women enjoyed it: 'The physical part of it was wonderful. It was a real challenge to my body' (221 F 1984). And, like their male co-workers, all of the women appreciated the benefits and relative protections afforded by the union: 'It was such a good job compared to any I had before. I was really glad the union was there to make sure I was treated fairly' (202 F 1984).

The massive lay-offs in the 1980s were a stark reminder that women's periodic successes in breaking out of the double ghetto are tentative, and especially vulnerable in periods of economic downturn.[2] What happened to women at Stelco was repeated throughout the Hamilton-Wentworth area and the rest of Ontario. For a brief period, between January 1978 and January 1980, the number of women manufacturing employees in Ontario rose 24.3 per cent, climbing steadily from 251,000 to 312,000. With the onset of the depression and the lay-offs, the number of women manufacturing workers dropped to 263,000 by January 1983 – a drop of 15.7 per cent in just three years![3] The short-term recovery in 1985 saw the employment of women in manufacturing rise to a high of 344,000 but immediately employment began to tumble back, to 272,000 by 1994. By 1996 employment of women in manufacturing had again reached the 1980 level of 312,000.

Restructuring in the 1980s and 1990s not only eliminated many jobs and imposed hiring freezes on most industries, it was accompanied by a conservative political climate in which earlier orientations to women's equality were eroded (Bashevkin 1998). Public campaigns to improve women's positions in the labour force faced growing indifference and opposition. One of the first actions of the Conservative government in Ontario after its 1995 election victory was to repeal employment equity legislation (Walker 1995: 7).

In that climate, it was not surprising that in the early 1990s various government and union-sponsored retraining initiatives focused on men.[4] In 1994 the majority of new jobs in Ontario were in manufacturing, where only 19 per cent of the workers were women. Given the absence of affirmative action and other special programs, 90 per cent of the new jobs went to men (Philip 1995). Thus, despite the victories of struggles such as the Women Back Into Stelco campaign, the economic recession and increasing political conservatism, combined with business and government restructuring throughout the 1980s and 1990s, meant that the majority of women were further confined to the double ghetto – to low-paid, insecure jobs in the labour force and to domestic responsibilities in the home.

Working Wives

The women living with men employed at Stelco were intimately familiar with that double ghetto. There were sharp contrasts between their work experiences and those of Stelco workers:[5] 'I was a "Stelco wife" for over twenty years! I had all the household responsibilities, I worked at any crummy job I could get that would fit in with his shifts and child care. When I saw what that job [at Stelco] meant for those women, I'd have done anything to be a Stelco worker instead of a wife. What's called "women's work" is the pits' (301 F 1996).

All of them had to juggle paid employment – often their own and always their partners' – with the demands of their household's domestic labour. They all were the primary domestic workers in their households. Almost all of them had had some type of paid employment since they had married, and most of them liked the advantages of paid employment – entitlement, money, sociability – and took pride in their capacities as workers. Unlike the men employed at Stelco, though, the women's work strategies were complicated by their double day.

In 1984, of the women we interviewed, seventy-seven (42 per cent) were full-time homemakers and more than half of them (108 out of 185) had paid employment: fifty-six (30 per cent) were employed part-time (of whom three were both employed by someone else and self-employed, and four were only self-employed), and fifty-two (28 per cent) were employed full-time (of whom three were self-employed).[6] Most did conventional 'women's' work in clerical, sales, and service jobs – in retail and wholesale (30 per cent), personal and business services (27 per cent), government (21 per cent), finances (9 per cent), manu-facturing (8 per cent), and transportation (4 per cent).[7] Only a few (9 per cent) had jobs in 'male' areas such as truck driver, transport opera-tor, or metal shaper. Where Local 1005 had established a long history of labour protection for Stelco workers, only 28 per cent of employed women were members of a union.[8] Many of them worked for minimum wage. The mean annual income for these women employed in 1982 was $9,484, which was very close to the national average.

The hours these women worked for pay each week ranged from three to sixty-eight.[9] Half of the women who had paid jobs were employed part-time, compared with the 1984 national average of 26 per cent (Sta-tistics Canada 1995b: 73). In some cases they would have preferred more hours, but full-time employment was not available because many employers prefer to hire part-time workers who are cheaper. For many women part-time employment was a strategy to help them balance the demands of paid employment and domestic labour. It made them more vulnerable, however, because employers generally do not have to pay benefits for part-timers. Most women (53 per cent) were employed dur-ing regular day hours; 18 per cent had varying hours of employment; 13 per cent were on afternoons; and 13 per cent had either two or three rotating shifts per week.

The labour force participation of these women reflected their respon-sibilities for child care; it was directly tied to whether they had children and to the age of the youngest child living at home. Nearly all women under thirty years of age who did not have children (88 per cent) were employed, about two-thirds of them (68 per cent) full-time. Similarly, about two-thirds of women over thirty without children (68 per cent) were employed full-time. In contrast, less than half the women with preschool-aged children (46 per cent) were employed, and only 14 per cent of them full-time. Women whose children were between five and fifteen were more likely to be employed (56 per cent), although only 21 per cent were employed full-time. Relieved of ongoing child care responsibilities, women whose children were over sixteen were more likely to have paid jobs (72 per cent), almost half (47 per cent) full-time. However, the twenty-two older women whose children had left home

TABLE 5.1
Women's work status by presence and age of youngest child (% in each work status by family phase)

	n	Full-time homemaker (%)	Employed part-time (%)	Employed full-time (%)
Pre-first child[a]	20	12	31	57
Age of youngest (years) ≤ 4	46	54	32	14
5–15	55	44	35	21
≥ 16	32	28	25	47
Empty nest	22	66	12	22
Childless	8	32	16	52
Number of women	183	78	52	53

[a]We differentiated among women with no children between those who were thirty years old or younger (per-first child) and those over thirty (childless).

were not as likely to have paid work: 34 per cent were employed, 22 per cent full-time. Not surprisingly, women with several children were more likely to be full-time homemakers, especially when the children were young.

Their work histories revealed the complications women experienced in their effort to manage the competitive demands of earning an income and providing domestic labour. There was considerable diversity both among the women and throughout individual women's lives. Of the seventy-seven women who were full-time homemakers at the time of the study, just seventeen (or 10 per cent of all the women) had been full-time homemakers since their marriage, and only ten of them said they wanted to continue as full-time homemakers. The others (90 per cent of all the women) had had paid employment for some period after marriage, and while some were looking for employment at the time, most said they wanted paid employment in the future. In addition, 25 per cent anticipated having to get paid employment in the next five years to make ends meet.

These variations reflect changing national patterns of women's work. The number of women who work as housewives their whole life has rapidly decreased; increasing numbers of women, on leaving school, work for pay until retirement. However, the majority of women move back and forth between paid employment and full-time homemaking, or engage in some combination of both, especially when their children are young. For example, by 1980 the majority of women living with male partners were employed outside the home. More significantly, by 1984 57 per cent of women with children under sixteen years of age and 44 per cent of women with children under six were in the paid labour force. By 1996 the participation rate for women with children under sixteen was 72 per cent, 66 per cent for women with preschool-aged children and 64 per cent for those with children who were less than three years old (Statistics Canada 1996a).

In our study, the changing patterns of work for married women were revealed by a comparison between the older women and younger women with children under sixteen. The older the women were, or the younger their children, the more likely they were to be full-time homemakers. Because older women had typically left school at an earlier age than younger women, they had started paid employment at a younger age. Some women aged fifty or more had started their first jobs as young as fourteen or fifteen; on average, such women had started jobs at seventeen. The older women had all had paid employment between leaving school and getting married, but four of them had not had paid work since marriage. Members of a generation who equated marriage with homemaking, they had little formal education and limited paid work experience, having spent less of their total working lives in paid employment.

In contrast, younger women had stayed in school longer; on average, women in their twenties had started paid jobs at nineteen and were more likely to continue to be employed except when they had young children. Of the 105 women with children under sixteen, 31 per cent left a paid job to have a baby, and of these, 52 per cent left that job permanently. However, 60 per cent returned to paid employment while the child was a preschooler, most when the child was about a year old. These women were younger and better educated. Being a full-time homemaker was not a vocation for them.

In the two years preceding the first interviews, only 35 per cent of the women had been employed continuously, and only 32 per cent had been full-time homemakers. The rest had changed what they were doing at least once. Between 1980 and 1996 most women changed their type of work, their workplaces, and hours of employment several times. A man described his partner's work history: 'She used to work at a retail store down at Jackson Square. She worked there for, well, since I've known her and when we moved down here, they closed up shop. She was on maternity leave and then she was off on unemployment, so she didn't work when we had [the baby]. And then when we came back to the city she was working full-time and with [the baby] it was kind of difficult. She chose the part-time' (140 M 1994).

The problems women had managing their conflicting responsibilities were revealed when less than half of all the women expressed satisfaction with their existing work arrangements. Full-time homemakers regretted their loss of income; employed women objected to the time pressures they were under. Quite a few envisioned self-employment as a possible solution, as they imagined it could be income-generating while permitting control over hours.[10]

The complexities of women's work are further complicated by the failure of both the formal categories used by government and employers and everyday common-sense language to acknowledge domestic labour as work. Despite a growing recognition that domestic labour is important, and a socially necessary work process, the term 'working women' usually implies employed women, as if homemakers do not work. All of the employed women were also homemakers, doing most of the domestic labour in their homes. To say that a woman is employed part-time, or full-time, does not convey the fact that she is also doing domestic labour.[11]

Women's own definitions reflect this confusion, as women who were doing exactly the same thing described their experiences differently. Some described themselves as homemakers who worked for pay part-time; others said they were employed part-time. Some described themselves as homemakers when they were on maternity leave, even though they planned to return to their paid job. Others explicitly described themselves as workers on leave. In talking about their unpaid domestic labour, they revealed the lack of an appropriate term for either the worker or the work. If pushed, older women were likely to call themselves 'housewives'; younger women used 'homemaker.' Most avoided a job title, saying instead, 'I'm at home' or 'I'm looking after my children.' They restricted the term 'work' to refer to paid employment and had no specific term for what they did in the home.

This discourse derives from the way being a homemaker, or housewife, is tied to marriage, family, and motherhood. Based on a naturalized notion that 'woman's place is in the home,' domestic labour has been closely associated with women as wives and mothers (Oakley 1974; Luxton 1980). In earlier decades, the majority of women did not 'choose' what type of work to do. They accepted the fact that, at least ideally, marriage meant staying at home. By the 1980s younger women had to make a decision about whether to forgo employment to work full-time as housewives. As full-time homemaking is perceived as one option among several, young homemakers sometimes felt expected to defend their choice the way their grandmothers had to defend having paid employment: 'And you meet the other wives and girlfriends. And the majority of them work; so of course the first question they say after hello is, "Where do you work?" And they look at me like I'm purple and green because I don't work outside the home' (108 F 1984).

The continuing association of women with domestic labour even when they are also employed was reflected in the ways in which women identified their occupations. When the women who identified themselves as full-time homemakers were asked when they first became a homemaker, 70 per cent said 'at marriage,' even though the majority of them were employed at the time. Another 21 per cent said they became a homemaker at the birth of their first child, even though the majority returned to paid work some time later.[12] There is a great deal of confusion about how to classify homemaking. When asked to identify their three main jobs, those who were full-time homemakers only listed their previous paid employment. In contrast, forty-eight of the 108 employed women (44 per cent) included homemaker as one of their three main jobs.[13]

This confusion reflects official policy. The 1991 census asked people to name their occupation but did not recognize any domestic labour category such as housewife or homemaker. One woman refused to answer and challenged the federal government to charge her, claiming that as a 'home manager' she was being discriminated against. The 1996 census responded to such challenges from women's groups by asking one question on unpaid household activities and others on labour market activities, still reserving the term 'occupations' for paid employment (Luxton and Vosko 1998).

Choices and Constraints at Work

Although economic necessity and the attractions of paid employment draw women into paid work, their decisions are complicated by gender and family ideologies, as well as the availability of jobs appropriate to their levels of education and training. A woman with several small children may have to devote her time and energy to domestic labour, even though it makes her economically dependent on either a husband or on state welfare payments. Another woman may put off having children because she cannot afford either to take time off work or to pay for child care. Someone else may find her work so enjoyable that she chooses not to have children because she wants no other demands on her time and energy, while another may happily leave paid work to stay home with young children, even though it means a considerable drop in income. A low-paid employee with no union protection may be required to work extensive overtime. A secure unionized worker may choose to work lots of overtime to make more money. A well-paid professional may work long hours for the prestige. In these cases, the demands of paid work leave little time or energy for domestic labour. However, despite the variations in the way daily life is organized, and the very real possibilities for individual choices, certain distinct patterns prevail.

Gender Ideologies and Family Values

Gendered discourses about the way divisions of labour promote family well-being and maximize household standards of living exercise considerable infuence on women's work strategies. While the activists and their union supporters who campaigned to get access to Stelco were deliberately challenging prevailing discourses and practices of family form, masculinity, femininity, and divisions of labour, most steelworkers, both men and women, and their partners, were less ready to abandon them.

For many of these couples, their acceptance of well-established sex/gender divisions of labour meant that women's decisions about whether to take paid employment were affected by their assessments of its impact on their husbands and marital relationships. Their commitments to their children were even more powerful in informing their work decisions. A mother of three young children said that she had left her demanding nursing job because she wanted to have more time and energy for her family: 'I didn't have enough of me left' (105 F 1984). She got work selling jewellery but left it because, when the other sales staff complained about their husbands, she caught herself doing it, too. She decided: 'I am getting out of this because my marriage is more important than selling jewellery' (105 F 1984). She finally settled on selling kitchen ware through house parties because it provided enough income without disrupting her domestic situation.

For other women the practical logistics of trying to maintain a relationship with a man who worked shifts discouraged employment. A woman, whose husband worked three rotating shifts with irregular days off, was available to spend time with him whenever he was at home: 'I don't work outside the home because of the shifts. When the woman works straight days and the man works shifts, they don't see each other too much. They're like ships that pass in the night. They are basically living two different lives. And that's why I don't work' (176 F 1984). Even for those who accept alternative views, the power of such notions of appropriate sex/gender divisions is very strong: 'I think it's fine for married women to go to work but lots of people don't. I really felt a lot of pressure to quit' (010 F 1984).

Masculinity and Income Earning

The ideal of the male income earner supporting a full-time homemaker wife has ceased to be the socially dominant one; nevertheless, it still retains a great deal of power (Luxton 1997a). For some couples, conformity to that ideal explained the woman's work strategy: 'I was working before we got married and I liked my job but he really felt his wife should be at home. He kept saying that's what a real marriage is – the man at work and the wife at home – so I'm at home' (069 F 1984).

Even in some households where women were employed, the ideal of the man as income earner remained important. It may explain why men were typically more reluctant than women to acknowledge the significance of women's financial contributions. The more women's earnings increased as a proportion of family income, the more likely both women and men were to report that it was easier for their households to make ends meet. In households where people said it had become easier to make ends meet over the previous two years, 65 per cent of men and 67 per cent of women identified increased income as a factor. However, women were more likely than men to attribute that increase to women's earnings.

Some men accepted their wives' employment, as long as it was not mainly to earn money. One man explained: 'My wife went out to work. She worked for six weeks, one time, in a restaurant, because she wanted to get out of the house. And I said, okay, but that was therapy, it was not to make money or anything like that. She went out and did her thing, and then she came back. I don't need my wife to work. If I can't support her, there's something wrong' (108 M 1984). Women married to men who held such views often either shared their views or went along with them because they felt the issue was not worth fighting over: 'If I went back full-time, I'd have to fight with my husband' (080 F 1984).

Gendered Discourses of Mothering

Women's work strategies were strongly determined by whether or not they had children and by their theories about appropriate child care. Those who shared the view that only mothers can provide the best care tried to stay home with their children: 'I want the best for my children, and that's me at home' (108 F 1984). So did those who had no sense that collective child care could benefit children or who resisted the idea of other people contributing to child-rearing: 'Somebody else is raising those kids. Where are your kids from 7 to 5? At day care. So they bring their kids home at 5 or 5:30, they make supper, they bath them, they put them to bed. That's not raising your child' (108 F 1984).

In contrast, most of the employed mothers (77 per cent) believed that their employment did not have negative effects on their children. A few were convinced that children were better off if they had several caregivers: 'Day care is so good for my child. He just stretches and grows with all that love and attention. And he has all those friends. He gets so much more than what I can give him' (221 F 1984). Their decisions about whether or not to take paid employment were made easier by their confidence that their children would thrive.

Economic Necessity

It was no coincidence that the majority of women steelworkers (twenty) relied on their own incomes for support. Ten of them were single parents providing the main financial support for their children. They needed well-paying jobs. Those women whose partners were employed at Hilton Works had some degree of financial 'choice' about whether or not to seek paid employment. For example, in 1982 the mean average income for men in Canada was $19,164, and for men employed full-time it was $25,137 (Statistics Canada 1989a: Table 2). For the 56 per cent of Stelco workers employed continuously in 1982, the mean average income was $27,900.

In 1982 government estimates set the low income cut-off figures for a family of four in urban centres such as Hamilton at $18,129 (National Council of Welfare 1989). Only about 13 per cent of the men in this study earned less than that. The total average annual dollar expenditure for a family of four in Ontario was $31,000; for larger urban centres, it was about $46,000.[14] While recognizing the arbitrary nature of such accounting, these figures suggest that most of the men interviewed for this study earned enough to support a dependent wife and children, and at least until the recession in the early 1980s, they had steady, reliable employment. In 1982 the average annual income for men married to full-time homemakers was $26,300, of men married to women who were employed part-time it was $26,000, and of men married to women employed full-time it was $25,800. For most of these people, the husbands' paid work provided a 'family wage' which reduced the significance of economic necessity in the wives' decisions about paid employment. By 1997 the average full-year full-time earnings of men was $46,108 (Drolet 1999: 25); for Stelco workers, it ranged between $40,000 and $60,000.[15]

However, economic need is a relative term. While the wife of a laid-off worker or a woman wanting to leave an unsatisfactory marriage may clearly need to have her own income, there is no absolute minimum necessary for survival, and thus economic need is a socially variable measure. What may be essential for one woman might be luxury for another.[16] When a man's family wage reduces his partner's need to have paid employment or women explain their participation in paid labour on the basis of economic need, it is essential to explore the complexity of those arguments.

Women identified economic necessity when the men's income-earning capacities seemed threatened. Many women got paid jobs during the 1981 strike: 'So I went there because of the strike and then I just stayed' (069 F 1984). Throughout 1982 and 1983, 53 per cent of the men interviewed had continuous employment; 47 per cent had been laid off for some time, ranging from just a few weeks (7 per cent) to over eighteen months (1 per cent).[17] Most of the people involved assumed the lay-offs were unusual and in their long-term planning took for granted that the men would continue to have regular employment at Stelco. However, as increasing numbers of men were laid off, their partners were compelled to look for paid employment. A young woman explained how her income sustained the household: 'It was hard for us when he was laid off. I would get my pay and we would have to pay the rent and there went my pay because I don't make great money. And the next time was the groceries, phone bill, hydro bill; there was no savings. My mom would slip me $20 bills. It used to make me feel so bad' (078 F 1984).

Our 1984 study of 234 steelworkers who had experienced indefinite lay-offs from Hilton Works found that 83 per cent of their partners had paid employment for part or all of the lay-off period. Half of the women who had been full-time homemakers before the lay-offs took paid employment; only 17 per cent of the women living with men on indefinite lay-off remained as full-time homemakers. As the pattern of lay-offs became more established through the 1980s, women were more likely to seek paid employment. The 1990 strike at Hilton Works pushed even more women to take paid employment: 'But it was kind of forced on us with the strike in '90. Then, she worked at an accounting firm doing secretarial work. She worked full-time because we were on strike' (089 M 1994).

Women also identified economic necessity when the men's earnings seemed insufficient to meet family expenses. For example, the less secure their housing, the more likely the women were to be employed full-time. A forty-three-year-old woman explained: 'I only went to work to get a down payment on a house but I stayed' (097 F 1984). Among the women whose homes were owned outright, 56 per cent were full-time homemakers, 40 per cent of those who had a mortgage were homemakers, while only 33 per cent of women whose homes were rented were full-time homemakers. In contrast, of those women employed either full-time or part-time, only 18 per cent owned their homes, 59 per cent had a mortgage, and 23 per cent rented their homes.[18] Thus, even when the man earned a family wage, there was sometimes economic pressure on the woman to get paid work to enable the couple to make a major purchase such as a house.

The Attractions of Paid Employment

Regardless of economic need, there are many attractions to paid work that explain the ongoing struggles by women who have stubbornly challenged dominant gender ideologies. Many women have demanded access to education and training, access to jobs, and the right to keep their jobs after marriage. As the appeal of employment at Hilton Works illustrated, paid work can be a source both of pleasure from socializing with co-workers and of the identity and prestige accorded to paid workers. A woman, who in the mid-1980s before she had children had planned to stay home with them, discovered that full-time homemaking was hard on her. She kept her paid work: 'When I stay home, I get like to the point I don't want to go out at all. It's because, you know, I'm doing this and I don't feel confident about myself. I seem to lose confidence somehow. But whereas when I get out, I have a good time and the people I work with are really good' (078 F 1994).

Paid employment can provide intellectual stimulation and variety: 'I really enjoy my work, and I enjoy getting out. I think it's really important to have something outside of the house. It might be so that people just don't become part of the house, a fixture in the house' (042 F 1984). It can also provide an antidote to the frustration and discontent many women have with the way domestic labour is organized, in particular the problems generated by economic dependency and social isolation. One man described his wife's employment as motivated by her unhappiness at home: 'One day I come in and there she is sitting in the living room crying. What are you crying about? I have got nothing to do. I said, well, why don't you go out and get a job?' (074 M 1984).

Available Employment: Labour Markets and Qualifications

Women's decisions about whether to take paid employment are strongly affected by local labour markets, the types of jobs they are qualified for, the quality of the job they can get and their assessments of its long-term prospects, and their future chances of getting such work if they are out of the labour force for a time. While good jobs and decent pay both justify and compensate for the loss of women's domestic labour, bad jobs and low pay may not be worth the costs at home.

For example, older women, with little formal education and limited paid work experience had few incentives to seek employment. The jobs that they had the chance of getting would be among the lowest paid. As their children were grown up, the financial pressures on them were reduced. Their husbands had high seniority and thus relative job security and steady incomes: 'When you've worked forty-five years and you've got your kids all away from home, and you've got your own home and everything's paid for – you don't need to be earning $16 an hour' (097 F 1984).

From the 1940s to the 1960s the female labour force participation rate in Hamilton was slightly higher than the national average. However, despite a steady increase in labour force participation, by 1981 the female rate for Hamilton was almost the same as the national average. Women in Hamilton lost their relatively higher participation rate because they were squeezed out of manufacturing and increasingly concentrated in a narrow range of sex-typed and lower-paying occupations.

By the 1980s women in Hamilton-Wentworth remained significantly under-represented in manufacturing and construction and had lower labour force participation rates and lower incomes relative to men than women provincially or nationally, and all of these relative indices worsened as the recession in the early 1980s wiped out the gains of women's struggles for access to industrial jobs (Csiernik and Cain 1985). In 1983 only 11 per cent of all manufacturing jobs in Hamilton were held by women compared with 41.9 per cent of jobs in trade and 38.9 per cent of jobs in the service sector. As a result, better paying jobs were not readily available. A woman revealed the experiences behind these statistics: 'My girlfriend who's on welfare wants a job so bad. But the only jobs she can find are like selling in a shoe store at minimum wage – she can't live on that' (069 F 1984).

By 1991 manufacturing accounted for 15 per cent of all jobs in Hamilton, and women were only about 19 per cent of the workers in that sector. In contrast, women were 61 per cent of service workers (Statistics Canada, 1991 *Census*), a pattern that continued through the mid-1990s and reflected national trends (Statistics Canada 1995b: 65–8). In 1996 a woman who had taken one of those jobs as a shoe clerk described the dilemma she faced: 'Since he was laid off [from Stelco] I've had to work. We can't get by without my income but we can't get by on what I'm making either. It's terrible. If I can't make enough to support us, I may as well stay home and take care of things there' (303 F 1996).

Jobs for women in Hamilton-Wentworth have never paid well compared with men's jobs. Table 5.2 compares the average employment incomes for women and men in Hamilton-Wentworth, Ontario, and Canada, and shows that women have consistently earned less than men. For example, steelworkers made an average of $17.74 an hour in 1994, in contrast with child care workers at $9.45 an hour. Women in female-dominated occupations lost ground between 1990 and 1995. The average annual earnings for twenty-five of the most frequently cited occupations for Canadian women declined by 5 per cent in this period (Brown 1999).

Although Hamilton experienced a lower unemployment rate than the rest of Ontario from 1976 to 1981, it was hit hard by the 1981–2 recession. During 1982 the unemployment rate in Hamilton region reached almost 12 per cent. Between 1976 and 1986 women consistently faced higher unemployment rates than men despite the lay-offs in heavy industry.[19] The shortage of jobs for women meant that in both 1982 and 1983 the percentage of women as part of the total labour force decreased significantly. The limited number of jobs and the low pay they offered explains why so few women looked for paid employment when their husbands were first laid off from Stelco, and why 15 per cent of full-time homemakers were unsuccessfully looking for paid employment. One woman commented: 'Mother's allowance and welfare are the last thing you would want. It's proper hell. What we need are more

TABLE 5.2
Average employment incomes comparing male and female incomes for Canada, Ontario, and Hamilton-Wentworth, showing the percentage (%) of female earnings to male earnings

Year	Hamilton–Wentworth		Ontario		Canada	
	Male	Female	Male	Female	Male	Female
1901			378	187	387	182
				(49)		(47)
1911			582	309	593	313
				(53)		(53)
1921			1,102	613	1,057	573
				(56)		(54)
1931	1,022	606	1,005	636	927	559
		(59)		(63)		(60)
1941	1,230	593	1,112 .	574	993	490
		(48)		(52)		(49)
1951	2,500	1,350[a]	2,308	1,372	2,127	1,221
		(54)		(59)		(57)
1961	4,251	2,075	3,933	2,137	3,625	1,990
		(49)		(54)		(55)
1971	7,552	3,213	7,213	3,328	7,004	2,948
		(43)		(46)		(42)
1981	18,656	9,410	19,076	9,802	18,516	9,522
		(50)		(51)		(51)
1991	25,308	12,337	25,145	13,422	23,265	12,645
		(49)		(53)		(54)
1996	36,323	21,713	33,599	21,048	31,917	20,162
		(60)		(63)		(63)

[a]These figures are approximately based on Census Canada (1951) vol. 5; Table 16-13 only gives the mid-point of $12,642 for women in the labour force in the upper 12% of $1,000–1,499 range and for men $31,690 at the low end of the $2,500–2,999 range.
Sources: Census Canada 1931; Statistics Canada, cat. no. 13-207; Census Canada (1986); Social Trends in Hamilton-Wentworth (1987: 75); Census Canada (1951), vol. 5, Table 16—13; 1996 Census; Statistics Canada, cat. no. 11-001E.
http://www.statcan.ca/english/census96/may12/tl.htm.

jobs. Most women I know on welfare would work if they could get jobs, but they can't. It's bad in Hamilton, even for men. I have girlfriends who are on mother's allowance and they hate it. They would rather be working. They should be able to get jobs if they want. That's only right, but they can't' (069 F 1984). By the mid-1990s the growth in jobs in community business and personal services, an increase of 23 per cent, meant

TABLE 5.3
Hamilton-Wentworth labour force participation rates of all men, all women, and married women 1941–1996

Year	All men	All women	Married women	Women as a % of the total labour force
1941[a]	71.9	25.0	n.a.	24.3
1951	81.5	29.5	18.6	26.6
1961	80.8	31.2	27.3	28.3
1971	81.3	41.8	40.5	34.4
1981	80.0	51.4	51.7	40.8
1986	77.7	56.6	56.7	43.6
1991	76.1	60	56.9	45.6
1996	71.9	58.4	55.9	46.6

[a]1941 stats are for 14+ years old, others are 15+ years old; 1941 stats do not include individuals in active service in the armed forces.
Sources: *Social Trends in Hamilton-Wentworth* (1987:65); *1941 Canadian Census*, vol. 6, *Earnings and Employment; 1941 Census*, vol. 7, Table 5; 1951 *Canadian Census*, vol. 5, *Labour Force*, and vol. 1, *Population; 1961 Census Canada*, vol. 3, Part 1, *Labour Force Occupations*, and vol. 1, Part 2, *Population; 1961 Census; 1971 Census; 1981 Census; 1986 Census; 1991 Census; 1996 Census; Census of Canada 1996.*

that there were relatively more jobs for women than in the previous decade (City of Hamilton 1995a: 13; 1995b). Table 5.3 compares the labour force participation rates for Hamilton-Wentworth for men, all women, and married women.

However, official unemployment rates of 9.5 per cent for women and 12.2 per cent for men (Statistics Canada 1991: 2B.2) continued to mask the fact that homemakers who are looking for work are not recognized in official unemployment rates and that many women wanted paid work but had given up looking: 'Since he was laid off, I've looked everywhere. At first I thought I'd have to convince employers to look at me because I've been at home for a long time. But I never even get that far! There just aren't any jobs!' (303 F 1996).

Women deciding whether to withdraw from the labour market must include in their deliberations their chances of getting a comparable job later. In some occupations, years out of the labour force cause the employee to fall behind, as new developments such as word processing systems or educational practices alter the field. Giving up a job in a fast-food outlet, where another will probably be available later, may be easier than quitting a unionized job and losing seniority, pension, and other benefits. A nurse describes her thinking: 'I was offered another job by a physician. But I can't quit the hospital now. There's no way. I've got a pension. I've got a good salary now because of the years. Could he give me four weeks holiday and a week at Christmas?' (097 F 1984).

In general, the more formal education a woman had, the more likely she was to have paid employment, and the better the job was likely to be. Educational expectations and attainment have changed over the past four generations for working-class women. Older women were less likely to have completed high school and were more likely to assume that they would work as housewives throughout their lives. Younger women were more likely to have completed at least high school, and most assumed they would mix homemaking and paid employment, although some, especially those with careers, expected to have paid employment throughout their lives.[20]

The less formal education women had completed, the more likely they were to be homemakers, regardless of whether they had children: 67 per cent of women with an elementary education were homemakers, compared with 43 per cent of women with some high school, 38 per cent with a high school diploma, and 27 per cent with some post-secondary education. Among the women who had a child under age five, 80 per cent of those with some high school were homemakers, compared with 15 per cent of women with post-secondary education. For women whose youngest child was between age five and fifteen, 60 per cent of those with an elementary education were homemakers, compared with 39 per cent of those with post-secondary education. For women whose youngest child at home was sixteen or older, 63 per cent with an elementary education were homemakers, while only 20 per cent with a high school diploma or any post-secondary education were homemakers.

Their level of education was also related to women's aspirations for future work and their assessments of their chances of getting it. While 23 per cent of full-time homemakers with an elementary education wanted paid work in the future, 53 per cent of those with some high school, 72 per cent of those who had completed high school, and 80 per cent of those with post-secondary education wanted paid employment in the future. This tendency is linked to whether the women thought they would have to take paid work to make ends meet. For example, only 7 per cent of women with elementary education thought they would need to take paid work, compared with 25 per cent of women with some high school, 33 per cent of those who had completed high school, and 44 per cent of those with some post-secondary education.

Of the women who had completed elementary school, 7 per cent of their husbands wanted them to get paid jobs, compared with 39 per cent of husbands whose wives had completed some high school, 41 per cent whose wives had completed high school, and 60 per cent whose wives had post-secondary education. For men married to full-time homemakers, there was also a close relationship between the husband's level of education and his desire for his wife to seek paid employment. Of these men who had completed elementary school, only 33 per cent wanted their wife to have paid employment compared with 44 per cent of men with a high school diploma.

The decisions women made about how much education to complete before having children reverberated throughout their lives. A thirty-nine-year-old woman with a Grade 8 education had had children when she was young. Once the youngest started high school, she wanted to get paid employment. However, reflecting on her lack of formal qualifications and experience, she gave a realistic assessment of her chances of getting decent employment:

> I'd like to. I would like to get into something, yeah. I mean the youngest one is going into high school in the fall now. But I don't know what I would want to do though, because I don't have the education either and you've got [Grade] 8 and pretty soon you are going to have to have 13 for God's sakes to work in [fast food] or something, you know. They are going to be able to pick and choose. But I'm not out to look specifically but if something ever came around, word of mouth or whatever, then I would consider part-time. I don't know if I would want to go full-time. You know, part-time is nice. (069 F 1994)

Women with more education were more likely to end up with the best jobs with the benefits those jobs entail.[21] The advantages of such jobs, especially over a lifetime, meant that women were more likely to keep them even when holding paid employment conflicted strongly with their domestic labour.

Grappling with the Contradictions

The wife at home making 'a real marriage,' the store clerk arranging her paid work to accommodate her family, and the steelworker organizing her domestic world to accommodate Stelco's shifts were each living the contradictions inherent in women's work. Their very different strategies reflect changes in sex/gender divisions of labour. As mothers increasingly remain in paid labour, they have fought for paid maternity leave. At the time of the 1984 interviews women who had been employed for twelve months by the same employer were entitled to seventeen weeks of paid maternity leave (Baker 1995: 156–85). Although this was better than nothing, it still did not solve ongoing child care problems. For most women, decisions about when to return to paid work depended on the amount of paid maternity leave they were entitled to, the length of unpaid leave, if any, they could negotiate and afford, the quality of child care available, and the costs of quality child care. For example, if child care costs used up most of her pay cheque, it might make more sense for her to stay home. However, for some women, long-term calculations made the heavy expenses of the pre-school years worth it for the overall benefits of having secure employment and seniority once the children were in school. A nurse explained: 'If the mother is going to work, cost of child care is something to consider. Once you start going to the sitter for a second child, you're adding that cost until they get to school age' (042 F 1984).

The pressures of coping with paid and domestic labour also affect women's decisions about whether to have children. Some women who expected to have paid employment full-time had just one child because they felt they could not manage or afford more. One woman explained that she and her husband had wanted a much larger family but had decided to stop at two: 'He's one of nineteen and we always thought we would have lots of kids, too, but after the second was born we realized that if we had more, I would have to go to work to pay for them and then who would look after them?' (089 F 1984). A teacher described how she loved her job so she limited the number of children she had in order to keep it: 'I always wanted lots of kids but I really love my job. I would hate to give it up and there's no way I could manage if I had more kids. So we just had the two' (061 F 1984).

One mother, whose two children were five and two years, described the rhythm of her week, showing how her paid work and domestic labour intersected. When she worked full-time, she said she was 'dead tired' in the evenings. Part-time work enabled her to do both jobs. She worked mornings Monday to Wednesday and all day Thursday as a librarian-teacher in an elementary school. Her husband, who was on days, got up first, woke the children, and left for work: 'I stay in bed until he leaves at 7:30 a.m., then I give the children breakfast, make lunch for the older boy, drop him off at the stop for the school bus, take the little one to the day care, and get myself to school.' She liked her job: 'My days are quite busy with meetings and planning special resources for each teacher as needed. I have a fair amount of discretion at work and I truly enjoy it.'

She looked after her youngest child in the afternoons except on Thursdays: 'I leave work around 1 p.m., pick up the little boy who has already had lunch, and we go home. Monday afternoon I generally relax. Tuesdays I take the little one to the library for story hour. Wednesdays are nothing special. Thursdays my mother comes here [to do child care] and we visit [after I get home from work]. Fridays are for cleaning.' Evenings she had energy for domestic labour: 'Every day I start supper around 4:30. Then after supper I make lunch for the next day or go out with the older boy on a bike ride' (080 F 1984).

Another woman, who worked as a telephone operator, took the afternoon shift from 6:30 p.m. to 1 a.m., even though it meant she did not get as much sleep as if she had worked nights. That way, either she or her husband could be at home with their five-year-old. She looked forward to the time when the child would be old enough to stay alone: 'I might work [night shift] in a few years when [the child] is old enough to be by himself ... but I couldn't right now because of our shifts. There is too much time in between' (046 F 1984).

For these women who had some means of support, their commitment to good mothering combined with a more general desire to conform to prevailing standards of respectability were important factors in their decisions to stay at home while their children were young.

Women's work strategies were also related to gender discourses. Since the 1970s, in Canada, there has been a gradual increase in support in principle for women's full participation in paid employment. By the early 1980s the majority of Canadian women and men expressed support for equal job opportunities for married women. In practice, many were more hesitant, and popular support for the various initiatives necessary to facilitate women's job opportunities was uneven, and the male income earner / dependent wife norms retain considerable power (Boyd 1984; Reid 1987). The various reactions to women's employment in general, and specifically at Hilton Works, revealed widespread confusion. This man's reaction was typical: 'Well, of course there are so many different things to look at today because of single parenthood. But sometimes I see women going in, taking jobs away from a family man or something like that. But I don't feel any animosity towards them. I guess everybody wants a job. The way it is today, it's hard to survive unless you have a job. So I don't know, I wouldn't say it's good and I wouldn't say it's bad. I just have a middle-of-the-road feeling about it' (151 M 1984).

Most people supported formal liberal notions about the rights of individuals to compete for jobs and earn equal pay. One man was firm: 'Me, I don't care if it is a man or a woman. Black, white, or purple, it don't matter to me, you know. I am not prejudiced about anything' (126 M 1984). But, like many, he hesitated when thinking about women in 'men's jobs,' raising issues that would never come up if the worker were male: 'If the woman wants to come with me driving the truck, and if she can do it ... There is only one thing. If she cannot do the job, then I think there should be something done about it, because then it is not fair' (126 M 1984).

The majority of male steelworkers and their partners (more than 70 per cent) agreed that 'if given the chance, women could and should do the same work as men now do, and men could and should do the same work as women now do (except for pregnancy).'[22] A male steelworker expressed that viewpoint: 'I figure the opportunity's there for everyone. It all depends on the individual. I think if a woman can do the job, I feel she should have it' (152 M 1984). The wife of a steelworker had a similar perspective: 'It's okay for a woman to want to do different kinds of work' (199 F 1984).

Steelworkers and their partners also indicated support (more than 85 per cent) for the principle of equal pay for equal work when they strongly disagreed with the proposition that 'women should not be paid the same as men': 'I think it should be equal pay for sure. There is no argument there for me at all. You know, if a woman does the job of men, then, pay her accordingly' (089 M 1984).

Despite this support in principle for women's right to paid employment and equal pay for equal work, attitudes towards more specific aspects of full sex/gender equality were much more mixed. Most men accepted the idea, that in principle, women and men are equal. However, despite the evidence of sexist discrimination at Stelco, many of them denied widespread systemic discrimination, assuming that the formal equality they believed in existed in practice. As the same man insisted: 'If women want jobs, let them apply. If they are qualified, they'll get the job' (089 M 1984). Another made a similar point, despite his recognition of the contradictions he expressed: 'If a woman wants a job, and she's qualified, she should get it. I think women who say they can't get jobs should stop whining, though I guess some didn't get hired at Stelco as were qualified. But anyway, no I don't think there's discrimination against women. If she can do the job, she'll get hired' (108 M 1984).

As a consequence, collective actions designed to overcome systemic discrimination were less readily accepted. Many men and a few women argued that employment equity and affirmative action programs were unnecessary. Even some of those who recognized how sexism and racism act to discriminate against women and visible minorities expressed a certain ambivalence:

> It is a male-dominated world so it's just natural that men would hire more men. But women should have the right to be hired the same as men. The minorities should have the same right. But I don't go along with [legislated requirements that] ... they have to hire so many minorities and everything. Like my son, he doesn't have hardly a chance of getting a job now and getting out in the workplace. Because he's white and he's in that group. So they have to hire minorities. I don't know, but what are you going to do, you have to get them in somehow. And people are prejudiced, so it's hard, the same as with women. (137 M 1994)

Some men who defended women's general employment rights expressed a distrust of women as reliable co-workers or as bosses:

> Philosophically, I have to agree that [women] have the same right in the marketplace as I do. In an environment like Stelco, I agree she has the right to be there, but in a life-threatening situation I wouldn't want my life being dependent on how she is going to react to that situation at that time, and we do get into some precarious positions. If you were to carry it a step farther, if you are going to allow them into the marketplace, you are going to have to at some time or other approach the subject of them in positions of supervision, and how well a female supervisor on a bull gang would go I really wouldn't even like to speculate. But we can't promote them all to the main office and we can't keep them all at the lower end. (149 M 1984)

Many men tried to reconcile their liberal support for individual rights with a more conservative affirmation of male income-earner rights: 'I believe in rights. People have rights. But I also believe that a man is the breadwinner and that the woman should stay home' (108 M 1984). From this perspective, unmarried women or women with husbands who were unemployed were acceptable Stelco employees: 'If a woman has a family to support and she wants some place where she is going to make some decent money, then she has got every right to be at Stelco that I do' (078 M 1984). But women married to employed men, especially those employed at Stelco or at equally well-paid jobs, were not, because they posed a direct threat to men's power as income earners: 'There were a lot of men who could do those jobs. We've had quite a few cases of women who have gone to Stelco to work whose husbands work there. There were a lot of men who have families who got laid off. That's what most guys object to – I was laid off, she's taking over my job. They were making $500 to $600 a week. You lose your house, you lose your car, you lose your wife ...' (097 M 1984).

Steelworkers and their spouses were aware of actual or threatened unemployment. However, the majority did not think about this in class terms. They did not criticize the existence of the class-based inequalities of wealth (Livingstone and Mangan 1996a). Instead, their fear and realistic assessments of the basic injustice of the unequal distribution of wealth engendered in many a strong sense that it is unfair that some households have two 'good incomes' while others have none: 'What really bothers me is where there are two breadwinners. That's not fair. I don't care who the breadwinner is, the man or the woman, but there shouldn't be two income earners in some families when some people have no jobs. I know everyone wants to get ahead, but it's not fair when some have no jobs' (069 M 1984).

The majority of male steelworkers with homemaker wives and the wives themselves agreed that men should have job priority. As one male steelworker insisted: 'Between a single mother with kids and a guy supporting a family, I would take the guy first' (097 M 1984). In contrast, the employed wives of Stelco workers, like women steelworkers, supported women's equal rights to paid jobs even in times of high unemployment: 'We need jobs, too, and there's no reason just because there's high unemployment that I shouldn't get decent pay. I've got to eat and pay bills' (201 F 1984).

The longer women had worked as homemakers, the less progressive were the views they expressed. They became more likely to agree that men should have priority for jobs during periods of high unemployment. They were also the most in favour of pensions for housewives. In contrast, the more involvement women had in the paid labour force, the more likely they were to agree that women and men could and should do the same work, that the proportion of women in traditionally male occupations should be increased through special training and hir-

TABLE 5.4
Women's work status by their attitudes to gender issues (% who agree with statement)

	Homemaker since marriage (%)	Homemaker now/was employed (%)	Employed part-time (%)	Employed full-time (%)
Men have job priority[a]	71	52	43	29
Homemaker pensions[b]	79	67	55	63
Women/men do same work[c]	69	80	82	76
Affirmative action[d]	42	56	63	56
Parental leave[e]	43	66	64	63

[a]In times of high unemployment, men should have priority for jobs.
[b]Homemakers should be entitled to pensions similar to those of paid workers.
[c]If given the chance, women could and should do the same work as men now do, and men could and should do the same work as women now do (except for pregnancy).
[d]The proportion of women in traditionally male occupations should be increased through special training and hiring initiatives.
[e]Paid maternity or paternity leave should be available for any employee who wants to care for a new baby.

ing initiatives, and that paid maternity or paternity leave should be available (see Table 5.4). Reflecting on her experience, a woman former steelworker commented:

What I learned is that when there were lots of jobs to go round, some guys were willing to support women trying to change, as long as we didn't do anything that would really change things. Like it was okay if a few women got jobs at Stelco, but not too many, and not if it meant guys couldn't get jobs. And it was okay if women had jobs that paid well, as long as they were single or had to support kids, but not if they just wanted decent pay like guys do – that was going too far. And it was okay if women had jobs as long as they kept on doing all that other so-called women's work – like looking after the kids, but it wasn't okay if we said someone else should do it. And it was okay if we tried to get hired on, as long as we didn't talk about sexism and discrimination. (224 F 1996)

Conclusion

Despite significant changes in women's work and in the divisions of labour between women and men, the fundamental incompatibilities between paid labour and domestic labour continue to generate enormous difficulties. By 1996 male income earner / female homemaker norms had changed a bit. An overwhelming majority of people in Canada believed that women should have equal job opportunities with men. There had also been a significant change in the discourses about parenting, from a position that assumed mothers were the best caregivers, to one that said either parent is acceptable. This linguistic shift from mother to the more gender-neutral term 'parent' rendered women's work invisible and implied that men were more involved than they used to be. In Canada 51 per cent of women and 49 per cent of men argued that only one partner should be an income earner while the other should stay at home and look after the children (Handelman 1996). One woman, who worked at home when her children were young, took part-time paid employment when the youngest started school. By the time her children were teenagers she was employed full-time: 'And now I think quite honestly we could both say that if one of us had a career where they were making enough money that we could leave then the other one would stay home. It wouldn't make any difference' (010 F 1994).

The change in climate has made it easier for women to feel that their paid employment is acceptable; however, the material circumstances have not changed to actually make things easier. Women still earn less than men. Individual parents have to make their own arrangements for child care until their children reach school age. Although the provision of schooling recognizes a limited collective social responsibility for children between ages six and sixteen, school hours are not organized to coordinate with hours of employment, and parents are individually responsible for arranging care around school times. Indeed, the economic uncertainty of the recession, the lack of quality child care, and the attacks on equity programs in the 1990s made things harder for people trying to manage paid employment and domestic responsibilities. Anticipating things would get even harder in the future, a woman worried that the next generation of women would not have the choice that she had had to stay home with small children: 'What kind of guarantees do they have? Like for my daughter and for my daughters-in-law that I am going to have. They probably won't have the chance to stay home with their families that I did. Because I can see things are just going to be too expensive. They can't afford a one-income family' (166 F 1994).

For the most part, it was women who continued to bear the brunt of the double day, which they experienced as fatigue, stress, lack of leisure time, and a general sense of overwork. Even though individual women and their families developed a variety of strategies to cope, individual work strategies can only mitigate partially the incompatibility between paid employment and domestic labour. It cannot be resolved except by structural changes in the organization of work and the sex/gender division of labour. A woman who had been active in the Women Back Into Stelco campaign concluded: 'Women are the shock troops for capitalism. We have to absorb all the ups and downs of capitalist profit-making, and when times are hard, women get hit the hardest. So when there was a boom, the courts and employers gave in and we won. Now there's a recession, it's back to the old ways – women lose even our little tiny gains like a few women working at Stelco' (300 F 1996).

6

Domestic Labour as Maintaining a Household

A full-time homemaker with two young children kept track of her daily activities when her partner was on day shift[1]:

Morning
6:30	Wake up, wash, get dressed
6:50–7:05	Prepare breakfast
7:05–7:20	Wake children
7:25–7:45	Eat breakfast, get children to eat breakfast
7:45–8:15	Get children ready for school
8:15–8:25	Make beds
8:25–8:30	Phone insurance company
8:30	Walk daughter to school
9:00–10:00	Volunteer at school
10:10	Return home from school
10:21–10:27	Clean bathroom
10:27–10:45	Vacuum carpets
10:45–10:55	Dust tables, etc.
10:55–11:00	Put away vacuum and dusting cloth
11:00–11:05	Load dishwasher
11:05–11:15	Take coffee break and talk on the phone
11:15–11:45	Pick daughter up from school
11:45–12:30	Make lunch and eat it, visit with daughter, talk with her about school, help her change into play clothes

Afternoon
12:30–2:00	Do several loads of laundry, folding it and putting it away, caring for daughter at the same time

2:00–3:00	Visit with mother while continuing to care for daughter, get her a snack, and finish laundry
3:30–4:00	Visit with sister and brother-in-law to celebrate my birthday
4:00–4:15	Welcome son home from school and make a snack for him
4:15–5:00	Prepare dinner, finish putting laundry away, make coffee for spouse, have coffee together and talk about our day, talk with children too
5:05–5:15	Serve dinner
5:15–6:00	Eat dinner with spouse and children

Evening

6:00–6:20	Clean up after dinner
6:20–7:00	Read newspaper
7:00–7:15	Discuss proposed household repairs with spouse
7:15–7:30	Play and talk with children and get them a treat
7:30–8:25	Give the children a bath, read them a story and put them to bed (brushing teeth, saying prayers, and cuddles)
8:25–8:35	Tidy bathroom
8:35	Get bread out of freezer to thaw for lunches
8:37–8:50	Fill out this form
8:50–9:20	Make lunches for the next day
9:20–10:00	Play a video game with my spouse
10:00–11:00	Watch a TV documentary about battered wives
11:00–11:30	Watch TV news
11:30–11:45	Lock up for the night, prepare for bed

(176 F 1984)

A nurse with a two-year-old worked three rotating twelve-hour shifts, three days a week. She described one of her days when she was on days and her spouse was on night shift:

5:30	Wake up, shower, get child up, have coffee, get child dressed
6:10	Drop child at sitter's
6:30	Arrive at hospital for 12–hour shift
7:00	Spouse arrives home after night shift
4:00	Spouse picks up child from sitter's, makes supper for himself and child and feeds child
7:30	Arrive home from hospital (after having supper at work, because 'I just feel it's so much nicer to come home and not

TABLE 6.1
Comparison of daily activities, full-time homemaker (176 F 1984) and nurse/homemaker
(042 F 1984)

Activities	Full-time homemaker	Nurse/homemaker
Sleep	6 h 45 min	7 h 10 min
Personal care	0 h 45 min	0 h 30 min
Paid work[a]	0 h	12 h 10 min
Volunteer work[a]	1 h 20 min	0 h
Housework	5 h 40 min	1 h
Child care[b]	3 h 55 min	2 h 10 min
Leisure	5 h 10 min	1 h
Total time reported	23 h 35 min	24 h

[a]This includes travel time to and from work.
[b]Child care was also done at the same time as other activities. This figure includes only
time spent exclusively on either caring for or playing and visiting with children.

	have all that [cooking and clean up] on top after 12 hours of work')
8:00–9:00	Put child to bed, do laundry, vacuuming, tidy up
9:00–10:00	Visit with spouse
10:00	Go to bed (spouse leaves for work later)

(042 F 1984)

Several things are revealed by this comparison. Both women had the major responsibility for domestic labour in their households and both did similar things. They did housework: cooking, cleaning, laundry, vacuuming, and general tidying up. They did child care, both the practical caretaking of waking, dressing, and putting to bed, and the delicate social interactions between people who love each other. They interacted with their spouses both as partners who cooperate in running a household and as intimates.

As Table 6.1 shows, the woman who combined homemaking with paid employment worked longer hours (about 3 hours and 25 minutes more) than the full-time homemaker, paid for child care, and spent less time with her child. But because she liked her paid work and the opportunity to have other interests ('I really enjoy getting out and working' [042 F 1984]) she came home excited to be with her child. In contrast, the mother who did all the child care before and after school got few breaks and sometimes felt swamped by her parenting work. The home-

TABLE 6.2
Comparison of time spent with children by full-time homemaker (176 F 1984), nurse/
homemaker (042 F 1984), and their spouses

While child is:	Full-time homemaker	Her spouse	Nurse/ homemaker	Her spouse
Awake	10 h 55 min	3 h 55 min	2 h 10 min	5 h
Sleeping	10 h 40 min	8 h 35 min	8 h 30 min	1 h 30 min
Total time	21 h 35 min	12 h 30 min	10 h 40 min	6 h 30 min
Total time without spouse	9 h 05 min	0	7 h 40 min	3 h 30 min

maker had time to visit with other family and friends in her home; the employed woman socialized at workplace breaks: 'The girls I see from work ... there's four of us that get together and go out for lunch' (042 F 1984). The homemaker also had time to volunteer in the community; the employed woman did not.

Because the employed woman was not available, her husband was more involved in caring for the child (prompted by the pragmatic need to reduce child care costs). He also did more housework than his co-worker, whose wife was a full-time homemaker. The homemaker's spouse could rely on her to be there and so had much less involvement with his children and did very little housework (see Table 6.2).

On days when she was at her paid job, the employed woman spent far less time on housework than the full-time homemaker (see Table 6.1). However, on her four days 'off,' she reverted to full-time homemaking, using that time to catch up on housework. The homemaker had greater flexibility to set her work pace. For example, she took two hours to get up and get her children off to school. The employed women worked under serious time constraints. She had forty minutes to get up and get her child to the sitter.

The day-to-day activities of both these women illustrate some of the complexities of domestic labour. As the labour that produces the means of subsistence for household members, it includes several discrete but interacting work processes. Housework and household maintenance keep up the physical space and provision the people living there. Other work processes such as financial planning and shopping transform the income available into goods and services, thus contributing to household standards of living. But domestic labour is more than just maintaining a household. At its heart is caregiving – the historically and culturally specific work of producing and sustaining members of the human species.

The Complexities of Domestic Labour

The central contradiction for domestic labour in working-class households is that it tries to produce and sustain people within the constraints of producing them as sellers of labour power.

Unpaid Domestic Labour and the Private Family Household

The organization of domestic labour as the unpaid work that sustains nuclear families in their private households affects the ways its labour processes and means of production have developed throughout the twentieth century. Unlike industrial capitalist enterprises like Stelco which, to remain profitable, have to stay competitive and so conform to industry-wide trends, family households, while affected by market forces, are not driven by them. The basic organization of domestic labour in wage earning households has remained unchanged since the early part of the twentieth century.[2]

Unlike businesses, households are not organized to maximize labour efficiency, and the technical changes that have transformed domestic labour over the past hundred years have been developed instead to maximize sales to consumers (Parr 1995). As a result, most household appliances are relatively inefficient, costly to operate, and do not take account of workers' health and safety.

Some of the most dramatic changes in household technologies occurred from the 1920s to the 1960s. New developments enabled people to link households to water and power sources such as electricity and gas. New household appliances such as washing machines, dryers, freezers, and vacuum cleaners, as well as ready-to-wear clothing and processed foods changed the types of labour and amount of time necessary to accomplish that labour (Oakley 1974; Luxton 1980; Strasser 1982). Since then, most developments, such as dishwashers, microwave ovens, or fast foods, have simplified the work by reducing both the time and skills required. As a result, men and children have taken on more domestic tasks, further reducing some of women's work (Goodnow and Bowes 1994; Bittman and Pixley 1997).

The organization of domestic labour as a private unpaid family activity also affects its divisions of labour and the status of the people who do the work. In contrast to paid employment, where the divisions of labour and the hours of work are clearly and often contractually known, domestic labour is task-oriented. The tasks involved vary significantly in how much time they take each time they are done and how frequently they are done: 'I don't know how much time it takes because, it just gets done. You know, you are always just doing it or planning what to do next, and there is always something, but if you sort of keep on top of things then you can miss something for a bit and do it a little later. But really I just keep doing everything' (069 F 1984).

As an informal unpaid work process, domestic labour has no standards regulated or enforced by an employer. The work itself is socially marginalized and low status as a result; the people who do it get little recognition for their work.[3] Aspects of it such as cooking or child care are familiar, but much of its social contribution is unnamed and unacknowledged. The boundaries between the work process and interpersonal relations are often obscure, so many domestic labour tasks – especially those relating to caregiving – are not recognized as work. Making tea for a housemate is work, yet it is just as likely to feel like an act of caring. Changing a baby's diaper is work, but it can also be a moment of intense love and delight: 'In a typical day I take care of my home and my family. It's not something you can describe exactly because, well, it's not like a job, eh? I mean, I play with the baby and clean up the kitchen; then I throw in a load of laundry and go do some baking. And then I vacuum the family room. And all the while I'm chatting to [the toddler] and keeping a close eye on the baby, and if either of the kids needs me, I drop everything else for them' (061 F 1984).

As domestic labour creates and maintains household life, its performance is inexorably tied to affirmations of relationships. One woman explained that she did all the domestic labour as a way of affirming her commitment to her marriage: 'That's what a wife is, I think. A wife makes a home for her husband and children' (010 F 1984). Another understood her husband's willingness to do domestic labour as proof that he was committed to their relationship: 'He does more than his share of work around the house. We share everything. That's part of a good relationship, that we share' (097 F 1984).

The way domestic labour is done, and who does it, are also ways that authority can be asserted, or love expressed. A woman steelworker recalled a co-worker's reaction when his wife packed him a lunch he disliked: 'He threw his lunchbox across the room so it smashed against the wall and the food splattered all over. He was screaming – like hysterical!

He really lost it. He kept shouting, "You fucking bitch! You're no wife of mine! I told you what to make in my lunch!" It was like he couldn't believe she hadn't done exactly what he said or that she didn't love him, or something. Geez – why doesn't he make his own lunch? Or give it to me – I'd love for someone to make me lunch' (222 F 1984).

Finally, because domestic labour is privatized and organized through individual households, it is difficult for individuals or individual households to intervene in its social organization. Many workers in paid employment have the possibility of organizing collectively in unions such as Local 1005 to challenge the conditions of their particular workplace. Through larger union associations such as the Ontario Federation of Labour or the Canadian Labour Congress, and through political parties relatively supportive of working people, such as the New Democratic party, many employed workers have fought to improve working conditions. Feminists have organized in the women's movement to fight for improvements for women in families, such as better protection of women and children from men's violence and improved divorce settlements and support payments. They have also fought for social recognition and valuing of their unpaid work at home (Luxton and Vosko 1998).

However, the challenges facing women and men who aspire to change sex/gender divisions of labour in the paid workforce are even more daunting in the context of renegotiating household divisions of labour. As women's attachment to the paid labour force is increasingly similar to men's, prevailing discourses assert that the double burden imposed on women by paid employment and primary responsibility for domestic labour will readily be alleviated by men's increasing participation in domestic labour. Widespread discourses, including a range of social science theories, mass media presentations, and popular common sense, repeatedly discuss changes in the sexual division of labour in optimistic terms that claim men are changing, promise happiness for women and men through marriage, and assert the emergence of gender equality (McMahon 1999: 66).

In contrast, hundreds of studies from a variety of countries, over more than thirty years, have shown that women still do the bulk of domestic labour, regardless of their involvement in paid employment. Several national studies have confirmed such trends in Canada. The 1992 Statistics Canada General Social Survey found that women continued to do more than men, even as teenagers. Women who were employed did more than their male partners; in fact, men living with employed women did a bit less than men whose wives were not employed! And women with children and paid jobs did more than anyone (Statistics Canada 1993). The 1996 census confirmed that this general pattern continued (Statistics Canada 1998).

These studies indicate that women cope with the double day, not because men are doing more, but because women decrease the amount of work they do and rely on other women, either unpaid exchanges with female friends and relatives (especially mothers and daughters) or paid female domestic help, if they can afford it. In contrast to prevailing claims, men in general exercise considerable choice about what, if anything, they do. Men who live with women do relatively little, and what they do is typically the more pleasant tasks such as playing with children. That existing gender divisions of labour are so resistant to change, and prevailing discourses are so unable to identify gender inequalities and name the oppression of women, suggests that the current social organization of domestic labour is deeply entrenched and difficult to change. Individual couples who aspire to more equitable divisions in their own homes face a formidable struggle. In a similar way, when even efforts to implement a national child care program meet strong resistance, initiatives to create alternative family and community forms such as collective living, or to socialize domestic labour through community kitchens, for example, are almost impossible to organize. Trying to implement significant changes in the way domestic work is organized is virtually impossible at this time. The only flexibility available is the way individual households arrange their own particular domestic labour.

Individual Household Strategies for Domestic Labour

At the level of individual households, negotiations about who does what and to whose standards, produce the practical resolutions people live with. They involve periodic discussions between spouses and other family members where they plan, schedule, assign tasks, clarify expectations, and negotiate agreements. The coping strategies of household members are both interpersonal and individual, cooperative and conflicted, openly negotiated and implicitly arrived at, the product of deliberate plans and decision-making, and the outcome of unconscious strivings. People have to make decisions and act in ways that combine and trade off duty and pleasure, sacrifice, and self-assertion.

The predispositions people have towards divisions of labour and caregiving practices have changed as specific historical periods shape individuals and differentiate generations. Women and men who were born in the 1910s and came of age in the 1930s are likely to have profoundly different gendered identities than those who came of age in the 1960s. Their different locations in the workplace and in the cycle of family and household formation, the ways they internalized changing cultural and ideological values about gender, work, and family, combine to produce general patterns of behaviour that correspond to age and generation. The older people of this study typically accepted a sharp sex/gendered division of labour, while younger people were more flexible. A father whose own gendered behaviours had changed as a result of his wife's insistence, expressed his expectations that his son would do things differently: 'He's not going to expect a woman's going to do all his cleaning, do all his work, come home and have his slippers ready for him. He's just not going to expect it because he sees I don't expect it because [my wife] won't tolerate it' (002 M 1994).

The diverse wants of family members are often difficult to harmonize. Even when both partners are committed to the family's welfare, they do not necessarily agree on what is best or how to pursue shared goals.[4] Many women complain that while their husbands are inclined to place their needs first, women are expected to subordinate theirs for the sake of the family's welfare: 'He says we have to put our kids first, and I agree. But that means me, not him. Like yesterday, I wanted to go visit my friend so he was going to come home right after work so I could go. But he went drinking with the guys instead and I was stuck here waiting and waiting. He never phoned or nothing' (010 F 1984).

Women typically recognize that the acceptance of familial obligation limits their exercise of self-interest both in relation to their husbands and to the world at large. One woman explained that both she and her mother struggled over whether to assert or subordinate their own needs in the context of their responsibility for their families' needs. She described how her mother, hesitant to spend family money on herself, dithered over a decision about buying a winter coat: 'I should get a coat? Well, really I should get a winter coat. No, this is January and in a couple of months I won't need a winter coat. Well I don't need a winter coat this year and then in September, well, I need a winter coat. I really should get a winter coat this year for sure. But it is not really cold, so I will wait 'til it is really cold out. It is February now and spring is just around the corner, so I really can wait until next year to get a winter coat. And that is how I grew up and that is how I think' (105 F 1984).

Divisions of labour and personal standards are caught between preferences – what people like – and limitations – what they are prepared to do or can pay for. Single parents, under pressure from the double day, were more likely than others to insist that their children take on domestic labour at an earlier age. Recognizing how stretched their parent is, children often comply more readily. A single mother explained: 'Both my boys were cooking and cleaning and just generally taking more responsibilty long before most of their friends. But as a single parent, I really needed help and they recognized that and pitched in' (208 F 1984).

Most people, like this man, acknowledged the importance of an agreed-upon division of labour: 'I think in a marriage you should be able to come to some kind of reasonable understanding of you do this and I'll do that' (308 M 1984). Coordination does not necessarily imply a democratic process where everyone has an equal vote; decisions may be taken unilaterally, and the purpose of communication may be simply to inform others of the plan. The same man noted that he sometimes overrode his wife when they disagreed: 'When it comes to some of the other jobs, a job I want to do outside, it's going to be done and I don't care if I have her approval. I've told her, it's got to be done and that's the bottom line. She doesn't agree 100 per cent ... I guess I make a ruling on those ones' (308 M 1984).

Most couples also insisted that their division of labour was based on sharing, by which they meant that they recognized the contributions of both as necessary to household survival. But there were marked differences in the way households organized these contributions. Typically, in households where women were employed, there was less domestic labour done, much of the work was simplified, and other household members did more work. However, in all households, even where men increased the amount of domestic labour they did, women remained responsible for overall management of advanced planning and ongoing task allocation, that is, ensuring that the myriad tasks got done and coordinating the interactions of the different labour processes. A woman described this dynamic: 'He's always, "What is there still to do?" And I'm, "Well, you know, we've got this to do and that to do, and this to do, and that to do." And then later on he'll say, "Why didn't you tell me you had all that stuff to do?" Well, come into the kitchen and you can help me doing dishes. Why don't you come in and help me? I hate to ask for you to do everything' (166 F 1994). Women do it and men 'help out.'

Initiatives to renegotiate divisions of labour are complicated by existing gender ideologies and by men's resistance to increased work. One man conveyed some of the gender confusion at the heart of these struggles: 'What's happening with the women and men in the workplace and just in day-to-day life, I'll never understand. I'll never be able to figure out women. I think women don't understand ... I know, it's sort of like slavery was. When they became free, they wanted everything' (002 M 1994). Such initiatives challenge existing notions of masculinity, but the strength of discourses about 'women's work' meant that only a few recognized it as a work process that can be learned by men as well as women: 'I cook. It was tough at first, you know, what to do and how to do it but as the years go on, the more experienced you get, the easier it gets' (151 M 1984).

Men who had learned these skills as children were most adaptable: 'I do a lot of housework. I do the vacuuming, my own ironing, I've always done that. My mom taught that, washing dishes, washing clothes. We share' (152 M 1994). But a father still felt it necessary to defend his son's training in housework: 'Teaching my son housework doesn't make him less of a man' (176 M 1994).

Such initiatives also involved persuading men to relinquish leisure and accept greater responsibility, something most were reluctant to do. A steelworker whose wife had been employed full-time since she was eighteen, as a secretary in a social service agency, described his feelings about doing housework when both of them were employed and they had no children: 'I don't like doing housework. I don't mind doing dishes but I don't like doing dusting. I don't mind doing the laundry. I'll do laundry' (090 M 1984). Subsequently they had two children and agreed to organize housework more systematically:

That's the cleaning schedule that the wife drew up. She just fills in each day as we go. On my day off, I've got to go grocery shopping and stuff like that, and I'll come in, like this morning I vacuumed the rug, so I will write down where it says D and V, dust and vacuum, so I just scratch that off as I do it, eh? And then if she is off Saturday, she can look at the list and say, well, okay, he hasn't done the kitchen floor, the hallways, so she can do that and she just crosses it off, so the whole house gets done on a regular basis. (090 M 1994)

Even in this household, where both had been employed full-time from the start, and where both now did all the housework tasks, she had the responsibility for designing the system and enforcing it.

However, during the period of this study, household divisions of labour and the amount done were affected by several contradictory trends. The increased participation of women in paid employment meant they were less available to do unpaid household work, which put more pressure on their partners and children to increase their contributions. Changing gender ideologies and practices meant that younger men were under pressure to be more involved in domestic labour than in previous generations.

While some households were relatively unaffected by the impact of neo-liberalism, declining real wages and household incomes meant that buying consumer goods and services became more difficult for many households, which increased the likelihood of them doing without or doing more work at home. For example, laid-off steelworkers responded to their drop in income by shopping more carefully, delaying purchases of costly items, and reducing their expenditures on entertainment and groceries (Corman 1993: 97). At the same time, cuts to social services increasingly imposed on private individuals and households work that previously had been done elsewhere. The impact of these trends on individual households was never straightforward or uniform, as changes in household organization and divisions of labour were prompted by a myriad of interacting forces.

Sometimes two households went through the same change but for very different reasons, for example, women took on full-time employment because their children were in school, they got an attractive job offer, or because their households suddenly needed more income. Some household changes were a result of life-course events – the birth of a new child or the departure of young adult children. Others were prompted by external events, for example, in households that were turned upside down when restructuring cost them their only source of income: 'When my husband lost his job, everything changed. I couldn't stay home any more. I got a job. And things at home were really tough' (303 F 1996). However, the cumulative effect was that most households were under pressure to increase their domestic labour while simultaneously increasing the number of people earning an income.

The Labour Processes of Domestic Labour

Housework and Household Maintenance

The aspect of domestic labour most clearly recognized as work is housework: cooking and cleaning up after meals, tidying, cleaning and maintaining the various rooms of the house and furnishings, shopping, laundry, mending and sewing, taking out the garbage, paying the bills. Domestic labour may also include household maintenance such as car upkeep, gardening, snow shovelling, and other yard-work. The skills required for, and the amount of housework and household maintenance done on a regular basis in any particular household, vary enormously and have changed significantly throughout the century (Strong-Boag 1986; Strasser 1982; Vanek 1974; Fox 1980). They depend on a complex interaction of factors such as the number and ages of the people living in the house; the amount of time, energy, and money they have available; the size and condition of the house; the type of household machinery available such as vacuums, washing machines, dryers, and microwave ovens; the personal standards of the people who live there; and even natural events such as snowfall or how quickly the grass grows.

One of the prevailing characteristics of housework is that it is only really noticeable when it is not done: 'I can clean up all day and no one sees it, but if I leave things even for just a bit, someone always says, "Wow, is this place a mess!" ... and I feel so bad' (061 F 1984). Another is that there is always more to do: 'And besides, I don't have a lot of time. I have a pile of mending that needs to be mended. I have got ironing that never gets finished. There is always a pile of ironing there. I can always round up enough laundry to do a load of wash' (105 F 1984).

There is great variation in both what and how frequently tasks are done, in whether they are considered chores or a pleasure, whether they are done automatically or put off. Some tasks are more imperative than others. Making meals and cleaning up after them takes place daily in most households, but the washer on the kitchen tap may need replacing only once every five years. If take-out meals are readily available, then the fact that no one shopped or cooked may be inconsequential. If overflowing garbage attracts mice and cockroaches, failing to take it out may be serious.

Housework can expand or contract depending on the circumstances. One woman explained that she had reduced the time she spent preparing meals: 'Because I get home usually between 6 and 6:15 ... cooking means just something simple like hot dogs or anything that is very simple, you know ... We do order out a lot of food' (078 F 1984). Another woman described how conflicting schedules dramatically increased the amount of work involved in getting meals and cleaning up after them: 'We tried eating dinner at noon when my husband worked afternoons, but the girls did not want a big meal at mid-day. Scheduling meals was a nightmare. The result was a kind of open kitchen where any kind of food could be prepared at any time of day – talk about a never-ending story' (301 F 1996).

Much of the labour involved in running a house is so automatic and taken for granted that people rarely consider it work. Opening the curtains in the morning to let in the light or shutting windows in a rainstorm may be 'just one of those things that gets done.' A homemaker with young children described the labour process involved in getting supper on the table. While the actual food preparation was relatively straightforward, a great deal of planning was required. She shopped every two weeks, a routine established because her husband only needed the car when he was on afternoons. Two weeks out of every three he would take the bus to work and leave her the car. Before each shopping trip she would plan menus for the next two weeks, taking into account the effect of his shifts and children's schooling on eating patterns: 'I have to think, well what shift is he on next week. Because we don't always eat the same when he is on a different shift. When he's on afternoons, rather than make a big meal, like I can't make supper at lunchtime because the kids are at school' (176 F 1984).

When her husband was on afternoon shift, she prepared something he could heat up at work. Each day, planning for supper began in the morning: 'I start thinking early in the morning what I'm having for dinner. I go and take something out of the freezer and then I start, depending on what we're having, come 3:00 or 3:30, I make supper' (176 F 1984). Explicit in what she described is their division of labour and the way housework had to be organized to accommodate the demands of jobs and school. Missing from her description are her efforts to acquire information and the capacity to interpret it that preceded those tasks, like anticipating her children's changing food preferences, juggling their choices with the food budget, or setting up and equipping the kitchen as a workspace.

Divisions of Labour in Housework and Household Maintenance

In households where the men were income earners and the women were homemakers, there was a clear division of labour: 'She looks after the shopping and the housework, no problem there. She doesn't work so she has the time to spend on the housework. She looks after that and I look after the cars and keep them running' (029 M 1984). Men typically did periodic maintenance, outdoor work, and car repair, tasks that permitted considerable discretion about whether or not and when they got done. In contrast, housework was women's responsibility, a terrain that men could explore if they chose. This pattern was so prevalent that women were appreciative if the men did any of the tasks considered 'women's work': 'I do all the cooking, laundry, and cleaning. I do all the breakfast and lunch dishes but not at night. The two older boys do that. They take turns. That's their job. My husband helps out a lot. He spends a lot of time with the children. He plays with the little one and often will put the kids to bed. He does more than his share. He really is responsible and great' (069 F 1984).

However, when women had paid employment as well, the allocation of all housework to women became increasingly burdensome: 'When I first started working part-time, I was home in time to prepare for dinner. Once I worked full-time, however, the others had to take turns cooking, and my husband did the grocery shopping himself. Other housework was also shared, so that I was no longer solely responsible – of course, by this time, the girls were in high school. Often when my husband didn't feel like cooking, we ordered fast food – a luxury unknown when I was a stay-at-home wife and mother' (303 F 1996).

Old long-established household patterns were hard to disrupt, despite new divisions of labour. A man in his fifties in 1994 said that when his wife got full-time employment, they reorganized domestic labour so that he did a greater share: 'I do a lot of the housework, so it's a real sharing thing' (080 M 1994). His wife recognized that when she began to allocate more time to paid employment, she did less housework, but she was less optimistic about how fair the division was: 'When I was employed part-time, I was home part-time, so it seemed like I did more housework. When I went back to work full-time, it went the other way a little more. The kids do a little more, too. I do all the shopping. I usually do all the laundry. And my husband will do some of the housework' (080 F 1994).

Some women insisted their men should do more. One argued that equal work loads were only fair: 'Both out to work, both earn good money, we both eat, we both sleep, we both wear clothes. I don't have a wife to come home to – to clean the house when I go out to work, so why should he? It's fifty-fifty. We both have to do it. And he doesn't like it – he can leave. Because I'm not doing it. It's a lot of work when you go to work all day. Some women come home and they have kids, and they have husbands that do nothing. I don't know how they do it' (097 F

1984). In fact, he usually only helped out if she had not done something or could not do it, especially because of her paid employment constraints: 'We share. If he needs clothes to go to work and I haven't got down to doing them, he washes his own clothes in the washer. The only thing he doesn't do is clean the bathroom. It's fifty-fifty. We do everything – he cooks, I cook. He doesn't iron' (097 F 1984).

Despite this woman's assertion that her husband had to share the housework fifty-fifty or leave her, and her insistence that he 'did everything,' her description of their division of labour showed that he still exercised more discretion, as he chose neither to clean the bathroom nor to iron. And the tasks he did were ones that directly affected his comfort and well-being if not done – cooking and laundry. Her comment that he washes his own clothes if she has not 'got down to doing them' suggests that he never did her laundry.

The concept of sharing complicates an analysis of who actually does the work and on what basis. Some people asserted that there was no sexual division of labour in their household, implying a pragmatic flexibility in which whoever was available would do whatever needed doing. For example, one man insisted that he and his partner shared the workload equally: 'Ours is split right down the middle. There's no set job for anybody. Everybody just does what has to be done. I cook, clean, do laundry, and she cuts the grass, paints, whatever' (047 M 1994). However, this claim ignored the reality that she was only employed for three hours a day Monday to Friday, while he was at Stelco on regular twelve–hour night shifts. His willingness to do 'whatever' obscured the fact that she was the one most of the domestic work fell to because she was home more of the time than he was.

The different ways women and men relate to the responsibility of domestic labour, particularly men's greater ability to exercise discretion, was expressed by a forty-nine-year-old steelworker who described his contribution to housework as a hobby: 'I do a lot of cooking because I like that. It is not that I have to, it is a hobby for me – the cooking. I always look for a new recipe. This is my choice. I don't have to do it' (126 M 1984). Another steelworker described what he did around the house on his days off: 'I usually do the vacuuming around this place, and the wife has never liked the vacuum cleaner so I use it. And I do the dishes and stuff like that. The wife does all the cooking but I do baking, like I sometimes make bread and I make muffins just about every week, and I make yogurt and stuff like this' (112 M 1984). He then qualified his response by noting that this happened more in the winter when he was inside. In the summertime, he preferred to spend most of his time outdoors.

Several women noted that men were more prepared to spend more money on labour-saving products than women: 'He gets fed up real easily and when that happens, it's well, let's buy fast food, a microwave, anything so he doesn't work so hard. If I get fast food, he complains. And spending money like that, I couldn't' (105 F 1994).

Some men expressed the prevailing male sense that housework was women's responsibility. One man said that he did a great deal of the housework, especially to help out when she was employed. He also insisted that men could never do housework as well as women:

I cook. I will make the supper when she is working. I get home at 3, I will barbecue or I will make supper first and I make beds and vacuum and wash the bathroom. Maybe it is not up to her standards but at least I will try and give it a shot, you know. No matter what you do, nothing is as good as a woman's touch in a house. A man can clean as much as he wants to, but a woman's touch is a different thing. I have seen it and that is true. If she wants me to vacuum, fine, I will vacuum for her, you know, or she wants the stove cleaned or whatever it may be. It gives her a break. (151 M 1984)

A second explained how he helped out: 'Well, it depends. If I am on days, you know, she will do the dishes and I will bath the kids or she will bath the kids and I will do the dishes. We share, eh? I don't just come home and sit and have a beer and do nothing, you know. I may fire a load of clothes in the laundry. We sort of share. She does most, more than I do for sure, because she is home more. But, you know, I try to do what I feel I should' (089 M 1984). Ten years later, his wife recalled that time differently: 'I was home to cook all the time. Suppers were ready when everybody came home. You know, the cleaning was done, the laundry was done, it was just very organized, the shopping was done' (089 F 1994).

The complicated relationship among masculinity, breadwinning, and domestic labour was posed more sharply when men were on strike or unemployed. One steelworker described how during the 1980 strike the prestige conferred by his union militancy reinforced his confidence in his masculinity and consequently his willingness to do domestic labour: 'I felt terrific! I'd come home after picket duty and help my wife with everything. I cooked, I cleaned. I especially liked looking after the kids. I was so involved with my family. It was great to have the time free and I loved it. I didn't care that it was "women's work"' (010 M 1984). But his lay-off three years later undermined his confidence and eroded his willingness to work at home: 'It just didn't seem right to be home doing housework or even looking after the kids. A man's the breadwinner. Without that you're nothing. And doing "women's work" just makes it worse' (010 M 1984).

The willingness to do domestic labour during the strike was not uniform. One man described how during the 1981 strike his wife took a job but he made no serious effort to contribute to housework:

> I didn't do much around the house when I was on strike. I suppose if I had more time, I could learn how to cook right. I can make bacon and eggs. The laundry part of it, well, she let me do the towels. But she doesn't trust me with anything else. She wants to keep the bed sheets the same colour as they are. I tried putting everything in the washing machine at the same time. I put the soap in, and put the bleach in and put the fabric softener in – and then you're done! Then the washing machine is bouncing all over the place. (049 M 1984)

Ten years later, despite the fact that both he and his wife were employed full-time, he was still incompetent in the kitchen: 'I try and do some of it but being a man ... and cooking, I fiddle around a little bit, but not really. I'm pretty good with hamburger helper and spaghetti' (049 M 1994).

Over the decade there was a growing sense, especially among younger couples, that the work involved in sustaining household livelihoods should be fairly divided. One woman's description of a fair division of labour was: 'If I'm still working, you should still be working' (166 F 1994). Another steelworker explained how the process of allocating responsibility for income earning and domestic labour changed in his household through the 1980s and 1990s: 'When I was laid off at Stelco I did all of the cooking and all the cleaning. When we were both working I did a fair share of the cooking. Now that she lost her job, she's doing more of the housework and everything' (015 M 1994). But women were still primarily responsible for all but a few specific tasks. It continued to be women, and rarely men or both together, who juggled the conflicting demands of domestic and paid labour.

What was unclear was the extent to which men were actively resisting or were actually incompetent, and whether this was because of a lack of skill and experience or because they did not get asked to do it more often. In some cases, the women may have judged men's performances on the assumption that only they knew how to do the work: 'I end up doing it all because it either gets done right or it never gets done' (046 F 1984).

Did women really believe the men could not do the job, or they were exerting their power over their own 'domain'? Some women exercised control over their houses, refusing to let others do housework: 'My wife wouldn't let me do that either. I wanted to wash up the dishes one time, and she says "no way." That is it. I am a good dishwasher. I was in a restaurant for five years. Everybody says I was very good. My wife says, "No." Not only me, she even says our daughter is no good. Nobody is good enough to wash her dishes' (004 M 1984).

Most women wanted their partners to spend more time at home and pay more attention to their children. The extent to which men helped out with the rest of domestic labour was a concern for many. However, most women did not argue overtly with their partners about it. Most homemakers (90 per cent) said they did not argue about it. Employed women were slightly less sanguine; 25 per cent of them said it was a source of dispute. In contrast, most men were feeling beleaguered; 80 per cent claimed that housework was a point of dispute.

Time Spent on Housework and Household Maintenance

Most couples agreed in their assessments of who did what work, although they were slightly more likely to agree on his performance than on hers. When they disagreed, it was usually because the man described himself as doing more than his wife thought he did[5]: 'My husband is always complaining that he is picking up after me and I complain that he doesn't do as much as he thinks he does' (105 F 1984). Or he tended to underestimate the actual amount of work the woman did: 'Well, now that the kids are gone, there's not that much to do and I help with the dishes' (199 M 1984).

The average amount of time women spent in housework varied with their work status.[6] Full-time homemakers on average estimated they spent twenty-seven hours a week on housework, compared with twenty-one hours for women employed part-time, and nineteen hours for women employed full-time. In contrast, the time men estimated they spent on housework was not significantly related to the employment status of their wives: twelve hours per week if their wives were full-time homemakers, fourteen hours where women were employed part-time, and thirteen hours where women were employed full-time. In households where both were employed full-time, the woman spent a total of sixty-two hours at work each week and the men fifty-seven hours – so the women spent five hours more than their husbands on housework and paid employment.[7] When child care was added in, the women spent far more time working than the men.

Men, and to a lesser extent, children, were drawn into housework in pragmatic ways, taking up tasks that immediately affected them and only rarely taking on the longer term work. For example, the more hours of paid employment a woman had, the less she was involved in meal preparation and clean-up. While men did not take up all the work women let go, they did prepare more meals and clean up afterward on a weekly basis. Husbands of full-time housewives did four meals each week and two clean-ups; husbands of women employed part-time or full-time did seven meals and three clean-ups[8]: 'When she is home on the weekends, she cooks but when I'm on nights and days, I usually try to have everything ready. It gives her a break. Because you know, if I wait for her to come home, we usually will end up eating around 6:30 or 7:00. So I usually help out quite a bit' (015 M 1984).

Other household members, especially older children, also did more meal preparation when women were employed: one meal each week where women were full-time housewives, three meals where the woman was employed part-time or full-time. The pattern was the same for cleaning up after meals and doing the dishes. Of the total meal preparation and clean-up, full-time homemakers did 81 per cent of meals and 62 per cent of dishes; women employed part-time did 68 per cent of meals and 48 per cent of dishes, and women employed full-time did 58 per cent of meals and 49 per cent of dishes. Men married to full-time homemakers did 16 per cent of meals and 14 per cent of dishes; men married to women employed part-time did 25 per cent of meals and 21 per cent of dishes, and men married to women employed full-time did 29 per cent of meals and 25 per cent of dishes.

A number of tasks (an average of thirty tasks in all households) such as making beds, dusting, sweeping and vacuuming, general tidying, cleaning bathrooms, and taking out the garbage, were done on a weekly basis in most households. Again, the number of these done by women decreased in relation to their hours of paid employment. Homemakers did twenty-two tasks, women employed part-time did nineteen, and women employed full-time did seventeen.[9] Their husbands increased the number of tasks they did from six for men whose partners were full-time homemakers to seven where women were employed part-time and

TABLE 6.3
Percentage of respondents who usually do household maintenance, by employment
status of the women

Tasks	Women			Men (Wife is/has)		
	Full-time homemaker	Part-time job	Full-time job	Full-time homemaker	Part-time job	Full-time job
Shopping	88	91	87	68	59	75
Laundry	99	98	98	19	20	29
Ironing	81	79	83	4	4	6
Mending/ sewing	86	82	83	10	14	6
Washing floors	90	95	79	18	18	19
Repairs	14	16	13	99	98	98
Yard work	50	48	46	93	96	98
Pay bills	61	70	69	64	59	73
Car	3	13	8	83	91	92

Note: Her report of her work and his report of his work. Percentage derived using total
number of respondents except for household repairs and yard work. In these cases,
people who designated these tasks as 'not appropriate' (e.g., apartment dwellers) were
excluded.

eight where women were employed full-time.[10] The number of tasks
done by others in the household remained about the same – three, four,
and three. Of the total tasks done, full-time homemakers did 75 per
cent of them, women employed part-time did 64 per cent, and women
employed full-time did 62 per cent.[11]

As Table 6.3 shows, household maintenance tasks such as laundry,
ironing, mending and sewing, washing floors, cleaning bathrooms,
house and car repairs, shopping, yard-work, or bill paying were done
with varying degrees of regularity. Overwhelmingly, however, there was a
clear division of labour between women and men, and most household
tasks were sex-specific. Women and men took equal responsibility for
paying bills. Close to half of women and men did yard-work and shopping, although more men reported yard-work and more women
reported shopping.[12] In all households, women were primarily responsible for doing laundry, ironing, mending and sewing, and washing
floors, men for fixing cars and doing household repairs.

Making Ends Meet

Another aspect of domestic labour involves 'making ends meet,' allocating the available income to the various needs and choices of household members, from paying the mortgage and buying the groceries to purchasing luxury goods and services. It also involves activities to obtain goods and services without paying money. Most of the people we interviewed needed general accounting and shopping skills, but had enough money to get away with small mistakes: 'If I want something I buy it if I have the money, you know, or use the charge card sometimes. It doesn't matter. If I want something, usually I get it' (126 M 1984).

However, for those households hit by unemployment, the drastic loss of income demanded new strategies for getting by. As the strikes and lay-offs revealed, working-class households were vulnerable: 'The strike of 1981 put many families in debt. Some lost their houses, cars, luxury items bought on credit. We had to borrow money from my parents when our savings ran out and use credit to buy Christmas presents for the children. It took many months of frugal living once my husband was back at work to pay back our debts. Other workers did not get called back to work after the strike – I can only imagine what that was like' (301 F 1996).

Instead of steady pay cheques, bolstered by overtime payments, these people tried to piece together a living through recalls, interim employment, and unemployment insurance premiums. They lived with job insecurity and had little control over the uncertainty imposed on their lives. A union official described some of the consequences: 'At the hall we talk to them on a daily basis. We hear stories of mortgage foreclosures or repossession, family breakdown and more.'[13] Another laid-off steelworker explained: 'Summertime. The living is supposed to be easy. But not at Stelco. For many the lack of work means delaying purchases. Houses and cars have to wait. Education plans are on hold. Debts increase.'[14]

Many households had to radically alter their ways of making ends meet. A steelworker described the impact of her lay-off: 'Suddenly my income dropped. I only had UI and not for that long. I had to cut back all over. I always paid the rent and made sure we had enough food, but treats were out. I had to stop driving for the kids' hockey car pool. The other parents didn't say anything, but I felt bad. And my youngest one didn't understand' (221 F 1984).

The 1984 survey of laid-off workers showed that people used all kinds of coping strategies to deal with their loss of income (see Table 6.4; (and Corman 1993). The most important were other income-generating activities. Almost all of them relied on unemployment insurance whenever possible as a partial buffer. Laid-off steelworkers looked for other jobs either permanently or to tide themselves over until they were recalled. Where possible they relied on their partners' incomes. Sixty per cent of men had partners, most of whom (66 per cent) had paid employment prior to the lay-off. Half of the spouses who had not had paid employment prior to the lay-offs took jobs. As the majority of women steelworkers were single, and only four had an employed spouse, they were even more vulnerable.

Laid-off steelworkers and their families drew on their savings, went into debt, used social assistance, and asked for help. They reduced their expenditures by shopping more carefully and cutting back on big consumer items, entertainment, and even grocery shopping. They also increased their domestic labour in the home by doing more mending and other repairs and cooking cheaper, but more labour-intensive meals: 'I just cut right back and worked really hard to make sure we ate okay. I soaked beans overnight and made vegetable stews. I even planted a garden so we could have fresh vegetables' (221 F 1996). Looking back over the years since his lay-off, another steelworker made this assessment: 'It's been tough times since the early 1980s. It's really changed our life at home. We just don't live as well as we did, and we have to work that much harder' (303 M 1996).

Financial Management

Household members handled resources, particularly income, in a variety of ways. At one extreme, the male income earner retained legal and practical control of all money, making his partner fully dependent on him. Twenty-three per cent of men and 20 per cent of women reported this option. At another extreme, both partners as income earners retained legal and practical control of their own money, each contributing to household expenses. The majority of women and men described a system of economic pooling and sharing. Forty-seven per cent of men and 52 per cent of women claimed that they shared: 'It is not my money or your money, or anything like that. It is our money, that is all' (126 M 1984).

TABLE 6.4
Use of coping strategies, by sex, marital status, and spouses' employment status (per cent)[a]

Coping strategy	All	Women	Men	Single men	Married men[b]	Spouse homemaker[c]	Spouse works full-tme
UI premiums	95	100	95	96	95	100	94
Savings	83	83	83	79	85	81	85
Debt	29	42	28	16	36	38	44
Social assistance	17	33	16	14	18	33	8
Get help	51	58	51	49	53	67	46
Repair	55	33	56	55	57	57	46
Shop	52	42	52	50	53	62	44
Big items	77	92	76	70	80	76	77
Entertainment	74	92	73	55	83	86	81
Groceries	32	42	32	17	42	38	33
N	234	12	222	92	118	21	52

[a]Relevant sample characteristics: (a) employment status of women's spouses: no spouse = 7, unemployed = 1, full-time job = 4;and (b) employment status of men's spouses: no spouse = 92, full-time job = 52, part-time job = 10, changed status = 16, full-time home-maker = 21, other reasons for no job = 16.

[b]The ten male steelworkers who became separated from their spouses after their layoff are not included in either the married or single category.

[c]All spouses are female, and homemakers did not have paid employment.

[d]All spouses are female, and these wives were employed full-time.

Source: Corman (1993).

For most, available income ensured a comfortable living, but once the basic bills were paid, there was little money left over: 'We don't budget. We exist. We don't save. We put $400 in the bank from my salary and that pays the taxes. I suppose it's because we're both working, and we don't have any reason to budget' (097 F 1984).

In the first few years living together, most couples established budgetary understandings that became household norms: 'I pay all the bills. He knows where the money is and he helps himself. I would never spend any money without discussing it with him first, not if it was say more than $100. We usually make those purchases together' (069 F 1984).

The Power of Male Income Earners

The dynamics of making ends meet reveal the economic inequality between women and men.[15] Marriages where men are income earners and women are homemakers are, economically, mechanisms of redistribution (Hartmann 1981). Workers who fought for and won a family wage were in effect paying their wives to stay home and look after them, their children, and homes. However, despite the ideology of the family wage, wages have always been the private property of the person who earns them. Various legal restraints have attempted to compel men to share their wages (Backhouse 1992). Women's groups and other reformers fought to change laws that gave control of married women's property to their husbands and for laws that recognize men's responsibility to support their families.

These laws are difficult to enforce, however. Men may earn a family wage, but there is no guarantee that they will redistribute their wages fairly. Indeed, there is extensive evidence that women are more likely to spend money on children, food, and daily living than men are (Pahl 1989). In families, women and children consistently have access to fewer resources than men (Oren 1974; Brannen and Moss 1987). Marriage breakdowns make this problem more visible; women have high rates of poverty after divorce, and men frequently fail to respect court orders to pay child support (Pulkingham 1994).

Earlier ideologies legitimating men's total financial power in marriage have largely disappeared. They have been replaced by discourses of sharing, a loose notion that income contributes to the subsistence of all household members and that everyone is entitled to a share. The majority of the couples we interviewed maintained that financial decisions were arrived at after lengthy discussions in which the concerns of both adults, and where appropriate, the children's, were taken into account: 'Fifty-fifty. We sit down, take a look at a bunch of different models of something you want to get and decide which one you are going to get. Like we talked about the microwave oven for I don't know how long. We don't argue over anything. We sit down and discuss it' (074 M 1984).

However, sharing need not imply any sense of equality, and collective decision-making may not be democratic. In 35 per cent of households where the man was the only income earner, he controlled the money, paid the bills, and gave his wife a housekeeping allowance. In some couples the man made most of the major decisions: 'We got a big car and I wanted a truck. And I traded the car for the truck. Momma didn't like me letting the car go, but the truck was something I wanted. So, I would say that I probably make the decisions. I don't mean to come off as chauvinist or a dictator or anything, but I think I make most of the major purchases and decisions' (108 M 1984).

In one case, the wife claimed they shared. But her description of practices revealed extreme male dominance: 'When he's working the pay goes directly into his account, and I write out all the cheques to pay the bills every payday and he signs them. I keep the chequebook balanced, and I do it real well. But then he goes and takes out money and never writes it in the book, so it never balances' (181 F 1984). He also decided which cheques to sign. Because he had put paying for repairs on his motorcycle before paying the heating bills, they had no heat through three months of the previous winter: 'It was too cold for us, especially for the baby [18 months old]. We wore all our clothes, even our outdoor coats but it was too cold, so finally I took the baby and moved in with my mother' (181 F 1984).

She went on to describe the particularly brutal way her partner exercised his wage-earner power: 'He does all the grocery shopping, and he won't let me have any money to do it. I never get any money. I make out a list and give it to him, and he laughs and says "you got to be kidding," and he just leaves the list on the table and goes out. Say I need dish soap and laundry detergent and floor polish. Well, he'll buy the food first and then the dish soap and probably the detergent, but he won't buy the floor polish' (181 F 1984). He justified his refusal to give her any money, even for personal things, by claiming that she was incompetent and could not 'handle money.'

Most couples have far less oppressive ways of allocating their money, but for women whose own income cannot support themselves and their children, survival depends on their husbands' goodwill. As long as they are the primary income earners, men have the ultimate control over spending. One man decided to buy a house, despite his wife's urging that they wait until they had saved more money: 'Well, I talked with the wife. That decision was mine because she didn't want to buy ... but I went ahead and bought the house' (004 M 1984).

The increased participation of married women in paid labour has shifted the balance of power, not just for women earning their own income but more generally for all women, as increasingly women are understood to be financial actors in their own right.[16] Among two-earner households, the majority (75 per cent) pooled their money in a common bank account; 14 per cent of employed women maintained their own accounts. In terms of family power relations, there is a close relationship between the proportion of total household income a woman generated, the length of time she had been earning money, and the degree of power she commanded in her household: 'If a mother is independent economically, she would have more say, more economic freedom. If there is a tight situation at home, women have more choice' (080 F 1984).

However, even when the women were earning relatively high incomes, there was a strong tendency for the couple to retain a gendered division of financial responsibility. Men's earnings were understood as sustaining basic or essential household needs – paying the mortgage or taxes – and women's earnings paid for 'extras' – holidays or special children's clothes or toys: 'I will look after the mortgage and the utilities. We always feel that her money brings in the extras. She basically looks after that. We have gone on a trip and she's paid for that' (151 M 1984). That pattern allowed men to retain their sense of breadwinner power and gave women the option of withdrawing from the labour market.

In 1984 a woman described how her household allocated her earnings: 'I have a separate account, but I use it to buy roasts instead of what we usually would get. If the kids need shoes, I will get them shoes, get myself a pair of loafers. I want to save up for a piano. [My son] wanted to have a bike for his birthday. He saved up for part of it. I saved the Canadian Tire money for part of it and the rest of it, I paid for. We wouldn't have been able to do it if I hadn't been doing sales. So it is sort of for extras' (105 F 1984). Ten years later, she had given up her paid work because it conflicted too much with her domestic responsibilities: 'I quit my part-time job because my spouse got involved politically in addition to still working at Stelco. Before he was involved in politics, he was also

out four or five nights a week. He comes home to eat, then he goes out.
I left work to take care of the kids who were alone at night. I do more of
the housework. I always have. My husband is good at doing dishes when
he is inclined' (105 F 1994).

Shopping and Consumer Culture

In nineteenth-century rural communities in Ontario, farming households produced much of what the household needed, especially in the
way of food (Cohen 1988). Staple foodstuffs such as sugar, tea, coffee,
and flour were typically purchased, as were household and farm imple-
ments, and fabric for making clothes. Shopping for consumer goods was
not a major activity. Well into the twentieth century, even in urban centres, people were able to produce many of the goods they needed for
household consumption (Katz 1975; Strong-Boag 1988).

Throughout the twentieth century, the purchased portion of household goods and services grew dramatically. Material standards of living
have reflected the increasing range of available goods and services. An
older woman gave a sense of how such changes had affected her understanding of society: 'My mother grew up on a farm, dirt poor. They
never had electricity or running water. And when I was growing up [in
Hamilton in the 1930s] – that was the depression then – we were working class. We didn't have much. So now I live real well. Now I'm middle
class. I have a modern house, a car, lots of nice things my mother could
never have dreamed of. In this society even working people can be part
of the middle class. That's why Canada is such a good place to live' (217
F 1984).

Significant generational experiences shaped the relationship to
money of the people interviewed for this study.[17] Those who came of
age during the depression in the 1930s tended to be careful financially
and to value frugality. The next generation, growing up in a much more
affluent period during the boom of the late 1940s and the 1950s, were
inclined to take relative economic security for granted. They were more
prepared to take out loans and use credit to get things they wanted. This
shift in the way people related to their money, to credit, and to buying
was part of the emergence of late twentieth-century consumer culture.
However, in the 1980s and for steelworkers after the 1981 strike, working people once again confronted a decline in real incomes that forced
many to reassess their spending practices: 'We don't charge now, we use
cash. We used to charge quite a lot. If you didn't have the money, you

put it on your account and charged it. But since the strike, we do the utmost to have the money first and then buy it' (097 F 1984).

With the economic downturn of the 1980s, the extent to which the Canadian economy, and particularly southern Ontario, depended not just on resource extraction and heavy manufacturing but on consumer shopping was clear. Just as the household produces (and reproduces) people who can go out as workers with labour power to sell to employers, the household also produces (and reproduces) consumers who go out as shoppers to purchase goods and services.

At one level, this is very straightforward. Because urban households cannot produce the goods and services their members need, they must purchase them. The contemporary Hamilton housewife cannot produce the evening meal from crops and animals grown on the family farm. Instead, she must go to a shop or market and use money to purchase supplies. What she confronts in these shops is markedly different even from what urban women found at the turn of the century. Then there was a relatively limited array of produce, and most of it was sold in bulk. Beginning around the turn of the century, there was a transformation in shopping equivalent to scientific management (or Taylorism) in manufacturing: 'The underlying effect of mass commodity packaging is to break sales down into standardized units, thus enabling commodity producers to have greater control over consumption and a more systematic means of exploiting the consumer through advertising. Prior to the 1890s there was no advertising for what would become Quaker Oats, because, if such advertising had existed, it could only have promoted oats in general' (Willis 1991: 2).

As Willis notes, the development of packaging permitted standardization of weights and measures and a proliferation of brands. Customers were forced to buy two kilograms of flour when they needed only 200 grams, for example. Whereas people had bought just flour, they were now able to choose among a range of flours. Presented through advertising as competitors and somehow significantly different, such 'choices' are often produced by the same company and intended to increase sales, not variety.[18]

In addition, throughout the twentieth century there was a dramatic growth in the range and types of commodities available, from inexpensive children's toys to household appliances like microwave ovens and gas barbecues. Industrial workers like those at Stelco earned enough money to pay for their basic subsistence needs and still had enough to purchase additional commodities for their homes, their children, and their own leisure time. This layer of the working class formed an important pool of consumers whose spending fueled capitalist growth through the mid- to late twentieth century.

The growth of consumer markets, all devoted to maximizing the number of people who purchase as many goods as possible, led to the emergence of what is called 'consumer culture' or 'consumer society' (Ewen 1976). The growth of corporate capitalism, and particularly its promotional or advertising wing, has transformed all aspects of social life, including family and household forms; concepts of women, men, and children; and even the needs and desires of potential consumers (Harvey 1989). Several features of this new cultural form were of particular significance to the evolution of domestic labour. The most apparent was that shoppers needed to learn new skills to assess the various products available, evaluate their relative worth in relation to household budgets, and determine where and how to get the best buys – how to shop efficiently: 'I find I want to go in the supermarket and I will be looking, you know, for different things that are cheaper. It is just something you learn as the years go by' (151 M 1984).

Skilled shopping includes not only knowing how to spend money, but how to resist temptation and not spend money: 'Some of our friends have nothing to show for what they got. They have got maybe $5,000 worth of stereo equipment. I might only have a $100-stereo. All I want to hear is music. Turn it on and it comes out. I am not going to go out and spend $1,000 on a radio system either. I feel I am practical' (021 F 1984). The availability of credit permits people to purchase things when they do not have the money available. As a result, 'living within one's means' has become much more difficult: 'I don't know if it is the right way or not. I figure sometime if you don't charge, you are not going to get the things if you try to save the money' (126 M 1984).

Like other aspects of domestic labour, shopping for household goods has been chiefly women's responsibility, and women in the study were more likely than men to cultivate the knowledge and skills: 'I could shop for hours and I can start in one store and see one thing but I have to go to check out everything else before ... Well it just drives him around the bend. He says, "If you like it buy it," you know. Well I said, "Well I might see something else out there that I like." Basically if he sees something and he likes it, he'll buy it. He won't shop around comparing' (042 F 1984).

Women often maintained that men did not know how to shop and that if they did it, they did it badly: 'I do not like him to go grocery shopping. I will make out a list and I will figure out how much it is going to cost and I give him that much. If I give him $10, he will spend it. If I give him $100, he will spend it. See what I mean – you can't have a grocery shopper like that. I can give him a list of ten items and he will get two items that are on the list and then the rest of the things for the money that he has; he thinks that he can buy whatever' (105 F 1984).

Households periodically make large economic decisions about purchasing a house, household appliances or furniture, a new car, an expensive vacation, a major career change. What is implicit when they are making these decisions is that adult household members have learned to accommodate their wishes and desires to what is possible. Many women and men echoed the woman who claimed: 'I usually get what I want' (069 F 1984). What would happen if she decided to mortgage the house, use the savings and credit to go back to school, to travel around the world, to buy a sports car, or play the lottery?

It is at the level of wishes and desires that domestic labour enters into the more complex levels of consumer society. Even basic needs are socially determined. While all people need basic nutrition to stay alive, the kinds of food they eat and the quantities are shaped by an interaction of factors such as the types of food available, their relative cost, cultural food norms and taboos, and the personal preferences of household members.

Within the confines of availability and cultural norms, the actual foods served in any particular household depend on the individual preferences of household members. In most households, meals are only partially intended to satisfy basic nutritional needs. Far more significant is the effort to make sure household members feel cared for and catered to and to create a sense of well-being and unity as a household or family (De Vault 1991). Thus, meal preparation not only requires matching the amount of money budgeted for food with the products available, it involves juggling household members' various likes and dislikes. To do this well, the shopper and meal planner must pay close attention to individual tastes which, especially in children, are often very narrow. They also have to consider competing preferences because family rivalries and hostilities are fueled if one person repeatedly feels that his or her preferences are subordinated. For most women, meal planning attempts to ensure that over a week everyone feels accommodated. For example, if one child hates fish, but loves hamburgers, a mother may serve fish one day while promising hamburgers the next.

The growth of consumer society has created a wide range of potential new needs and desires. Where working-class children at the turn of the century might have been resigned to having only two sets of clothing, one for 'good' and one for play, and only a few toys, or books, contemporary children typically have a range of clothes, toys and books. Similarly, while studies of turn-of-the-century living show that working people rarely had money beyond what would purchase housing, food, and clothing, as well as a few small pleasures such as beer, cigarettes, or make-up, contemporary Hamilton households have far more to choose from: 'Look at all the stuff in this house! My kids have every toy imaginable. I never had such stuff when I was a kid. Maybe we didn't have the money; maybe there was less stuff to have, I don't know. But now kids expect to have everything' (221 F 1984).

As numerous studies have shown, one of the key features of consumer capitalism is the way in which advertising is designed to foster endless dissatisfaction (Wernick 1991). Advertisements create new needs which they claim can only be satisfied by purchasing new products. All aspects of human life – from bodily appearance to interpersonal relationships – are transformed into longings that particular products promise to satisfy. As Reiter (1991) has shown, the fast-food industry has captured the longings many people have for caring family relations, skilfully portraying the idea that if families eat at their local fast-food outlet, 'all will be well.' For many, the anticipation of the use value of whatever they buy far outweighs its actualization (Willis 1991). This not only breeds discontent, but feeds the notion that next time, a different purchase will make everything all right. One man described this process in his family: 'Vacations are something of a disaster in this house because it seems like every year we decided to do something different, and every year we do it, it doesn't seem as good as what we used to do' (075 M 1984).

By creating new desires and needs, consumer capitalism draws people even further into the commodity goods market, a process that strengthens their need for earnings. The more a sense of well-being rests on acquiring material goods, the more private consumption promotes competition. A man described how this dynamic created tensions for him as he struggled to reconcile two conflicting impulses: 'My son wants me to pay for his college and he wants that I support him through two years there. It's a good plan, and I'd like to. But I've had lay-offs for years. We've had to dip into our savings. If I give him the money, I won't have it for when I retire' (069 M 1998).

One of the challenges facing people inundated by the pressures to buy more is to figure out how to juggle competing desires both within individuals and among household members and how to mediate, repress, or restrain desire. There is a clear tension between earning more money so that it is possible to buy more things and earning less, but having more time to enjoy life. An older steelworker whose children had left home talked of his plans to move to a lower-paying, but less-demanding job: 'I have no children now to speak of. I think Mom and I can get along on a lot less than $35,000 a year. I really don't need to make that money anymore, I don't think' (108 M 1984).

For older people who have benefited from years of steady earnings, this trade-off is relatively easy. An older woman explained that she would prefer to have time off work rather than more money because 'as you grow older and you have everything, there's less things that you need. Now we're just replacing things that break down, whereas before we had to get a whole room furnished. We don't need things really' (097 F 1984).

For younger people, or those lacking material security, the demands of making ends meet are in constant tension with the desire to have more time and energy for social relations. An older man recalled: 'Years ago, I worked at Stelco when I first came out of school. When I was single, I spent eight or nine months there. I said, "This is stupid, for a single guy to work shifts." So I went back to sell shoes and I had my weekends off' (061 M 1984). When he married, he returned to work at Stelco.

Conclusion

The day-to-day activities of housework, household maintenance, and making ends meet involve a series of relatively discrete labour processes. The different tasks require different skills and exert different pressures. In combination they are often harder, and sometimes they undermine the caregiving they are supposed to sustain. A mother ironically described some of her difficulties when she had to combine shopping and child care: 'Oh! It's lots of fun when I have the kids with me! I end up almost killing them. If I don't have to have them with me, I will not, because they are uncontrollable in the store' (105 F 1984).

Efforts to reconcile the various demands of maintaining a household and meeting the requirements of paid employment, in order to meet the needs of individuals and the household as a group, are central to the way domestic labour is organized.

As the labours that ensure household subsistence, they are the means available to individual households to exert some (limited) control over standards of living. They also provide the basis for caregiving.

Just as the kind of involvement people have in domestic labour affects their participation in paid employment, the kind of attachment they have to the labour force affects their participation in domestic labour. Men who have a sense that they have met their familial obligations by bringing home a pay cheque and who are worn out after a long day on the job have reason to resist demands that they put in a second shift at home. Women who are in a similar situation typically have less power, whether from economic clout or supporting gender discourses, to resist the double day. Some women push for a more equitable division of labour; others prefer to do the work themselves rather than fight. Most are somewhere in between. A few men resist or refuse outright; others make a conscious effort to change, preferring this to constant hassles, and most are somewhere in between.

Despite important changes in the division of labour between women and men in family households, most men still benefit from the power prerogatives of income earning, and most women are still economically dependent on marriage. In spite of increasing variation in the work that women do in the paid labour force, they remain primarily responsible for domestic labour.

Struggles to reduce gender inequities in the home were complicated by economic restructuring as the outcome of increases in class inequalities was to alter the balance of work – both paid and unpaid – and family life for these working-class households.

By working harder, women modify the effects of attacks on their households' standard of living. Central to the process of capital accumulation in general, and to recent international economic restructuring policies, domestic labour serves as a residual labour, replacing or filling in when other resources are unavailable. Women act as a reserve army of unpaid workers, absorbing more unpaid work in the home when public services are not available or the costs of paying for services are too high.

7

Domestic Labour as Caring for People

In 1984 a woman tried to put into words what looking after her husband and young child meant to her. She pointed out that she had taken marriage and children for granted: 'Why did I get married? Well, I don't know, really. I always assumed I'd get married, and when I met a guy who seemed right, we just went ahead. It was just a natural thing to do. I always wanted kids' (208 F 1984). Her declaration of emotional commitment to them revealed ambiguities and tensions between loving or caring about others and looking after or caring for them: 'That's what family is about; it's about caring about your husband and your kids. If you get married and have kids, then you have to care for them. After all, you love them, naturally you would look after them. And I do love them. I want to care for them' (208 F 1984). She noted the social pressures that encouraged conformity: 'But you should, too, because it's just the right thing to do. And if you don't, people will think badly of you' (208 F 1984).

She expressed frustration with the demands that caring imposed on her: 'I feel pulled in all directions at once. I want to be more attentive, more loving, and I want to scream. I don't understand why I don't like being with them more or why it makes me crazy when I love them so much' (208 F 1984). A decade later, she had a slightly different perspective: 'When I was younger I really thought as a good wife and mother, I had to put my husband and child first. I thought if I loved them, I had to take care of them. Now, I don't think one person can be everything to someone else. It's too much' (208 F 1996). But she regretted the demands on her time that made it difficult to give them the attention she wanted to: 'I don't remember back then ever feeling so busy, even though [the child] was little. We just seem to have to work harder and

harder. I never have enough time for myself or anyone else. It's very sad'
(208 F 1996).

One of the main reasons that people live together is that they care
about each other, and they demonstrate that by taking care of each
other; so caregiving is the heart of domestic labour. Caregiving includes
everything people do to sustain themselves and the people they care for,
day-to-day and over a lifetime. A central contradiction for domestic
labour is that, while caregiving is an expression of the strong emotional
ties that bind people together, it is also a demanding labour process,
embedded in unequal divisions of labour. That contradiction is deepening in working-class households, where caregiving tries to produce and
sustain people within the constraints of producing some of them as sellers of labour power. A union activist described this tension: 'We work at
Stelco because of the money. The money gives us a chance to live a
decent life. But there's always that kicker, you're living a decent life only
to go back to Stelco the next day where you work your butt off and
maybe risk your life and health so you can have a life' (310 M 1984).

This tension gets played out in class struggles over standards of living
and the extent to which individual or family members, employers, or
public or state sectors should be responsible for the care of children and
other dependent people. It is intensified by gender struggles, as women
try to alleviate the oppressive aspects of their responsibility for unpaid
domestic labour by socializing more of it and redistributing more of it to
men.

Caregiving as a Labour Process

The demands of caregiving as a labour process are frequently obscured
by discourses of romantic love, parental dedication, and family devotion. Caregiving is most clearly understood as work when it involves
looking after those who cannot look after themselves – especially children or those who are ill, elderly, or have special needs. The recognition
that companionate marriage assumes that spouses love each other, and
that love is expressed through ongoing, mutual expressions of care,
make it harder to see the labour aspects of caregiving between cohabiting adults.

One woman described the tensions these competing dynamics posed
when her husband was injured and needed care: 'Of course I wanted to
look after him. He's my husband after all, but it was too much. I love
him. I care about him, but he needed someone with him all the time

fetching and carrying, giving him his medication, and I thought, this isn't love any more. Other people get paid to do this' (069 F 1984).

The tensions between the social relations and the work process are exacerbated by the contradiction between caregiving as a private and a public responsibility, especially as the way families and households are organized puts stress on caring relations and makes it difficult for most people to extend such caring beyond their immediate circle. While most people acknowledge some responsibilities and obligations to others beyond their immediate household or family members, the boundaries are unclear: 'I do a lot for his mother. She's old and needs a lot of help. Everyone just assumes I'll do it because she's my mother-in-law, but sometimes I don't see why I have to. She should get taken care of, but I shouldn't have to just cause we're related. And when I feel bad about having to ... then I'm not very nice to her' (010 F 1984).

Most people find it easier to contemplate taking on caregiving responsibilities if they know the dependent person has other resources available; taking on the full responsibility can feel overwhelming: 'When I had to take care of [my mother-in-law] myself, I got so I just hated her and dreaded having to do anything. Then when we got her into the day care program, and I knew it wasn't just me doing it all, and I got a break each day, then it was much easier and I didn't mind taking care of her' (208 F 1984).

This public–private contradiction intensified in the 1990s, as cutbacks in social services reduced public support. For the women in this study, the cuts came just when more of them had paid jobs and therefore less time available for providing unpaid caregiving: 'I had just got things all worked out with my new job and a babysitter for after school, and it looked like we were going to be able to make it financially with what I earn and the costs of the sitter and all, when the school board decided to cut junior kindergarten. Now I don't know what to do. We need my job to get by, but who will look after the children?' (303 F 1996).

At the same time, changing gender practices meant that some men were more involved in caregiving work, generating new assumptions about their capacities as nurturers. A steelworker described generational differences among his co-workers: 'I'm thirty-five and there's quite a few guys in my age bracket, say from forty down and then, there's the forty above. And it's like two different species ... There might be six guys around the lunch table and for three, there's no problem changing diapers, in that respect, the relationship between men and women – in that age bracket, there are no stereotypical roles' (047 M 1994).

The type of work, its intensity, and how the caregiver experiences it all depend on the quality of the relationship at the time: changing soiled bedding for an ill adult can be a miserable, unpleasant task that breeds resentment, or it can be a tolerated necessity that expresses deep loving. Caregiving is also shaped by the degree of dependence and the nature of the care needed: comforting an adult who is grieving a death takes different skills than reassuring a three-year-old who is afraid of thunder. Raising a child involves different dynamics than nurturing an elderly person who is dying.

Child Care[1]

A mother of two young boys neatly captured the contradictions many parents face when raising children: 'The society tells you, you have to have kids and have to raise them right and blames you if they get into trouble, but at the same time, it tells you, you are on your own, and don't ask for society to help you because you chose to have them. But make sure they grow up to be the kind of people who will fit into society, but no one will tell you how to do that, or even what kind of person will succeed in the society that might be when they are grown up' (069 F 1984). She went on to explain how those contradictions played out in her own life:

> Before I had kids, I just took for granted that I would, and that because being a mother was natural, I'd just know instinctually how to raise my kids, and what was right for them – that's what being a mother is all about. Boy was I wrong! There's nothing natural about it at all. Like they're my kids alright, but the whole world affects them no matter what I do and everybody out there has an opinion about how I should raise them. They're quick to interfere if they don't like how my kids are, but they sure aren't there to help with the everyday stuff. (069 F 1984)

As this mother points out, the private and social aspects of parenting are intensely contradictory. Because it is seen to be 'natural,' or instinctual, parents usually receive little or no preparation or training. It is assumed to be up to individual parents to raise their children, so they are left largely to their own devices and get virtually no social support.[2] At the same time, parenting is profoundly social, shaped by the panoply of normative expectations and legal requirements about having children and how to raise them.

Families form the main social relationships within which infants develop as intersubjective beings, that is, the way children develop as human subjects in their relationships with other people through language, behaviours, observations, and their experiences of the world around them. As part of the process of social reproduction, child-rearing is at the same time the way individual parents raise their children and part of what produces the next generation. Through their child-rearing practices, adults significantly shape the psycho-social environment in which subjectivity is formed in relation to specific gender, race, ethnic, or national and class identities.

Despite their assumption that having children was a natural thing to do, most of the people we interviewed agreed that child-rearing was something that had to be learned. One woman acknowledged that her previous child care experiences looking after her younger siblings and her nephew had helped her as a new mother: 'So being around kids is just natural for me' (176 F 1984). Her partner, however, had had no previous experience and 'he was scared to death' (176 F 1984).

Precisely because it is so widely assumed that parenting is natural, there is very little social support for learning parenting. Most parents learn on the job, trying to balance pressures to conform to prevailing notions of appropriate familial relations and child-rearing practices with what their own predispositions and circumstances make possible.

Who Looks After the Children?

As Table 7.1 shows, mothers were far more involved in child care for children under five years of age than fathers were, regardless of the women's employment, and of all the child care activities, fathers were more likely to be playing with their children than providing physical care. While mothers who were with their children all day spent more time diapering and playing with their children than employed mothers, there were no differences in the amount of time mothers spent on the tasks done once a day such as getting children up, putting them to bed, dressing or bathing them, and looking after them during the night.

Men had more choice about whether, when, and to what degree they did child care. The clearest expression of this difference was revealed by how women and men described what they were doing. Women talked about raising their children or staying at home with them; most men talked about 'watching' or 'babysitting.' A mother pointed out the problem with this formulation: 'I said, well, it's not really babysitting. It's

TABLE 7.1

Number of times (and percentage by parent) in a typical day parents did specific child care activities for children under 5 years of age, by women's employment status (means)

Child care activity	Father times per day	Mother times per day	His percentage	Her percentage
Diaper				
N = 32	1.6	5.8	23	75
Full-time homemaker (17)	1.4	6.7*	22	78
Both employed (15)	1.9	4.8*	25	72
Dress				
N = 44	1.0	2.3	29	70
Full-time homemaker (20)	0.8	2.5	26	73
Both employed (24)	1.1	2.1	32	67
Bathe				
N = 41	0.4	1.1	21	79
Full-time homemaker (19)	0.3	1.1	19	81
Both employed (22)	0.4	1.1	22	77
	Hours per day	Hours per day		
Play				
N = 47	2.2	3.3	39	55**
Full-time homemaker (23)	2.2	4.0***	35	61**
Both employed (24)	2.2	2.6***	43	50

Significance is between women of different employment status or between men married to women of different employment statuses. Significance (*P*): * = .1; ** = .05; *** = .01; **** = .001 (steelworkers).

Only families who actually engage in the activity are counted, so the number of families for each activity varies. Figures are based on his report of his activities and her report on her activities. The activities of others are not included, so percentages do not add to 100.

your daughter you're looking after' (042 F 1984). A full-time housewife praised her partner for his unusual willingness to 'help out' with the children.[3] His involvement after the birth of their first baby was aided by the fact he was not going out to work at the time: 'When the oldest was born, he was on sick leave so he helped a lot. I don't know what I would have done if he hadn't helped because the oldest was the runt of the litter, and he needed feeding every two hours and I was young and so tired. I was just seventeen and I'm not sure I could have done it without him' (069 F 1984). His involvement continued as the children grew older, perhaps because they were boys involved in hockey: 'My husband helps out a lot, especially he is so involved with the kids' hockey. He spends a lot of time with the children. He plays with the little one and often will put the kids to bed' (069 F 1984).

An employed mother insisted that both she and her husband shared child care: 'Child care is shared between the two of us because of our shifts, and the babysitter, and sometimes, as I say, my mum, more than the babysitter. Child care is with both of us' (042 F 1984). But it was clear that he was less constrained by child care responsibilities than she was: 'Some days, depending if it's [her husband's] day off and he has something planned and I have to work, she sometimes will go to the sitter on those days so he has the day off to do as he wants to do. I never do that. But he appreciates the day off, and he says it's not really a day off if he has to look after [the child]. Some of these guys are really funny about this kind of thing' (042 F 1984).

Another full-time housewife and mother of a preschooler explained that her partner did virtually no child care: 'He doesn't do much for the child. He won't bathe her or take her to the washroom. Even when she was toilet training, he would never take her. If he's sleeping, I never ask him to watch her. I'll ask a neighbour rather. If he is up I might ask him, but most of the time he's working in the garage so he wouldn't see her if she went off' (181 F 1984).

Some men seemed to have difficulty caring for babies; men's willingness to take an active role in caring for their children appears to increase as the children get older. However, full-time homemakers took the major responsibility for school-aged child care. Where mothers of school-aged children were employed, they continued to do more child care than fathers, although children themselves took on more responsibilities when mothers were employed. As Table 7.2 shows, women did most of the caregiving for school-aged children. If their partners were employed, men whose shifts meant they were home were likely to supervise lunch times and after school. Otherwise their involvement with child care was unrelated to their partners' employment.

As Table 7.3 indicates, both mothers and fathers set and enforced rules in most households, although where women were full-time homemakers they were more likely to be the active enforcers. Both parents typically took children to the dentist and attended parents' nights at school. Mothers were typically responsible for shopping for children's clothes. When children got sick, it was overwhelmingly mothers who

TABLE 7.2
Number of times (and percentage by parent) in a typical week parents did specific child care activities for children between 5 and 16 years of age, by women's employment status

Child care activity	Father times per day	Mother times per day	His percentage	Her percentage
Up for school				
N = 61	0.9	4.6	12	84
Full-time homemaker (28)	0.5	5.2****	7**	91***
Both employed (33)	1.1	4.0****	17**	77***
≤ 29 h (24)	0.9	4.1	13	79
≥ 30 h (9)	1.6	4.0	27	79
Available after school				
N = 67	2.7	4.5	33	64
Full-time homemaker (35)	2.4	5.3****	25***	75****
Both employed (33)	3.0	3.7****	41***	54****
≤ 29 h (24)	2.3	4.0	32	62
≥ 30 h (9)	5.0	3.0	63	31
Supervise lunch				
N = 48	1.3	4.4	25	72
Full-time homemaker (26)	0.8***	5.6****	11****	89****
Both employed (22)	2.0***	3.0****	43****	51****
≤ 29 h (15)	1.7	3.0	41	49
≥ 30 h (8)	2.6	3.0	46	54
School Work				
N = 54	1.6	3.1	34	64
Full-time homemaker (29)	1.5	3.2	29	69
Both employed (25)	1.7	3.0	40	58
≤ 29 h (18)	1.7	2.2	38	59
≥ 30 h (7)	1.8	2.4	44	56

Significance is between women of different employment status or between men married to women of different employment statuses. Significance (P): * = .1; ** = .5; *** = .01; **** = .001 (steelworkers).

Only families who actually engaged in the activity are counted, so the number of families for each activity varies. Figures are based on his report of his activities and her report of her activities. The activities of others are not included, so percentages do not add up to 100.

TABLE 7.3
Responsibilities of parents for specific activities for children between 5 and 16 years of age[a]

Child care activity	1 Father (%)	2 Mother (%)	3 Both (%)	4 Other (%)	5 Father Total (1 + 3) (%)	6 Mother Total (2 + 3) (%)
Tend sick child						
N = 102	4	76	11	9	15	87
Full-time homemaker (49)	0	92	5	3	5	97
Both employed (53)	7	62	16	15	22	78
Part-time (34)	8	57	21	15		
Full-time (19)	6	71	7	15		
Take to the dentist						
N = 102	7	52	39	2	46	91
Full-time homemaker (49)	10	50	38	3	40	88
Both employed (53)	5	53	40	2	45	93
Part-time (33)	4	57	40	0		
Full-time (19)	6	47	40	6		
Shop for clothes						
N = 101	2	69	22	6	24	91
Full-time homemaker (49)	5	63	27	5	32	90
Both employed (52)	0	75	17	7	17	92
Part-time (33)	0	87	20	11		
Full-time (19)	0	69	14	0		
Attend parents' night						
N = 73	5	42	51	2	56	93
Full-time homemaker (35)	11	39	47	4	58	86
Both employed (38)	0	45	55	0	45	100
Part-time (25)	0	44	56	0		
Full-time (13)	0	47	53	0		
Set rules						
N = 95	9	18	73	0	82	91
Full-time homemaker (44)	11	18	70	0	81	88
Both employed (51)	7	17	76	0	83	95
Part-time (33)	0	15	85	0		
Full-time (18)	19	20	61	0		
Enforce rules						
N = 95	16	31	53	0	69	84
Full-time homemaker (44)	9	39	53	0	48	62
Both employed (51)	22	24	54	0	66	78
Part-time (33)	16	19	65	0		
Full-time (18)	32	33	36	0		

[a]This table is based on reports provided by mothers; the reports provided by fathers are similar.

cared for them, although when mothers were employed fathers were more likely to help out.

An employed mother of a six-year-old boy asserted her conviction that men ought to take responsibility for their children: 'And they should too, really. Yeah, oh yeah, he has done his share. Mind you he didn't do much when he was a baby. I had a babysitter then, but now he is doing more because [the child] can pretty well take care of himself' (046 F 1984).

A father who took active care of his small son contrasted his behaviour with that of his father: 'Things have changed quite a bit. My dad is a little, ah, he doesn't like to change him that much or stuff like that. He likes to take them out all the time ... and when it is time to change him, that is grandma's job' (187 M 1984). He maintained that younger men were increasingly participating in child care. This change in men's behaviour he explained partially by the fact that families had fewer children than in earlier generations: 'But I do think it has changed quite a bit as far as watching kids are concerned. I think it was a little harder years ago, because they had more kids. It was a little harder to take care of them – five, six, or seven. But they are no trouble at all, really' (187 M 1984).

Some men were able to develop a relationship with their children because they were unemployed: 'But things worked out pretty good because when my wife and the baby came home from the hospital I was home. I really helped out. I really enjoyed it. I really like kids, so we had a really good time' (015 M 1984). Later that year, when he was again unemployed for several months, he assumed responsibility for child care full-time while his wife was at her job: 'My wife was working and I looked after our son and it was really good. He made my day every day. I didn't mind babysitting, we had a really good time' (015 M 1984).

In a context where child care is still considered women's responsibility, having fathers look after the children when the mother cannot has several important advantages. It does not cost money, it does not involve leaving the children with a 'stranger' (an odd term for people who may spend hours each day with the child), it does not require transporting children to and from a sitter's, and it eases mothers' guilt about leaving their children. Most importantly, it fosters greater intimacy between fathers and their children. For couples beginning to challenge the notion that child care is women's responsibility, this last point is significant. But if men and women organize their paid employment so that they can each do child care, there are some decided disadvantages.

There is little time available for both parents and children to spend together or for parents to go out either separately or together.

Some fathers looked after their children, but their involvement was limited and often lasted only a few hours at a time. If they were feeding the children or putting them to bed, mothers often left food and clothes ready, on the assumption that fathers would not know what to do. Fathers often filled in a gap between the time the mother left for her job and the time he left for his, when he would drop the child at the sitter's on the way. One employed mother described her husband's difficulties: 'When she was little, he found it very difficult to pick her up from the sitter, feed her – because she was still on the baby routine kind of thing – and yet cook something for himself. He found that really difficult' (042 F 1984). But once men had actually taken on child care, the nature of their relationship with their children shifted and often became more significant. Some men began to cherish the time they were alone with their children and to increase it. One father who 'filled in' from the time his wife left for her job initially took the baby to the sitter shortly after his wife left. Gradually, he lengthened the time: 'I usually keep my son until I'm ready to go in on afternoon shift. I keep him till 1:30, then before I go to work, I drop him off' (015 M 1984).

In a context where good parenting is considered the responsibility of parents (perhaps with a little help from their kin), and where the only alternative child care costs money, most parents struggle to provide that care themselves. When combined with the demands of paid employment, individual child care arrangements can be endlessly complex and demanding. As women's employment patterns change and social attitudes to women's and men's roles and parenting become more fluid, the range of child care practices and arrangements becomes more varied.

Juggling Child Care and Paid Employment

Many women accept the ideological position that mothers provide the best care. For some, the decision to stay home was shaped by their childhood experiences: 'My mother worked when I was a kid and my grandmother raised me. I was never as close to my mother and father as I was to my grandmother. I don't think it's so good a mother working. I swore I'd never do it. A mother should be at home raising them. I think it's better for them' (069 F 1984). For others, it was shaped by the conviction that the most desirable situation is one where parents have full control over child-raising: 'And they look at me like I'm purple and green because I don't work outside the home. I'll say to them – well, you have kids, but you're not raising them' (176 F 1984).

For many parents, however, the strongest motivation for having the mother stay at home was a combination of convenience, economics, and concern for quality care. For example, as one man noted, he could always rely on his wife to look after the children, unlike some of the men whose wives were employed: 'That is why she doesn't work. That is the purpose of having her home, I guess. When I am at work, she is around with the kids, you know. There is no organization, like we don't have to plan – are you going to be home with the kids? – because she is always here' (089 M 1984).

On the other hand, parents who had other child care arrangements that they trusted expressed their delight, not only that their children had good care when they had to be at paid jobs, but that the children had a chance to know other people, to have a range of experiences, and to develop relationships independently. One mother described their daughter's sitter: 'She's wonderful. She is really, really fantastic. And she has had her since she's been three months. As soon as I went back to work, she's had her, so she's practically been her second mother' (042 F 1984).

Employed mothers were just as strong as full-time homemakers in their assertions that child care was important. What mattered to them was that their children received loving attention from all their caregivers; they simply did not believe that it required their personal full-time attention: 'It's important to have quality time with your kids. They are little people, not little things' (080 F 1984).

In contrast to the dilemmas women faced, it was taken for granted that men's employment took priority over their involvement in parenting. While this might be noted with regret in some cases, it was not understood as anything that could be altered. This pattern was particularly true for young men who, with less seniority, had less control over their schedules.[4] Many were tied to rotating shifts, days off that rarely fell on weekends, and holidays that rarely coincided with school breaks. Thus, the men were most restricted by shift work when their children were young. Many achieved enough seniority to work steady days, get more weekends, and have their holidays during July and August just at the point when their children were leaving home. One woman described how she and her husband were committed to spending as much time as possible together with their two children. When her husband worked day shift, they cooperated:

After dinner we both clean the table off. The kids take their own plates in. And we both clean up the kitchen. And I'm lucky enough to have a dishwasher now, so we load the dishwasher. This gives me more time with him. And now that the nice weather's here, we'll go outside and work in the garden. And we'll play with the kids. And it's bath time at 7:30, and she usually goes in first, cause it takes longer to dry her hair. And then my son goes in and we put the kids to bed together. We have baths and we brush teeth, and if there's time, we have stories, they say their prayers, and they say good night. And then we change rooms – he'll be in one room and I'm in the other room and then we'll change. And then the two of us come downstairs and I usually make lunches after the kids are in bed and put them in the fridge. And then we watch a movie on TV or we'll play cards. Then it's time for us to go to bed. (176 F 1984)

However, when he worked other shifts, their family togetherness was ruptured: 'When he goes from day shift to afternoon shift, my whole day changes. Because he's here all morning, then he goes to work before my son comes home from school. And then he's not here when the kids go to bed' (176 F 1984). His commitment to his children prompted him, when he was on afternoons, to cut short his sleep and get up before 8:30 to have a chance to see them before they left for school.

A steelworker noted sadly that he had never been able to coach his son's hockey team and had rarely made it to games because of his shift work. He also noted that this dynamic reinforced mothers as the ones responsible for the children and strengthened their emotional ties with their children: 'The problem is that games are predominantly on the weekend; and you never know when they are. So strictly you're an observer, when you can be there. You're an observer. A shift worker's wife is usually the kid's biggest fan. She's the one that's got to be at the arena 5 Saturday morning 'cause Dad's on days, or is coming off nights, and so on' (075 M 1984). He noted the irony of the impact of men's employment on their relations with their children. In his view, most men worked at Stelco in order to earn enough money to support their families: 'There isn't anything else. Most of the people I work with have very strong family relationships. Anyone who takes a job on a unit, the one I work on, which goes on twenty-four hours a day, seven days a week, is not a playboy. You have picked a job strictly for the money' (075 M 1984). However, while the job paid enough to support family life, its demands undermined family relations: 'That's the only thing I find now – like my son's in second year high school – is that I don't have the evening time. Like now his only free time really is evenings, and I'm only available in the evenings one week out of three' (075 M 1984).

The demands of paid employment combined with assumptions that child care is women's work means that many men do not know their children very well and are unsure of how to care for them. These gender differences mean that parental labour is not neutral; one parent cannot simply substitute for the other, because parents develop different levels of skill.[5] Discussing their neighbours who took their children out of day care while the Stelco strike was on, one woman commented on men's lack of experience: 'While he was home, she didn't put the kids in day care anymore. Dad's home to look after them, save money there. But Dad doesn't know how to handle these things all day long. Because he hasn't spent any time with them before. And all of a sudden, Dad's got these kids that he's only known for a few hours each day' (176 F 1984).

An older man whose children were adults discovered the painful consequences of this specialization long after his children had left home: 'What I found out about working shift work, I really didn't ever know my children. When you get to my time of life and you have worked shift work all your life, you realize you didn't really know your own children' (112 M 1984). Some men whose children had grown up realized too late what they had missed by not being more involved in child care: 'I should have spent a lot more time with my kids than I ever have spent. I feel kind of guilty at times. I try to spend time with them, you know, but I wish I could have spent more' (151 M 1984).

Sharing the Caring

The lack of adequate day care, particularly for parents who work shifts, means that a high proportion of parents create their own informal child care arrangements. A 1981 Statistics Canada national survey found that children under five years of age whose mothers were in the paid labour force were cared for mainly by friends, neighbours, or paid sitters (41 per cent), or by relatives (31 per cent) (Ram 1986). By 1990, 31 per cent of children using additional care were in licensed or workplace child care centres; 30 per cent were cared for by friends, neighbours, or paid sitters, while 38 per cent were cared for by relatives (Statistics Canada 1995b). By 1996 the National Council of Welfare estimated that more than half of all children in Canada experienced some form of non-parental child care (1999: 38) but only 8 per cent were in regulated care (1999: 48). The majority of the parents interviewed for this study made arrangements to fit with available employment, babysitters (both voluntary and paid), and personal beliefs about 'alternative care.'

While fathers were considered to be important caregivers, the exigencies of work at Stelco meant that very few couples could divide the care between the two of them. The majority needed at least one other caregiver to cover the times when both parents' paid work overlapped. For example, one couple with a three-year-old juggled his three rotating shifts and her three twelve-hour shifts a week, relying on whichever parent was available, a babysitter who was very flexible, and the woman's mother, who would keep the child overnight or for several days.[6] Another couple with a preschooler faced the same situation of the man's rotating shifts at Stelco and the woman's three twelve-hour shifts. Between them, they were able to cover most of the time and their mothers filled in when necessary: 'When I am on nights, I usually stay up and watch him, and if she is on days, I will stay up and she gets home around 2. When she is on afternoons, she will take off to work around 12, and I will watch him until it is time to go to work. And just drop him off at mom's when it is time to go to work, and she can pick him up at 5' (187 M 1984).

Female relatives, especially children's grandmothers, were the preferred caregivers, if they were available. As women and experienced mothers, they were often considered preferable to inexperienced fathers. Like fathers, they rarely demanded payment for the service. Because they were 'family,' women felt relieved of any guilt about leaving their children, and the generalized reciprocity between parents and adult children made it relatively easy to ask for such help. The father of a baby boy relied on both grandmothers for child care: 'My mom just lives over on [a street nearby], and her mom looks after him, too' (187 M 1984).

An employed mother paid her mother to look after her small son one day each week (080 F 1984). Another employed woman depended on several female relatives who all lived nearby: 'my mother or my sister or his sister' (051 F 1984). Several women and men talked about how reliable their mothers were and how much their children enjoyed staying with their grandmothers. For some grandparents, regular or periodic responsibility for grandchildren can offer great pleasure. An older man described his delight at having his grandchildren over to visit regularly: 'For the last while we have had grandchildren here pretty well. We count on them showing up on a Saturday morning. There would have been four grandchildren with grandpa and none of their parents here. Two of them spent the night' (149 M 1984).

However, with high rates of migration, many couples did not live near other female relatives. Even when older female relatives live nearby, they are not always available for child care. Some, especially younger women, have paid employment themselves. Others, especially older women who have raised several children of their own, feel either too old and tired to take on a baby or think they have done enough child care in their time and want no more of it. Some women were reluctant to leave their children with their own mothers because their ideas about how to bring up children were so different. Others knew their mothers disapproved of employed mothers and so were unwilling to ask them for help.

Other (especially female) relatives may be drawn on in a similar way, but this strategy is less popular because of the reciprocal obligations it implies (Finch 1989). A man noted that although both his and his wife's parents lived nearby, none of them had provided any support at points when they really needed it: 'They never, like when we were laid off and on strike, they never offered assistance, so I wouldn't say they are a major part of our life' (089 M 1984). As a result, he preferred not to ask them for help in child care: 'If we need babysitters – sometimes her mother or my mother – but there are two boys who live next door. I get them to babysit. I just pay them. It is just as easy' (089 M 1984).

When volunteers are unavailable, parents find someone – often a woman – who is willing to babysit for payment. Many considerations go into the selection of a regular sitter. The most important is that the sitter will provide safe, affectionate, and stimulating care. The ideal is someone who becomes so attached to the child she is like a second mother. Other factors include the rate she charges and whether she wants 'under the table' cash payments or will offer income tax receipts; the location of her home in relation to the child's or to the routes parents travel to paid jobs; whether there are other children in the home; and how flexible she is. As the majority of women who offer child care in their homes are not doing other paid work, they are often willing to be flexible, keeping the child beyond the regular hours if the parents are delayed, allowing the child to sleep over occasionally when parents' shifts overlap, perhaps even keeping the child for several days while parents take a holiday. When such arrangements work well, they can be very satisfactory.

However, when employed parents rely on a sitter for child care, they are vulnerable. If the sitter decides to stop taking their child, or if she gets sick or goes on holiday, the arrangement may be abruptly termi-nated. If the sitter treats their child in ways they are uncomfortable with, they may feel trapped if no alternatives are readily available. As Sharpe notes: 'It is clearly a sensitive area, a minefield of potential differences about things like discipline, food, manners, etc., and this may generate conflict ... Parents' exclusive responsibility for their children often makes them less tolerant of the way other adults treat children, and chil-dren themselves may be quick to play on this' (1984: 107).

Child care centres and nursery schools eliminate many of these prob-lems, but there are very few of these in Hamilton, the fees are high, and they do not take young infants (many will only take children who are toi-let trained). Moreover, in 1984 only one day care centre in Hamilton accommodated shift work, and it closed after a few years.[7] Child care workers are among the lowest paid in the country, which often results in high staff turnovers, and means that the quality of care depends on the devotion and self-sacrifice of the (mostly) women who work there. In the face of systematic government refusal to establish a national child care policy and to adequately fund quality non-profit child care centres, there are very few day care places available and few parents see day care as a viable option.[8] As a consequence, few children have access to group care.

However, parents whose children went to day care frequently discov-ered that their child blossomed, thriving on the experience of collective care: 'He has been going there for two and a half years. He gets bored at home. This year I had kept him out when he went to kindergarten. About three weeks after, he asked to go back to nursery school in the afternoon because there was no one to play with' (046 F 1984).

Once children are five years old, schools provide free organized care, although kindergarten children only go for three hours a day, and grade school children attend from 9:00 a.m. to 12:00 p.m. and from 1:30 p.m. to 3:30 p.m., Monday to Friday, September to June. Schools are closed on holidays and professional development days. These hours are a major concern for employed parents, but they can be a problem for mothers at home full-time as well: 'I dread the summer when the kids are at home all the time, and they eat all the time, and they are bored, and I'm at my wits end in no time' (069 F 1984).

Schools in the Hamilton-Wentworth region were uneven in their pro-vision of junior kindergarten (for four-year-olds). One mother was hop-ing to enrol her daughter, but was embroiled in a fight to get the school board to provide enough spaces: 'There are forty-six kids at one place in

Grimsby, ready for junior kindergarten, and they just didn't plan right. So we are fighting desperately with the board to try and get it into this year' (042 F 1984).

Some school boards recognized that organized child care was needed before and after school, at lunch time, and on weekdays when schools are closed. Most Hamilton schools, however, were organized on the assumption that someone, typically the mother, was available to take young children to and from school, to care for kindergarten children the rest of the day, to mind the children over lunch time, prepare and feed them lunch, and to be available to care for them once school has ended at 3:30, or when it is closed for holidays or for teachers' meetings. Few paid jobs have hours that accommodate such demands.

The pressure on individual parents increased as the government cut funding for such programs in the mid-1990s. As employment became more precarious, asking employers for more flexible hours became riskier. Many women took part-time employment so that they could be available for child care; others made a variety of arrangements with neighbours, other parents, or sitters.

Child Care as Socially Essential Labour

Debates about child-raising address a number of issues: What family forms are best? Who is responsible for what aspects of child care? What arrangements provide the best care? What are the relationships among care, socialization, and education? Yet because child-rearing is typically seen as a private choice, a crucial issue is often obscured: the fact that child care (like the rest of domestic labour) is not recognized as a labour that contributes to productivity or to national economic well-being. It is not included in calculations of the gross national product (Waring 1988), although since signing the 1985 U.N. *Forward-Looking Strategies* and the 1995 U.N. *Platform for Action,* the Canadian government has agreed to measure and value domestic labour and has developed tentative efforts at equating parental child care with its market equivalents (Chandler 1994; Status of Women 1997). In 1996, for the first time, the census included a question on unpaid housework, child care, and care for seniors, but policies recognizing the social value of this labour have not been developed (Luxton and Vosko 1998).

The consequences of the social refusal to recognize child care as an essential social labour and not the private hobby of individual parents (and particularly mothers) are profound. They trap women either in economic dependency on a wage-earner husband or state welfare or in difficult working conditions juggling paid employment and domestic labour. As Sharpe has argued: 'Each working mother is individually responsible for the arrangements by which she combines her job with her family commitments. The almost total absence of state daycare provision for both the under-fives and the over-fives makes a mockery of the concept of equal opportunities for women. In consequence, women work in jobs and for hours that they would never consider if they did not have children to care for' (1984: 132–3). Furthermore, as long as care by anyone other than immediate family members is seen only as substitute or alternative, as clearly second best, then the possibilities of developing genuine communities are eroded: 'While care outside the home is always assumed to be second best to that within it, and while we try to reproduce the conditions of mothering in the family rather than extending relationships of love, trust and stability into other caring environments with other children and adults, we are denying potentially enriching experiences to all those concerned' (Sharpe 1984: 134).

When babysitters, child care workers, and teachers – who spend hours each day in intimate contact with a child – can be described as 'strangers,' how easy is it for parents to find out about alternatives? How can anyone accept that child care collectives might offer good care or that collective living arrangements might be as good as, or preferable to, nuclear families, or that communities might share responsibilities for children? This is an illustration of how the discourse of natural and inevitable parenting works to contain both the imagination and political possibilities.

Simultaneously, privatized parenting imposes on individual parents (and their children) workloads and emotional strains that are difficult, sometimes impossible to manage. Thus, working-class parents absorb many of the costs – the money, time, and energy – of reproducing the next generation of workers for capital. One man recognized the ways in which government policies in Canada force these costs onto individuals and, in so doing, reproduce class inequalities:

[In other countries such as Holland] they give you incentives, and they help you. Better to help you a lot more if you stay in school than, you know ... the tuition fees are a lot lower, whereas here they're rising like crazy. You know, this is how it's structured in Canada now. All the poor people who can't afford to go to school are going to remain poor and they're going to all remain in the bottom scale; and all the people that are rich and can afford to put the kids through school, all those kids are gonna become rich. So that's where you're gonna have the rich looking down on the poor. (011 M 1994)

As well, the privatized organization of child-rearing produces children who, as adults, tend to assume that only immediate family can provide the caring, economic cooperation, and commitment so necessary for human life, thus perpetuating emotional predispositions to nuclear families.[9]

Finally, the tension between the private and social aspects of parenting stimulates so many contradictions that few parents know how to reconcile their personal desires, aspirations, and practices with their children's needs and demands – and with the social forces shaping their lives. As one mother insisted: 'There's nothing natural about it at all' (069 F 1984). But until its fully social character is publicly acknowledged, and child-rearing is reorganized to take account of it as a socially essential labour, individual parents and their children will find themselves caught in the contradictions of parenting. Despite the political emphasis on privatization and cuts to social programs, one steelworker in 1994 held on to a vision of a future in which child care, and especially higher education, would be seen as a collective responsibility: 'That's where I hope Canada will change, where they'll invest in children. Like we have to do it, it's all privately done now but I'm hoping that, down the road, Canada will choose to invest in its own people, and to invest in the children to get an education' (011 M 1994).

Successful Child-Rearing

Parents typically assess their child-rearing by measuring their child against their interpretation of current standards on a range of things such as correct or appropriate behaviour for that age and sex, popularity, academic success, social status, and later, economic achievement or class attainment: 'She's [youngest daughter] doing pretty good in school right now, and the other two are straight A students. We've done something right!' (021 F 1994).

Just as ideas about appropriate family forms are contested, so are prevailing age and sex standards and notions about what kind of future adults parents should be aspiring to generate. A steelworker mother of two was puzzled: 'I want the best future possible for my kids so I push them. "Get good grades! Learn music, French!" But maybe what they really need to learn is how to organize the workplace, how to be union militants. French won't help them get jobs in steel. I don't know if I'm doing good by them' (221 F 1984). By 1996 the children were in their late twenties. She reiterated her confusion: 'So [one] is a musician. He loves it, but it's no living, and [the other] works for minimum wage at [a fast-food restaurant]. Could I have done something different? If I'd made them do better in school would they have middle-class professions? Did I fail my kids if they have to work at shit jobs all their lives?' (221 F 1996).

This mother indicated her own personal confusion about class-appropriate child-rearing and suggested that there was no widespread social consensus available for her to draw on.[10] At various times, and in different places, dominant discourses are clear about the qualities parents are expected to produce in their children. From the 1860s to the 1940s in Quebec, for example, francophone women were urged to exact 'the revenge of the cradle' by raising French-speaking, Catholic Québécois(es) nationalists (Maroney 1992). In post-war Britain, working-class and middle-class parents were cajoled to raise democratic citizens who would eliminate class hierarchies and provide capable workers for a meritocracy (Walkerdine and Lucey 1989).

In the late twentieth century, in Canada, there was no straightforward agreement about appropriate methods or ends of child-raising for working-class parents. Instead, there is a vague notion that parents should produce a well-adjusted member of society, but just what that entails remains unclear.

On a day-to-day basis, as parents look after their children, they are simultaneously living their daily lives, raising the next generation, and reproducing the social relations of advanced capitalism. They are also, of course, reproducing the species. But only certain aspects of that process are socially recognized. New parents almost inevitably announce the birth of their child by identifying its sex – 'a baby girl' – and they often recognize and reinforce kin ties – 'a new sibling for ...' or 'proud grandparents ...' They are unlikely to proclaim 'a new Canadian citizen,' even less 'a future Stelco worker,' a 'white, working-class baby,' or 'a continuation of the species.' They will acknowledge the importance of children and how they 'drop everything else for them.' They may talk about how important it is to teach children to believe in their parents' religion, but they are unlikely to conceive of their activities as reproducing compulsory heterosexuality (Rich 1980) or personalities most suited to carrying out alienated labour (Seccombe 1986).

Sex/gender differences are aspects of child development that are clearly recognized. Most of these parents had strong ideas that sex differences are significant and warrant gendered child-rearing practices: 'Of course, I came from a family of three girls. [My husband's family] had four boys and two girls, so I think that my upbringing would have been stricter than his was' (105 F 1984).

While feminist challenges to sex-role stereotyping have reduced some of the previously sharp distinctions, all the adults interviewed for this study grew up in sex/gender–differentiated ways. A woman described her high school experience in the early 1970s: 'I can remember when you started high school you had a test to see what subjects you should be enrolling in, what things you excelled in. And I can remember everyone being so devastated when my report came back that I should be in a mechanical field. Well, hey, you're in Grade 9, you're a girl. You have to take typing and bookkeeping. I hated typing. But then in about Grade 10, that's when you were able to wear blue jeans to school, and things started to change for women. I took carpentry, drafting, auto mechanics, electricity' (208 F 1984).

Most parents still differentiated between girls and boys. A few planned pregnancies, hoping to have a child of the desired sex.[11] For example, the mother of a three-year-old daughter wanted a son: 'I wanted a boy and we tried for two years and nothing happened. I will keep trying until she is five' (181 F 1984).

Other aspects of child-rearing are less clearly recognized. One of the features of liberal-democratic, capitalist societies is that the systemic inequalities such as sex/gender, sexual orientation, racialization/ethnicity/nationality, and class, which are in fact essential features of such societies, are masked by the concepts of choice, merit, and equal opportunity. For parents trying to raise children, the social denial of structural inequalities can be confusing. Because these people were almost all white, and unlikely to advocate explicit racial segregation or discrimination, few of them considered race an issue in their child-rearing practices, unlike those groups subject to racist discrimination. Those from Southern and Eastern Europe had often run up against ethnic and linguistic stereotyping, but most of their children as a second generation going to Canadian schools were spared the worst of it. However, unless parents made explicitly anti-racist efforts, their child-rearing practices were likely to reproduce existing racisms in their children.

As heterosexuals, these people did not experience homophobia directed against themselves. Many of them, in fact, perpetuated heterosexism when they took for granted that their children would be hetero-sexual, get married, and have children. Informed by the political struggles of gays and lesbians, by the mid-1990s, a few recognized the possibility that their children might prefer same-sex partners. One man talked about how important it is to avoid homophobic behaviour in front of children: '[My son] could grow up to be gay! Like who can say ... I see some friends of mine and with their kids around talking about that kind of stuff [homophobic talk]. I'm looking at the kids thinking, "Well, what happens if this poor little guy grows up to be gay?" He's going to think his father's going to hate him. And it could happen. It could. Everyone out there, in Toronto, and San Francisco, everyone has got parents somewhere' (002 M 1994).

Notions of class are rarely explicit, except in the vaguest sense of rais-ing children who hold 'appropriate' expectations or fearing a child has 'gone bad.' A few parents recognized that growing up as 'working mid-dle class' had consequences for their children, but held on to the hope that they would get education and jobs that would propel them into higher professional positions in the middle class.

For most of these working-class parents, one clear criterion for suc-cess was that their child at least complete high school without 'getting into trouble': 'Fortunately, I've had no problems around the kids at school. They both seem to enjoy it. They go. They never talk about quit-ting school or anything like that' (029 M 1984).

Then, depending somewhat on sex, age, and personal preferences, the young adult should prove to be a reliable and steady worker. She or he should have a personal life that does not seriously violate social con-ventions, and should accept the basic structures and premises of capital-ist society and liberal-democratic politics[12]: 'I don't care what they become. I don't want them to end up in jail, okay, but if they want to do something, then that is fine. If they want to be a doctor, let them be a doctor. If they want to be a fireman, let them be a fireman ... I just hope that they – that, number one, they can get a job, and number two, that they don't work like some people and give up a job every time they don't like it' (105 F 1984).

Many parents had aspirations that their children should do as well or better than they themselves had, and they hoped they could influence their children's futures: 'I think parents are capable of moulding their children's futures, more than they think ... We try to show the kids, the first thing you have to do is get good report cards. We've got them both in there in the process of becoming lifeguards. So that they can work in the pool and not flipping hamburgers. There is no reason why, because we're middle-class working people, that those two kids can't come out and be upper class if they want to be. They might choose to be on welfare, I hope not. It's not going to be through any promotion of ours, though' (089 F 1994).

At the same time they believed that adult children should make their own decisions about what they do with their lives. A man talked about his hopes for his young adult children:

> My kids, I don't know what they expect. I was hoping they would do better than I would, get better jobs, and not have to work shift work. But the boy is kind of leaning that way. It looks like he's gonna try and get into Stelco or Dofasco. The only thing is, he's got a better education than I have. He's finished his high school, and I want him to go further, but that's entirely up to him. And if that's what he thinks he wants to do, is work for Stelco, there's nothing I can do there either. You just have to let him go. The daughter, well, she might get somewhere. She has the ambition. She wants to. Whether it'll pan out that way, or not, I don't know.' (029 M 1984)

Most people held a strongly cherished belief in 'choice' – the faith that in Canadian society, people have 'choices' and 'can be and do anything they want, if they try hard enough.' As this father said, 'That's entirely up to him.' At the same time, most people also realized that there are constraints and limits beyond the control of most individuals – luck, opportunity, God's will, or systematic discrimination can prevent individual achievement no matter how strong the will and ambition. 'Whether it'll pan out that way, or not,' the father cannot predict.

Another father of grown children was firm in his realization that social constraints block individual aspiration. Despite his own activism in his union, he felt that the economic recession had undercut the possibilities for individual and collective action. He said he did not think his children were happy and that they would like something better, adding: 'They don't seem to be doing a helluva lot to change where they are. But then there's not much you can do nowadays, to change things' (176 M 1984).

Even those parents who had hoped to change things for themselves acknowledged that it might be harder for their children because of 'the ways things had gone.' Another father had a clear sense of the external constraints imposed on children by the class location of their parents, but no faith in the possibilities for change:

I am definitely part of a class system. Anyone who feels this is an equal opportunity country is very sadly mistaken. I believe anyone who thinks that a son of a doctor has the same things that he can look forward to as my son is a fool. If you're a steelworker, unless your son is brilliant, or your daughter, and gets a scholarship on merit, she's going to the university you can afford to send her to. She's going to meet the people she can afford to meet. He's going to meet the people he can afford to meet. Yes, rank has privilege, there's no doubt about it ... If my children want more than I have, they have a very limited means of getting it. (075 M 1984)

By the mid-1990s this sense of a limited future was even stronger for many parents: 'I think what we're going to have is a situation where your kids and my kids are not going to have one full-time job. They might have three or four part-time jobs. Not necessarily all related to one another, because of benefits and whatever else. You get two visions of your kids, one vision is that they stand there and say, "I would like to thank the Nobel Peace Prize for selecting me for my award," and the other vision is, your kids shouting out, "Do you want fries with your hamburger?"' (047 M 1994).

This growing insecurity generates greater confusion and anxiety for parents, as they struggle to figure out the best ways of raising their children in an uncertain present for an unknowable future. In a context where parents know vaguely what they hope for their children but have no firm model to follow to assure their children's future, they do what they can.

Generational Reproduction and the Transition to Adulthood[13]

Working-class parents, in general, find it difficult to prepare their children for adulthood because the parents' ability to orchestrate the transition from dependent childhood to independent adulthood is largely out of their control. Unlike farm or business owners, who can incorporate their children into family enterprises, wage labourers cannot guarantee a job for their children. In marked contrast to propertied families, where inheritance plays a strong role – as family businesses and substantial holdings are passed from generation to generation – in working-class families inheritable wealth does not amount to much (Barrett and McIntosh 1982). Because of the small amounts involved, and the fact that these domestic savings are not bound up with children's future livelihoods, the anticipation of possible inheritance is unlikely to be a determining factor for parent–child relations.

Because the wage form is fully individuated (as a payment to a person who is entitled to spend it as he or she see fit), young people are free to leave home as soon as they have secured sources of income. They can live with whomever they wish, even marry a partner of their own choosing. When employment is hard to come by, children may remain dependent on their parents, for much longer than any of them want. Attaining independent adult status depends on the child's ability to secure a steady income, an eventuality that most parents cannot orchestrate. Working-class young people have to seek jobs on their own initiative, hoping to be hired on their merits. As future workers, children's prospective jobs, and their ability to support themselves, are tied to the economic fluctuations of the capitalist labour market.

In the late nineteenth century, when there were relatively high birth rates and lots of jobs, employers recruited young children to work in industry and voraciously consumed their labour power before they had matured.[14] In the late twentieth century, economic restructuring engendered the opposite problem, delaying and blocking young people's entry into employment, even as birth rates dipped well below replacement levels. Many of the same companies that reduced employment opportunities for young people in Canada did so by relying on child labour in other, Third World, countries.[15]

The obstacles placed before young people in making the transition to adulthood are different for boys and girls, although less starkly differentiated than they were in the past. In the male income earner / dependent housewife family economy of the early twentieth century, marriage reinforced men's connection with the labour force, while interrupting women's attachment to it or severing it altogether. Most young single women took short-term jobs and remitted their pay almost entirely to their parents. They were not typically oriented to long-term employment prospects because they expected to marry, ideally a man who would not only make a decent wage, but bring it home reliably and share it with them and the children. Soon after marrying, most young women would quit paid work to become full-time homemakers. The poorer a young woman was the more likely she would work for pay, at least sporadically after marriage. By the 1950s the single income earner / homemaker family form had become a widespread norm.

Young men in working-class families typically had a variety of ways to find employment. Some moved from job to job, avoiding long intervals of joblessness while picking up new skills on each job that compensated for their lack of post-secondary education or specialized training. Many youth from the Maritimes and Ontario, for example, headed west in response to employment opportunities in the oilfields or on construction sites in Alberta. Another career strategy was to stay in school, try to identify a durable niche in the labour market, obtain formal training and credentials in a specialized vocation, and seek entry into a skilled trade or profession. Others moved into the same plants as their fathers. One of the attractions of industrial jobs for working-class men was that employers were often willing to hire the children of steady workers. Thirty-five per cent of those interviewed had applied to Stelco because they had family or friends at the plant.[16]

From the 1940s to 1970s thousands of young men entered Hilton Works in their teens, fresh out of high school; for many it was their first full-time job. Describing his father's experience, and his own, a steelworker pointed out the consequences of these changes: 'He left half-way through Grade 11 and got a job and thank the good Lord, twenty-three years later he's still there. You couldn't even get that kind of job down there now with Grade 11, and actually he doesn't. He's got only Grade Ten education' (069 M 1994).

Throughout this period, the labour force was expanding; hiring was more or less continuous in the plant's 'dirty work' departments, the coke ovens and the blast furnaces, because of high quit rates. But a significant minority of young workers ended up staying. They hung on and became long-time steelworkers. Young men who held down a steady job demonstrated that they had the capacity to become a reliable income earner. Men with secure employment could marry young[17]: 'And I was sixteen when we got married, so, I mean, we saved and bought our first home before I was two weeks shy of my eighteenth birthday' (069 M 1994).

In the four years from 1989 to 1993 the labour force participation of young people in Canada (aged fifteen to twenty-four) fell from 63 per cent to 52 per cent. This drop offers clear evidence that instead of conducting a futile search for paid work (and joining the ranks of the officially unemployed), vast numbers have stayed in school, or dropped out to live on family support or on the streets as part of the underground economy. Youth unemployment remained very high, almost twice the national average. An older steelworker compared his entry into the labour force in the 1970s with the job market facing young people in the 1990s: 'When I started at Stelco in '77, I had worked at [three other companies]. I had worked at all these jobs, and it was not a problem. Apply for a job and you were hired. Kids can't do that now – not even coming out of university. Where are they getting their summer jobs? It's pumping gas some place, or working at [a fast food] place, you know?' (078 M 1994).

What is clear is that young working-class men in Hamilton in the 1990s had a far more difficult time finding good jobs than their elders did; very few could expect to succeed by following their fathers' employment strategies:

> For the younger people just starting off, I think it's going to be really difficult. You pick a trade or something you want to get into and then, by the time you get there, it's too many people or there's not enough jobs. When I grew up, there was always the Stelcos and the Dofascos and the Harvesters, and there were always jobs there. If you didn't like this job, you could go to another job. I think right until 1980, things were all right. But after that, things are just changing. Seems like every time you get the paper, somebody's closing down and technology has taken a huge bite out of it, no doubt about it. But, I don't know. It's going be hard for the kids. You keep telling them to get an education but the jobs aren't there. It's not going to help. (140 M 1994)

Young working-class women continued to have difficulty finding good jobs and were unlikely to find male partners able to support them. By the 1990s young women were staying in school much longer, and yet when they entered the labour force they were likely to get stuck in poorly paid jobs with few avenues of promotion. The difference was that the dearth of career employment opportunities was a concern for them in a way that it had not been thirty years previously, when the expectation of lifetime financial support by a future husband was much more plausible. A mother of three children, herself no longer able to stay at home with the younger children, predicted: 'They probably won't have the chance to stay home with their families that I did. Because I see things are just going to be too expensive. They can't afford a one-income family' (166 F 1994).

In the recent past most young people left home to set up their own households in their early twenties. By the 1990s they were likely to continue living with their parents longer, often because they were unable to find steady work: 'I know a lot of people that I worked with are students. I was married at twenty-one; these people are twenty-three and twenty-four, and they don't own a home. They're still living with their mom and dad, whereas I wasn't. I was working from the time I was sixteen on' (078

F 1994). And when young people did get employment, it was often harder than it used to be to support a family: 'There's jobs out there, but are they going to be able to provide for their families? It used to be one person could provide for their family, now it's two and sometimes two can't even do it' (152 M 1994).

One woman worried about her twenty-four-year-old son's ability to establish an independent household and have a family: 'Whether it's from the economy or whatever, I don't know, but you take kids like [her son aged twenty-four], they are not interested in going into a relationship and having kids, not interested at all. And there are a lot of them like that. And that's sad. That's sad. Yeah, I need grandchildren, you know. But it's too easy now not to have that' (075 F 1994).

A report by the Social Planning Council of Hamilton-Wentworth confirms her fears: 'The combination of declining incomes and high unemployment for our youngest workers is a disturbing trend. At a time when the newest participants in the workforce may be paying down large student loans, paying rent and possibly a mortgage that is at its highest amount, having and caring for young children, and purchasing a car to get to work, they are now making 11 per cent less than their counterparts did ten years ago' (1999: 34). Workers who are unable to reproduce themselves from day to day may cease to reproduce themselves generationally.[18] The economic crisis generated by restructuring may prefigure a crisis in the reproduction of families. It certainly made the transition to adulthood more difficult.

Adult Caregiving

Caregiving between adults expresses their relationship. It can affirm love, sexuality, and interdependency. It may be an area where power struggles get acted out, leaving people feeling hurt and unloved (Stacey 1990; Hochschild 1989). The responsibilities and obligations that develop as part of any intimate relationship also entail work: 'Well it's also about, you know, like, I guess, about taking care of people. If you are making a home and a family life, well, part of that is taking care of everybody. And of course that's not work, except that sometimes when I feel I have to do it, then it feels a lot like work' (010 M 1984).

People who live together provide ongoing services and assistance, from providing company to comforting in a crisis. A divorced man described adult caregiving: 'I left my marriage. But then I realized what you lose when you stop living together, even when the marriage is no good. Having someone to talk to, having someone bring you coffee, the sex, of course, just a sense that someone would look out for you' (310 M 1996).

Because the social relations between parents and children are life-long, parental caring, responsibilities, and obligations continue after children become adults. Sometimes parents offer adult children help in setting up their own households. One woman explained that she and her husband had bought the house next door to theirs, which they rented to their daughter and her partner: 'With her husband, there was no way they could buy a home, and apartment rents keep going up and up, so they might as well pay us the rent as somebody else. They don't pay all the rent. We still have to put something in it. We'll never get any-thing out of it because how can you kick them out?' (097 F 1984).

Grandparents provided child care for their grandchildren: 'I have my grandkids over as often as possible. I love having them, and I know it's a break for their parents' (221 F 1996).

Parental responsibilities for their adult children increased during the 1990s, as young adults had more and more trouble finding secure employment. In Canada the percentage of twenty-five to thirty-four-year-olds living with their parents increased; 33 per cent of women and 40 per cent of men in 1996, up from 23 per cent and 28 per cent in 1984 (Statistics Canada 2000: 8). Their precarious employment situation cre-ated deep anxieties for their parents. One steelworker lamented that his son's friend, trained as an accountant, 'is working ... shipping pizza, and that breaks your heart' (075 M 1994). He appreciated how lucky both his children were to have jobs. But he knew that neither hard work nor formal qualifications were a guarantee. He also recognized that his chil-dren's success at finding work affected the whole family: 'We've been extremely lucky in our family' (075 M 1994). Yet it was striking that despite the fact that both had jobs, neither was living independently: 'My son is living at home, yes. He left for a while but the money he was making he couldn't make a go of it, so he came back. He's been back probably a year now, and my daughter has, well, she's living with her parents-in-law' (075 M 1994).

As children remained economically dependent for longer periods, parents found themselves providing all kinds of unanticipated adult car-egiving. The imposed prolongation of children's transition to adult-hood generated tensions and conflicts. Parents felt obligated to provide support, but then assumed it entitled them to participate in the chil-dren's decision-making. A man described his frustration with his son and wondered when he could legitimately tell his son to leave home: 'He's been back and forth a few times when he was younger, and he was back actually a year this time ... so that kind of did it when he said he's quit. I said, "Well we can't help you anymore." I mean, he was making good money, and he was hardly paying anything to the house ... "so go out on your own. Give me peace. Come and visit me on Sundays ..." Oh, gee! They drive you crazy!' (069 M 1994).

Similar ties of responsibility and obligation link adult children to their parents.[19] Quite a few people cared for widowed, elderly, or sick parents who lived elsewhere: 'My mother is widowed. My mother comes here almost every day' (186 M 1984). It can also involve younger siblings in the process of leaving their parental home: 'Four out of seven nights my younger brother is here' (078 M 1984).

While immediate family and kin typically have priority in terms of reciprocal obligations and caregiving, many people are also tied into very important relationships with other housemates, neighbours, or friends. Two women had lived in communes for a number of years. One described the resulting ties: 'Our commune broke up years ago, and we've all moved to different places. But the ties are still there. When I got laid off, three of my former housemates sent a big cheque, like I mean a really big cheque, to tide me over' (221 F 1996). More typically, people talked about neighbours and friends who over the years developed ties that were available for caregiving: 'I have lived in this community for a long time, and I have lots of friends. I know I could call on them if I needed to' (069 F 1984).

While most people were reluctant to make too many demands on such relationships, their existence was valued: 'The last ten, fifteen years, I've come to see how important my friends and neighbours are. I don't think I would have survived the lay-offs if I hadn't known I had real friends I could call on if I had to. I didn't, but knowing they were there kept me going' (089 M 1994).

Conclusion

The caregiving work people do is central to the relationships they forge out of their day-to-day interactions. For most people, the importance of those relationships makes the work worthwhile and provides the impetus to keep on doing it. A woman described her take on this dynamic: 'There are days when I don't know why I keep at it. I get frustrated and pissed off. I imagine just walking out the door and going to live somewhere else with no one to look after but me. But then I have to laugh, because I would miss them so much. I love them, and that makes it all okay, doesn't it?' (208 F 1996).

But while most people focus on their immediate relationships – making a marriage work, raising their kids, looking after an ailing friend – their activities are simultaneously sustaining and reproducing the complex social relations of their communities and their society. The focus on interpersonal relationships often obscures the underlying social structure that shapes those relationships. As a result, people usually look at their relationships in terms of personal attributes, rather than in terms of the ways in which those relationships are socially constructed. A woman may evaluate her husband's contribution to child care as evidence that he is a good man and a loving father, without questioning the underlying sex/gender divisions of labour that give him the ability to choose how involved he would be with his children's care. In a similar way, parents may hope that the labour market will produce jobs for their children, but they are unlikely to assert that, as parents, they have contributed to the production of a necessary labour force.

Just as a focus on family relationships can mask the way labour power is treated as a commodity, apparent cross-class similarities in family forms and the organization of domestic labour obscure the important differences inherent in producing and sustaining people of different classes. The caregiving done by working-class people, especially women, simultaneously sustains their daily lives, ensures generational continuity, and reproduces the labour power necessary for capitalist economies.

8

Making a Life: Leisure and
Social Activities

A former steelworker and single mother described one of the greatest pleasures of her day: 'When I've got home from work, the kids are safely off, either at school or in bed, I've cleaned up and suddenly, there it is, a couple of hours that are all mine, to do whatever I want. Often I just sit down, heave a great sigh and enjoy the feeling of not having anything to do' (223 F 1996).

Free time or leisure, when the demands of employment, domestic labour, and other obligations are not pressing, is time when people have the greatest discretion about what they do and how involved they are with other people.[1] As one man said, 'When I come home from work, that's when the fun starts' (029 M 1994). He went on to describe what leisure meant for him: 'I'm into everything. I'm heavily involved with several community organizations, hours every day. Once I got involved in what I could do about the community and I started working with other people on it, it just evolved, and now it's a full-blown program for me. I have a lot of fun, I meet a lot of people. I deal with a lot of kids and stuff like that. It's very interesting' (029 M 1994). In contrast, one woman said that she and her husband preferred to spend their free time together at home: 'We set up a gym in the basement. One uses the machine and the step-up, and the other uses the treadmill and then we just switch ... about four nights a week' (075 F 1984).

Despite such variations in how individuals used their free time, certain patterns influenced what they did and which people they did things with.[2] Typically people used their free time to engage in a variety of activities: to rest up and recuperate from work, forge family relationships, build friendship, community, or other social and political ties, to do whatever interested them – and to have fun. As they made decisions about what to do in the free time available to them, they had to take into account the constraints of their own and their partners' work, their family responsibilities, and their commitments to their friends and communities. They had to determine their own preferences, while trying to accommodate the often competing demands of partners, children, and friends, as well as other obligations. Through these personal interactions and activities people negotiated their identities, developed group or collective identities, and engaged with the discourses that informed their understanding of life.

The Social Construction of Ties and Activities

Work and family life provided access to particular social networks, activities, and resources that tended to dominate the choices people had available to them. Because social ties are intensified and, to a certain extent, are easier to maintain if people meet each other regularly in their daily activities, most of the people we interviewed identified families, neighbours, and co-workers among their most important social ties. Given the prevailing relative ethnic and racial homogeneity of marriage patterns, Stelco's labour force and most Hamilton neighbourhoods, these social networks tended to be predominantly white, Anglo-Celtic, and English-speaking.[3]

Workplaces and neighbourhoods also tended to reinforce class similarities. As a consequence, most people's ties were with people who shared important social and cultural similarities, something that was often only noticeable when it was disrupted: 'When I got involved in the union, I got to be friends with other activists. Now I have friends who are lesbian, a black guy, someone who's Polish, all sorts. I never knew my friends from before were so much the same as me' (213 F 1996).

Gendered divisions of labour meant that women and men had different access to free time and different appreciations of what free time meant. While many men celebrated the end of a shift, anticipating free time until the start of the next, lots of women said they had no free time. A woman with young children exclaimed: 'Free time, what's that?' (176 F 1984). Her point that domestic labour is unending was reinforced by a man who enjoyed spending time with his wife, but failed to recognize that his leisure rested in part on her work. He claimed: 'Once I leave the work area, there are no real commitments on my time. We do whatever we just choose. The rest of the day is ours to use as we see fit' (149 M

1984). He then went on to say, apparently unaware of the contradiction, that he wanted his dinner ready for him as soon as he got home.

The demands of employment and the private, individualized organization of domestic labour combined to limit the kinds of social and political activities as well as the range of social ties people were involved in, setting in motion dynamics that strengthened their orientation to their families: 'I work with a close friend. But I very seldom see any other people [from work]. I talk, on an irregular basis, to maybe half a dozen friends that I grew up with. I see them semi-regularly. I run into them or something ... there is one other guy, we have been to parties at his place. But mostly it is just our family. We don't socialize a lot' (078 M 1984).

As the increasing demands of making a living cut into free time for many, leisure became even more elusive. Larger friendship circles and communities became more difficult to sustain: 'I used to have way more time for my friends. We all seem so busy now, we hardly see each other. I miss it, the good times we had together' (301 F 1996).

The Impact of Work on Social Ties and Activities

Most workplaces bring people together and offer at least some relatively discretionary time when they are able to combine work with enjoyable activities and socializing. Women at home talked about doing the laundry in the evening, freeing the afternoon for a visit with a friend. They listened to the radio or watched television while doing the housework and chatted with their neighbours while pushing their children on the park swings.

Steelworkers described ongoing chess and card games both in the lunchrooms and on the job when work was slow. Most workers described the socializing with co-workers as one of the attractions of paid jobs. Even when work demands prevailed, workers confided in each other, comparing notes about the workplace, their families, or life in general and, in the process, often developed strong long-term ties. A retired machine operator described the importance of Stelco co-workers in his life: 'When I was part of that 14,000 workforce, I was part of a very large family. There were always a lot of things going on. Being on my own now, you don't get the big family feeling that you had when you were part of the steel company' (075 M 1994).

Paid employment and domestic labour impose fairly strict demands on time and energy, significantly determining not only what free time people have, but the energy, resources, and inclinations they have available for it. Because paid work consumes people's labour power, employees have to use some of their time off to rest and recuperate, needs determined by the way they feel at the end of a shift. Some left work keen to take up their favourite sport or to 'party': 'I'm always happy when I get off work. There's always something happening, a party, my baseball league' (202 F 1984). Others needed that time to recuperate: 'I am getting older. I find more and more that I am napping for an hour or two. Generally from about 5 p.m. to 7 p.m. I am just physically not capable of going out unless I make a concerted effort. I watch television in the evenings' (149 M 1984).

The pleasures some of them derived from their work energized them: 'Days when I don't work, it's much harder to do stuff. I have to drag myself out of the house. But on the days I work, I have such a good time at work that I'm just full of beans when I come home. Then you can't hold me back because I'm just raring to go' (069 F 1984). But any stress they brought home with them affected the ways they unwound: 'I enjoy myself [at home listening to music] because I forget. I know the problems are still there, but give yourself a couple of hours to forget' (126 M 1984).

Domestic labour is more flexible, permitting greater discretion in the allocation of work and free time, but caregiving may impose continuous obligations, seriously challenging free time. Parents caring for young children are subject to frequent and unpredictable interruptions. For those doing infant or elder care, free time may come at nap time, which is usually irregular and of unpredictable duration. And caregivers remain responsible and on call: 'On [his] afternoon shift, that was my free time. The kids would go to bed and he wasn't home. I could do what I wanted' (075 F 1994).

Stelco Makes (and Breaks) Families and Friends

Although Stelco as an employer was indifferent to the personal lives of its employees away from work, most Stelco workers and their partners insisted that its organization deeply affected their personal lives. The shift schedule was a dominant organizing principle that established and disrupted the routine of their daily lives. Stelco's shifts encouraged a family orientation on the part of its employees, while simultaneously undermining family relationships. To a lesser extent, Stelco shifts also fostered social ties among Stelco workers, while reducing their ability to sustain other community networks.

Shift work meant that steelworkers could not regularly attend social and community activities, nor could they count on participating in activities planned for weekends: 'I play baseball. I miss afternoon shift games. I am left out of things with friends. Like even parties, maybe she can go, family birthday parties and stuff, she can go and I can't. I have to go to work' (109 M 1984). These recurring disruptions created numerous problems: 'I get three weeks with at least one weekend day off. Then I go half a year without. What happens is that after my third week, some of our friends realize that I have weekends off. The phone starts to ring. I have three weeks of riotous living. I'm out prowling all night long and partying. Then the phone keeps ringing for the next few weeks but I keep telling the people, "No, I'm on nights. It's all over, see you in six months." Then I've got thirteen weeks when I putter around the house' (075 M 1984).

Shift workers explained that even when they were actually free, they often could not enjoy social activities because they had to go to work later: 'If I have got to go to work, my mind is not going to have a good time. It is basically thinking of going to work. If I have to go to work I do not like to go out and socialize or go to a party. I am very conscious of having a drink. I don't like doing it, and I don't do it. Your stomach and that. I don't feel your system was made to keep turning around like that' (151 M 1984). This pattern easily created tensions between partners if one wanted to go to events that were organized for couples: 'If there is a dance going on Saturday night or something like a party, unless I am off, sometimes she has got to drag me to go. I just don't want to go' (151 M 1984).

Some steelworkers ended up socializing more with co-workers because they understood and accommodated the vagaries of shift changes. A few steelworkers, determined to play sports they liked despite shift work, organized sports leagues with other co-workers: 'The guys get together. They have quite a hockey league, a slow pitch league and stuff like that. But it's mostly production people. We have a couple of guys in our department [maintenance] who play hockey. They play because they love it, they don't play to socialize' (108 M 1984).

For women steelworkers, gender politics made even these workplace-centred activities relatively inaccessible. One woman joined the baseball league but was harassed, especially by wives of her male co-workers who resented the men's activities and found her presence a threat: 'The wives hated me. You could just feel them at it. You could just feel the hole in your back. It got to be so petty and bad. I pulled my own weight on that team, but the men were being reprimanded [by their wives] for having me in the circle. First of all I've got to earn your respect, and now I've got to earn your wives' respect' (213 F 1984).

Many steelworkers responded to the constraints on their free time by turning to social activities that could be done anytime, such as playing darts at the local pub or pick-up golf. But even coordinating these pastimes with friends proved difficult: 'I like to play golf. One guy says, "Let's go golfing." "Okay, when?" "Well, let's go next Thursday." "I'm working." "Oh well, what are you doing two weeks Friday?"' (090 M 1984). Because it was hard to sustain social activities with friends and community groups, shift workers tended to spend much of their free time at home: 'So if days off are during the week we usually putter around the house' (029 M 1984).

Despite this orientation to the home, steelworkers complained that their conflicting schedules eroded domestic life. On certain shifts fathers and children rarely saw each other: 'It's anti-social, just no social life. The kids are going to school and you're on afternoons, you don't see them for a week at a time' (108 M 1984). Their wives and partners complained about the impact shift schedules had both on their family life together and on the women's social life. Schedules ruined important festive events and allowed them very little family time: 'Christmas morning you would have to get up at 4 in the morning because Dad had to leave at 6 for day shift. It was totally abnormal' (069 F 1994).

As couples were expected to socialize together, wives and partners of steelworkers were drawn together too: 'Stelco husbands have Stelco wives. The husbands have friends from work and they hang out and party together or whatever, and the wives have to hang together, too. I don't really get along with the wives of his friends, but we get stuck together. If there's a party and he's invited, I don't really want to go. His friends give him a hard time if his wife doesn't go to parties' (181 F 1984). When the men were not available, their partners learned either to forfeit a social life or go ahead alone: 'Life with him has never been routine. I learned a long time ago that if I wanted to do things, I had to do them. I can't wait around for him to have free time' (105 F 1994).

The more irregular shift schedules and job demands were, the more home and community relations were affected – with household routines upset, family outings and friendship gatherings disrupted, relaxation and sleeping patterns unsettled. These practices increased as management cut the labour force, undermining previous seniority arrangements: 'You might plan something for his first Saturday–Sunday off, and he'll get switched, he's back to Wednesday–Thursday. So he doesn't get the weekend which you really were looking forward to. You plan things for those free weekends. When friends are getting married or anything, you look at the old schedule and try to figure out when you'll be free' (176 F 1984). Others complained that the twelve-hour shifts left them so tired they slept for much of their time off.

When lay-offs or unemployment removed the restrictions of the Hilton Works shift schedule, people confronted imposed free time. They suddenly had leisure, but unemployment deprived them of both the money and the state of mind to enjoy themselves.[4] They had time for their favourite activities; they had the time they needed to visit and participate in social events. These options were overshadowed, however, by the grim threat of long-term unemployment: 'It was tough for me to go out with the boys. We didn't have much money. We didn't know how long it would last. My friends didn't have any money' (140 M 1984).

With less money for entertainment, leisure activities tended to become even more home-based than they had been before. But activities such as watching television or gardening were less enjoyable when they became ways of passing time. And imposed time together put stress on most couples: 'During my lay-off we saw a lot of each other, sometimes too much' (140 M 1984).

In search of work, some of the unemployed steelworkers took jobs at Stelco's plant on Lake Erie. In 1994 a steelworker explained that he and his family were forced to move during an economic downturn, to sever ties with their former community, to lose money on the sale of their house, and to give up their 'pretty well-settled' lives: 'It wasn't easy. There's quite a few of us out there came from Hilton Works and we still have big mortgages and it's like starting over again' (140 M 1994).

Some families broke up under the strain of unemployment. A thirty-eight-year-old steelworker, with five years seniority who had been unemployed for twenty-four months explained: 'I felt inadequate, and I felt I couldn't live up to my wife's expectations. I had chronic headaches and gastritis brought on by my stress and depression. My debts increased. After the separation I moved back to my folks and my wife moved in with her sister.'[5]

A former steelworker reflected on Stelco's impact on his social life: 'Stelco loomed large over my whole life. Some of my best friends were guys I met at work, and one woman too. But when I was working, it seemed like I had no time to have a life, to hang out with them, and when I did have time, they didn't. Then when I was laid off, I had all the time in the world, but no life' (303 M 1996).

Women's Work Makes (and Breaks) Families and Friends

Women's work similarly had an impact on the kinds of social activities they engaged in and the types of people they socialized with. Full-time homemakers focused their attention on their immediate families; the more women were involved in the paid labour force, the more likely they were to have a different orientation to social life. Their families were important to them, but they also spent relatively more time with friends.

Whatever leisure time a full-time homemaker had was organized in relation to her husband's and her children's, often conflicting, schedules. A number of women described similar pressures, as they tried to respond to their husbands' desires for company while the demands of child care left them too tired: 'I used to find that it was a long day. He would leave at 2 p.m., I was up until 11 at night and I would be tired. I would be sleeping when he came home, and he would want me to stay up. It wasn't bad when the kids were babies, because then you could sleep in the morning, but once they got older they had to get up for school' (151 F 1984).

Women based at home watched more television than employed women, used the phone as a way to connect with their friends more often, and spent more time visiting with friends at home.[6] Alone with small children for much of the day, and eager for adult company, they typically put pressure on their husbands to spend most of their free time with them. Nights were particularly hard for some women: 'He likes afternoons, but I hate them. I don't like being at home alone at night, especially with the children. I get scared alone at night' (069 F 1984).

Women managing the double day had the least amount of free time. Their work days often left them with little time or energy: 'With her working, when she gets home she's tired and she's quite happy to sit and sew and watch *Star Trek*. Three hours of *Star Trek*' (045 M 1994). At the same time they were more socially active outside the home than full-time housewives. Employed women went out more often (on average two times more each week), and they were involved in a wider range of social activities than full-time housewives. Their employment gave them their own money to spend and located them in work-based social networks, undermining somewhat the anti-social character of family life, and orienting them to activities and relationships independent of their families.[7]

A nurse described her friends at work: 'I am more connected with my friends rather than as couples. It is only the girls. It's not with the husbands. In that respect the hospital life is basically mine' (042 F 1984). She went on to argue that a couple's relationship is strengthened when both people have separate interests and friends: 'It's important for both of us to be out on our own, to have a private life as well. And private interests are important. I feel that's good therapy for yourself. I can be quite happy doing things on my own' (042 F 1984).

Women's work had an impact on the way their partners spent their time. Men living with full-time homemakers could count on their wives to be available whenever they were free. Men whose wives were employed spent more time independently, typically at home alone, sometimes going out on their own or with friends.

The typical homemaker's strategy of making family relationships primary reinforced family ties, but it also intensified pressure on family relationships to satisfy needs for intimacy, support, and socializing. The employed women's practice of having more diverse ties reduced pressure on the one relationship, but also introduced competing demands for time and attention. In both cases, women's work was central to building and maintaining family ties. At the same time, the demands of their work often conflicted with efforts to socialize with their families. It was even harder for them to find time for their friends and communities.

A woman steelworker noted that when her children were young her double day constrained her social life: 'When the kids were small, it was just work, work, work. I'd go to work, come home, do the housework, look after the kids. Any time I had I spent with the kids' (223 F 1984). Once her children were a bit older, her social life expanded. Laid off by Stelco, she had found work in another steel mill, where she worked long hours and was active in her union and in a feminist group that met weekly. She described her leisure time: 'There's never enough time for what I want to do. I just love having time to visit my friends, to play. I have tons of things I want to do, from learning French to volunteering at the Rape Crisis Centre. I get such a good feeling when I get off work and I just think about all the terrific things I can do before I have to go back to work' (223 F 1984).

Years later she complained that the increasing demands of her job imposed too many constraints. She had less free time and it was not as much fun: 'I don't think I've got any free time. I get time off, but lots of it goes in all those little errands and things you just have to do – go to the doctor, pick up a prescription, take my car in to the garage. Then I always have friends I ought to see. They phone up and complain that they haven't seen me in a long time, and, of course, I want to see them but there's never enough time. Sometimes I almost dread my time off because it just feels like more pressure. I just don't have a life any more' (223 F 1996).

Choices and Constraints Shaping Social Ties and Activities

For many, social life is filled with contradictions. A man reflected on some of the contradictions of social life: 'It's strange, eh. You think it's your free time, so you can do what you want, but you can't, not really. Not unless you don't want much! And you don't have anyone who you have to see. I guess it's only "free" time if you are alone' (303 M 1996).

People do have a lot of discretion about what they do in their time off and who they do it with. Some passed their free time in activities requiring few resources, little advanced planning, and minimal social interaction – dozing in front of the television or having a drink on the porch. Others passed their time in extensive socializing, for example, by sharing large meals with extended friendship networks or in active involvement in formal organizations.

But social activities and ties are also shaped by networks of caring and obligation, available resources, and the spatial dimensions of daily life. Memberships in organizations such as unions or churches carry expectations of participation. Many activities require specialized resources, such as an ice rink for hockey teams or curling leagues, and ball players are more likely to join the league if the field is nearby.

People were quick to recognize how financial resources affected what they could do: 'We see the neighbours. It is expensive for the two of us to go out drinking. You can spend a lot of money' (109 F 1984). This point became even more obvious for the men who were laid off during the 1980s: 'Moneywise, we were tight ... like entertainment, that just stopped. There was nothing to do' (089 M 1984).

Many had used their savings up during the strike that preceded the layoffs: 'We didn't have any savings left, just a couple of months ahead in rent. I didn't like staying at home. You couldn't do anything you used to do. The money wasn't there. I babysat, lay around, and got lazy' (109 M 1984).

As employment became more insecure through the 1990s, steelworkers were forced to cut back on leisure-related expenses they had taken for granted earlier: 'My seven-year-old wants to play this year. I said, "Well, okay but we have to see how much money we've got. If I get laid off, I'll have to save my money during the summer so I can buy all your hockey equipment and have money left over if anything comes up." The ten-year-old kind of understands. The seven-year-old occasionally will say, "Why can't I do that?"' (090 M 1994).

People's leisure activities also depended on what was available. Residential neighbourhoods differ in the resources they offer, and the use of parks, rinks, and community centres varies with the ease of access. The older, crowded Hamilton east end offered fewer parks and play spaces than the newer suburbs. As municipal governments cut back on spending through the 1990s, some recreational facilities cut their hours or charged user fees, making them less accessible: 'It's such a shame. My kids used to go to the local pool all the time. But now there's a fee, so they can't go. They really miss it' (303 F 1996).

Seasonal variations significantly affect what activities are possible: 'We'll go snowmobiling in the wintertime if we can. In the summertime we go up north to our cottage, and we spend as much time up there as we can' (029 M 1984).

For women, concerns about safety often curtailed their activities at night and limited the places they could go. One of the women steelworkers talked about how women were not able to socialize after work with their co-workers as easily or unself-consciously as men: 'I always made sure I took my own car, that is, I had my own escape' (221 F 1984).

Shopping malls, especially in the suburbs, with their convenient locations, security guards, the protection from the weather, and their array of services, apparently offer public spaces for people to gather: 'Sometimes I like to just get out for a while. That is why I go to the grocery store. I know I won't spend too much money in the grocery store' (105 F 1984). But as that speaker implies, efforts to make malls attractive places to spend time are prompted by commercial interests aimed at encouraging consumption. Malls are actually private property, and the right to be there is predicated on spending money, as the harassment and banishment of those, such as teenagers deemed to be just hanging around, shows.

Spatial proximity has an impact on the ways people interact, though proximity only offers a possibility and its absence acts as a hurdle. When intimate friends live far from each other, contact may be harder to sustain, but it is not impossible, while frequent contact increases the possibilities for conflict. A man who drives right by his mother's house each day on the way to work is more likely to drop in on her than if she lives an hour out of his way, but if he is estranged from her, he may drive by her house each day and never stop. On the other hand, if he enjoys her company, a visit may be worth a two-hour drive.

Once people have chosen to become involved in certain relationships or activities, other options are precluded. The man who volunteers to coach his son's hockey team is committed to being at the rink at a set time each week. He has the possibility of meeting and befriending other parents or coaches, but he is unable to go to a union social held at the same time, and so he misses an opportunity to strengthen his ties with his union steward.

Throughout their lives, as their circumstances change, people's patterns of activities and socializing also change. At the same time, friendship ties and types of activities that get established by young adults often become habits that continue even when the original reasons for them no longer exist (Guilmette 1992). The duration of social relations has its own dynamic. A forty-one-year-old woman who had lived in Hamilton all her life described her situation: 'All over this city I've got family and friends. It's great. I'm just walking along or in the mall, for sure I'll see someone and it's "Hi! How are you? Let's go for coffee." Me and a bunch of girls were in grade school together and we still hang out. We get together for a beer every month. It's a habit, I guess, but it's fun' (205 F 1984).

The Importance of Families

The strong commitment most of these couples had to companionate marriage meant that most (87 per cent) identified their spouse as their main companion. They assumed that partners should and would socialize together and couples tended to do very similar things[8]: 'He's my best friend. Of course, I want to spend my time with him. It's not as much fun without him' (061 F 1984). A woman affirmed a similar commitment to her lesbian partner: 'We're a couple which means she's the one I want to spend my time with and if I want our relationship to work, I have to make sure to spend lots of time with her' (226 F 1984).

When two people first become a couple they have to renegotiate friendship networks to take their new relationship into account. Typically, marriage disrupted the previous friendship networks of both partners: 'A lot of my friends that I hung around with years ago when I was single, we all got married, and it got to be, well I met this woman and you leave the boys at the bar. Now there's some of them I haven't seen in years' (049 M 1984). New partners and old friends were under pressure to accommodate each other: 'He may like my girlfriend but he doesn't care anything for her husband. Or the same thing with me. I may meet some of his friends from work, and I might like the guy or I might like the girl and not care anything for the guy. Those ones are left by the wayside' (042 F 1984).

Many, especially in households where women were full-time home-makers, took for granted that husbands and wives should socialize together and felt threatened if one partner had a separate social life: 'My husband, he couldn't stand it [when I went out drinking beer once a month with former school friends]. He said I should spend more time with him' (205 F 1984). Some assumed that only single people or those having marital problems would go out independently: 'It is usually the same bunch of guys who will go out once or twice a week, and it is usually after the 3 to 11 shift. If you are single or ... a lot of guys with shaky marriages don't care to go home after work' (089 M 1984).

Others, especially in households where women were employed, took a different position, assuming that separate friends were important sources of support: 'I really enjoy seeing my girlfriends from work. It is a lift. Because everyone has their problems and everyone has their funny experiences to tell you. And you realize that you're not in this thing alone. It's really good to get together with them. As soon as you lose your workplace friends, you have only your husband's friends. And you don't have that other outlet who understand how you think, or you could talk to and laugh' (042 F 1984).

Having children together strengthened the ties between parents and further bolstered a nuclear family orientation. A mother of two, who had left her paid job when she and her partner had children, described how their lower income and new child care responsibilities curtailed their outings and made them more homebound: 'It used to be it didn't matter what we did. We could stay out all night and sleep all day. We could go on the spur of the moment. Now, you've got to say, "Okay, what are we going to do?" We can't go away without the kids. Before we could say, "Okay, let's go to Toronto for the weekend." We just can't do that any more' (078 F 1994).

On average, young women without children went out nine times a month, while men went out eleven times; both participated in a wide range of activities (averaging 3.2 different activities a month). In contrast, women and men with children went out about five times a month, and their activities usually included their children.[9] Parents gave priority to their children's activities and often combined their own apparent leisure time with child care, in part because they really had no other options and in part because they enjoyed being together: 'We spend a lot of time together with the kids. We're a very "family" family, the traditional kind of old-fashioned family, do everything together. My son plays hockey, so we all go to the hockey games. She was into dancing and then we'd all go to the recital' (176 F 1984).

Some activities, especially those only suitable for adults, became more difficult for parents. They had less time and paying babysitters added to the costs: 'We haven't gone out together for a long time. We used to. But with the kids ...' (109 M 1984).

Some parents adapted their activities so they could include their children in everything: 'We usually take our son [twenty months] everywhere we go' (015 M 1984). Over the years these parents continued this practice, even after the birth of a second child. Ten years later they had well-established family-based leisure activities: 'It's really just the four of us ... we always do it [leisure], the four of us' (089 F 1994). He elaborated: 'We try to play together. The kids raced go-carts one summer. We try to do things where everybody's involved' (089 M 1994).

A number of people noted that when they had children, former friends withdrew, leaving the new parents more socially isolated: 'After work two or three friends would come up to the house. Since we had our son [aged one] they've all kind of stayed away. I keep telling them to come up, but ever since our son was born, they don't. Maybe they think they are intruding or something' (015 M 1984). Ten years later his social life was even more narrowly focused on home-based activities; his one regular outside activity involved taking his eleven-year-old son to hockey.

Once children started school, their schedules also had to be taken into account, both on a daily basis and throughout the year. When both partners were employed and their children were school-aged, mismatched schedules made it nearly impossible for them to find free time together. For parents who did not have enough seniority to get holidays during the summer, vacations away from home became impossible: 'You can't go away anywhere because the kids are in school and you have to stay home with them' (029 M 1984).

Parents who were able to tended to organize summer vacations and weekend activities around their children's interests: 'We used to have a trailer and every weekend in the summer we'd go up north, and it was great for the kids. We'd take them waterskiing, sailing, swimming. They could ride their bikes for miles and be safe, not like in the city. [This year] we are going to do little trips like fishing or Ontario Place or all the other places kids like to go. The kids have a list of places' (069 F 1984). In many families, the children's activities took priority: 'During the summer I'm very seldom [at the Legion] because of the kids. They're so wrapped up in things that you can't. You know, everything conflicts' (090 M 1994).

For mothers, in particular, the boundaries between child care and leisure are very ambiguous because children can both be leisure companions and act as constraints. Full-time homemakers with young children rarely had truly discretionary time with complete freedom from commitment for the welfare of others. They typically had their children with them most of the time. Because employed women had less time available to be with their children, they and their husbands tended to make deliberate efforts to be involved with their children when they were with them. One couple who had three teenage boys both had paid employment: 'I'm involved with children's baseball and my wife's involved now, too. I'm on the executive of the league and I coach. We're in the park six out of seven days. In the winter it is hockey' (069 M 1994).

Children drew their parents into new activities and linked them to social networks with other parents at the playground or at children's sports games: 'The only thing that we're really doing is, my son is involved in a lot of sports. We go out, we take him out to the games and then with the other families, we talk to them, and sometimes we have a house party that we go to. Once my son got involved in sports we've been out a lot more. We've met more people and we've actually gone to more parties and get-togethers' (015 M 1994).

As social actors, children often set the agenda, both by choosing their own friends and preferred activities and by introducing new friends into the network. Many parents found their social activities and relations shaped by their children's. A father described how his child's intervention changed his social orientation: 'The biggest difference is my son. I could take the car and go over to the Legion and socialize for three or four hours. But it is not fair to him. My son doesn't want me to go to work. I talk to him on the phone from work. He wants me to come home right now' (049 M 1984). Ten years later this man described how similar dynamics still governed his life: 'I don't do community activities. My shifts don't allow it. Also other family responsibilities come into it, too. And my parents are older now, and now and then they need something done. We keep in touch with them once a week' (049 M 1994).

One of the consequences of this orientation to nuclear families is that while growing children pulled their parents into wider networks, once the children were grown up, many couples found themselves less involved with outside networks and more reliant on each other. One man reflected: 'The fishing club kind of dried up [when the children stopped going]. It was kind of just a bunch of old guys going away on a fishing trip and the fun went out of it. I came back the last year and said it's all over. It's no fun anymore' (075 M 1994). His wife explained that they stayed home more: 'I don't think we [see our friends] as much. There's longer gaps between the times' (075 F 1994).

Companionate marriage often makes the spouses emotionally dependent on each other, making each vulnerable when the other is not available. Some men in particular are very reliant on their wives for social support. One man described how he missed 'doing things together' and how unsettled he was when his wife was out at work: 'I have cleaned up or whatever and have all my stuff done. Then I sat around the house. I would go to my mother's, or I would go to my sister's and have tea or whatever and I read a book, but then I would find after two or three days of this I was getting kind of bored' (166 M 1994). Another man described the isolation he encountered when his marriage ended: 'I had no life, no friends. They are all couples and don't really want a single guy tagging along. My kids live with my wife, so I don't have them. I used to go to their hockey and skating' (140 M 1994).

Staying Home and Going Out

For people whose first priority is their family, other friendship and community connections are easiest to sustain if they welcome or accommodate families.[10] But especially in a context where the demands of paid employment and domestic labour leave little time for other activities, a family-centred focus is often at the expense of other friendship and community connections. Commitments to families, the demands of paid work, and the kinds of resources available meant that staying at home, combining relaxation and leisure activities, family socializing and domestic labour was one of the most popular ways of spending free time: 'I like to do things around the house, that's my enjoyment. I love to putter' (166 M 1994).

Yet when people spend their free time at home, the distinctions between leisure and domestic labour are quickly blurred. Household needs often disrupt free time, and activities chosen for pleasure may slide into obligation. A father whose children are playing in a nearby park may have leisure time, but he is on call and must keep track of their expected time of return. A mother may insist that she watch her favourite television show each afternoon uninterrupted, but if her children do interrupt, she will have to deal with them. If she invites them to watch the show with her, and they cuddle together talking about it, she may be simultaneously relaxing, overseeing the health and safety of her children, educating them, and enjoying their company. The different aspects of the activity are indistinguishable.

An activity such as fixing the car may be undertaken with lots of enthusiasm for the pleasure of the task: 'If I want some time to myself, leisure, I just go work on my car in the garage' (089 M 1994). It can quickly turn into drudgery and obligation if other household members expect the job to be done as a contribution to household maintenance.

Shifting work demands and their orientation to family life made people reluctant to get involved in formal organizations. The majority, like this man, were not involved in community activities: 'No, my shifts don't allow it. And really I just wouldn't have the commitment to it. There's a lot of times that I'm working late. I'm working on my day off or something. Like a lot of other guys ... also other family responsibilities come into it, too. And my parents are older' (049 M 1994).

The two leisure activities with extensive appeal were churches and sports. A homemaker described her involvement: 'I coach two of the kids this year, one night of practice and one night a game. So that's four nights a week. I'm on a committee at church. I'm on the baseball executive, church choir at Christmas and Easter, and a blood donor every three months' (166 F 1994). Churches are explicitly family-oriented, so church involvement was compatible with family responsibilities. Church organizations were designed so that people could move in and out of active involvement as their time and inclinations moved them. About a fifth of the people we interviewed were involved in church committees and groups (23 per cent of women and 17 per cent of men).

As young adults, many enjoyed playing in organized sports such as baseball or hockey. They continued playing as long as possible, although men were twice as likely to play on adult teams (40 per cent of men and 21 per cent of women). Many gave up team sports when they had children and then encouraged their children's participation in team sports. More than a third of parents were involved with their children's sports, taking the children to practices and games and sometimes even coaching (35 per cent of women and 37 per cent of men with children between the ages of five and fifteen living at home).

One man described his changing priorities. In the early 1980s he had been involved in a baseball team with his buddies. By 1994 he had two children: 'I'm not going to play because it interferes with my son's playing. I'd like to see his game. I like playing, but I think it's more important to be there for his game than for me to do it' (078 M 1994). His experience was typical. Other parents, especially of preteen children, dropped out of their own teams because they were busy with their children's activities: 'I played baseball for about five or six years and gave that up when the girls got into all their things [swimming, baseball, gymnastics, and school sports]' (089 F 1994).

As their children grew older, parents often withdrew even more: 'Well, we were [involved in community activities] but the kids have grown up now, so we haven't really been involved in anything' (163 M 1994).

Other activities held little attraction for most people. Fewer than 15 per cent of the women and men were involved in organizations such as charity groups, co-operatives, ethnic associations, lodges, trade union socials, neighbourhood associations, home and school groups, or political organizations.

Over the years, as rotating shifts took their toll and family-oriented activities became established habits, even those whose seniority assured them steady days and whose children were grown up continued to spend most of their free time at home. Older women and men whose children had left home went out only four times a month and typically participated in a limited range of activities.[11] Those with enough money invested in home improvements or various entertainment resources; once they had made these investments, they were more inclined to stay at home: 'We barbeque. We stay home in the summer because we have a pool. In the winter we go for a lot of TV, read a lot' (097 F 1984).

Fragile Friendships and Casual Communities

Because they are almost entirely voluntary, unsustained by formal or institutional structures (unlike marriage or parent–child relations), individual friendships and community networks both depend for their survival on people's deliberate efforts. It is indicative of the importance people attribute to their friends and communities that, despite the counter-pressures, these networks continue to survive and even thrive: 'There are days when I'm just too swamped. I'm tired. I haven't spent time with my family and I'm desperate for some time alone for myself. And a friend calls. She wants me to listen because she's got problems, or she wants me do something – organize a protest or send a letter or something. And part of me is screaming "No way!" as I say, "Yes, of course." Because I may not survive without some down time, but I will perish without my community' (223 F 1996).

Extended Kin Ties

Relationships with extended kin are often important, but discretionary. There is considerable variation in people's involvement with their parents, siblings, and other family members: 'We do a lot with her family, not so much with my family. I've got a sister I'm fairly close to and I see her fairly often. We have a lot of fun with my wife's family' (166 M 1994).

In the 1984 interviews 42 per cent of women and 37 per cent of men said they had spent time with an extended family member in the past month. Full-time homemakers were the most likely to report spending time with kin. Women employed full-time spent about the same amount of time as men did with their extended families. The only relatives that people mentioned on a regular basis were parents and siblings. Aunts, uncles, and other relatives were seen at formal occasions such as weddings and funerals.

When kin enjoy each other's company, they socialize for the pleasure of it. One woman said: 'I enjoy spending time with my family [her mother and sisters]. I get up to see Mom as much as I can' (042 F 1984). For people with a strong commitment to their nuclear families, the ties can be very strong: 'We see each one of them [parents] at least once a week. Well, family is very important to us, there's no doubt about it' (152 M 1984). Other people have more casual relations: 'With my family, everybody's got their own life. We will all get together for a birthday, and say, "Hi, how are you? I haven't seen you in a couple of months"' (090 M 1994).

Kinship discourses imply that families have obligations to help each other, especially with financial and other material assistance. Close relatives, especially parents and children, may have a history of generalized reciprocity – of offering help without expecting an immediate return. As a result, it is often easier to ask kin for help than anyone else. During the 1990 strike and subsequent lay-offs, for example, a man with three children relied extensively on his brother, sister-in-law, and parents for assistance. He and his partner shared potluck dinners with siblings, moved in with parents, boarded with a brother-in-law, and asked a sister-in-law to provide child care.

When young people first set up their own homes, they may retain close ties to their parents' homes, both for practical support and for socializing. One young couple, for example, rented an apartment close to the man's parents' house, where they could keep their dogs, which were forbidden at their apartment: 'We have dinner and then we just go down the street and see our dogs, or my brother will come over and play targets or something like that' (078 M 1984).

Once they had young children, a shared interest and pleasure in the babies, as well as the practical help of babysitting, reinforce people's tendencies to remain connected with extended kin who live nearby. However, making such demands puts strain on relationships that may lead to conflict: '[We spend] very little time with her [mother]. We've had too many disputes with that lady over the kids, so we don't bother anymore. We don't even let her babysit any more' (090 M 1994).

When the children become teenagers, babysitting services are no longer required, and teenagers may be busy with activities that do not involve grandparents. Families may visit less frequently. However, when parents and siblings live nearby and share interests in common, the likelihood of spending time together increases: 'A lot of [our social life] is family-oriented. My wife's family, most of them are close to my age. And there's a lot done with them' (049 M 1984). Ten years later the man reported that he was still seeing both sets of parents once a week and, because his parents were aging, he was offering them assistance.

When kin do not live close by, or when they do not share interests in common, there is often little interaction, except perhaps at formal occasions such as important holidays, weddings, or funerals: 'My dad is dead. I see my mom I guess once a month. I have one sister up north, I haven't seen her for a year now. One brother I see about once a week. He lives around the corner from me and the other ones [three other siblings living in Hamilton], I see them at family functions, five or six times a year. I have a bunch of aunts and uncles, I don't know how many. I see them at funerals or weddings' (061 M 1984).

Extended kin ties were strengthened when kin were neighbours or co-workers or if kin had other day-to-day experiences in common. For many, working together at Stelco was an important factor in keeping up kin ties: 'My dad and brothers all worked at Stelco, so I used to bump into one of them at work. And they'd say, "Hey! How're doing? Why don't you come by after work?" And I miss that now. I just don't see them as often now I'm not working there' (213 F 1996).

Friends

Given the restrictions imposed by jobs and family obligations, other social ties were not that easy to maintain, although about 60 per cent of the people interviewed said they regularly spent time with (non-kin) friends. Homemakers, who were the most likely to spend time with kin, were the least likely to spend time with friends; only 54 per cent of homemakers had spent time with at least one friend in the preceding month, compared with 65 per cent of women employed part-time, and 71 per cent of women employed full-time. Men's socializing with friends reflected a similar pattern. Just over half of men married to homemakers reported spending time with at least one friend in the preceding month, compared with 65 per cent of men married to women employed part-time and 71 per cent of men married to women employed full-time.[12] Full-time homemakers and their partners were more likely to socialize with friends as a couple; couples where the women were employed were more likely to do things with friends on their own, especially when they worked different shifts. Not surprisingly, men whose partners were employed were more likely to spend time with their co-workers than men whose partners were full-time homemakers (40 per cent compared with 24 per cent).

One of the important features of friendship that distinguishes it from kinship is that people do not expect friends to provide material support (Side 1997). Instead, friends are expected to offer emotional support and company. While the people we interviewed did not spend that much with friends, many of them had a network of friends who were important to them.[13] They maintained contact by telephone, enjoyed the periodic times they did get together, and derived great pleasure from the relationships.

While friendships can form in any number of ways, proximity and shared experiences were important sources for many of the people we interviewed: 'We've been friends with the neighbours next door. I have been friends with a fellow since grade school. And there is another couple we see, a friend of mine from work that just lives over here. And I'll drop in for coffee a lot' (166 M 1994). Working together often generated friendship: 'I have one really good friend that I hang around with.

I work with him, but other than that no. We get together, depending on how his schedule works out with mine' (090 M 1984).

The Stelco lay-offs disrupted plant-based friendship networks, eroding long-established social networks and community life: 'Sure I feel demoralized. I feel rotten, you feel there is nothing out there. You don't see your friends because you don't have any money to spend. It gets me angry.'[14]

Friendships for workers left at the plant were also disrupted: 'With the lay-offs, I lost most of my close friends. They're just not around anymore. It's pretty lonely at work, and even my hockey team has fallen apart' (305 M 1996). In a similar way, couple-based friendships are hard to maintain if the marriage ends. A woman who had left two marriages, divorced, and remarried said it was hard to maintain her previous friendships: 'I don't feel like we have friends' (011 F 1994).

Neighbours

Just as women's employment undermines the anti-social character of family life, the fact that family households are located in neighbourhoods embeds people in potential social networks:[15] 'He enjoys being out with other people. He enjoys socializing, he loves to socialize. I could be out in the backyard digging and he'd be out there talking with the neighbours' (021 F 1994). The longer people have lived in a neighbourhood and the more they work in the neighbourhood, for example, as homemakers, the more likely they are to know people in the neighbourhood.

Most neighbourhood friendship networks are informal. Some people are naturally gregarious and enjoy getting to know as many neighbours as possible, while others are shy. Nevertheless, meeting people in the street, chatting over the fence, running into each other in the local shops, all create familiarity among co-residents. Indeed, about half of the people interviewed knew nine or more neighbours by name, suggesting that at least casual friendship networks linked them together. An average of 67 per cent of women and 69 per cent of men insisted that if they had to move from their present home, they would prefer to remain in the same neighbourhood.

Women are key to linking their households to others in their neighbourhoods. The type of involvement in their neighbourhoods depends on a variety of factors, in addition to basic personality, such as the length of time they have lived in the neighbourhood, the number of their relatives who live there, their employment history, and the ages of their children. The more women are involved in paid employment, the more likely they are to have other social ties available to them, and the less time they have around the home to socialize with neighbours.

In contrast, women working at home full-time may experience their neighbours as the equivalent of co-workers and may rely on them in ways that employed women do not. Full-time homemakers were the most likely to know seven or more neighbours by name (71 per cent). Women employed part-time were less likely (64 per cent) to know so many, and women employed full-time (49 per cent) were the least likely to know many neighbours by name. Women who had been homemakers in 1984, but were employed a decade later, explained that they missed the neighbourhood camaraderie afforded full-time homemakers: 'I think we saw our friends socially more than we do now. Ten years ago a lot of my friends or neighbours where we used to live weren't working. Now everybody's working. It's rare that people will drop by. Some of them work shifts, or they'll say they drove by and didn't see the van so they knew I was at work' (089 F 1994).

The longer people had lived in an area, the more involved they were with it. Of women who had lived in an area for five years or less, only 42 per cent knew seven or more neighbours by name compared with 76 per cent of those who had lived in an area six years or more. Only 34 per cent of men who had lived in an area five years or less knew seven or more neighbours by name, compared with 70 per cent of men who had lived there longer. Both women and men with preschool-aged children were slightly more involved in local neighbourhoods than parents of older children. Men tended to be connected to neighbourhood networks through their wives, so both the number of neighbours that men knew and their sense of their neighbourhood as a community followed their wives' pattern.[16]

While the resources available in any particular neighbourhood vary enormously, and are largely beyond the control of individual residents, the parks, recreation facilities, community centres, and range of people and activities all combine to form a backdrop for potential community involvement. To the extent that people can and do mobilize resources and social connections, they challenge the predominance of the private nuclear family household.

In Search of Collective Social Relations

Despite the pressures on them to focus on immediate family and informal activities, some people put considerable effort into building and maintaining larger community networks and organizations. They got involved for all kinds of reasons – a sense of social responsibility, the satisfaction of public involvement, or the pleasure of hanging out with friends. Some were active for decades; others moved in and out of various commitments as the mood hit them or when opportunities arose. In addition to widespread interest in church groups and sports, at the time we interviewed them, some were volunteer firefighters, several were active in the women's crisis centre, and a few were involved in municipal, provincial, or federal politics.

Some people felt strongly that a collective or community orientation was an important antidote to prevailing tendencies to individualism: 'When it all becomes broken down into small individual things going on, then there's got to be some way of getting it back as a community' (075 M 1994). Others got involved in specific groups, such as their union, or other social or political movements, as part of an effort to protect or improve their circumstances: 'I got active in the women's liberation movement when I was about twenty. When I heard these women talking about women's oppression and about fighting for liberation, what they said just made sense of all the confusions I'd had. So I started going to their meetings and demos and stuff and made friends. I came to understand the world in a new way. I've been a feminist ever since' (223 F 1996).

One woman explained why collective action was important to her: 'Alone, you can maybe change yourself a bit, learn to react to things differently maybe. But if you get together with other people, you actually have a chance to change the world so you can live in it differently' (224 F 1996).

Marching with many of his former co-workers in the Day of Action, the laid-off steelworker who claimed that economic restructuring had turned his world upside down said that the demonstration gave him a sense of community: 'I feel so alone. It's so hard trying to get by and I feel such despair. But here, it's great. There are so many like me. I'm not alone and when thousands of us like this get together, I know I can hold on because we're all in this together' (303 M 1996).

Conclusion

People had considerably more discretion in the choice of their leisure activities and companions than they did in their activities and associates at their paid workplace or at home. Despite this latitude, people's choices of leisure activities and companions were constrained by their gender and class and tended to reproduce their ethnic and racialized networks. Social ties and activities were also shaped by the resources available to them, their own labour force participation and their partner's, their shift schedule, the ages and activities of family members, their own age, and their domestic labour responsibilities.

In general, the sex/gender division of labour, particularly the importance of men's financial contribution to the household and the habitual pattern of women doing most of the domestic labour, gave men more leisure time. It constrained opportunities for women who were full-time homemakers, at least until their children grew up. But the pressures on men constrained them, too. Given this context, friendships and informal networks were difficult to sustain and community networks were chancy. Both depended on voluntary sustenance. They were rarely supported by structures that ensured their continuation. If nothing in the day-to-day activities brought people together, their relationships were likely to be inactive.

In significant ways, dependence on Stelco made it difficult for people to maintain friendships or get involved in building collective community networks. People in couples were in general bound up in a set of constraints that left them focused on their spouses and children and on home-based or child-based activities. Where they engaged in other activities it was typically things to which spouses and children could also belong, such as a church or children's sports activities.

Despite the pressures of market-driven individualism, private consumerism, and family introversion, people strove to develop and maintain networks of kin, friends, neighbours, and co-workers. By manoeuvring around the constraints of work schedules and the disincentives imposed by nuclear families, some actively engaged in activities with other friends and contributed to sustaining networks, organizations, and communities.

9

Dreams and Dilemmas:
Trying to Make Sense of It All

Following the 1996 Hamilton Day of Action, a woman whose partner was a former steelworker reflected on the changes she had lived through over the previous two decades: 'Things have got harder instead of better since the 1980s. Me and my friends are doing okay, but not like we used to or what I expected for my future. And there are so many people not doing okay – there's way more people begging on the streets – and then, like the banks, and the CEOs, they make so much money. But all our things we used to take for granted, just cuts, cuts, cuts – like my kids' school doesn't have any money and the hospital's been cut ... So many changes' (304 F 1996). Then she expressed a sense of confusion, shared by many of her contemporaries: 'And the government says the cuts are necessary and the changes will make things just fine, but the labour movement and other people say no – I don't know how to make sense of it all' (304 F 1996).

The period between 1980 and 1996 was one of greater change and disruption of social, political, and economic life than any period since the 1939–45 war. The costs of social reproduction were increasingly forced onto individual working people, destabilizing their livelihoods, and putting their children's futures at risk. By the late 1990s the Hamilton working class was characterized by a still-diminishing and increasingly insecure group of aging steelworkers, along with many former heavy industry workers who had found some form of steady work in new light industries, and a burgeoning contingent labour force, increasingly forced to seek temporary employment in the service sector – for generally lower wages and fewer benefits.[1] There were also growing numbers of poor, unemployed, and street people, a haunting reminder of the lack of jobs and the failure of existing social security programs. Between

1986 and 1996 the number of families living in poverty in Hamilton-Wentworth increased by 4.4 per cent to 23,815 families, and the number of single people living in poverty increased by 5.5 per cent to 27,880 individuals (Brown 1999). In Hamilton-Wentworth 21.9 per cent of the total population lived below the poverty line, as compared with 17.7 per cent for all of Ontario (Brown 1999). As a result, the number of people relying on general welfare for an income, increased 48 per cent between 1987 and 1997 (Brown 1999).

While the families who still had someone working at Stelco maintained a comfortable life, many of their friends, their children, and their neighbours were adjusting their standards of living to cope with less money and/or less time. Some had the resources to ensure their lives continued largely unchanged. A union executive who took early retirement spoke for many former male steelworkers when he said: 'There's a thirty-and-out clause, so some of our members who started young and have been there all along, they can retire in their fifties. Some, like me, took early retirement when Stelco offered it. We're okay, you know. My house is paid for. I don't have any other debts. I've been living a good life since I left Stelco' (310 M 1996).

One of the women offered a more cautious assessment. She pointed out that many of the men who left Stelco by taking early retirement, or who then got other jobs, were older workers with years of secure earnings behind them and adequate pensions. Her own circumstances left her in a much more precarious position, and she warned of greater hardships to come: 'Lots of the folks I worked with there are doing okay. But I'm not sure I am. I'm just getting by right now, but I've no benefits, no sick leave, no dental plan, no pension, and no savings. I can't afford to get a toothache. If I get sick for just a week, I'll lose my job, my place, and we'll be on the street. More and more people are in that position. Things could get really bad here' (221 F 1996).

Between 1980 and 1996 many prevailing discourses were transformed, challenging assumptions that sustained the routines of daily life and undermining possibilities for critique or opposition. The shift, from presumptions that the well-being of the economy depended on the well-being of the people who were part of it, to those which gave priority to the well-being of the corporate sector, strengthened others that valued individual and family responsibilities over collective ones and private profit-making over public services. For ordinary working people, the range of available discourses to explain their new circumstances was increasingly limited, making it harder to make sense of what was happening.

Sober Concerns: Confronting New Problems

As a former steelworker put it, people were forced to confront tough choices: 'Back then [the early 1980s] I just took life for granted. Things were the way they were, because that's how they were. And I just went along, making the best of things. I didn't think much about it. But now, for working people like me, we face lots of sober concerns, new problems I never thought I'd have to face' (010 M 1994).

Most people could easily identify a series of problems that had arisen in recent years to undermine their security and peace of mind. One steelworker reflected on the way the changes at work had wreaked havoc on the personal lives of some of his co-workers: 'Some of it I blame on management down there, the stress they put the workers under, on that restructuring. I have known three guys in my department, all have been divorced in the last year. I would still say it's a lot to do with what's happening in their job' (021 M 1994). They readily identified general job insecurity and the declining social security net as major problems: 'Nothing's for sure anymore, and you can have the greatest job, but no matter where you live, nothing's for sure. And I think everyone knows that now. And it's not just Hamilton, it's not just St Catharine's; it's everywhere' (152 M 1994).

Closely related was their recognition that the cost of living was increasing, while their incomes were not: 'You get so damn frustrated with everything all the time. Like, even going to a store. You go on Monday, and the price of bread is twenty-five cents. You go on Tuesday, now it's a buck. Look at the gas. The price of gas for your car, one day it's forty-seven cents, the next day it's fifty-three, but the guy that owns the gas station says he only makes a penny on every litre' (090 M 1994). Many also had a strong sense that they were working harder, for longer hours, with less reward: 'Everything is always so rushed now. It used to be, I'd work hard, but at the end of the day I had time to relax and enough money to have some fun. Now I just work all the time, and it doesn't feel like I have much money, and it's getting harder to have fun' (306 M 1996).

Some talked about the way even a steady income was insufficient to prevent the erosion of their standard of living: 'Like I can't even afford to fix this place up. So you just keep putting it off, putting it off. It keeps getting worse, and all of a sudden, you're poor ... Look at that house! Look at that mess! He can't afford to fix it up. He doesn't have the money to fix it up' (090 M 1994).

Many of them linked their growing insecurity to their perception that they were part of a class that was increasingly bearing a disproportionate share of the tax burden: 'I'd say I'm middle class, the "paying class" I'd guess you'd call it. Everybody above us is not paying anything, and people below us are taking it, and we're the ones that just keep paying it' (047 M 1994). Many stressed that the upper class, or the rich, and their banks and corporations, were paying few or no taxes, while the numbers of poor who need assistance were growing and their poverty deepening: 'The upper class was getting away with a lot and the lower class families that needed the support through social assistance or whatever were not getting it. It was always the middle class that was being hit to help pay for everything' (015 M 1994).

As a consequence, they had a growing feeling of insecurity: 'My life feels, well, more on the edge, like I could fall off at any moment' (306 M 1996). It was fed by their appreciation of growing poverty and their fear that they were just a lay-off away from poverty themselves: 'There's people out there that were once middle-class people that are sitting there with nothing. Twenty years ago you figured you start at Stelco, you're set for life. But nobody's ever set anywhere anymore. I mean, you hear about it on the radio and TV, people that were once, I mean, your money only goes so far once you lose a job' (069 M 1994). These concerns fuelled support for the idea of one job per family: 'It depends on the breadwinner. If it's the woman that's taking care, then she should have it. If the guy's wife is at home, then he should have it. Otherwise you are going to have one on welfare and one way up here' (166 M 1994).

One thing that helped working people get by in the period from 1946 to the late 1970s was their strong conviction that things were getting better, that if they hung in and worked hard, their own material conditions would improve and that, if it did not work for them, at least they would have achieved something for their children. As that sense of a better future unravelled, it undermined one of the strongest forces motivating people: 'Before, when I didn't think I could cope, I would think, "You're doing this for your kids. Hang in there. You can do it." And I would. For your kids, you can do anything. But now, what's the point? I don't think there's much of a future for me. I don't think there's going to be much of one for my kids. So what's the point?' (303 M 1996).

People were able to articulate their deepest anxieties about their futures when they talked about what they wanted and what they anticipated for their children. Implicit in their concerns for the next generation were their own fears for themselves. When they talked explicitly about their immediate situations in the 1990s, and anticipated their futures, most people were circumspect, less willing to give voice to their fears, more ready to insist on their capacities to cope. Despite their descriptions of rising levels of insecurity, time pressures, rigidities of work-time scheduling, conflicted demands, and difficult trade-offs that caused personal stress and interpersonal tensions, people were quick to add a more optimistic qualifier: 'But I can't complain' (010 F 1994) or 'But we'll manage' (223 F 1996) or 'We're coping' (225 F 1996).

One woman offered an insight into this tendency to downplay their concerns and fears: 'No one will really say they think they will be on the streets, or poor, or destitute, even if they think it might happen. The worse off I am, the more I insist things will be okay. It's like saying it might make it real – so you say the good stuff and just block out the fear' (224 F 1996). Another pointed out the bottom line: 'Things can always be worse. If you've got your health, and a roof, and food – well, things could be worse' (301 F 1996).

Tough Choices: Making Sense of Getting By

While most of the people we interviewed clearly understood the effects of the changes on their lives, they were less certain about the causes or sources of those changes. Starting from their own experiences, comparing them with what they knew about others' experiences, and drawing on available discourses to articulate their knowledge, people in subordinate positions can observe the discrepancies between ideologies about the way society works and their own reality. But unless they have access to larger networks of information beyond their specific experiences, it is difficult to develop broader, more comprehensible analyses, envision effective alternatives, or develop viable strategies for change.

Collective movements and organizations such as the labour and women's movements, union locals, and women's centres have the potential to pool a range of information, develop shared analyses, and generate specific political demands and even long-term transformative strategies. Certainly, during the period of this study, dozens of national, bi-national, or provincial and territorial organizations such as the National Action Committee on the Status of Women (NAC), the Canadian Labour Congress (CLC), the Ontario Federation of Labour (OFL), the National Anti-Poverty Organization (NAPO), and thousands of smaller local or issue-oriented groups organized against neo-liberal and neo-conservative policies and offered alternative political visions and strategies.[2] But when power holders exert enormous efforts and resources to contain and undermine such groups and their views, when prevailing discourses both ridicule their analyses and dismiss them as 'special interest groups,' when mainstream media refuse to make their perspectives known or even deliberately misrepresent their views, it is not easy for such groups to reach people who are not already in contact with them.

Only a few of the people we interviewed had access to the types of resources that collective movements and organizations offered. One of the former women steelworkers noted that, in the normal course of day-to-day life, she was unable to get critical insights: 'It takes a lot of learning and I don't think I have really learned it yet. But I am aware of it which is a lot more than I was. You were totally surrounded by inequalities all your life but never aware of it. It is like you are in this shell, you don't know what is out there. I knew nothing of the women's movement or the union. All you know is what you see or hear. It just goes in this ear and out the other if you are not involved, or it doesn't relate to you somehow – if you don't know that it relates to you' (213 F 1984). She described how her experience as a woman at Stelco changed her life precisely because it gave her access to critical perspectives and to organizations where she could work collectively:

> It changed my whole life, because of the union and the women I met down there. It changed everything. I learned a lot about women's struggles. The union was such a learning experience for education about the world, the Irish, the Palestinians, the war in El Salvador. Sooner or later you have got to say to yourself, how does all this relate to me? How do I fit in here? And then you take everything that has happened to you. Why couldn't I get a loan two years ago? Why did I have to have a man sign for this? This stinks, you know. It's only because you are a woman. All that didn't really bug me until you become more conscious. It became a thirst. You had to learn more. I think the biggest learning experience was, the women fought really hard to get in. (213 F 1984)

Caught up in the important demands of getting by day by day, and in the dynamics of their personal networks and social activities, most people have few opportunities to become aware of alternatives. Unless something specifically draws them into their union, other organizations, or activist politics, or they have friends who make alternative perspectives available to them, most people remain disconnected. Pushed by our interview to examine how she thought about social relations, a woman gave a complex analysis but concluded by insisting that she rarely gave such matters much attention: 'So that's how I look at it. I usually don't look at it. I haven't delved this deep in a long time. I usually don't look at the social end of it, you know' (181 F 1994).

Despite the clarity of their understanding of what had happened to them, most of the people we interviewed were unsure about what, if anything, they could do to resist the changes or improve their situations, although most agreed with the assessment expressed by this steelworker: 'And we have to make choices about what kind of life we want, and we have to make choices about how we go about trying to get that life' (010 M 1994).

The ways people cope and adjust reflect the resources available to them; they also have implications, not just for themselves but for the shape of the larger society. A steelworker who refuses overtime sacrifices additional income, but he also lays a basis for more mutually supportive and egalitarian relations both at work, as the time is available for others, and at home, where he is available to do more domestic labour. In contrast, if he accepts the overtime, he implicitly supports management's downsizing strategies and recreates the male income earner scenario that increases inequalities between spouses. Even if people avoid getting involved in politics, if they define themselves as apolitical, become inactive and retreat, then that, too, becomes an alignment of sorts, because they are supporting dominant ideologies and practices. One steelworker implied that their resulting inactivity could be seen as acceptance: 'We're too complacent. We are being shoved around and nobody seems to want to do anything. They just sit back and take it' (112 M 1984). In the 1990s that meant favouring market-driven atomism and the search, among those who could afford it, for private solutions to public problems.

One of the women who had been active in the Women Back Into Stelco campaign pointed out: 'It's not simple, but really, working-class people are under attack and we have two choices. We can hang tight, look after ourselves, and hope we get by. Or, we can fight back' (221 F 1996).

For most people trying to get by in hard times, neither the options of hanging tight nor of fighting back is as straightforward as this woman implied. Because people have multiple, layered, and cross-cutting identities, as workers and as mothers, as union activitists and individuals working overtime, as family income earners and as part of the bridge-playing gang, they have many potential and conflicting allegiances. The way they align themselves is complicated; the priorities they give their various allegiances can change.

Shifting Class Relations

In the years between 1946 and 1980 steelworkers made significant gains in the workplace through their collective union activities, improving their pay and working conditions, and forging themselves into important players in the Canadian labour movement. The post-1980 crisis in the steel industry undercut that terrain by leaving many workers concerned for their jobs and, therefore, for the survival of the plant. These changing conditions produced an increasing receptivity among the workers to negotiations with and concessions to the employer. New union tactics reflected this shift. Rather than taking a more militant stance or risking a long struggle, like the 1981 strike, the union tended to try to work with management to ensure plant survival.

Over the years, the union developed a less confrontational, more cooperative relationship with management, punctuated by challenges such as the 1990 strike. A union activist described this stance: 'But I honestly believe that the company and the union are working together now to get the job done. And that's what you need' (029 M 1994).

Nevertheless, Hilton Works was still subject to serious competitive pressures. Lake Erie Works continued to increase its semi-finished steel productivity, and continental market pressures to reduce person hours per ton to U.S. levels also continued. The future productivity of Hilton Works would be partly contingent, of course, on how effective Hilton engineers and sales staff were in designing and selling lighter, stronger, and cleaner steel products in an ever-changing marketplace.

It would also be dependent on the extent to which current employment guarantees could be sustained. Despite the fact that labour productivity, corporate profits, and executive pay were steadily rising by the end of the 1990s, workers did not receive a share of their firm's prosperity in the form of real wage increases.[3] Instead, their cooperation was sustained by the threat of unemployment. If that threat were to persist, unrelieved by substantial positive incentives, even workers who were not predisposed to labour militancy might conclude that they had no alternatives but to fight back to defend their interests.

Certainly, many unionized workers recognized that there are clear limits to cooperation with employers and that they needed collective nization to avoid being played off against other workers. A steel-worker still at Stelco in 1994 made this point: 'I help out a lot of people that are in non-union shops with the knowledge that I got out of the union. They've got no representation or anything. I have seen too many non-union shops and what the guys are going through in there. It's either do this or you ain't got a job. I mean, if they're telling me I got to do something unsafe, there is just no way. The contract, it's like a bible, eh?' (029 M 1994).

A retired Stelco worker's comparative experience made him even more conscious of the need for worker solidarity against management:

> The companies I've been working with since Stelco are largely non-union, smaller businesses. The owners have complete control. As I watch the way they run the operations, they don't care about the welfare of their employees. I guess with the recession and hard times you begin to think maybe workers are asking for too much. Then you see a little core group of owners and managers. It just blows my mind the way these people take care of themselves – and don't take care of their employees. It's the attitude in all these companies that, "Well, you know times are tough and if you don't like it, there's the door." And it will be for a long time because they know that for everyone that leaves there's a hundred and fifty that will come in the door. That's sad and it's frightening. (075 M 1994)

The Hilton Works case study illustrates the changing dynamics of class relations in a period of economic restructuring, when neo-liberal policies were reinforcing and deepening class, race, and gender inequalities (Seccombe and Livingstone 2000; Ricciutelli, Larkin, O'Neill 1998; Ralph, Regimbald, and St Amand 1997). It shows how powerful capitalist employers are, not only in determining whether or not there are jobs and what happens to workers on the job. In their hiring practices and on-the-job policies, employers affect race, ethnicity, and gender politics by either reinforcing or undermining discriminatory practices. In their decisions about the organization of their workplaces, they can significantly affect the standards of living, not only of their workers, but of the larger community as well.

In a climate where the few new jobs were typically not unionized, low-paid, with few benefits or protections, and often precarious and part-time, where the social safety net was full of holes, and the political discourses deadened alternative visions, the relative power of capitalists, the owners and controllers of wealth, was strengthened. Vulnerable to threats of job loss and the consequent insecurities, workers in particular workplaces found their capacities for resistance undermined.

For some Stelco workers, the way the shift in power from workers to management constrained political action during the period of restructuring was illustrated by Local 1005's position on the Hamilton Day of Action in February 1996. A high point of mutual accommodation between Stelco management and the union leadership occurred as Local 1005 publicly supported the days of protest, but agreed not to picket the plant (Prokaska, 24 January 1996). The many Hilton workers who wanted to participate were allowed to take some of their holiday time to do so, while the plant remained open and functioning with reduced staff (Poling, 24 February 1996). One of the participants at the demonstration drew a dispirited conclusion: '1005's position is telling. We don't have the political strength to fight effectively right now. And management knows it. They've got us over a barrel. So they can generously let guys like me take a holiday to protest, but how effective is that? I give up a holiday; Stelco's still making its profits, so it's under no pressure to change current policies' (304 M 1996).

Shifting Gender Relations

The period from 1980 to 1996 was a transformative period for women, as their two major options became increasingly hard to realize. Women who aspired to secure support from husbands to stay at home to look after their families typically had to find paid employment to help their households get by. Women in the paid labour force who aspired to secure, well-paid jobs found that the employment available to them was more likely to be precarious and poorly paid. The majority of women, coping with the demands of paid employment and domestic labour, in a period where both were intensifying, were working harder with fewer resources just to get by.

Employed parents continued to piece together child care arrangements because the promised national child care program was shelved. Getting child care for people who worked shifts in Hamilton remained difficult. The Child Care Information Line (1997: 2) reported many cases of women who had unmet needs: 'A single mother who works twelve-hour shifts is looking for licensed child care for three children. She is unable to find centre or home-based licensed care that can be flexible about her hours. Consequently, she is feeling very stressed over the lack of monitored care for "shift workers."'

The changing sex/gender divisions of labour in the paid labour force have had an impact on general gender relations. Women's place in the labour force has changed in response to widespread recognition that women's employment is necessary, and the awareness of women's success in a growing range of occupations and the ongoing efforts of women in the labour and women's movements to improve women's situations. One of the most prominent changes is the acceptance in principle of women's right to paid employment in any occupation. A former woman steelworker explained how economic changes had combined with women's political initiatives to change gender politics, not just in the workplace but in family households and in the community:

Things have really changed for women, and men are slowly coming to accept that's the way things are now. When I applied to Stelco my dad went ballistic. 'No daughter of mine ...!' He wanted I should get some little job just 'til I got married and had kids. But now, he says, 'Times are tough. You go out there and get the best job you can and I'll support you all the way.' And the guys I know, my friends, they're cool about women working now. They all know we need the jobs. (221 F 1994)

The growing acceptance of women's labour force participation has serious limitations, however. While women's struggles for pay and employment equity have secured better jobs and pay for some women, the labour market remains highly sex-segregated, and the majority of women are ghettoized in a limited number of occupations, most of them low-paid and vulnerable (Statistics Canada 1996 *Census*). In 1996 women still earned considerably less than men, on average about 65 per cent of men's earnings. Reductions in the wage gap were not the result of pay equity but of the decline in men's wages – between 1990 and 1996 average income for men dropped 7.8 per cent, for women 2 per cent (Drolet 1999). An apparently increasing gender equality that is based on men's loss of income and job security is both fragile and undesirable. And while paid employment undermines women's economic dependence on marriage, being forced to take a job to ensure family subsistence is hardly liberating.

The growing acceptance of formal gender equality in the labour market, confirmed by many legal rulings, was offset by growing resistance to initiatives to ensure greater actual equity in the labour market.[4] In 1984, while over 70 per cent of men and women interviewed agreed that women can do the same work as men, only 43 per cent of men and

57 per cent of women supported the idea of affirmative action measures to help women get jobs in former male preserves.

As jobs became more scarce, support for men's 'breadwinner' prerogatives increased, opposition to women's demands for greater equality in the labour force hardened, and many men became more cautious in their support for gender equality in the workplace. A steelworker who supported women at Stelco argued in 1984: 'It's perfectly natural. I had a woman on my crew. I don't think she made any difference. I think it's natural' (075 M 1984). Ten years later he was less sanguine: 'What I see happening now terrifies me. I worked for years with women and felt completely comfortable. But now I find that lots of things, like sexual discrimination and sexual harassment and things of this nature, are working to the detriment of men. I don't feel comfortable working with a woman now because I feel threatened. Now I constantly have to think if I'm doing anything that is wrong or can be perceived as harassment of any sort. I feel very, very threatened now working with a woman' (075 M 1994).

This man's expression of growing tensions between women and men in the labour force may well have reflected his experience at Stelco, where most of the women had lost their jobs, leaving Hilton Works an almost exclusively male preserve once again. Typically, the more gender-integrated a workplace is, the less likely there are to be gender hostilities; employees cease to be 'women' or 'men' and become individual co-workers. But this man's change of perspective may also reflect another widespread phenomenon – men afraid of losing jobs could blame globalization or intensified capitalist profit-making, but women are closer to hand and men-as-breadwinner discourses are more readily available.

Different dynamics operated in households. One of the major victories of the feminist movement has been the widespread recognition that what women do in the home is socially important work. This success is indicated by United Nations agreements to measure and value unpaid work and to consider women's unpaid work in gender equality measures designed to assess the extent to which government policies increase gender equality (Status of Women 1997). As domestic labour has been reconceptualized from a feminine attribute to a labour process, and as women increasingly work in the paid labour force, there has been increasing pressure on men to do more domestic labour. Notions of formal gender equality have fostered a growing willingness to acknowledge that men as well as women can, and perhaps should, do domestic labour, yet typical work and family gender relations undercut men's participation in domestic labour.

Unlike paid employment, where workers can organize collectively, mount public campaigns, and negotiate with employers, co-workers, and governments to improve their working conditions, domestic divisions of labour remain private. Individual women and men renegotiating their gender division of household labour tend to experience their struggles as interpersonal, reflecting either the character of the other or the depth of their love and commitment to the relationship. A former steelworker who was active in the feminist movement offered this insight. She explained that in workplaces, the combination of collective action and institutional practices supported women who were trying to change sexist behaviours and offered men ways to change without humiliating them:

> In the union, we could say, 'There's discrimination going on here,' and there were lots of other women and some men who would agree and who would help us try to change it. And there were policies and laws and stuff. And years of the women's movement. So you could go to some guy who was being a real pain and say, 'Hey man, you can't do this and here's why.' And if he didn't change, you had lots of ways of dealing with him, like other guys would talk to him, or he could be charged, or whatever. And you could always make him feel like it wasn't him that was a jerk, even if he was. You could say, 'This is how things are done here. Like it or lump it.' (214 F 1996)

She contrasted that with the dynamics in private family relations:

> But in the home, it's his home, it's his wife. What's she going to say? She can't just say it's not on for men to sit around while their wives do all the work because society doesn't work that way anymore. She doesn't have any union to say we have policies that men have to do their share of the housework or legislation that says she has a right to pay equity in the home if she wants to go shopping. No. Instead it's like her saying, 'I don't like who you are anymore.' She has to be really mad before she'll go that far. And he sure won't find that easy to hear. (214 F 1996)

And while increased sharing of domestic labour reduces some of the workload on women, it does so by increasing pressures on men, who in this period, were often already under pressure to work longer on the job. It does little to address the basic problems – that working-class households must work longer and harder to hold on to a standard of living that keeps declining, that the two subsistence labours remain incompatible, and that capital accumulation depends on working-class women's and men's unpaid and underpaid labour.

Dreams and Dilemmas: Strategies for Change

It is hard for people as individuals to make sense of changes in their immediate workplaces and households, in the context of the globalization of capitalism. Since the way people make sense of their world shapes their visions of alternatives, and therefore the strategies they advocate, the available analyses of the socioeconomic and political organization of society are crucial.

For many, the most obvious alternative to the hard times was their memory of the relatively better pre-1980 period. Their assessment of what they wanted and what was possible was informed by that earlier experience, and yet, in many ways, the changes of the 1980–96 period were such that strategies that worked in the earlier period had become less effective. In the period between 1946 and 1980 working people won certain protections by making demands on both employers and the state for better protective legislation and social security. The organized labour movement and the women's movement were central in that struggle, but as post-1980 employers and neo-liberal states proved less open to such demands, and the growing right-wing movement posed an even more oppositional challenge, such struggles became more difficult (Luxton and Reiter 1997). At the same time, such backward gazing, which easily romanticized what they had in the 1970s and before, reflected the lack of any sense of viable progressive alternatives.

While the corporations, business interests, and others advocating neo-liberalism rejoiced at increasing profits, growing privatization, and lower taxes, there was considerable popular resistance to deteriorating working conditions and deep government cuts. The 1996 Day of Action in Hamilton was one moment in that resistance. What brought thousands of people onto the street on Hamilton's Day of Action in February 1996 was their sense that government and business economic restructuring was undermining the stability of daily life. Their demands were clear – stop the cuts, restore social programs, and ensure jobs for all. Marching to protest government support of the corporate agenda, a laid-off steelworker explained that the changes had undermined his confidence in the way society works. He joined the march to protest, something that previously he would never have imagined himself doing:

'But here I am [at the protest demonstration]. I feel like my world's turned upside down. Now we bounce from crisis to crisis every day. And I think people should have a right to a decent job, enough money to live and care for their family and everybody' (303 M 1996). This man's demands for full employment, a living wage, and the resources to provide caregiving to those who need it were basically demands for a return to the conditions of daily life that had been available to him just a decade previously.

A former steelworker described how her new precarious work situation made her daily life unstable. Her brief experience as a steelworker had given her an appreciation of what well-paid secure employment meant, especially for women. She also had a sense that the possibilities and constraints shaping her life reflected corporate and government policies that could be challenged. 'When I got hired at Stelco, I was set. It was hard work but I could do it and the pay was so great! I thought I was set for life. Then this new corporate agenda stuff – the lay-offs ... and there's no jobs, and my day care centre is closing because of funding cuts. And this job I've got now – I never know my schedule 'til the day before, and they often make me stay late. It's a disaster. And this Harris government is making it worse. We have to stop it!' (221 F 1996).

As McQuaig (1998) has argued, however, in the aftermath of restructuring, there were few discourses available to help those who wanted to resist the changes. The most public and readily available explanation about what was happening to the global economy was the neo-liberal agenda that denies class exploitation and inequality, and encourages people to feel impotent, leaving them open to blaming others and supporting right-wing policies. As part of the cultural mainstream, many of the couples we interviewed found some resonance between their experience of being under attack and neo-liberal and right-wing discourses.

Certainly, the analysis of class available to most offered no appreciation of class conflict, undermined critiques of class inequality, and provided no analysis of the importance of class struggle. In the 1984 interviews most people made clear distinctions between three classes – upper, middle, and lower – based on socioeconomic status, differing mainly in how fluid or rigid they saw the divisions between them:

There are different classes for sure, the typical upper, middle, and lower classes. You drive down my street and you can see it. Everyone on this block are steelworkers. Most of them make around $30,000 a year. Down the street they are making less, up the street they are making a lot more. The whole country is made up of it. I guess it's a way of life. It's always going to be that way. A lot has to do with your family before you. If your family made a lot of money, then you are pretty well going to maintain that class of living. (089 M 1984)

In the 1994 interviews most people reiterated the same tripartite model, but expressed concern about growing poverty and assumed that the rich upper class was getting richer, imposing a greater burden on the middle class: 'There have always been rich, middle, and poor classes. But there are more poor in the past few years – food banks all over. You never had food banks when I was a kid. People who are higher class don't help the lower, the middle class do. The middle is carrying the burden for everything' (176 M 1994).

There were only two explanations offered by most people for the growing class inequalities. The first was employment insecurity: 'Yes, you don't think, well, gee, I'm going to be here for the rest of my life. You hear too many people who had good jobs and they don't have them anymore. You can plan, maybe for next month' (152 F 1994). The second was the way government tax policies allowed the upper classes tax relief, while imposing increased taxes on the people in the middle: 'The middle class I think take the brunt for basically everything. The rich are only going to get richer; there are too many tax loopholes for them to get through. The middle takes the brunt for that with taxes, and the brunt for the welfare class. It lands here' (181 F 1994).

This socioeconomic status model of class tended to obliterate any appreciation of ruling class exploitation. The soaring profits made by shareholders and the high salaries of senior management were either shrugged off as inevitable or subject to moral condemnation. The discourses that deny class exploitation leave people few resources for a critical perspective on class inequalities or conflict. In fact, in the 1984 survey, it did not occur to two-thirds of Stelco workers and even more of their partners to identify class conflict as an important form of group conflict in Canadian society. A critical class analysis of ruling-class wealth as an extraction of surplus labour from the working class was rarely offered.

While they remained critical of elites, in the absence of a clear discourse about class struggle, the people we interviewed became increasingly preoccupied with threats from below, often arguing that movements of the oppressed were 'going too far.' In face of dwindling jobs and reduced social programs, many of them perceived feminist and

anti-racist challenges as threatening. In this context, support for principles of social equity, still upheld in the abstract, became increasingly difficult to reconcile with maintaining personal security (Seccombe and
Livingstone 1996). Against progressive arguments for collective social
responsibility and entitlement, and for a more equitable redistribution
of social wealth, some accepted a market rationale where everyone com-
petes as an individual for scarce resources. Others, based on their experience, remained ambivalent.

In such ways, economic restructuring pitted subordinated peoples
against each other. Employed people became increasingly aware of the
threat posed by those who, because they were under- or unemployed,
were forced to accept lower-paying, less-secure jobs. Since visible minorities and immigrants were more likely to be part of the reserve army of
labour than white workers, economic insecurity easily fed the long history of racism. As hard times persisted, many steelworkers and their
partners, like many others in Canada, became increasingly likely to perceive challenges to their established rights and identities in terms of the
behaviours of visible minorities, implying that the minorities posed serious threats to established Canadian cultural traditions and arguing that
racial and ethnic conflicts were the most important social problems.[5]

One man expressed concerns about what he considered to be reverse
job discrimination against his son and his friends. Although he
expressed shock at the strength of their racist views, he accepted their
sense that the problem was not a lack of jobs but that they could not get
jobs because others got special priorities: 'My son and a lot of his friends
have very red-neck tendencies. These kids are well educated, but there's
a bitterness. You know, a fellow is working at a pizza place and can't get
another job because somebody has quotas they have to have. When they
are all here and a lot of his friends say things, it's frightening. But it's a
way they perceive things because they go out looking for jobs and there
are a lot of doors closed that are open to other people' (075 M 1994).

While he tried to distance himself from their 'frightening' views, he
also distinguished between 'my country' and 'other people' and insisted
that immigrants adapt to what they find in Canada without making any
demands: 'If you come to my country, you are more than welcome to
become part of my country. Don't come to my country and set down
rules that say I came here but I will still have this and this and this legis-
lated as being my right because I brought it here from another country.
I don't know if I am right or wrong. It's my answer. I think we're probably going to see more ethnic conflict in the next while' (075 M 1994).

The tendency to attribute blame for ethnic or racial conflict to those who protest against it was widespread and readily led 'white Canadians' to call for tighter immigration controls and an end to anti-racist initiatives:

> When I hear 'social groups' it kind of segregates into a racial thing. And I guess that's been a lot worse in the last ten years than better, unfortunately. I think they should be a little more selective in who they're letting into the country. That plays a major part in a lot of social issues that the average person has to deal with – you know, crime and even preferential hiring. So, what's a white Canadian going to do? If they're segregating right now for government jobs, I don't know. It's pretty scary. (047 M 1994)

Another steelworker agreed that there was increased racial and ethnic conflict: 'It's sad, but I guess you'd have to say there's lots of racial conflict. The French in Canada has been going on for years. I feel so sorry for the Pakistanis, and I don't know what they did to anybody, but everybody seems to hate the poor things. It amazes me that people are still that prejudiced against the Jewish people. It's phenomenal. So I would still say the Jews have a hard haul of it, like the Pakistanis or the Indians [South Asians]' (002 M 1994). He expressed his fear that to leave racism unchallenged invites its growth: 'I can handle the downright racists because I can confront them and say, "Why? What have they done? Let's talk about this." It's the people that don't care that get me. It's just sort of a non-caring, and those people scare me because those are the ones that would, if something like [German Fascism] ever happened again, they would fall right in and go along with it' (002 M 1994).

Certainly, over the decade, what this man called 'non-caring' increased. As people became increasingly concerned about their own security and about the loss of their own traditional prerogatives in the labour market, they became less empathetic to recent immigrants and visible minorities, and more hostile to the efforts of political movements to redress existing inequalities: 'I think the women's movement has gotten totally out of hand. When [the government] says you have to have *x* number of women, *x* number of men, why? It should be everybody that is a hundred per cent qualified' (075 F 1994).

Although affirmative action measures, such as the 1993 Ontario Employment Equity legislation, were designed explicitly to ensure that people were hired based on their ability and qualifications for the job, and not just because they were white, able-bodied men, there was widespread resistance to them.[6] While some opposed such measures from a neo-conservative position that white, able-bodied men deserved special privileges, most opposition was grounded in deeply held ideologies of liberal individualism. For people who strongly believed that they deserved their jobs, and had acquired them on their own merit, acknowledging the need for affirmative action measures was difficult.

Prevailing ideologies maintain that Canada is a democratic society where people who work hard can succeed on their own merit. To recognize systemic discrimination was to admit that jobs had been available to them in part because others – such as women, Aboriginals, people of colour, gays and lesbians, and people with disabilities – had been denied jobs for reasons unrelated to their ability or qualifications. Against the claims of activists in Aboriginal, anti-racist, gay, disability, and women's movements, race- and gender-neutral discourses articulated liberal individualism by insisting that everyone should be treated the same: 'It's the way I look at people. I don't look at men or women, I look at people' (029 M 1994).

Discourses opposing affirmative action measures mobilized both the difficulties people had in acknowledging their comparative privileges and gender-neutral discourses to generate hostility to affirmative action; they succeeded in turning its claims upside down. By claiming that affirmative action measures forced employers to fill quotas with people from designated groups rather than hiring people based on their qualifications, these discourses opposing affirmative action dubbed it 'reverse discrimination.' Despite the fact that Canadian initiatives did not have quotas, and despite the fact that systemic discrimination meant people in the designated groups were repeatedly denied jobs despite their qualifications, these discourses found quick reception among large segments of the population. A steelworker who actively had supported women at Stelco in the early 1980s articulated this position: 'To me, if you are capable of doing the job, it's yours. I don't like the idea of this quota hiring of women. I'm against that. No I don't agree with quota hiring. I feel it should be on their merit, their knowledge' (029 M 1994).

The Ontario Conservative party capitalized on these concerns in the 1995 election, and shortly after forming the government, it passed Bill 8 to eliminate 'job quotas' and restore 'merit based employment practices' (Noce and O'Connell 1998: 14).

Reflecting anxieties and insecurities about the loss of prerogatives enjoyed by white, male, 'mainstream' Canadians, one woman was hostile to affirmative action initiatives both for women ('Why should she get the job because she is a woman?') and for racialized people of colour:

'Somewhere, somebody has to start standing up for the non-minority. We're becoming extinct. We have no rights anymore. Like look at my son, he couldn't get a job if he tried in the police force. It's no longer your ability, your education, or whatever. It's your colour and that's not right' (075 F 1994). Implicit in her complaints was an assumption that affirmative action and employment equity policies, rather than attempting to redress the inequalities of racism and sexism, were partially responsible for the difficulties young white men were experiencing in looking for employment. Worried about her underemployed son and his friends, she claimed recent immigrants were taking jobs away from Canadians: 'The people that are getting jobs haven't been held back. They're barely off the boat. They haven't been discriminated against. Half of them haven't earned the right to get a job' (075 F 1994).

Nevertheless, this woman recognized the racism of her position: 'I don't know. Maybe that's racist.' Her avowed commitment to equality ('Everybody should be equal and that means everybody'), and her recognition of the impact of racism ('There was discrimination against the minority, always has been, and that's not right'), left her ambivalent about solutions: 'It's a delicate issue, and I understand their side, too, you know.' She concluded by linking hostility to women's employment and racism to high rates of unemployment: 'If there wasn't the unemployment, you wouldn't have the anger. You wouldn't have the problem' (075 F 1994). Her insight that if there were jobs for all, sexism and racism would be undermined is an important one. Implicit in it is an understanding that competition among working people divides them, pitting different groups against each other. However, she had no sense of how to fight for greater economic security for all.

A former Women Back Into Stelco activist articulated a different worldview, but a similar lack of clarity about what to do. Informed by anti-racist, socialist, feminist politics, she identified capitalist exploitation in combination with sexism, racism, homophobia, and other systems of discrimination as the source of the problem. She described the way capitalists make profits at the expense of working people: 'Capitalists – the people who own the wealth – they make their profits by ripping workers off. On the job, they pay as little as they can and make a big profit for themselves off the work workers do. They sell stuff we need for way more than it costs them to make it, and they pocket that profit, too. Then they create all this desire for other stuff we don't really need to get us to buy even more so they make even bigger profits' (223 F 1996). She argued that business elites exercised political power to support their special interests: 'Because they control the government, they make sure taxes and trade deals, and all that benefits them, not the majority of Canadians. That's class society – the elites own so much they have the power to just keep making more money off of the rest of us' (223 F 1996).

She explained how class is linked to other forms of oppression: 'Class is part of it. But there is also sexism, racism, homophobia – lots of different systems of discrimination and inequality, and they are all interrelated and tied up together. So a Black upper-class woman probably just isn't as powerful as a white upper-class guy but they are both more powerful than any working-class person of any variety. And if she's a lesbian, well, if she's rich she can probably buy privacy and not get hassled, but ...' (223 F 1996). She understood that when people come together collectively they have more power to challenge the systems of inequality: 'Alone, people can't do much. We have to organize together, like in unions, the women's movement, the gay and lesbian movement, and all those movements united. You know, if we had a general strike in the country – if every worker refused to work, we could bring down the government' (223 F 1996).

This woman recognized that there was little support for such initiatives: 'People aren't up for that at this time.' But she did have a sense of what might foster a greater willingness to fight back collectively: 'I don't know what to do right now, how to get people demanding their rights, but I do know two things; the position we take on every issue has to take account of the most oppressed and improve things for them or we will continue to be divided, and if we fight for things that make life better for most people, it will be harder for them to take it away' (223 F 1996).

It was a period when doing nothing was supporting the changes, where not resisting was to give legitimacy to those who advocated the new neo-liberal social, political, and economic organization of life in Canada. Yet, the lack of obvious alternatives made resistance or fighting back difficult. A participant in the Day of Action captured the complexities involved. He noted that the demonstration sent a warning to the ruling powers: 'There were a hundred and twenty thousand of us, or more. That's a lot of people in a country where people don't usually protest! We sent a loud message to the government here in Ontario and to the federal government, and to big business with its super profits. It's a warning that we won't put up with these attacks on working people's lives' (306 M 1996). More importantly, it strengthened working people's solidarity and made public the depth of anger and frustration many people felt: 'It was terrific being in such a crowd, from all over, steel-

workers, teachers, auto workers, government workers, my neighbours ...
It reminded me that I'm not alone, there's lots of folks who feel like me.
And so many people at one demo – it made it easier for people who
don't usually protest in public to see that it's okay. When so many are
pissed off, we have to do something' (306 M 1996).

The dilemmas expressed by these speakers capture the political climate of the mid-1990s, in Hamilton, in Canada, and elsewhere.[7] As Judy
Darcy, president of the Canadian Union of Public Employees, the largest public sector union in the country, put it (1995: 236–7): 'Large numbers of workers in both the private and public sectors don't see
themselves as part of the working class and are unsure where their
interests lie. We are divided – between younger and older, part-time and
full-time, employed and jobless, public and private, activists and non-
activists, those who see the struggle for equality as the struggle for fair-
ness for all workers, and those who don't see it as their struggle. We are
all anxious about the future and many of us feel that we've lost control
of our lives.'

Five years later, Darcy was more optimistic.[8] 'I think there is an incred-
ible resurgence of working people, especially in the labour movement.
After years of cutbacks, people are saying "We aren't going to put up
with it any more." And they are organizing resistance and fighting back.'

Writing about such end-of-the-century politics in Britain and the
United States, Sheila Rowbotham argues (1997: 576): 'The political and
social responses of women and men to these dilemmas of the late twentieth century will have a crucial effect on the shape of life in the twenty-
first century. There could be a new impetus for rethinking work, time,
the social forms of technology, the utilization and distribution of
resources and power, the role of the state, the bringing up and educating of children – or the feeding of an anger that lashes out at scape-
goats. As the twentieth century draws to a close, there are signs of both.'

Conclusion

We suggest that, while the political dilemmas identified by Rowbotham
may be more or less sharply posed in different periods, they reflect fundamental conflicts inherent in any society where capitalist economic
relations predominate. This case study, of a particular group of people
living through a specific historic period, illustrates the way class, race,
and gender inequality and conflict are at the heart of capitalist economics. Capitalists employers individually, and collectively as the business

sector, strive to keep their labour costs low enough to ensure profits. Workers, whose livelihoods depend on wages, strive to secure as high a standard of living as possible.[9]

The conflict between employers trying to reduce labour costs and workers struggling to ensure their livelihoods means that social reproduction is in conflict with the process of capital accumulation and profit maximization. At stake is the way the costs of social reproduction are met. There are various ways of doing so; each generates different types of conflict and accommodation. Higher productivity – widespread between 1946 and 1980 – keeps the costs of mass consumer goods relatively low, allowing workers relatively comfortable standards of living, while ensuring profit-making. State provision of services and transfer payments – the welfare state – paid for by tax-generated general revenues, subsidizes the costs of individual social reproduction, creating a minimum standard of living for the majority and reducing workers' demands for pay increases.

The development of a widespread, but lower-paid service sector, whether public or private, also subsidizes the labour costs of other sectors. Reducing standards of living and creating a climate of insecurity, as happened in the period between 1980 and 1996, also serve to reduce the likelihood of workers' demands for higher wages. Finally, the costs of social reproduction are reduced for the business sector to the extent that families and households absorb them and bear the costs themselves. Conversely, the more working people are able to insist on collective responsibility for social reproduction, funded by personal and corporate taxes, the higher their standards of living and the less profit individual capitalists can appropriate for themselves.

Because social reproduction is in conflict with processes of capital accumulation, the outcomes of these conflicts, or class struggles, determine the particular standards of living available. Pivotal is the degree to which working people bear the costs themselves. These fundamental conflicts shape daily life for the majority who depend for their livelihood on the combination of paid employment and domestic labour. Expressed discursively as the problem of balancing work and family, the conflicts are, at one level, problems of scheduling, of arranging alternative care for dependents, of the fatigue of the double day. However, the conflicting demands of work and family are more than that. At a deeper level, working-class households embody the contradictions between the process of producing and sustaining people and the process of maximizing profit.

These conflicts are also entangled with, and get played out through, gender relations. Gender divisions in both the paid labour force and the household, typically, reinforce each other to the detriment of women. Households based on a conjugal contract establish arrangements for individual and family livelihoods based on sex/gender and age-based divisions of labour which, typically, reproduce gender inequalities. Even when both people in a female-male couple aspire to equality in their relationship, gender divisions of labour are not gender-neutral. There are intrinsic differences which develop as learned practices and are internalized as femininity or masculinity. These are reproduced and reinforced by extrinsic differences such as access to jobs, pay rates, child care supports, and discourses about women and caregiving. As a result, it is hard for individuals to renegotiate divisions of labour in their own households.

In the paid labour force, women continue to be restricted to certain sectors of the labour force, and certain occupations within those sectors. Within those jobs, women are typically lower paid, have poorer working conditions, are defined as less skilled, and are rarely in positions of authority. At the same time, most women also work in unpaid household-based activities and often have access to fewer resources than the men they live with. As a result, most women work longer hours than men do to attain a lower standard of living than men have. The subordination of women played out through sex/gender divisions of labour puts them at the centre of these struggles.

When the family household bears the main responsibility for producing and sustaining daily life, the dynamics of paid employment and domestic labour easily orient people towards their own families and undermine their capacity to build and sustain strong friendship networks and community organizations and to organize collectively such as in protest movements. The weakness of those extra-familial ties and their inability to ensure support reinforces an orientation to the family. In this way, as Barrett and McIntosh have argued, the family is anti-social: 'The family sucks the juices out of everything around it, leaving other institutions stunted and distorted (1982: 78).

The more working people are able to establish collective responsibilities for social reproduction, the stronger collective or community ties become, linking specific family ties to larger community networks. The stronger those ties, the easier it is to fight for a wide range of changes that foster greater equality. What happened to people working in the 1980s and 1990s in Hamilton, shows how easily secure livelihoods can be disrupted and how important collective efforts are for getting by.

Appendix A:

Data Collection Strategies

The data for this book come from four surveys, five different sets of open-ended, in-depth interviews, and one time budget study.

The Surveys

Survey 1: The 1983–1984 Survey of Steelworkers and their Partners

From the December 1982 membership list of United Steelworkers of America Local 1005 we drew a stratified random sample of steelworkers. We specified that we were only interested in interviewing steelworkers who:

1 Were members of Local 1005 employed by Stelco at Hilton Works at the time of the 1981 strike, and who were either still employed at Hilton Works at the time of the interviews or were laid off but prepared to work there if recalled (at the time we did the interviews, eight steelworkers were on lay-off from Hilton Works); and
2 Were living with a spouse or partner who also agreed to be interviewed, or with a child under sixteen years of age; and
3 Were living in the Census Metropolitan Area (CMA) of Hamilton, which included the following townships adjoining the City of Hamilton: Grimsby, Stoney Creek, Glanbrook, Ancaster, Flamborough, Dundas, and Burlington. This geographic demarcation excluded less than 10 per cent of the 1005 list and meant the population of our study was directly comparable with the population of Hamilton CMA.

The Local 1005 membership list was divided into three groups: (1) union executive officers, (2) stewards and other activists holding non-executive posts in the local, (3) and regular members. We excluded the executive and randomly sampled the others, oversampling to include more stewards and activists (43 stewards and 153 regulars). We interviewed 196 steelworkers (2 women and 194 men); 187 with a partner (2 men and 185 women) and 9 men who were single parents. All survey results are weighted to reflect the stratified sampling procedure, unless otherwise stated.

The survey was administered by Social Data Research of Hamilton in face-to-face interviews between October 1983 and February 1984. People in couples were interviewed separately. The interview included about 200 questions on: biography, work history, household composition, domestic labour, household economics, and the respondents' social networks, community involvement, and social attitudes.

Survey 2: The 1984 Survey of Unemployed Steelworkers

From the Local 1005 list of laid-off steelworkers in the summer of 1984, we drew a random sample of 234 (222 men and 12 women). The interviews were conducted thirty months after the first wave of lay-offs and included people who were laid off during the first eight months of 1982. This survey was conducted by telephone and people were asked about: their lay-offs, their subsequent unemployment, recalls, and job searches; their household and family coping strategies; the impact of unemployment on household economics, domestic divisions of labour, and social activities.

Survey 3: The 1984 Survey of Unemployed Steelworkers and their Partners

Fifteen laid-off steelworkers who participated in Survey 2, the 1984 survey of unemployed steelworkers, and their partners, agreed to be interviewed using the same interview schedule employed in Survey 1, the 1983–4 survey of steelworkers and their partners. These interviews enabled us to make some comparisons between those steelworkers who were still employed and those who had been laid off.

Survey 4: The 1984–1985 Hamilton Work and Family Study

Between November 1984 and February 1985 we interviewed one person from each of 798 households. These households, with two cohabiting adults between the ages of 18 and 65, were randomly selected from within the greater Hamilton Census Metropolitan Area. The York University Institute for Social Research conducted interviews with 393 men and 405 women using an adapted version of the questionnaire used in Survey 1. The 1983–4 Survey of Steelworkers and their Partners that included about 100 questions.

The Open-Ended, In-Depth Interviews

In-Depth Interviews 1: The 1984 In-Depth Interviews with Male Steelworkers and their Partners

From the people who participated in Survey 1, the 1983–4 steelworkers and their partners survey, we selected 44 individuals, based on their responses to the first survey, and did face-to-face, open-ended, in-depth interviews with each of them. We selected people whose responses indicated their different positions on a range of topics including: location at Hilton Works, women's employment status, household composition and family phase, division of domestic labour, union involvement, and social attitudes. These interviews were taped and transcribed. Quotes from these interviews are identified in this book by an identification number between 001 and 199, M (male) or F (female), and the year of the interview.

In-Depth Interviews 2: The 1984 In-Depth Interviews with Women Steelworkers

In 1984 we interviewed five women involved in initiating the Women Back Into Stelco campaign and twenty-one women who at the time were or had been steelworkers at Hilton Works. In open-ended, in-depth, face-to-face interviews, they were asked about the campaign to hire women and their experiences as steelworkers. Respondents were located using a snowball technique. Quotes from these interviews are identified by an identification number between 201 and 226, F (female), and the year of the interview.

In-Depth Interviews 3: The 1994–1996 Follow-Up Interviews

In 1994 Dr Belinda Leach conducted interviews with individuals who had originally been interviewed in Survey 1, some of whom had also been interviewed in In-Depth Interviews 1 (the 1984 in-depth interviews with male steelworkers and their partners) (Leach 1997). Members of the project team also interviewed some of these individuals for a total of thirty interviews. In addition, we re-interviewed six of the women steelworkers. These interviews asked people about changes in their work status, household composition, and family phase; the impact of Stelco lay-offs, and a variety of social issues. Quotes from these interviews are identified by the original 1984 identification number, M (male) or F (female), and the year of the interview.

In-Depth Interviews 4: The 1989 Middle-Class Wives Study

In 1989 Elizabeth Asner interviewed fourteen women who had previously been interviewed in Survey 4, the 1984–5 Hamilton work and family study. She selected middle-class married women and interviewed them about their employment choices (Asner 1993). Quotes from this study are indicated by reference to Asner 1993.

In-Depth Interviews 5

Throughout the period of the study a few individual steelworkers, and a few woman living with steelworkers, discussed our work with us, and commented on our study and their assessment of what was happening in the steel industry, at Hilton Works, in Local 1005, and in the Hamilton community. Interviews from these people are identified by an identification number between 301 and 310, M (male) or F (female), and the year of the interview.

The 1984 Time Budget Study

The forty-four individuals who participated in the first round of open-ended, in-depth interviews were asked to complete time budget schedules; forty did so. Their spouses were also asked to complete them; twenty-three did so. They were asked to fill out a form covering twenty-four hours divided into fifteen-minute sections, indicating what activities they were doing, when the activities began and ended, who was with them, and when they expected to do those activities again.

Appendix B:

Hilton Works

Stelco Inc. is the largest steel producer in Canada. In 1998 Stelco owned four steel-producing units: Hilton Works in Hamilton, Lake Erie Steel Company Ltd. in Nanticoke, Ontario, Stelco-McMaster Ltée. in Contrecoeur, Quebec, and AltaSteel Ltd. in Edmonton, Alberta. It also owned a number of steel-fabricating businesses. Hilton Works continues to be Stelco's largest operation.

Hilton Works is an integrated steelmaking and processing complex situated on 1,110 acres in Hamilton, Ontario. Hilton Works' docks and its access to the harbour, provide a direct link with the Great Lakes–St Lawrence Seaway system and major raw materials sources in Canada and the United States. As a major supplier of steel products to the North American marketplace, this business unit has earned top quality awards from General Motors and the Chrysler Corporation (including the Gold Pentastar Award), as well as environmental honours from the government and other agencies. All of Hilton Works' rolling mills are ISO 9002 certified.

Components and Facilities

Steelmaking

Primary production facilities include coke oven batteries, a pulverized coal injection facility, two blast furnaces (54,004 and 64,707 cubic feet working volume), a three-vessel basic oxygen furnace shop (160-ton furnaces), and a ladle metallurgy / continuous casting complex (one slab caster and one combination slab/bloom caster). Semifinished steelmaking capacity is approximately 2,700,000 tons per year.

Plate and Strip Business

Steel for flat rolled products is hot-processed through a 148-inch plate mill or a 56-inch coilbox-equipped hot strip mill. Steel from the hot strip mill destined for the cold mill is pickled on one of three pickle lines. The plate mill and strip mill both fly General Motors' Mark of Excellence Award flags in recognition of the outstanding performance of the two mills in the areas of quality, cost, leadership, delivery, and technology.

Cold Rolled and Coated Business

Cold finishing facilities at the Hilton Works business unit include an 80-inch, 4-stand, 4-high tandem mill, and a 56-inch, 5-stand, 4-high tandem mill. Two batch annealing facilities and two continuous annealing lines precede three temper mills. Coating facilities include three hot-dip galvanizing lines and two electrolytic tinning lines. A General Motors' Mark of Excellence Award has also been presented to this unit. Hilton Works provides management and operations services to the joint venture Z-Line Company, one of North America's premier facilities for zinc-coated sheet steel for automotive products.

Rod and Bar Business

Long products are processed through a bloom and billet mill and then either through the world-class bar mill or the rod mill.

Products and Services

Hilton Works manufactures an extensive range of products, shipping approximately 3,000,000 tons annually. These steel products include plate, hot and cold rolled sheet, galvanized sheet, rods, and bars.

Markets and Sales

Hilton Works' products are sold in a variety of markets, with major penetration in the automotive, steel service centre, construction, pipe and tube, and wire and wire products sectors.

Source: http://www.stelco.com/profile 6/28/98.

Notes

1: A World Turned Upside Down

1 The Hamilton protest was one of a series of 'Days of Action' demonstrations organized by labour unions and community groups to protest the harsh policies of the Conservative government led by Premier Mike Harris. The march included a group of retired steelworkers who, fifty years before, had been part of a long and bitter strike against Stelco for union recognition and a first contract. They followed the same route taken by workers in 1872 during a fight for the nine-hour day (McLeod 1999: 4).

2 For newspaper accounts of this event see Pietropaolo (1999).

3 The information in brackets following quotes from people we interviewed for this book include an ID number, an M (male) or F (female) and the year of the interview, 1984, 1994, or 1996.

4 Neo-liberal economic policies, implemented first in the early 1980s in Britain by the Thatcher government and in the United States by the Reagan government, have come to dominate economic policies of most states and leading international economic organizations such as the World Bank and the International Monetary Fund. The main policy of neo-liberalism is to reduce government intervention in the profit-making initiatives of capitalist investment by reducing state economic regulation (such as environmental protection or health and safety legislation), encouraging increased international trade, and reducing state spending, particularly on social services. For a discussion of neo-liberal policies in Canada, see Brodie (1996).

5 Marxist feminists have argued that women serve as part of the reserve army of labour, that is, as capitalist larbour markets expand and contract, women can be drawn into the labour force or expelled, leaving or returning to the household (Connelly 1978). More recently, feminists have also argued that women

act as a reserve army of unpaid labour, expanding or contracting their domestic labour depending on what extra-household services are available.

6 We thank Anne Molgat for pointing this out.

7 City of Hamilton (1980: 5).

8 Stelco was formed as an integrated steel company by a merger with a number of plants in Hamilton and Toronto (Kilbourn 1960). Dofasco was founded in Hamilton in 1912 but remained a small, locally owned specialized manufacturer reliant on purchased iron and scrap until after 1945. Stelco stressed the application of proven technologies, including oxygen lancing and self-fluxing sinter for blast furnaces, which served to prolong the competitive life of its open hearth mills into the 1960s. In contrast, Dofasco was the North American pioneer in implementing the more efficient basic oxygen furnace vessel technology in 1954; it has generally been more daring in its use of new technology and has become an integrated producer with a wide array of products (Livingstone 1996).

9 For information on the depression of the 1930s, in Hamilton, see Archibald (1992, 1996, 1998).

10 Norflicks Productions has produced a video about the 1946 strike called *Defying the Law* (1997).

11 For a discussion of this capital–labour accord, see Guest (1980).

12 Stelco, Dofasco, and Algoma ranked among the largest 100 steel companies in the world, led by Stelco, which was ranked fortieth in 1995. Data cited here are drawn from International Iron and Steel Institute (1995 and prior years), and Ministry of State, Science and Technology (1988). For accounts of the development of the Hamilton steel companies, see Kilbourn (1960), J. Weaver (1982), and Storey (1993). For postwar production share data, see Woods, Gordon and Co. (1977).

13 Henry (1965) documents the presence of Japanese and 'negroes' living in Hamilton during the 1950s. Half the Black population had been born in Hamilton; very few had jobs in heavy industry.

14 Neither Stelco nor Dofasco make public records of the sex, racial, or ethnic composition of their workforces, so it is not possible to determine the exact figures. Stelco's sexist discrimination was demonstrated at law by the 1980 human rights ruling, but racist or ethnic discrimination has never been legally demonstrated.

15 The term 'green-field' refers to farmlands outside cities where companies (re)locate.

16 Other new technologies such as developments in direct reduction systems and ladle technology, thin slab casting, and mini-hot strip mills also facilitated the production of superior quality steels in low volumes at lower costs.

17 Canada is the seventh largest steel producer among the advanced capitalist countries (behind Japan, the United States, Germany, Italy, France, and the United Kindom, respectively).

18 T.E. Dancy, vice-president, Sidbec-Dosco Inc., as cited in H.E. Chandler (April 1985: 55).

19 Figures are from Stelco Steel Turnover Report, 6 Oct. 1989, and Dofasco 1989 Annual Report.

20 Http://hamilton.london.hrdc-drhc.gc.ca/english/lmi/profile/compro/comprof.html (13 Feb. 1998).

21 See *Globe and Mail Report on Business,* July 1998: 87–8.

22 *Toronto Star,* 2 April 1998: D3, reported that 'Stelco Inc. Chief James Alfano's pay jumped 64 percent to almost $1 million last year.' *Globe and Mail Report on Business Magazine,* July 1998: 84, 88 listed James Alfano as ranking forty-ninth of the fifty best paid CEOs earning a 254 per cent increase over his 1996 salary, for a 1997 total of salary, and bonus of $2,125,477.

23 When discussing people who are easily identified, such as union executive members, women steelworkers, and racial minorities, we have changed some details to ensure confidentiality.

24 In the 1960s Stelco introduced a high school diploma as a requirement for employment.

25 The Revolutionary Workers' League / Ligue Ouvrière Révolutionarie was the Canadian branch of the Fourth International. For its political position supporting radical women's work in industry, see Revolutionary Workers' League (1979). For a review of the political analysis typical of the Fourth International, see Mandel (1977).

26 The feminist movement comprises a variety of political currents, including those concerned about liberal equal rights, those concerned about women in racialized ethnic and national groups, and radicals and socialists fighting for women's liberation (Rowbotham 1992). The current with the greatest awareness of class oppression was the women's liberation movement, which linked the fight against all forms of inequality with sexual liberation and personal self-determination. Slogans and banners of this current stressed that the liberation of women depends on the liberation of all.

27 For a discussion of gender, race, ethnicity, and class in settler societies see Stasiulis and Yuval-Davis (1995).

28 This heritage is itself stratified by class, ethnicity, and gender.

29 In his analysis of the relationship between capitalists and workers, Karl Marx [1867](1976) distinguished between the activity of work – labour – and the capacity to work – labour power. The sale and purchase of labour power does not imply the transfer of ownership of the worker to the capital-

ist, but of the opportunity for the capitalist to use the worker with his or her consent.

30 While this study focuses on households dependent on wage labour, it is not the only form of income generation available. Farming- and fishing-dependent households, for example, generate income by either growing or hunting produce that can be sold (see Binkley n.d.).

31 Picchio argues that housework produces people, rather than their labour power, as commodities. We disagree, assuming with Marx [1867] (1976) that one of the defining characteristics of capitalist economies is that the labouring population is free (not slaves) but, lacking any other way to make a living, must sell their capacities to labour for wages. Employers do not own their workers; they only have the right to command their labour for the duration of the work contract.

32 The concept of discourse was developed by Michel Foucault, who argued that discourses involve the production of meaning or the processes that make the knowledge or 'truth' that orders the social world, that make possible what can be spoken about and how people speak. Discourses, he argued (1974): 'can be seen as sets of "deep principles" incorporating specific "grids of meanings" which underpin, generate and establish relations between all that can be seen, thought and said' (cited in Shilling 1993: 75). We acknowledge and appreciate our conversations with Gail McCabe which helped us clarify our thinking on discourses.

33 Terry Eagleton reviews the multiple ways that ideology has been defined, arguing that one main definition of ideology is that it signifies: 'the ideas and beliefs which help to legitimate the interests of a ruling group or class' (1991: 30). We have followed this definition in this book. We thank Heather Jon Maroney for her help in clarifying our thinking on discourses and ideologies.

34 For a discussion of Huron society, see Karen Anderson (1991).

35 The term 'sex' has typically referred to physiological characteristics that are used to distinguish two main groups: female and male. The term 'gender' is used to refer to the socially constructed, culturally specific characteristics of femininity and masculinity. We use the term sex/gender following Rubin's definition (1975: 159): 'the set of arrangements by which a society transforms biological sexuality into products of human activity.'

2: Families at Work

1 Religious-based intentional communities such as the Doukhobors, Hutterites, and Mennonites are the best-known examples of such communities that have survived into the present in significant numbers. There were also some

socialist communes in the early 1910s and 1920s that settled on Vancouver Island and in other remote parts of the country.

2 The Canadian census does not collect data on lesbians or gay men, so there is no accurate record of how many same-sex families there are or how many children are living with same-sex parents.

3 In 1996, 89 per cent of spousal assaults reported to police were attacks by men on women (Statistics Canada, 1996b). In 1996, 20 per cent of physical assaults and 32 per cent of sexual assaults against children under 18 years were by family members. Of these, fathers were responsible for 73 per cent of physical and 98 per cent of sex assaults (Statistics Canada, 1996b).

4 Assuming women are adults at eighteen and that active parenting continues until the child is eighteen years, women who had their first child at eighteen and had four children about two years apart completed active parenting by forty-four years of age. Assuming a life expectancy of seventy such women were active parents for 50 per cent of their adult lives. In contrast, a woman who had her only child at twenty-four, stopped active parenting at forty-two, and lived to be seventy-five would spend about 30 per cent of her adult life in active parenting.

5 For example, immigration through the family category is tightly restricted to a definition of the family that includes spouse, dependent children, and parents (Hathaway 1994a).

6 In some municipalities, bylaws prohibit more than three unrelated people living together. Typical house construction is designed on the assumption that the inhabitants will be an adult couple and their children. Hospital rules may limit visitors to the very ill to 'immediate family,' automatically including an opposite-sexed lover but excluding a same-sex lover: including kin who may not be the primary support for the patient, while excluding friends who may be. Since the nineteenth century, and continuing to the present, groups that have attempted to live communally have faced systematic opposition from neighbours, social welfare, and law-enforcing agencies.

7 In the past thirty years gay and lesbian organizations and individuals have fought hard to win legal protections and have increasingly made important gains (see Arnup 1995, 1997; Gavigan 1997).

8 This notion of the breadwinner husband/father and the economically dependent housewife/mother is a component of a larger ideology of 'familialism,' which includes concepts of appropriate femininity and masculinity, of compulsory heterosexuality, and of a sex/gender division of labour. See Barrett and McIntosh (1982).

9 The term 'breadwinner' has been widely used to imply the person, usually the man, whose earnings provide the mainstay of the household. It is a

culturally specific term which assumes that the staple food is bread, so we have used the more neutral term, income earner.

10 See Dunk (1991) for a discussion of consciousness and culture among working-class men in Northern Ontario.

11 For a discussion of the situation of nannies, see Arat-Koc (1990) and Bakan and Stasiulis (1997).

12 For a discussion of African Canadian women's history, see Brand (1983) and Bristow et al., (1994).

13 As the domestic division of labour became increasingly conflicted, it became a subject for research. In the late 1960s and through the 1970s sociologists and home economists, particularly those informed by feminist research questions, conducted a variety of studies in Canada and Quebec, the United States, and Britain. These include sample surveys: for the United States: J. Robinson (1977) a national survey conducted in 1965–6; M. Geerken and W.R. Gove (1983), forty-eight contiguous states, 1974–5; S.F. Berk (1985), a national survey of cities over 50,000, 1976; J. Huber and G. Spitze (1983), national telephone survey, 1978; for Canada: M. Meissner et al. (1975) in Vancouver, 1971; William Michelson (1985); Szalai (1972) compared time use in twelve countries, not including Canada. They also include in-depth interviews of small numbers of informants – for Britain: H. Gavron (1966); A. Oakley (1974); P. Hunt (1980); for Canada: M. Luxton (1980, 1983); P. Kome (1982); for the United States: M. Komarovsky (1962); H. Lopata (1971); L. Rubin (1977, 1994).

14 There are literally thousands of such studies. None of them has satisfactorily addressed a fundamental question about how to assess these topics. What measures indicate whether or not a woman's employment has a negative impact on her child? The typical measures used – the child's success at school or relating to peers – are themselves difficult to assess and may not be appropriate measures at all. The typical measure of marital satisfaction assumes that it is always best for a couple to remain together and attributes marital breakdown (a bad thing) to women's employment. Yet the end of a marriage may not be a bad thing, and couples who remain married may not flourish. There is also evidence to show that women whose marriages end describe themselves as much better off, even when they are considerably poorer financially (Graham 1987).

15 The neo-conservative politics that developed during the 1980s share with neo-liberal policies a commitment to economic deregulation, but in addition have a relatively coherent social programme based on what has been termed 'family values,' that is, a commitment to ensuring heterosexual nuclear families remain at the centre of social policy (Luxton 1997a).

16 In contrast, in 1997 Quebec introduced a comprehensive new family policy which offered child care to all preschool children at $5 a day (National Council of Welfare 1999: 39).

17 Neo-classical economists have traditionally interpreted this loss as the price the couple must pay for refusing to 'specialize' their labour contributions, an argument which simply naturalizes the market's unequal pay bias.

18 While this form of conjugal power is distinct to employees, it parallels men's control of profits and other forms of income among the propertied classes.

19 We are indebted to Wally Seccombe for his contributions to this section.

20 Employers who rely on women workers, especially those who have invested in training, are more willing than most to accede maternity and parental leaves and other 'family friendly' policies to accommodate workers' family responsibilities. For examples of such policies, see Ontario Women's Directorate (1990), de Wolff (1994), and Johnson (1995).

21 Contrast the dynamics of wage labour with farming where, during the era of pre-mechanized farming, there was an incentive to have lots of children to provide unpaid labour on the farm. Inheritance of land provided an inducement for adult children to care for elderly parents.

22 Claude Meillassoux (1979: 14) writes of France's minimum wage (s.m.i.c): 'The smicard is a celibate labourer in that he has neither wife nor children. He is an employee who labours without interruption for all the working hours of the year. That is, he never falls ill and he is never unemployed. And he dies at the age of retirement. He is really an ideal wage labourer for the employer. Under these conditions, of course, the hourly wage covers the minimum needs of the labourer. But which needs? Those of the daily reconstitution of labour-power and no more.'

23 The OECD is the Organization for Economic Co-operation and Development. It includes: Australia, Austria, Belgium, Canada, the Czech Republic, Denmark, Finland, France, Germany, Greece, Hungary, Iceland, Ireland, Italy, Japan, Luxembourg, Mexico, the Netherlands, New Zealand, Norway, Poland, Portugal, the Republic of Korea, the Slovak Republic, Spain, Sweden, Switzerland, Turkey, the United Kingdom, and the United States (www.oecd.org).

24 For a fuller discussion of the problems inherent in purchasing labour or services to provide domestic labour, see Luxton (2000).

25 As Marx put it, 'People [our translation] make their history, but they do not make it just as they please, they do not make it under circumstances chosen by themselves, but under circumstances directly encountered, given, and transmitted from the past' (1977:300). The German *Menschen* has conventionally been translated as 'men'; here we have used a gender-neutral term, 'people.'

3: Working for Stelco

1 For a discussion of working at Hilton Works see, Corman et al. (1993).
2 There are slight discrepancies between the numbers reported for 'plant totals' and 'total workers' for 1981, 1989, and 1996 in Tables 3.1, 3.2, and 4.1 because the data were collected in different months.
3 Local 1005 had a history of struggles between internal factions and during the mid-1980s went through a particularly difficult faction fight (Freeman 1982).
4 Adoption of a twelve-hour shift schedule was subject to approval by 70 per cent of the employees in designated departments (*Stelco-1005 Basic Agreement July 20* 1993: 243–56).
5 See Leslie and Butz (1998) for a discussion of similar issues in the auto industry.
6 This section extends the arguments made in Livingstone and Luxton (1989) and Luxton and Corman (1991).
7 The ID number for this man is incorrect to protect his identity.
8 See Sugiman (1994) for a discussion of the gender dynamics in the auto industry.
9 There were also women working in the cafeteria. They were subject to frequent verbal and physical harassment. Eventually management installed protective transparent barriers to protect them from having food thrown at them.
10 For an analysis that compares Canadian and U.S. experiences of feminist organizing in the United Steelworkers of America, see Fonow (1998).

4: Restructuring Hilton Works

1 Some of the material in the remainder of this chapter is revised from Corman et al. (1993) and Livingstone (1996).
2 There has been much celebration by workplace researchers of the merits of leaner production systems, especially the 'Japanese model,' which offers lifetime security to a committed core workforce (e.g., Womack et al. 1990). What is typically ignored is the underside of this labour system. Efficient production remains dependent on a contingent labour force available for occasional hire on non-routine jobs and for short-term regular hire during market upturns, that is, a highly flexible industrial reserve army of labour. The Japanese auto industry, for example, continues to rely on poorly paid temporary workers, notably in its various non-unionized supply industries (Cusumano 1985).

3 For comparative analyses of the operation of lay-off–recall systems in long-established unionized industries, see Berg (1981), esp. 153–86, 219–48.

4 See, for example, 'Contracting Out Committee,' *Steel Shots* Jan.–Feb. 1987: 8.

5 Interview with USWA Local 1005 officials, 3 Dec. 1984.

6 In 1985 concern over lay-offs prompted national trade union leaders to propose a new joint labour–management institution for the steel sector. With the federal government they established the Canadian Steel Trade and Employment Conference (CSTEC). CSTEC provided retraining to help laid-off workers find other work and 'upside retraining' to older, still-employed workers to ensure they could operate the increasingly capital-intensive computerized technology in the plants.

7 The 'Braverman debate' provoked by Braverman's (1974) work about labour process deskilling or upgrading has been plagued with numerous conceptual and empirical confusions. For critical overviews, see Spenner (1983: 824–37), Livingstone (1987: 1–30), and Wood (1989).

8 For a review of the relevant research and discussion of the dimensions of underemployment and economic alternatives to close the education-jobs gap, see Livingstone (1998b).

9 Documentation on the increasing awareness of underemployment among different occupational class groups in Ontario is presented in Livingstone (1996) and Livingstone et al. (1997).

10 For accounts of the development of Hilton's workplace culture, see Heron (1988), Heron and Storey (1986), Storey (1981a, 1987), and the union magazine's special issue on the fortieth anniversary of the 1946 strike and the associated regular issue on its current relevance in *Steel Shots,* July 1986.

11 For a detailed account, see Livingstone (1996).

12 For the most prominant case pursued by the Ontario Ministry of Labour, see Papp (1991: A10).

13 For a detailed account of these coercive tactics at Hilton Works during the 1980s, see Corman (1990: 85–109).

14 These shifts have been consistent with general trends in the international and Canadian steel industries (OECD 1987; Ahlburg et al. 1987; Warrian 1989).

15 Steel companies internationally have slowly recognized this need to regenerate their aging workforces (OECD 1987; Kleiman 1995).

5: Women's Work

1 In 1984 the hourly wage at Hilton Works for class 1, the lowest paid category, was $10.39 an hour, compared with the minimum wage in Ontario of $4.00.

By 1996 employed steelworkers at Hilton Works in class 1 made $18.00 an hour compared with the minimum wage of $6.85 in Ontario.

2 The two spheres of women's work have been identified as a 'double ghetto.' The concept of a double ghetto was presented by Pat Armstrong and Hugh Armstrong (1st ed., 1978). It refers to the sex segregation in both domestic labour, where women do most of the work, and in paid employment, where women are concentrated in a limited number of occupations.

3 See Statistics Canada, No 71-001 Labour Force, 1978 to 1983b.

4 In response to criticisms from women's groups that all government initiatives were directed to men, the federal department of Human Resources Development established a committee of government, labour, and business to study clerical workers in Metro Toronto (de Wolff 1998).

5 The random sample of Stelco workers generated two women; one had a male partner who also worked at Stelco. Apart from him, most of the other wives or partners of Stelco workers had no experience at Stelco or other heavy industrial workplaces.

6 For the purposes of our analysis we have adopted the Statistics Canada definitions: twenty-nine hours per week or less is considered part-time and thirty hours or more is considered full-time. A comparison of this designation of women's work status and their own shows the degree of similarity:

	Full-time homemaker	Employed part-time	Employed full-time
Statistics Canada	77 (42%)	56 (30%)	52 (28%)
Self-reporting	74 (41%)*	63 (34%)	45 (25%)

* Two women who identified themselves as currently unemployed and one who was on maternity leave are included in the full-time homemaker category.

7 Only 17 per cent of all the women interviewed had ever been in a supervisory position. At the time of the study, only 4 per cent were supervisors.

8 In 1983 29 per cent of Canadian women workers were unionized, and they constituted 35 per cent of all union members. Membership in a union makes a great difference for women in terms of job security, benefits, capacity for collective action, and wages. In 1985 the average hourly pay for unionized workers was $15.23 and for non-unionized workers $12.38. By 1992 31 per cent of women workers were unionized, and they comprised 41 per cent of all union members (Statistics Canada 1995a: 68; Luxton and Reiter 1997). In 1997, 26.6 per cent of women workers were union members, and women represented 45 per cent of all unionized workers. The average hourly pay for union employees was $18.57, and the average hourly

pay for non-union employees was $14.04 (Statistics Canada 1997c, cat no. 75-001-XPE, 45–51).

9 The woman who reported sixty-eight hours of paid employment each week looked after neighbourhood children in her home and also made and sold crafts.

10 The attractions of self-employment for women are more apparent than real. In 1995 the average annual income of self-employed women age fifteen years and over was $19,600 (Statistics Canada 1997b: 25), just 62 per cent of the average income of $31,506 of full-year, full-time women workers (Drolet 1999: 25).

11 Feminism has increasingly challenged this way of denying the social worth of domestic labour. Marilyn Waring documents the development of the international system of accounting which excludes so much of women's work from calculations of GNP (1988). In 1981 Statistics Canada estimated that housework equalled 36 per cent of GNP (Kingston 1991). In Canada, various women's groups have called for women's unpaid work to be included in the census. Court cases have begun to recognize the monetary worth of domestic labour; for example, in 1991 Vera Fobel was awarded $79,000 for 'the future loss of her housekeeping capacity' (Kingston 1991).

12 Nine per cent said they became a homemaker at some other event.

13 This held true for women of all ages.

14 Compiled from Statistics Canada, cat. no. 62–555, *Family Expenditure in Canada*, Table 7: Summary of Family Expenditures by Family Composition, Canada, 10 Provinces, 1982; Table 33: Detailed Average Expenditure by Region and Province, Canada, 10 Provinces, 1982; Table 34: Detailed Average Expenditures, by City, Canada, 1982; and Statistics Canada Catalogue 62-010, *Consumer Prices and Price Indexes October–December 1983a*, Table 8: Consumer Price Index for Canada, All Items, not Seasonally Adjusted, 1972–1983. For family expenditures, there are no direct data for Hamilton, so this figure averaged the costs for Toronto ($48,894.27) and Thunder Bay ($44,441.49).

15 This figure is based on information from the 'Basic Agreement dated July 20, 1993 between Stelco Inc. Hilton Works and Local 1005 United Steelworkers of America' which covered the period between the date of the contract and 31 July, 1996 (p. 115). It provided a standard hourly rate for job class 1 of $17.54 and an increment between job classes of 19.7 cents (p. 19); 28 job classes (p. 179); and a normal work week of 40 hours (p. 10). Assuming job class 14, for which workers get paid about $21 per hour times 40 hours per week for 50 weeks a year, mid-range steelworkers earn roughly $42,000. Some earn less than that, and most older workers with considerable seniority earn quite a bit more.

16 The social definition of economic necessity is starkly revealed in divorce settlements of the rich where courts rule that women must receive each month, to maintain their standard of living, amounts greater than the average annual income of women.

17 Those steelworkers whose seniority was lowest and whose chances of being recalled were slight were not employed at Stelco by the time we did the study and so they are not included in this group. For a discussion of the unemployed, see Corman (1993).

18 The significance of Chi square for women's work status and home ownership is .0778.

19 For example, in 1984 the unemployment rate for women was 10.5 per cent and for men, 9.2 per cent.

20 Just 15 per cent of the women had only completed elementary school, and their average age was fifty years. Thirty per cent had completed some high school and 33 per cent had completed high school; their average age was thirty-four years. The remaining 22 per cent had some post-secondary education.

21 There is a distinction between 'good jobs' in the primary labour market and 'bad jobs' in the secondary labour market. Primary labour market jobs have relatively high wages, good working conditions, employment stability and job security, equity and due process in the administration of work rules, and chances for advancement. Secondary labour market jobs have low skill requirements, low wages, poor working conditions, low security, few advancement opportunities, low status, and a high risk of unemployment.

22 There were significant correlations of youth and higher educational attainment with more egalitarian views on women's employment rights for both men and women, whether the wife was employed or not.

6: Domestic Labour as Maintaining a Household

1 An earlier version of this section appeared in Luxton (1997c).

2 These findings parallel other research regarding domestic divisions of labour; for example, many of these patterns are similar to those described in Meg Luxton's (1980) book based on a study of domestic labour in Flin Flon, Manitoba, in the 1970s.

3 See Frederick (1995), INSTRAW (1995), Jackson (1992), Nakhaie (1995), and Swinamer (1982) for a discussion of putting a value on housework.

4 The way families 'share' has important implications for measuring poverty (see Phipps and Burton 1995).

5 This pattern has been found in a number of studies (Berk and Shih 1980: 200).

6 In calculating measures of housework and household maintenance for each household we have relied on each of the women and the men to report on their own time and on the women to report for any other helpers.

7 Travel time to and from work is included in paid work time.

8 This difference is statistically significant at the level of .000 for meals and $P = .005$ for dish clean-up.

9 This difference is statistically significant at the level of $P = .000$.

10 This difference is statistically significant at the level of $P = .05$.

11 This difference is statistically significant at the level of $P = .000$.

12 In 1996 the Food and Consumer Products Manufacturers of Canada reported unexplained fluctuations in the amount of shopping done by men. In 1987, 13 per cent of shoppers were men. This increased in 1991 to 21 per cent and then fell in 1996 to 15 per cent (Strauss 1996).

13 For more details, see Sutherland (1985).

14 For more details, see Baker (1982).

15 One of the best examples of how popular culture, particularly the media, undermines feminist politics is on the issue of economic inequality. Feminists developed a range of analyses showing that beneath a popular ideology of family unity lay an economic basis for male domination. These studies showed how women's economic dependence as housewives was central to their subordination. This revelation was quickly inverted by those hostile to feminism and re-presented as a simplistic claim that feminism is 'anti-family,' contemptuous of housewives, and hostile to children (Luxton et al. 1990).

16 Battles in the 1970s and 1980s – around women's right to hold credit cards in their own names or to take out mortgages; around pensions for housewives and more equitable divisions of family property on marital dissolution; around legal recognition that housewives contribute economically to their households – have all produced a changed climate.

17 We are grateful to Larry Campbell for pointing this out.

18 Harriet Rosenberg (1990: 137) has shown this about laundry detergents, for example. Three companies control the market; each produces various products that are presented as if they are in competition with each other.

7: Domestic Labour as Caring for People

1 An earlier version of this section appeared in Luxton (1997b).

2 See Skrypnek and Fast (1996) for a discussion of work and family policy in Canada.

3 This man was from a culture that put a high value on extended kin relations. He was part of a very large extended family. It may be that his cultural back-

ground and his own family experience fostered his particular capacity for child care.

4 See Brayfield (1995) for a discussion of the impact of schedules on fathers' care of children.

5 Heather Jon Maroney pointed this out to us.

6 As the grandmother lived in a nearby town, this arrangement would work only until the child started school.

7 Information provided by Child Care Information Line, Interview, July 1999.

8 The costs of day care (typically offering five days a week from 8 a.m. to 6 p.m.) are very high. In Ontario, where day care workers are among the lowest paid employees (i.e., where day care workers subsidize the system), the annual cost for infant care is around $12,000 and for over-twos is $7,000. If actual spaces were available for every child whose parents wanted it, or for every child in the province, the costs would be more than could be sustained by tax revenues from working-class incomes. Inevitably these costs would have to come from profits and taxes on businesses and wealthy people. Over the past decade, opposition to day care has shifted away from arguments that it is bad for children to arguments that it costs too much and in the current discourse of debts and deficits, this argument resonates.

9 Nancy Chodorow, in *The Reproduction of Mothering* (1978), has shown how heterosexual couples in which mothers are primarily responsible for child care reproduce gender divisions and 'create' girls who desire to become mothers. We suggest a similar pattern applies to single or dual parenting; the psychic experience of dependency on one or two parents predisposes the next generation to assume (emotionally) that similar parenting patterns are 'the best.'

10 For a discussion of social class and parental involvement in education, see Lareau (1989).

11 As medical testing has become adept at identifying the sex of the fetus, increasing numbers of people have aborted fetuses of the 'wrong' sex. We have no evidence of this practice among the people interviewed for this study.

12 Novelist Faye Weldon captures this ideological concept of ideal child behaviour: 'Little children should all sit down quiet and good in one place and learn to take the world for granted, and not attempt to change it' (1990: 48).

13 This subsection is informed by work done by Wally Seccombe.

14 See the *Report of the Royal Commission into Capital and Labour* (Government of Canada 1899).

15 For a discussion of contemporary child labour, see Springer (1997).

16 Jennifer Keck (1998) shows that the same practice in the mines at Inco

provided workers with a sense of pride in their ability to get their sons (and daughters) hired on.

17 In 1960 the mean age of men in Canada at first marriage was 25.4 years; in 1990 it was 27.9 years (Vanier Institute 1996: 39).

18 Declining birth rates suggest this may be happening. In 1971, 7.8 per cent of Canadian women between the ages of thiry-five and forty-four did not have children. In 1981, it was just 8.4 per cent, but by 1998 it has risen to 15 per cent, a higher rate than ever before. The 1996 rate of 1.5 babies per woman was the lowest ever (Ram n.d.).

19 Various studies done by the Social Planning Council show that family care of the elderly in Hamilton became more common as publicly funded services became strained. In Hamilton, 14 per cent of the population was over the age of sixty-five years in 1982 and 45 per cent of seniors had incomes that fell below the poverty line (Jaffray et al. 1997). Caring for family members also extends to those with disabilities or mental health disorders. In 1996, in Hamilton-Wentworth, 13,638 people had severe mental illness and in 1991, 10,225 had severe disabilities (Jaffray et al. 1997).

8: Making a Life

1 The original meaning of leisure conveys its links to servitude. From the Latin 'licere,' to be permitted, it came to mean in English, 'freedom or opportunity to do something,' 'opportunity afforded by unoccupied time' or 'the state of having time at one's own disposal, free time' (*Shorter Oxford English Dictionary on Historical Principles* 1973).

2 Wellman (1985, 1988, 1992, 1999) has written extensively on how large-scale divisions of labour affect the organization and content of interpersonal ties in Canada. See also Shaw et al. (1991) and Chambers (1986).

3 In 1996 only 5.2 per cent of the Hamilton population had ethnic origins from Asian, African, or Arab countries. Only 0.3 per cent were Aboriginals (Statistics Canada, 1996 Census).

4 The implications of unemployment for survival, family relations, and leisure activities is well documented. See Bensman and Lynch (1987), Donaldson (1991), Glyptis (1989), Harris et al. (1985), Morris (1990), Packard (1978), Rubin (1994), Schultz (1985), and Targ and Perrucci (1990).

5 Interview with laid-off steelworker, study of 234 unemployed steelworkers, Hilton Works, 1984.

6 For a review of the literature on home-based leisure, see Glyptis and Chambers (1982) and Allan (1985); see also, Harrington (1989) and Bella (1990, 1992).

7 The benefits of employment for women's social activities and friendships is not clear from the research. Deem (1986), Gloor (1992), and Wellman (1985) argue that employed women are in a position to draw better boundaries between leisure and household obligations. Deem (1986) found that paid employment gave women not only access to their own money so that they could go out, it gave them self-confidence, a pool of potential friends with similar resources, and legitimized their going out of the house. However, Shaw (1985) and Firestone and Sheldon (1988) found that increases in women's paid work time decreases leisure if domestic labour time is not decreased.

8 There was almost perfect correlation between wives and husbands in naming their spouse as a leisure companion. It is striking how high the statistical correlations (over .50) are between what each partner reported for going to the movies, sports games, dances, pubs, restaurants, and parties. Women employed full-time and their partners were not as likely to report going to the same number of movies (.27) or parties (.17).

9 For discussion of the relationship between children and leisure, see Deem (1986), Green et al. (1987), Harrington et al. (1992), Henderson and Allen (1991), Henderson et al. (1989), Horna (1994), Rubin (1985), Shaw (1988, 1992), Wearing (1990), and Wimbush (1986).

10 Horna (1985) found in a Calgary study that 86.1 per cent of respondents reported that family was the most important thing in their life. Rubin (1994) argued that working-class families in the United States were turning inward, impelled by the sharp separation between family life and wage labour. She explains how individuality is eroded by the 'coupled world,' yet marriage does not completely fulfil women's social and emotional needs. For these reasons, Oliker (1989) found that many women had deep, rewarding friendships with women.

11 This pattern was reflected in the relationship between age and the frequency of social outings for women (corr = −.32, P = .000) and for men (corr. = −.37, P = .0000) and also for the total different types of social outings where the correlation for women is −.35 (P = .000) and for men −.32 (P = .000). The correlation between number of outings and age for men married to homemakers is −.35 (P = .001); men married to women employed full-time, −.54 (P = .000); and men married to women employed part-time −.13. The correlation between number of outings and age for homemakers is −.24 (P = .01 significance); women employed part-time, −.30 (P = .01), and women employed full-time, −.51 (P = .001).

12 A comparison of number of friends reported by spouses reveals a symmetrical pattern of friendships. The correlation between all spouses is high at .72.

Women employed part-time most highly resemble their husbands, with a correlation between number of friends of .85, compared with .69 for women employed full-time and .54 for full time housewives.

13 This experience is fairly typical in North America, especially for couples. Wellman's (1999) review of the research indicated that couples in urban North America have floating, loose-knit friendship networks, maintained by women. Socializing is home based and conversations are about domestic or personal concerns.

14 Interview with unemployed steelworker from the study of 234 laid-off workers at Hilton Works, 1984.

15 This analysis draws on Rodrigues (1990).

16 Men's informal neighbourhood ties were related to their partners' work status (with a statistical significance of 0.05). The percentages of men who knew seven or more neighbours by name were: 41 per cent of men married to women employed full-time, 60 per cent of men married to women employed part-time, and 65 per cent of men married to full-time homemakers.

9: Dreams and Dilemmas

1 For an analysis of the growth of contingent employment, its organization and its impact on workers, see Vosko (2000).

2 One example is the Canadian Centre for Policy Alternatives (CCPA). Set up by the labour movement and other progressive groups to provide an alternative perspective more oriented to social justice, and greater economic and social equality for working-class people, it publishes the *CCPA Monitor.*

3 In the period April to June 1998 Stelco recorded an after tax gain of $11 million (*Globe and Mail,* 'Steel,' 8 May 1998; B9).

4 On 29 July, 1998 the Canadian Human Rights Commission released its ruling on a complaint filed by the Public Service Alliance in Canada, the union of federal government employees. The commission found that the federal government had discriminated against its women employees for years and called on it to pay compensation to ensure equal pay for work of equal value for federal employees. This ruling offered major legitimation of the argument that women have been discriminated against in the labour force and of the union strategy of pay equity as one way of redressing discrimination (CBC Radio 8a.m. *News,* 29 July, 1998).

5 A 1993 poll by Decima of 1,200 people in Canada found that 72 per cent said immigrants should adapt to Canada's values, many said they were 'tired of ethnic minorities being given special treatment,' and half said they were 'tired of ethnic minorities complaining about racism' (Bergman 1993: 42).

6 See Fudge and McDermott (eds.) (1991) for an analysis of pay equity.

7 For an interesting discussion of these issues, see Leach (1998).

8 Judy Darcy, President, Canadian Union of Public Employees, personal communication, 15 October 2000.

9 Segmented labour markets work to keep labour costs relatively low. While a few workers in certain industries may win relatively high wages, other workers earning much lower wages both subsidize the higher paying industries and serve to produce pools of lower paid workers whose existence acts as a brake on wage demands. Segmented labour markets also produce race, ethnicity, and gender specific types of jobs. The more jobs are specific to certain types of workers, the more likely those workers are to defend their occupations against efforts to extend access to those jobs to others. Competition between workers reduces competition between workers and employers, undermining the capacity of working people to force capitalist employers to redistribute the wealth produced by their efforts (Vosko 2000).

References

Adams, Mary Louise. 1997. *The Trouble with Normal: Postwar Youth and the Making of Heterosexuality*. Toronto: University of Toronto Press.

Adams, R.J. 1988. 'The "Old Industrial Relations" and Corporate Competitiveness: A Canadian Case.' *Employee Relations* 20(2): 3–7.

Adams, R.J., and I. Zeytinoglu. 1987. 'Labour-Management Dispute Resolution at the Hilton Works.' Pp. 71–99 in T. Hanami and R. Blanpain (eds.), *Industrial Conflict Resolution in Market Economies*. Boston: Kluwer Law and Taxation Publishers.

Ahlburg, D.A., A. Carey, B. Lundgren, S. Barrett, and L. Anderson. 1987. 'Technological Change, Market Decline, and Industrial Relations in the U.S. Steel Industry.' Pp. 229–45 in D.B. Cornfield (ed.), *Workers, Managers and Technological Change: Emerging Patterns of Labour Relations*. New York: Plenum Press.

Akin, David. 1998. 'Hamilton Steel Forges Ahead.' *St Catharines Standard*. 13 Feb.: D5.

Akyeampong, Ernest. 1986. '"Involuntary" Part-Time Employment in Canada: 1975–1985.' *The Labour Force*. Ottawa: Statistics Canada (Dec.): 143–70.

Albright, Robert. 1995. 'A Mature Rivalry: Labor Relations in the American Steel Industry.' N.p. in A. Verma, A. Frost, and P. Warrian (eds.), 'Workplace Restructuring and Employment Relations in Canadian Steel Industry,' in *International Conference on Workplace Change: Human Resources and Rationalization in the Global Steel Industry*. Toronto, 5–6 June.

Allan, Graham. 1985. *Family Life: Domestic Roles and Social Organization*. Oxford: Basil Blackwell.

Allan, J. 1982. Speech to the Conference Board of Canada Seminar. 8 October. Reported in the *Hamilton Spectator*, 9 Oct. 1982.

Allessandri, Steven M. 1992. 'Effects of Maternal Work Status in Single-Parent

Families on Children's Perception of Self and Family and Achievement.' *Journal of Experimental Child Psychology* 54: 417–33.

Anderson, Karen. 1991. *Chain Her by One Foot: The Subjection of Women in 17th Century New France.* London: Routledge.

Anderson, William. 1987. 'The Changing Competitive Position of the Hamilton Steel Industry.' Pp. 202–21 in M. Dear, J. Drake, and L. Reeds (eds.), *Steel City: Hamilton and Region,* Toronto: University of Toronto Press.

Arat-Koc, Sedef. 1990. 'Importing Housewives.' Pp. 81–103 in Meg Luxton, Harriet Rosenberg, and Sedef Arat-Koc (eds.), *Through the Kitchen Window.* Toronto: Garamond.

Arendt, Hannah. 1958. *The Human Condition.* Chicago: University of Chicago Press.

Archibald, Peter. 1998. 'Do Status Differences among Workers Make a Difference during Economic Crises? The Case of Depression Hamilton.' *Canadian Review of Sociology and Anthropology* 35(2): 125–63.

– 1996. 'Small Expectations and Great Adjustments: How Hamilton Workers Most Often Experienced the Great Depression.' *Canadian Journal of Sociology* 21: 359–402.

– 1992. 'Distress, Dissent and Alienation: Hamilton Workers in the Great Depression.' *Urban History Review* 21: 3–32.

Armstrong, Pat, and Hugh Armstrong. 1996. *Wasting Away: The Undermining of Canadian Health Care.* Don Mills, Ont.: Oxford University Press.

– 1978. *The Double Ghetto: Canadian Women and Their Segregated Work.* Toronto: McClelland and Stewart.

Arnup, Katherine. 1997. 'In the Family Way: Lesbian Mothers in Canada.' Pp. 80–97 in Meg Luxton (ed.), *Feminism and Families: Critical Policies and Changing Practices.* Halifax: Fernwood.

– 1995. *Lesbian Parenting: Living with Pride and Prejudice.* Charlottetown: Gynergy Books.

– 1994. *Education for Motherhood: Advice for Mothers in Twentieth-Century Canada.* Toronto: University of Toronto Press.

Asner, Elizabeth Ann. 1993. 'Class, Gender and Generation: A Life Course Approach to Married Women's Employment Choices and Feminist Consciousness.' Unpublished doctoral thesis, Ontario Institute for Studies in Education.

Backhouse, Constance. 1992. 'Married Women's Property Law in Nineteenth-Century Canada.' Pp. 177–98 in Bettina Bradbury (ed.), *Canadian Family History.* Toronto: Copp Clark Pitman.

Badcock, B.A. 1984. *Unfairly Structured Cities.* Oxford: Basil Blackwell.

Badenhorst, Ruth. 1987. *Social Trends in Hamilton-Wentworth: Update.* Hamilton: Social Planning and Research Council of Hamilton and District.

Bakan, Abigail B., and Daiva Stasiulis. 1997. *Not One of the Family: Foreign Domestic Workers in Canada.* Toronto: University of Toronto Press.

Baker, Maureen. 1995. *Canadian Family Policies: Cross-National Comparison.* Toronto: University of Toronto Press.

Baker, Tom. 1982. 'Strategy for Jobless Relief.' *Steel Shots* (6): 14.

Bakker, Isabella, (ed.). 1996. *Rethinking Restructuring: Gender and Change in Canada.* Toronto: University of Toronto Press.

Bakker, Isabella, and Katherine Scott. 1997. 'From the Postwar to the Post-Liberal Keynesian Welfare State.' Pp. 286–310 in Wallace Clement (ed.), *Understanding Canada: Building on the New Canadian Political Economy.* Montreal and Kingston: McGill-Queen's University Press.

Balloch, J. 1988. 'Losing Jobs.' *Steel Shots* (22): 22.

Barrett, Michele. 1980. *Women's Oppression Today.* London: Verso.

Barrett, Michele, and Mary McIntosh. 1982. *The Anti-Social Family.* London: Verso.

Bashevkin, Sylvia. 1998. *Women on the Defensive: Living through Conservative Times.* Toronto: University of Toronto Press.

Bella, Leslie. 1992. *The Christmas Imperatives: Leisure, Family and Women's Work.* Halifax: Fernwood.

– 1990. 'Women and Leisure: Beyond Androcentrism.' Pp. 151–79 in E. Jackson and T.L. Burton (eds.), *Understanding Leisure and Recreation: Mapping the Past, Charting the Future.* State College, Pa: Venture Press.

Bensman, David, and Roberta Lynch. 1987. *Rusted Dreams: Hard Times in a Steel Community.* New York: McGraw-Hill.

Berg, I., (ed). 1981. *Sociological Perspectives on Labour Markets.* New York: Academic Press.

Bergman, Brian. 1993. 'A Nation of Polite Bigots?' *MacLean's* 106(52): 42–3.

Berk, Sarah. 1985. *The Gender Factory: The Apportionment of Work in American Households.* New York: Plenum Press.

Berk, Sarah, and A. Shih. 1980. 'Contributions to Household Labor: Comparing Wives' and Husbands' Reports.' Pp. 191–227 in Sarah Berk (ed.), *Women and Household Labor.* Beverley Hills, Calif.: Sage.

Bezanson, Kate. 1996. 'This Little Tory Went to Market: Gender and Restructuring in Ontario.' Master's thesis, York University.

Binkley, Marian. n.d. 'Set Adrift.' Unpublished manuscript, Department of Sociology and Social Anthropology, Dalhousie University.

Bittman, Michael, and Jocelyn Pixley. 1997. *The Double Life of the Family Myth: Hope and Experience.* St Leonards, Australia: Allen and Unwin.

Bowen, P. 1976. *Social Control in Industrial Organizations: Industrial Relations and Industrial Sociology: A Strategic and Occupational Study of British Steelmaking.* London: Routledge.

Boyd, Anne. 1982. 'Women's Work in Canada.' Unpublished paper. Department of Sociology, McMaster University, Hamilton, Ontario.

Boyd, Monica. 1984. *Canadian Attitudes towards Women: Thirty Years of Change.* Ottawa: Supply and Services Canada.

Boyer, Patrick, and Daniel Drache (eds.). 1996. *Do Nation States Have a Future?* London: Routledge.

Bradbury, Bettina. 1995. 'The Home as Workplace.' Pp. 412–76 in Paul Craven (ed.), *Labouring Lives: Work and Workers in Nineteenth-Century Ontario.* Toronto: University of Toronto Press.

– 1993. *Working Families: Age, Gender, and Daily Survival in Industrializing Montreal.* Toronto: McClelland and Stewart.

Brand, Dionne. 1983. 'A Working Paper on Black Women in Toronto: Gender, Race and Class.' *Fireweed* (16): 149–55.

Brannen, Julia, and Peter Moss. 1987. 'Dual Earner Households: Women's Financial Contributions after the Birth of the First Child.' Pp. 75–95 in Julia Brannen and G. Wilson (eds.), *Give and Take in Families: Studies in Resource Distribution.* London: Allen and Unwin.

Brannen, Julia, and G. Wilson (eds.). 1987. *Give and Take in Families: Studies in Resource Distribution.* London: Allen and Unwin.

Braverman, Harry. 1974. *Labor and Monopoly Capital: The Degradation of Work on the Twentieth Century.* New York: Monthly Review Press.

Brayfield, April. 1995. 'Juggling Jobs and Kids: The Impact of Employment Schedules on Fathers' Caring for Children.' *Journal of Marriage and the Family* 57(May): 321–32.

Breaton, Steve. 1998. 'The Grey Area.' *This Magazine* 31(4): 15.

Bristow, Peggy, Dionne Brand, Linda Carty, Afua P. Cooper, Sylvia Hamilton, and Adrienne Shadd. 1994. *'We're Rooted Here and They Can't Pull Us Up': Essays in African Canadian Women's History.* Toronto: University of Toronto Press.

Brodie, Janine, (ed.). 1996. *Women and Canadian Public Policy.* Toronto: Harcourt, Brace.

Brown, Suzanne. 1999. *Poverty Profile.* Hamilton: Social Planning and Research Council.

Calliste, Agnes. 1991. 'Canada's Immigration Policy and Domestics from the Caribbean: The Second Domestic Scheme' Pp. 136–68 in Jesse Vorst, Tania Das Grupta, Cy Gonick, Ronnie Leah, Alan Lennon, Alicja Muszynski, Roxana Ng, Ed Silva, Mercedes Steedman, Si Tvansken, and Derek Wilkinson (eds.), *Race, Class, Gender: Bonds and Barriers.* Rev. ed. Toronto: Garamond Press and the Society for Socialist Studies.

Campbell, Maria. 1973. *Halfbreed.* Toronto: McClelland and Stewart.

Canada. Human Resources Development Canada. 1994. Advisory Group on

Working Time and the Distribution of Work. (Headed by Arthur Donner). *Report of the Advisory Group on Working Time and the Distribution of Work.* Ottawa: Minister of Supply and Services.

Canada. Ministry of State, Science and Technology. 1988. *Industry Profile: Primary Iron and Steel.* Ottawa: Department of Regional Industrial Expansion.

Canadian Steel Trade and Employment Congress (CSTEC). 1996. *Report.*

– 1993. *Report.*

Carey, Elaine. 1998. 'Women Closing Wage Gap but Young Workers Lose Out.' *Toronto Star,* 24 March: A2.

– 1997. 'Common-Law: The New Trend.' *Toronto Star,* 15 Oct.: A1, A28.

Chambers, Deborah A. 1986. 'The Constraints of Work and Domestic Schedules on Women's Leisure.' *Leisure Studies* 5: 309–25.

Chandler, H.E. 1985. 'A Profile of Canada's Steel Technology.' *Metal Progress* (April): 55–71.

Chandler, William. 1994. 'The Value of Household Work in Canada, 1992.' *Canadian Economic Observer.* Statistics Canada. Cat. No. 11-010 (April), 3.1–3.9.

Chess, Stella, and Alexander Thomas. 1984. *Origins and Evolution of Behavior Disorders: From Infancy to Early Adult Life.* New York: Brummer/Mazel.

Child Care Information Line. 1997. *Unmet Needs Report, 1996/1997: Hamilton-Wentworth.* Hamilton: Child Care Information Line, P.O. Box 2700, Hamilton, Ontario.

Chodorow, Nancy. 1978. *The Reproduction of Mothering.* Berkeley: University of California Press.

Christmas, B. 1990. 'Guess Who's Going to Dinner? Stelco Changing Relations with Workers by Taking Them Out for "Pizza and Wings."' *Hamilton Spectator.* 21 Sept.: B7.

Chunn, Dorothy. 1995. 'Feminism, Law and Public Policy: Politicizing the Person.' Pp. 177–210 in Nancy Mandell and Anne Duffy (eds.), *Canadian Families: Diversity, Conflict and Change.* Toronto: Harcourt, Brace.

City of Hamilton. 1995a. *More! Hamilton Facts and Figures.* Hamilton: Planning and Development Department. Oct.

– 1995b. *Report of the Hamilton-Wentworth Economic Development Department.*

– 1980. *Report of the Treasurer and Commissioner of Finance.* 31 Dec.

– 1970. Reports: Treasury Department 1960–1970.

Clement, Wallace, and John Myles. 1994. *Relations of Ruling Class and Gender in Postindustrial Societies.* Montreal and Kingston: McGill-Queen's University Press.

Cockburn, Cynthia. 1983. *Brothers: Male Dominance and Technological Change.* London: Pluto Press.

Cohen, Marjorie. 1997. 'What Women Should Know about Economic Fundamentalism.' *Atlantis: A Women's Studies Journal* 21(2): 4–15.

– 1994. 'The Implications of Economic Restructuring for Women.' Pp. 103–16 in Isabella Bakker (ed.), *The Strategic Silence: Gender and Economic Policy.* London: Zed Books.

– 1988. *Women's Work: Markets and Economic Development in Nineteenth-Century Ontario.* Toronto: University of Toronto Press.

Connelly, Patricia. 1978. *Last Hired, First Fired: Women and the Canadian Work Force.* Toronto: Women's Press.

Corman, June. 1993. 'Living on the Fringe: Reemployment for Steelworkers after an Indefinite Layoff Notice.' Pp. 75–101 in June Corman, Meg Luxton, D.W. Livingstone, and Wally Seccombe (eds.), *Recasting Steel Labour: The Stelco Story.* Halifax: Fernwood.

– 1990. 'Dissension within the Ranks: The Struggle over Employment Practices.' *Studies in Political Economy* 32: 85–109.

Corman, June, Meg Luxton, D.W. Livingstone, and Wally Seccombe (eds.). 1993. *Recasting Steel Labour: The Stelco Story.* Halifax: Fernwood.

Crone, G. 1988. 'Mood at Stelco "Volatile," Says Union.' *Hamilton Spectator,* 6 Sept.

Csiernik, Rick, and Winsome, Cain. 1985. *An Overview of the Impact of the Recession on Women in Hamilton-Wentworth.* Hamilton: Social Planning and Research Council of Hamilton and District.

Cusumano, M.A. 1985. *The Japanese Automobile Industry.* Cambridge, Mass.: Harvard University Press.

Darcy, Judy. 1995. 'Afterword: Shades of Grace.' Pp. 232–9 in Susan Crean (ed.), *Grace Hartman: Woman for Her Time.* Vancouver: New Star Books.

Das Gupta, Tania. 1995. 'Families of Native Peoples, Immigrants and People of Colour.' Pp. 141–74 in Nancy Mandell and Ann Duffy (eds.), *Canadian Families: Diversity, Conflict and Change.* Toronto: Harcourt, Brace.

Davie, M. 1996. 'Hamilton 9002, Stelco: A World-class Ranking.' *Hamilton Spectator,* 20 Feb., D10.

– 1992a. 'Hold On, 1005 Tells Stelco: Layoff Plans Too Fast, Martin Says.' *Hamilton Spectator,* 16 Oct., C6.

– 1992b. 'Cooperation the Key as Steelworkers Decide.' *Hamilton Spectator,* 14 Nov., C9.

– 1990. 'Stelco Studies Outright Sale, Mill Closings.' *Hamilton Spectator,* 21 Sept., B7.

Day, Shelagh, and Gwen Brodsky. 1998. *Women and the Equality Deficit: The Impact of Restructuring Canada's Social Programs.* Ottawa: Status of Women.

Dear, M.J., J.J. Drake, and L.G. Reeds (eds.). 1987. *Steel City: Hamilton and Region.* Toronto: University of Toronto Press.

Deem, Rosemary. 1986. *All Work and No Play? The Sociology of Women and Leisure.* Milton Keynes: Open University Press.

Desoer, David. 1995. *Employment by Industry Sector.* City of Hamilton: Greater Hamilton Economic Development Department, 20 Sept.

De Vault, Marjorie. 1991. *Feeding the Family.* Chicago: University of Chicago Press.

Deverell, John. 1985a. '2 Stelco Workers Charge Coverup by Firm's Doctors.' *Toronto Star,* 21 Aug., A4.

– 1985b. 'Stelco Ordered to Comply with Health Law.' *Toronto Star,* 11 Nov., A15.

de Wolff, Alice. 1998. 'The Clerical Workers Project.' Paper presented at the Learned Society, Ottawa.

– 1994. *Strategies for Working Families.* Toronto: Ontario Coalition for Better Child Care.

Dofasco. 1989. *Annual Report.* Hamilton.

Doherty, G. 1995. *Quality Matters: Excellence in Early Childhood Programs.* Don Mills, Ont.: Addison-Welsey.

Donaldson, Mike. 1991. *Time of Our Lives: Labour and Love in the Working Class.* England: University of Wollongong.

Drolet, Marie. 1999. *The Persistent Gap: New Evidence on the Canadian Gender Wage Gap.* Income Statistics Division, Statistics Canada, Cat. no. 75F0002MIE-99008. Ottawa: Ministry of Industry.

Duffy, Ann, and Norene Pupo. 1989. *Part-Time Paradox: Connecting Gender, Work and Family.* Toronto: McClelland and Stewart.

Dunk, Thomas. 1991. *It's a Working Man's Town: Male Working-Class Culture in Northwestern Ontario.* Montreal: McGill-Queen's University Press.

Eagleton, Terry. 1991. *Ideology: An Introduction.* London: Verso.

Easson, Jeannette, Debbie Field, and Joanne Santucci. 1983. 'Working Steel.' Pp. 191–218 in Jennifer Penney (ed.), *Hard Earned Wages: Women Fighting for Better Work.* Toronto: Women's Press.

Elson, Diane. 1992. 'From Survival Strategies to Transformation Strategies: Women's Needs and Structural Adjustment.' Pp. 26–48 in Shelly Feldman and Lourdes Beneria (eds.), *Unequal Burden: Economic Crises, Persistent Poverty and Women's Work.* Boulder, Col.: Westview Press.

Estock, D. 1987. 'Steel Takes Stock.' *Hamilton Spectator,* 30 May: B1.

Evans, Patricia. 1997. 'Divided Citizenship? Gender, Income Security, and the Welfare State.' Pp. 91–116 in Patricia Evans and Gerda Wekerle (eds.), *Women and the Canadian Welfare State: Challenges and Change.* Toronto: University of Toronto Press.

Ewen, Stuart. 1976. *Captains of Consciousness: Advertising and the Social Roots of the Consumer Culture.* New York: McGraw-Hill.

Field, Debbie. 1980. 'Introducing: Local 1005 Women's Committee.' *Steel Shots* (Nov.): 5.

Finch, Janet. 1989. *Family Obligations and Social Change.* Cambridge: Polity Press.

Firestone, Juanita, and Beth A. Sheldon. 1988. 'An Estimation of the Effects of Women's Work on Available Leisure Time.' *Journal of Family Issues* 9(4): 478–95.

Fonow, Mary Margaret. 1998. 'Women of Steel: A Case of Feminist Organizing in the United Steelworkers of America.' *Canadian Woman Studies* 18(1): 117–22.

Fowlie, L. 1992. 'Stelco to Cut 1200 Jobs at Hilton Works,' *Financial Post,* 24 Sept.: 3.

Fox, Bonnie. 1997. 'Reproducing Difference: Changes in the Lives of Partners Becoming Parents.' Pp. 142–61 in Meg Luxton (ed.), *Feminism and Families: Critical Policies and Changing Practices.* Halifax: Fernwood.

– 1980. *Hidden in the Household: Women's Domestic Labour Under Capitalism.* Toronto: Women's Press.

Frankenberg, Ruth. 1993. *White Women, Race Matters: The Social Construction of Whiteness.* Minneapolis: University of Minnesota Press.

Fraser, Nancy. 1997. 'After the Family Wage: A Postindustrial Thought Experiment.' Pp. 41–66 in *Justice Interruptus: Critical Reflections on "Postsocialist" Conditions.* New York: Routledge.

Frederick, Judith. 1995. *As Time Goes By ... Time Use of Canadians.* Ottawa: Statistics Canada, Ministry of Industry.

Freeman, B. 1982. *1005: Political Life in a Union Local.* Toronto: Lorimer.

Freeman, B., and M. Hewitt (eds.). 1979. *Their Town: The Mafia, the Media, and the Party Machine.* Toronto: Lorimer.

Friendly, Martha. 1997. 'Child Care Policy.' Pp. 107–13 in Nandita Sharma (ed.), *The National Action Committee on the Status of Women's Voters' Guide.* Toronto: Lorimer.

Frost, A. 1996. 'Labour-Management Collaboration over the Redesign of Work: The Impact of Alternative Approaches.' Paper presented at CLAMS/CWRN Conference, University of British Columbia, Vancouver, 18–19 Oct.

Frost, Ann, and Anil Verma. 1997. 'Restructuring in Canadian Steel: The Case of Stelco Inc.' Pp. 82–112 in A. Verma and R. Chaykowski (eds.), *Contract and Commitment.* Kingston: IRC Press.

Fudge, Judy, and Patricia McDermott (eds.). 1991. *Just Wages: A Feminist Assessment of Pay Equity.* Toronto: University of Toronto Press.

Gaskell, Jane, Arlene McLaren, and Myra Novogrodsky. 1989. *Claiming an Education: Feminism and Canadian Society.* Toronto: Our Schools / Ourselves Education Foundation.

Gaskell, Jane, and Arlene McLaren (eds.). 1987. *Women and Education: A Canadian Perspective.* Calgary: Detselig.

Gavigan, Shelley A.M. 1997. 'Feminism, Familial Ideology and Family Law:

A Perilous Menage à Trois.' Pp. 98–123 in Meg Luxton (ed.), *Feminism and Families: Critical Policies and Changing Practices.* Halifax: Fernwood.

Gavron, Hannah. 1966. *The Captive Wife: Conflicts of Household Mothers.* London: Routledge and Kegan Paul.

Geerken, M., and W.R. Gove. 1983. *At Home and at Work: The Family's Allocation of Labour.* Beverley Hills: Sage.

Gilman, Charlotte Perkins. [1898] 1966. *Women and Economics* Ed. Carl Degler. New York: Harper Torchbooks.

Globe and Mail. 1998. 'Report on Business News Bulletin's Steel,' 8 May: B9.

– 1998. 'Canadian Business News Bulletins – Steel,' 4 Feb.: B8.

– *Report on Business Magazine.* 1998. '50 Best-Paid CEOs.' (July): 87–8.

Gloor, Daniela. 1992. 'Women versus Men? – The Hidden Differences in Leisure Activities.' *Society and Leisure* 15(1): 39–60.

Glyptis, Susan A. 1989. *Leisure and Unemployment.* Milton Keynes: Open University Press.

Glyptis, Susan A., and Deborah A. Chambers. 1982. 'No Place Like Home.' *Leisure Studies* 1: 247–62.

Godfrey, J. 1990. 'Stelco Workers Suffer Burden of History.' *Financial Post* 8 June: 11.

Golz, Annalee. 1993. 'Family Matters: The Canadian Family and the State in the Postwar Period.' *Left History* 1(2): 9–49.

Goodnow, Jacqueline, and Jennifer Bowes. 1994. *Men, Women and Household Work.* Aukland: Oxford University Press.

Gordon, P. 1981. 'A Report from the Chairman of the Board.' *Stelco Annual Report,* 2–3.

Government of Canada. 1899. *Report of the Royal Commission into Capital and Labour.* Ottawa: King's Printer.

Graham, Hilary. 1987. 'Being Poor: Perceptions and Coping Strategies of Lone Mothers.' Pp. 56–74 in Julia Brannen and Gail Wilson (eds.), *Give and Take in Families: Studies in Resource Distribution.* London: Allen and Unwin.

Gray, Stan. 1984. 'Sharing the Shop Floor.' *Canadian Dimension* 18(2): 17–32.

Green, E., S. Hebron., and D. Woodward. 1987. *Leisure and Gender: A Study of Sheffield Women's Leisure Experiences.* London: Sports Council / Economic and Social Research Council.

Guest, Dennis. 1980. *The Emergence of Social Security in Canada.* Vancouver: University of British Columbia Press.

Guilmette, Ann Marie. 1992. 'Women of Age and Leisure: A Celebration of the Possible.' *Journal of Leisurability* 19(3): 18–24.

Hall, Stuart. 1980. 'Race, Articulation and Societies Structured in Dominance.' Pp. 305–45 in *Sociological Theories: Race and Colonialism.* Paris: UNESCO.

Hallman, M. 1990. 'Stelco Slashes Dividend, Cuts Managers' Salaries.' *Financial Post*, 19 Sept.: 56.

Hallman, M. 1987. 'Documents Show Stelco Knew Overtime Was Illegal: Mackenzie.' *Hamilton Spectator.* 17 Dec.: A1.

Hamilton, Roberta, and Michele Barrett (eds.). 1986. *The Politics of Diversity: Feminism, Marxism and Nationalism.* London: Verso.

Handelman, Stephen. 1996. 'Family Values Best for Country: Poll.' *Toronto Star.* 27 March: A1, A26.

Harrington, Maureen. 1989. 'The Work-Leisure Relationship of Three Occupational Groups of Working Women.' Paper presented at *American Sociological Association.* Department of Leisure Studies, University of Ottawa.

Harrington, Maureen, Don Dawson, and Pat Bella. 1992. 'Objective Constraints on Women's Enjoyment of Leisure.' *Society and Leisure* 15(1): 203–21.

Harris, C.C., R.M. Lee, and L.D. Morris. 1985. 'Redundancy in Steel: Labour-Market Behaviour, Local Social Networks and Domestic Organizations.' Pp. 154–66 in Bryan Roberts, Ruth Finnegan, and Duncan Gallie (eds.), *New Approaches to Economic Life.* Manchester: Manchester University Press.

Hartmann, Heidi. 1981. 'The Family as the Locus of Gender, Class and Political Struggle: The Example of Housework.' *Signs: Journal of Women in Culture and Society* 6: 366–94.

Harvey, David. 1989. *The Condition of Post Modernity.* London: Basil Blackwell.

Hathaway, Jim. 1994a. *Report of the National Consultation on Family Class Immigration.* Convened by the Department of Citizenship and Immigration, Government of Canada and Refugee Law Research Unit, Centre for Refugee Studies, York University.

– 1994b. *Towards a Contexualized System of Family Class Immigration.* Convened by the Department of Citizenship and Immigration, Government of Canada and Refugee Law Research Unit, Centre for Refugee Studies, York University.

Hayden, Dolores. 1981. *The Grand Domestic Revolution.* Cambridge, Mass.: MIT Press.

Hayes, Cheryl, and Sheila Kamerman (eds.). 1983. *Children of Working Parents: Experiences and Outcomes.* Panel on Work, Family, and Community, Committee on Child Development, Research and Public Policy. Washington, DC: National Academy Press.

Henderson, Karla, and Katherine K. Allen. 1991. 'The Ethics of Care: Leisure Possibilities and Constraints for Women.' *Society and Leisure* 14(1): 97–113.

Henderson, Karla, M. Deborah Bialeschki, Susan M. Shaw, and Valeria Freysinger. 1989. *A Leisure of One's Own: A Feminist Perspective on Women's Leisure.* State College, PA: Venture Press.

Henry, Franklyn J. 1965. *Perception of Discrimination among Negroes and Japanese-*

Canadians in Hamilton. A report submitted to the Ontario Human Rights Commission. Department of Sociology and Anthropology, McMaster University, Hamilton.

Heron, Craig. 1988. *Working in Steel: The Early Years in Canada 1883–1995.* Toronto: McClelland and Stewart.

Heron, Craig, and Robert Storey. 1986. 'Work and Struggle in the Canadian Steel Industry.' Pp. 210–44 in C. Heron and R. Storey (eds.), *On the Job: Confronting the Labour Process in Canada.* Montreal: McGill-Queen's University Press.

Hicks, D.A. 1985. *Advanced Industrial Development: Restructuring, Relocation and Renewal.* Boston: Oelgeschlager, Gunn and Hain.

High, Steve. 1998. 'The Gender of Displaced Industrial Workers.' Paper presented at the Learned Society Meetings. University of Ottawa. June.

Hochschild, Arlie, with Anne Machung. 1989. *The Second Shift.* New York: Avon Books.

Holt, Jim. 1996. 'Six-Year Contract Offered to 1005.' *Hamilton Spectator* 26 March: A1.

Horna, Jarmila. 1994. *The Study of Leisure.* Toronto: Oxford University Press.

– 1985. 'The Social Dialect of Life, Career and Leisure: A Probe into the Preoccupators Model.' *Society and Leisure* 8(2): 615–30.

Hossie, Linda. 1985. 'Stelco Workers Cite 62 Incidents of Sexual, Other Harassments.' *Globe and Mail* 17 Sept.: 3.

Houseman, Susan N. 1991. *Industrial Restructuring with Job Security: The Case of European Steel.* Cambridge, Mass.: Harvard University Press.

Houser, Angela. 1988. *Job Losses / Job Gains in Hamilton-Wentworth.* Hamilton: Social Planning Council of Hamilton and District.

Huber, Joan, and Glenna Spitze. 1983. *Sex Stratification: Children, Housework and Jobs.* New York: Academic Press.

Human Resources Development Canada. 1998a. *Annual Average Unemployment Rates: Hamilton CMA.* 31 March.

– 1998b. http://hamilton.london.hrdc-drhc.qc.ca/english/1mi/profile/comporo/comprof.html. 13 Feb. 1998.

Hunt, Pauline. 1980. *Gender and Class Consciousness.* London: Macmillan.

International Iron and Steel Institute. 1995. *Annual Report.*

INSTRAW (International Research and Training Institute for the Advancement of Women). 1995. *Measurement and Valuation of Unpaid Contribution Accounting Through Time and Output.* Santo Domingo, Dominican Republic: United Nations.

Jackson, Chris. 1992. 'The Value of Household Work in Canada, 1986.' *National Income and Expenditure Accounts.* Ottawa: Statistics Canada, Catalogue 13-001. xxxiii–lii.

Jaffray, Don, Tania Alexander, Susanne Brown, Mark Fraser, and Susan West. 1997. *Social Change in Hamilton-Wentworth: 1997.* Hamilton: Social Planning and Research Council.

Joe, Rita. 1996. *Song of Rita Joe: Autobiography of a Mi'kmaq Poet.* Charlottetown: Ragweed.

Johnson, Laura. 1995. *Changing Families, Changing Workplaces: Case Studies of Policies and Programs in Canadian Workplaces.* Women's Bureau, Human Resources Development Canada: Minister of Supply and Services.

Katz, Michael. 1975. *The People of Hamilton, Canada West: Family and Class in a Mid-Nineteenth Century City.* Cambridge, Mass.: Harvard University Press.

Keck, Jennifer. 1998. 'Twenty-five Years of Women Working at Inco.' Paper presented at the Learned Society Meetings, University of Ottawa. June.

Kervin, J., Morley Gunderson, and Frank Reid. 1984. *Two Case Studies of Strikes: Final Report.* Toronto: Centre for Industrial Relations, University of Toronto.

Kilbourn, William. 1960. *The Elements Combined: A History of the Steel Company of Canada.* Toronto: Clarke Irwin.

Kingston, Anne. 1991. 'The Court on Homemaking: It's More than Physical Labour.' *Financial Times of Canada* 80(17): 17.

Kleiman, Bernard. 1995. 'Information from the United Steelworkers of America,' in A. Verma, A. Frost, and P. Warrian (eds.), *International Conference on Workplace Change: Human Resources and Rationalization in the Global Steel Industry.* Conference Papers. Toronto: 5 and 6 June.

Knox, Gary. 1998. 'Contracting Out.' *Steel Shots* (April): 14.

Komarovsky, Mirra. 1962. *Blue-Collar Marriage.* New York: Vintage Books.

Kome, Penny. 1982. *Somebody Has Got to Do It: Whose Work Is Housework?* Toronto: McClelland and Stewart.

Land, Hilary. 1980. 'The Family Wage.' *Feminist Review* 6. 55–78.

Lanthier, J. 1990. 'Stelco Workers Head for Strike.' *Financial Post* 7 June: 3.

Lareau, Annette. 1989. *Home Advantage: Social Class and Parental Intervention in Elementary Education.* New York: Falmer Press.

Leach, Belinda. 1997. 'New Right and the Politics of Work and Family in Hamilton.' *Atlantis* 21(2): 35–46.

– 1998. 'Citizenship and the Politics of of Exclusion in a "Post"-Fordist Industrial City.' *Critique of Anthropology* 18(2): 181–204.

Lebowitz, Michael. 1991. *Beyond Capital.* New York: St Martin's Press.

Lefaive, D. 1990a. 'It Paid Off, 1005 Boss Says.' *Hamilton Spectator* 5 Nov.: C1.

– 1990b. 'Stelco Axes over 300 Salaried Workers: More Terminations Imminent.' *Hamilton Spectator* 13 Dec.: D1.

– 1990c. 'We Have to Stop Fighting.' *Hamilton Spectator,* 5 Nov.: A1, A2.

Lefaive, D., and R. Hughes. 1990. 'Who Goes on Pogey?' *Hamilton Spectator,* 1 Nov.: A1.

Leslie, D., and D. Butz. 1998. '"GM Suicide": Flexibility, Space and the Injured Body.' *Economic Geography* 74: 360–78.

Little, Margaret Jane Hillyard. 1998. 'No Car, No Radio, No Liquor Permit.' *The Moral Regulations of Single Mothers in Ontario, 1920–1997*. Toronto: Oxford University Press.

Livingstone, D.W. 1999. '1005 Disaster Scenario: Hire or Die.' *Steel Shots* (Feb.): 21.

– 1998a. 'Renewing the Hilton Work Force.' *Steel Shots*. (Aug.–Sept.): 26.

– 1998b. *The Education-Jobs Gap: Underemployment or Economic Democracy*. Boulder, Col.: Westview Press; Toronto: Garamond Press.

– 1996. *Steel Work: Recasting the Core Workforce at Hilton Works, 1981–1996*. Report to Local 1005, United Steelworkers of America, Ontario Institute for Studies in Education, Toronto.

– 1993. 'Working at Stelco: 'Re-Tayloring' Production Relations in the Eighties,' Pp. 13–53 in June Corman, Meg Luxton, David Livingstone, and Wally Seccombe (eds.), *Recasting Steel Labour: The Stelco Story*. Halifax: Fernwood.

– 1987. 'Job Skills and Schooling.' *Canadian Journal of Education* 12(1): 1–30.

Livingstone, D.W., and Elizabeth Asner. 1996. 'Feet in Both Camps: Household Classes, Divisions of Labour, and Group Consciousness.' Pp. 72–99 in D.W. Livingstone, and M. Mangan (eds.), *Recast Dreams: Class and Gender Consciousness in Steeltown*. Toronto: Garamond.

Livingstone, D.W., and Meg Luxton. 1989. 'Gender Consciousness at Work: Modification of the Male Breadwinner Norm among Steelworkers and Their Spouses.' *Canadian Review of Sociology and Anthropology* 26 (May), 240–75.

Livingstone, D.W., and Marshall Mangan. 1996. 'Men's Employment Classes and Class Consciousness: An Empirical Comparison of Marxist and Weberian Class Distinctions.' Pp. 15–51 in D.W. Livingstone and Marshall Mangan (eds.), *Recast Dreams: Class and Gender Consciousness in Steeltown*. Toronto: Garamond.

– 1993. 'Class, Gender, and Expanded Class Consciousness in Steeltown.' *Research in Social Movements, Conflicts, and Change* 15: 55–82.

– (eds.). 1996. *Recast Dreams: Class and Gender Consciousness in Steeltown*. Toronto: Garamond.

Livingstone, D.W., D. Hart, and L.E. Davie. 1997. *Public Attitudes towards Education in Ontario 1996: Twelfth OISE/UT Survey*. Toronto: University of Toronto Press.

Lopata, Helena. 1971. *Occupation: Housewife*. London: Oxford University Press.

Luxton, Meg. 1988. 'Family Coping Strategies: Balancing Paid Employment and Domestic Labour.' Pp. 403–20 in Bonnie Fox (ed.), *Family Bonds and Gender Divisions Readings in the Sociology of the Family*. Toronto: Oxford University Press.

– 1997a. 'Feminism and Families: The Challenge of Neo-Conservatism.'

Pp. 10–26 in Meg Luxton (ed.), *Feminism and Families: Critical Policies and Changing Practices*. Halifax:Fernwood.

- 1997b. "Nothing Natural about It": The Contradictions of Parenting.' Pp. 162–81 in Meg Luxton (ed.), *Feminism and Families: Critical Policies and Changing Practices*. Halifax: Fernwood.

- 1997c. 'The UN, Women, and Household Labour: Measuring and Valuing Unpaid Work.' *Women's Studies International Forum* 20(3): 431–9.

- 1993. 'Review.' *Signs* 19(1): 260–4.

- 1983. 'Two Hands for the Clock: Changing Patterns in the Gendered Division of Labour.' *Studies in Political Economy* 12: 27–44.

- 1980. *More than a Labour of Love: Three Generations of Women's Work in the Home*. Toronto: Women's Press.

Luxton, Meg, and June Corman. 1991. 'Getting to Work: The Challenge of the Women Back Into Stelco Campaign.' *Labour / le Travail* 28: 149–85.

Luxton, Meg, and Ester Reiter. 1997. 'Double, Double, Toil and Trouble ... Women's Experience of Work and Family in Canada 1980–1995.' Pp. 197–221 in Patricia Evans and Gerda Wekerle (eds.), *Women and the Canadian Welfare State: Challenges and Change*. Toronto: University of Toronto Press.

Luxton, Meg, Harriet Rosenberg, and Sedef Arat Koc. 1990. *Through the Kitchen Window: The Politics of Home and Family*. Toronto: Garamond.

Luxton, Meg, and Leah Vosko. 1998. 'Where Women's Efforts Count: The 1996 Census Campaign and "Family Politics" in Canada.' *Studies in Political Economy* 56(Summer): 49–81.

Macrury, Al. 1996. 'Stelco and Dofasco still Largest Single Employers.' *Hamilton Spectator*, 26 Feb.: B3.

Mandel, Ernest. 1977. *From Class Society to Communism*. London: Ink Links.

Mandell, Nancy. 1995. 'Family Histories.' Pp. 17–43 in Nancy Mandell and Ann Duffy (eds.), *Canadian Families: Diversity, Conflict and Change*. Toronto: Harcourt, Brace.

Maroney, Heather Jon. 1992. "Who Has the Baby?" Nationalism, Pronatalism and the Construction of Demographic Crisis in Quebec, 1960–1988.' *Studies in Political Economy* 39: 7–36.

Maroney, Heather Jon, and Meg Luxton. 1997. 'Gender at Work: Canadian Feminist Political Economy.' Pp. 85–117 in Wallace Clement (ed.), *Understanding Canada: Building on the New Political Economy*. Montreal and Kingston: McGill-Queen's University Press.

Martin, J. 1989. 'President's Comments.' *Steel Shots* (Dec.): 2.

- 1988. 'Dental Plan Restored.' *Steel Shots* (Oct.): 3.

Marx, Karl. 1977. *Selected Writings*. Oxford: Oxford University Press.

- [1867] 1976. *Capital*, vol. 1: *A Critique of Political Economy*. Reprint. London: Penguin Books.

Maurice, M. 1995. 'The French Steel Industry: Industrial Development and Social Regulation.' N.p. in A. Verma, A. Frost, and P. Warrian (eds.), *International Conference on Workplace Change: Human Resources and Rationalization in the Global Steel Industry. (Conference Papers).* Toronto; 5 and 6 June.

May, Martha. 1982. 'The Historical Problem of the Family Wage: The Ford Motor Company and the Five Dollar Day.' *Feminist Studies* 8: 406.

McCreadie, Malcolm. 1988. 'Overtime.' *Steel Shots* (July): 20.

McKnight, W.A. 1999. 'The Crazy Gang of Eight.' *Steel Shots* (Feb.)

McLeod, Catherine. 1999. 'Introduction.' Pp. 1–6 in Vincenzo Dietropaolo (ed.), *Celebration of Resistance: Ontario's Days of Action.* Toronto: Between the Lines.

McMahon, Anthony. 1999. *Taking Care of Men: Sexual Politics in the Public Mind.* Cambridge: Cambridge University Press.

McManus, G.J. 1988. 'Getting Down to One Manhour Per Ton.' *Iron Age* 3 Oct.: 34.

McQuaig, Linda. 1998. *The Cult of Impotence: Selling the Myth of Powerlessness in the Global Economy.* Toronto: Penguin.

– 1995. *Shooting Hippo: Death by Deficit and Other Canadian Myths.* Toronto: Viking.

– 1993. *The Wealthy Banker's Wife: The Assault on Equality in Canada.* Toronto: Penguin Books.

Meillassoux, Claude. 1979. 'Historical Modalities of the Exploitation and Over-exploitation of Labour.' *Critique of Anthropology* 4(13/14): 9–27.

Meissner, Martin. 1986. 'The Reproduction of Women's Domination in Organizational Communication' Pp. 51–67 in L. Thayer (ed.), *Organization – Communication: Emerging Perspectives* vol. 1. Norwood, NJ: Ablex.

Meissner, Martin, Elizabeth Humphries, Scot Meis, and William Scheu. 1975. 'No Exit for Wives: Sexual Division of Labour and the Culmination of Household Demands.' *Canadian Review of Sociology and Anthropology* 12(4): 424–39.

Michelson, William. 1985. *From Sun to Sun: Daily Obligations and Community Structure in the Lives of Employed Women and Their Families.* Totawa, NJ: Rowman and Allenheld.

Miller, Jack. 1984. 'Shift Work Could Tick Years off Your Life by Throwing the Body's Clock off Schedule.' *Toronto Star,* 24 Sept.: C20.

Mills, C. Wright. 1961. *The Sociological Imagination.* New York: Grove Press.

Mitchell, Alanna. 1997. 'Women's Evolving Role Confuses Canadians.' *Globe and Mail,* 17 Sept.: A1.

Mitchell, P. 1984. 'John Allan Takes Over a Streamlined Stelco.' *Hamilton Spectator,* 1 May.

Mitchell, P., and M. Wickers. 1982. 'Stelco 2001: Lake Erie May Overstream Aging Hilton.' *Hamilton Spectator,* 5 Jan.

Moloney, Joanne. 1986. 'Recent Industry Trends in Employment: Canada and the Provinces.' *The Labour Force.* Ottawa: Statistics Canada, 83–127.

Monture-Angus, Patricia. 1995. *Thunder in My Soul: A Mohawk Woman Speaks.* Halifax: Fernwood.

Morris, Lydia. 1990. *The Workings of the Household.* Cambridge: Polity Press.

Morrison, J. 1992. 'Opening the Books to Union Sets Precedent at Stelco.' *Hamilton Spectator,* 6 May: F5.

Municipality of Hamilton-Wentworth, Economic Development Department. 1980. *Directory and Buyers' Guide.* Hamilton: Alfin Publishers.

Nakhaie, M.R. 1995. 'Housework in Canada: The National Picture.' *Journal of Comparative Family Studies* 16(3): 409–25.

National Council of Welfare. 1989. *Budget and Social Policy.* Ottawa.

National Council of Welfare Preschool. 1999. *Children to Keep: A Report by the National Council of Welfare.* Ottawa: Minister of Public Works and Government Services.

Noce, Louise, and Anne O'Connell. 1998. *Take It or Leave It: The Ontario Government's Approach to Job Insecurity.* Ottawa: Caldeon Institute.

Oakley, Ann. 1974. *The Sociology of Housework.* Bath: Martin Robertson.

O'Brien, Dennis. 1989. 'Look at the Idea of Multicrafting.' *Steel Shots* (April): 20–1.

Oliker, Stacey. 1989. *Best Friends.* Berkeley: University of California Press.

Onions, C.T., (ed.). 1973. *The Shorter Oxford English Dictionary on Historical Principles.* Oxford: Clarendon Press.

Ontario Federation of Labour. 1979. *Minutes* (November).

Ontario Public Service Employees Union (OPSEU). 1979. *OPSEU News* 14(9):

Ontario Women's Directorate. 1990. *Work and Family: The Critical Balance.* Toronto: Ontario Women's Directorate.

Oren, Laura. 1974. 'The Welfare of Women in Labouring Families: England 1860–1950.' Pp. 226–44 in M. Hartman and L.W. Banner (eds.), *Clio's Consciousness Raised.* New York: Harper and Row.

Organization for Economic Co-operation and Development (OECD). 1987. Working Party of the Steel Committee. *Study of the Age Structure and Technical Qualifications of the Steel Industry Workforce.* Paris: OECD.

Packard, Steve. 1978. *Steelmill Blues.* San Piedro: Singlejack Books.

Pahl, Jan. 1989. *Money and Marriage.* Basingstok: Macmillan.

Palmer, Rodney. 1986. 'Stelco Workers Seek Medical Tests after PCB Scare at Hamilton plant.' *The Globe and Mail,* 20 Oct: A14.

Papp, L. 1993. 'Three-Year Deal Reached for 6,000 Workers at Stelco.' *Toronto Star,* 3 May: A10.

– 1991. 'Firm, Staff Not Guilty of Excess Overtime.' *Toronto Star,* 6 April: A10.

Parr, Joy. 1995. 'Shopping for a Good Stove: A Parable about Gender, Design and the Market.' Pp. 75–97 in Joy Parr (ed.), *A Diversity of Women: Ontario, 1945–1980*. Toronto: University of Toronto Press.

Peters. 1990. 'Looking Ahead.' *Steel Shots*. 4 Oct.: 3.

– 1980. 'Peters Report.' *Steel Shots*. Nov.: 2.

Petersen, J., and Robert Storey. 1986. *Final Report Prepared for Local 1005 on Technological Change*. Hamilton: McMaster University.

Philip, Margaret. 1995. 'Male–Female Income Gap Widens.' *Globe and Mail*, 20 Dec.: A10.

Phillips, Anne. 1987. *Divided Loyalties: Dilemmas of Sex and Class*. London: Virago.

Phipps, Shelley, and Peter Burton. 1995. 'Sharing within families: Implications for the measurement of poverty among individuals in Canada.' Paper presented at *Canadian Economics Association*. Feb.

Picchio, Antonella. 1992. *Social Reproduction: The political economy of the labour market*. Cambridge: Cambridge University Press.

Picot, Garnett, and Ted Wannell. 1987. 'Job Loss and Labour Market Adjustment in the Canadian Economy,' in *The Labour Force* (March): 85–135.

Pierson, Ruth, and Marjorie Cohen (eds.). 1995. *Canadian Women's Issues*. Vol. 2. *Bold Visions*. Toronto: Lorimer.

Pierson, Ruth, Marjorie Cohen, Paula Bourne, and Philinda Masters (eds.). 1993. *Canadian Women's Issues*. Vol. 1. *Strong Voices*. Toronto: Lorimer.

Pietropaolo, Vincenzo. 1999. *Celebration of Resistance: Ontario's Days of Action*. Toronto: Between the Lines.

Poling, David. 1996. 'Protest Shuts Down Factories.' *Hamilton Spectator*, 24 Feb.: B2.

Pollard, J.S. 1989. 'Gender and Manufacturing Employment: The Case of Hamilton.' *Area* 21(4): 377–84.

Porter, John. 1961. *The Vertical Mosaic*. Toronto: University of Toronto Press.

Prentice, Alison, Paula Bourne, Gail Cuthbert Brandt, Beth Light, Wendy Mitchinson, and Naomi Black. 1988. *Canadian Women: A History*. Toronto: Harcourt, Brace.

Prokaska, L. 1996a. 'How Stelco Deal with 1005 Died.' *Hamilton Spectator*, 4 April: A1.

– 1996b. 'Layoffs at Hilton Works.' *Hamilton Spectator*, 25 April: B1.

– 1996c. 'Local 1005 Backs Labour Protest.' *Hamilton Spectator*, 24 Jan.: B2.

– 1996d. 'Stelco Workers Irate over $1.68.' *Hamilton Spectator*, 29 March: C1.

Pulkingham, Jane. 1994. 'Private Troubles, Private Solutions: Poverty among Divorced Women and the Politics of Support Enforcement and Child Custody Determination.' *Canadian Journal of Law and Society* 9: 73–79.

Ralph, Diana, Andre Regimbald, and Neree St-Amand (eds.). 1997. *Mike Harris's Ontario Open for Business Closed to People*. Halifax: Fernwood.

Ram, Bali. n.d. 'Family Structure and Extra-Parental Child-Care Need in Canada: Some Projections.' Unpublished paper, Demographic Divisions, Statistics Canada.

– 1986. 'Women's Labour Force Participation in Canada: Socio-Demographic Aspects.' Paper presented at the Eleventh World Congress of Sociology, New Delhi, India.

Reid, Angus. 1987. *Canadians' Views of the Role of Women in Society.* Winnipeg: Angus Reid Associates.

Reiter, Ester. 1991. *Making Fast Food: From the Frying Pan into the Fryer.* 2nd ed. Montreal: McGill-Queen's University Press.

Revolutionary Workers' League. 1979. *RWL/LOR PanCanadian Preconvention Discussion Bulletin* 2(4).

Ricciutelli, Luciana, June Larkin, and Eimer O'Neill (eds.). 1998. *Confronting the Cuts: A Sourcebook for Women in Ontario.* Toronto: Inanna Publications and Education.

Rich, Adrienne. 1980. 'Compulsory Heterosexuality and Lesbian Experience.' *Signs* 5(4): 631–60.

Roberts, W., (ed.). 1981. *Baptism of a Union: Stelco Strike of 1946.* Hamilton: Labour Studies Program, McMaster University.

Robinson, J.P. 1977. *How Americans Use Time: A Social-Psychological Analysis.* New York: Praeger.

Rodrigues, Denyse. 1990. 'The Relationship between Women's Employment Status and the Participation in Local Neighbourhoods: The Case of Hamilton Steelworker Households.' Master's research paper, Department of Geography, York University.

Rosenberg, Harriet. 1990. 'The Kitchen and the Multinational Corporation: An Analysis of the Links between the Household and Global Corporations.' Pp. 123–50 in Meg Luxton, Harriet Rosenberg, and Sedef Arat Koc. (eds.), *Through the Kitchen Window: The Politics of Home and Family.* Toronto: Garamond.

Rowbotham, Sheila. 1997. *A Century of Women: The History of Women in the United States and Britain.* London: Viking.

– 1992. *Women in Movement: Feminism and Social Action.* London: Routledge.

Rubin, Gayle. 1975. 'The Traffic in Women: Notes on the Political Economy of Sex.' Pp. 157–210 in Rayna Reiter (ed.), *Toward an Anthropology of Women.* New York: Monthly Review Press.

Rubin, Lillian. 1994. *Families on the Fault Line: America's Working Class Speaks about the Family, the Economy, Race, and Ethnicity.* New York: Harper Collins.

– 1985. *Just Friends.* New York: Harper and Row.

– 1977. *Worlds of Pain: Life in the Working-Class Family.* New York: Basic Books.

Sanger, M. 1988. 'Transforming the Elements: The Reorganization of Work and Learning at Stelco's Hilton Works.' Master's thesis, University of Toronto.

Schor, J. 1991. *The Overworked American: The Unexpected Decline in Leisure.* New York: Basic Books.

Schultz, Julianne. 1985. *Steel City Blues.* Ringwood, Australia: Penguin.

Scott, Emily. 1998. 'The Effects of the Cuts on Poor Women and Their Families in Thunder Bay.' Pp. 120–3 in Luciana Ricciutelli, June Larkin, and Eimer O'Neill (eds.), *Confronting the Cuts: A Sourcebook for Women in Ontario.* Toronto: Inanna Publications and Education.

Seccombe, Wally. 1992. *A Millennium of Family Change: Feudalism to Capitalism in Northwestern Europe.* London: Verso.

– 1986. 'Marxism and Demography: Household Forms and Fertility Regimes in the Western European Transition.' Pp. 23–55 in James Dickinson and Bob Russell (eds.), *Family, Economy and State: The Social Reproduction Process Under Capitalism.* Toronto: Garamond.

– 1974. 'The Housewife and Her Labour under Capitalism.' *New Left Review* (Jan.–Feb.) 83: 2–24.

Seccombe, Wally, and D.W. Livingstone. 2000. *'Down to Earth People': Beyond Class Reductionism and Postmodernism.* Aurora, ON: Garamond.

– 1996. '"Down to Earth People": Revising a Materialist Understanding of Group Consciousness.' Pp. 131–94 in David Livingstone, and Marshall Mangan (eds.), *Recast Dreams: Class and Gender Consciousness in Steeltown.* Toronto: Garamond.

Sharpe, Sue. 1984. *Double Identity: The Lives of Working Mothers.* London: Penguin.

Shaw, Susan M. 1992. 'Introduction: Feminine Perspectives on Leisure.' *Society and Leisure* 15(1): 17–20.

– 1988. 'Gender Differences in the Definition and Perception of Household Labour.' *Family Relations* 37: 333–7.

– 1985. 'The Meaning of Leisure in Everyday Life.' *Leisure Sciences* 7(1): 1–24.

Shaw, Susan, Arend Bonen, and John McCabe. 1991. 'Do More Constraints Mean Less Leisure? Examining the Relationship between Constraints and Participation.' *Journal of Leisure Research* 23(4): 286–300.

Shilling, Chris. 1993. *The Body and Social Theory.* Thousand Oaks, Calif.: Sage.

Side, Katherine. 1997. 'In the Shadow of the Family: Women's Friendships with Women.' Unpublished doctoral dissertation, York University.

Skrypnek, Berna, and Janet Fast. 1996. 'Work and Family Policy in Canada: Family Needs, Collective Solutions.' *Journal of Family Issues* 17(6): 793–812.

Social Planning and Research Council of Hamilton-Wentworth (SPRC). 1999. *Understanding Youth Unemployment in the Hamilton-Wentworth HRDC Management Area.* Hamilton-Wentworth: SPRC.

– 1993. Tracking Community Trends in Hamilton-Wentworth. Hamilton-Wentworth: SPRC.

– 1987. *Social Trends in Hamilton-Wentworth: An Update.* Hamilton: SPRC.

Spenner, K. 1983. 'Deciphering Prometheus: Temporal Change in the Skill Level of Work.' *American Sociological Review* 48(6): 824–7.

Springer, Jane. 1997. *Listen to Us: The World's Working Children.* Toronto: Roundwood.

Stacey, Judith. 1990. *Brave New Families: Stories of Domestic Upheaval in Late Twentieth Century America.* Santa Clara, Calif.: Basic Books.

Stasiulis, Daiva, and Nira Yuval-Davis. 1995. *Unsettling Settler Societies: Articulations at Gender, Race, Ethnicity and Class.* Thousand Oaks, Calif.: Sage.

Statistics Canada. 2000. *Canadian Social Trends,* issue no. 56. Catalogue no. H11-008, Spring.

– 1998. *Daily Catalogue.* 11-001E (17 March).

– 1997a. 'Age, Sex, Marriage Status and Common Law: Canada, Provinces and Territories.' Electronic media release, 14 Oct.

– 1997b. *Labour Force: Update.* Cat. no. 71-005-XPB.

– 1997c. *Perspectives on Labour and Income.* Cat. no. 75-1-SPE.

– 1996 Census. www.statcan.ca/english/Pgdb/ People/Population/demo28f./htm

– 1996a. *Labour Force: Annual Averages.* Cat. no. 71 220 XPB.

– 1996b. *Family Violence in Canada: A Statistical Profile.* Cat. no. 8X-224-XIE.

– 1995a. *Historical Labour Force Statistics.* Cat. no. 71-201.

– 1995b. *Women in Canada: A Statistical Report.* 3rd ed. Cat. no. 89-503E.

– 1993. 'Employed Parents and the Division of Housework.' *Perspectives on Labour and Income.* Ottawa: Minister of Industry.

– 1978–96. *Labour Force.* Cat. no. 71-001.

– 1992. *Profile of census tracts in Hamilton, Part A.* Publication no. 95-341.

– 1989a. *Earnings of Men and Women.* Cat. no 13217 annual.

– 1989. *Catalogue Characteristics of Dual Earner Families.* Publication no. 13-215.

– 1985. *Quarterly Estimates of Population for Canada and Provinces.* Publication no. 91-001.

– 1983a. *Consumer Prices and Price Indexes.* Oct.–Dec. Cat. no. 62-010.

– 1983b. *Employment, Earnings and Hours.* Publication no. 72-002.

– 1982. *Family Expenditure in Canada.* Cat. No. 62-555.

Status of Women. 1997. *Economic Gender Equality Indicators.* Canada: Federal–Provincial / Territorial Ministers Responsible for the Status of Women.

Steel Shots. 1987. 'Contracting Out Committee.' (Jan.–Feb.): 8.

– 1986. Anniversary Issue (July).

Stelco. 1989, 1995. *Annual Report.* Hamilton: Stelco.

– 1989, 1996. *Hilton Works Personnel Reports* (Oct. 1989 and Nov. 1996).

– 1989. *Steel Turnover Report* (6 Oct.).

Stelco–Local 1005 Tentative Agreement. 1996, April.

Stelco–Local 1005 Basic Agreement. 1993, 20 July.

Stewart, Katie. 1981. 'The Marriage of Capitalist and Patriarchal Ideologies: Meanings of Male Bonding and Male Ranking in U.S. Culture.' Pp. 269–311 in Lydia Sargent (ed.), *Women and Revolution*. Boston: South End Press.

Storey, Robert. 1994. 'The Struggle for Job Ownership in the Canadian Steel Industry: An Historical Analysis.' *Labour / Le Travail* 33(Spring): 75–106.

– 1993. 'Making Steel under Free Trade.' *Relations Industrielles / Industrial Relations.* 48(4): 712–30.

– 1987. 'The Struggle to Organize Stelco and Dofasco.' *Relations Industrielles / Industrial Relations.* 42(2): 366–84.

– 1981a. 'Workers, Unions and Steel: The Shaping of the Hamilton Working Class.' Doctoral dissertation, University of Toronto.

– 1981b. 'The Dofasco Way.' Pp. 145–8 in Craig Heron, Shea Hoffmitz, Wayne Roberts, and Robert Storey (eds.). *All that Our Hands Have Done*. Oakville: Mosaic Press.

Storey, R., and J. Petersen. 1987. *The Impact of Technology at Hilton Works*. Ottawa: Labour Canada.

Strasser, Susan. 1982. *Never Done: A History of American Housework*. New York: Pantheon.

Strauss, Marina. 1996. 'Men Getting Scarce in Grocery Stores.' *Globe and Mail,* 23 Oct.: B5.

Strong-Boag, Veronica. 1988. *The New Day Recalled: Lives of Girls and Women in English Canada, 1919–1939*. Markham, Ont.: Penguin.

– 1986. 'Pulling in Double Harness or Hauling a Double Load: Women, Work and Feminism on the Canadian Prairies.' *Journal of Canadian Studies* 21(3): 32–52.

Sugiman, Pamela. 1994. *Labour's Dilemma: The Gender Politics of Auto Workers in Canada, 1937–1979*. Toronto: University of Toronto Press.

Sutherland, Ed. 1985. 'Editorial Comment,' *Steel Shots* (Dec.): 2.

Swinamer, Janet. 1982. 'The Value of Household Work in Canada, 1981.' *Canadian Statistical Review* (March). Ottawa: Statistics Canada, Cat. no. 11-003E.

Szalai, A., (ed.). 1972. *The Use of Time: Daily Activities of Urban and Suburban Populations in Twelve Countries*. The Hague: Mouton.

Targ, Dena, and Carolyn Perrucci. 1990. 'Plant Closings: Unemployment and Families.' *Marriage and Family Review* 15(3–4): 131–45.

Taylor, C. 1982. 'Equal Partners.' *Steel Shots* (Jan.): 1.

Teghtsoonian, Katherine. 1993. 'Work and/or Motherhood: The Ideological Construction of Women's Option in Canadian Child Care Policy Debates.' *Canadian Journal of Women and the Law* 8(2): 411–39.

Toronto Star. 1998. 'Stelco Chief's Pay up 64% Last Year.' 2 April 2, D3.

– 1996. 'Pay Packets Fatter, as Job Ranks Shrink.' 30 Aug., E3.

Ursel, Jane. 1992. *Private Lives, Public Policy.* Toronto: Women's Press.

Vanek, Joanne. 1974. 'Time Spent in Housework.' *Scientific American* 231: 116–20.

Van Harten, Peter. 1979a. 'Stelco Hires Women for Plant Jobs.' *Hamilton Spectator,* 1 Nov.: 7.

– 1979b. 'Stelco's Woman MD Has Men Red-Faced.' *Hamilton Spectator,* 16 Aug.: 7.

Vanier Institute of the Family. 1996. *Transitions* (March).

Verma, Anil, Ann Frost, and Peter Warrian. 1995. 'Workplace Restructuring and Employment Relations in the Canadian Steel Industry' In A. Verma, A. Frost, and P. Warrian (eds.), *International Conference on Workplace Change: Human Resources and Rationalization in the Global Steel Industry* Conference Papers. Toronto, 5 and 6 June.

Villa, P. 1987. 'Systems of Flexible Working in the Italian Steel Industry.' Pp. 307–41 in R. Tarling (ed.), *Flexibility in Labour Markets.* Toronto: Academic Press.

Vosko, Leah. 2000. *Temporary Work: The Gendered Rise of a Precarious Employment Relationship.* Toronto: University of Toronto Press.

Walker, James. 1995. 'No Retreat at the Revolution.' *Financial Post,* 19 Aug. 7.

Walkerdine, Valerie, and Helen Lucey. 1989. *Democracy in the Kitchen: Regulating Mothers and Socialising Daughters.* London: Virago.

Wardoch, J. 1986. 'Wardoch Report.' *Steel Shots* (5 Jan.): 2.

Waring, Marilyn. 1988. *If Women Counted: A New Feminist Economics.* San Francisco: Harper Collins.

Warrian, Peter. 1989. 'Industrial Restructuring, Occupational Shifts and Skills: The Steel and Manufacturing Cases.' Background Paper prepared for Study Team Two, Colleges and the Changing Economy, Vision 2000, Ontario Council of Regents.

Wearing, B.M. 1990. 'Leisure: The Crisis of Motherhood.' Pp. 122–55 In S. Quah (ed.), *The Family: An Asset.* Singapore: Time Academic Press.

Weaver, John. 1982. *Hamilton: An Illustrated History.* Toronto: Lorimer.

Webber, Michael, and Ruth Fincher. 1987. 'Urban Policy in Hamilton in the 1980s.' Pp. 238–57 in M.J., Dear, J.J. Drake, and L.G. Reeds (eds.), *Steel City: Hamilton and Region.* Toronto: University of Toronto Press.

Webber, M. 1986. 'Regional Production and the Production of Regions: The

Case of Steeltown.' Pp. 197–224 in A Scott and M. Stroper (eds.), *Production, Work, Territory: The Geographical Anatomy of Industrial Capitalism.* Boston: Allen and Unwin.

Weldon, Faye. 1990. *Darcy's Utopia.* London: Collins.

Wellman, Barry. 1999. 'From Little Boxes to Loosely Bounded Networks: The Privatization and Domestication of Community.' Pp. 94–114 in Janet L. Abu-Lughod (ed.), *Sociology for the 21st Century: Continuities and Cutting Edges.* Chicago: University of Chicago Press.

– 1992. 'Men in Networks: Private Communities, Domestic Friendships.' Pp. 74–114 in Peter Norch (ed.), *Men's Friendships.* Newbury Park, Calif.: Sage.

– 1988. 'The Community Question Re-Evaluated.' *Comparative Urban and Community Research* 1: 81–107.

– 1985. 'Domestic Work, Paid Work and Network.' Pp. 159–61 in S. Duck and D. Perlman (eds.), *Understanding Personal Relationships: An Interdisciplinary Approach.* Beverly Hills: Sage.

Wernick, Andrew. 1991. *Promotional Culture.* Newbury Park, Calif.: Sage.

Westell, D. 1992. 'Stelco Local Waves Olive Branch.' *Globe and Mail,* 2 April: B2.

White, Julie. 1993. *Sisters and Solidarity: Women and Unions in Canada.* Toronto: Thompson Educational Publishing.

Williams, Claire. 1993. 'Class, Gender and the Body: The Occupational Health and Safety Concerns of Blue Collar Workers in the South Australian Timber Industry.' Pp. 57–91 in Michael Quinlan (ed.), *Work and Health: The Origins, Management and Regulation of Occupational Illness,* South Melborne: Macmillan Education.

Williams, Raymond. 1983. *Keywords: A Vocabulary of Culture and Society.* London: Fontana Press.

Willis, Paul. 1979. 'Shop-Floor Culture, Masculinity and the Wage Form' Pp. 155–94 in J. Clake, C. Critcher, and R. Johnson (eds.), *Working Class Culture: Studies in History and Theory.* London: Hutcheson.

Willis, Susan. 1991. *A Primer for Daily Life.* London: Routledge.

Wimbush, Erica. 1986. *Women, Leisure and Well-Being.* Edinburgh: Centre for Leisure Research.

Womack, J.P., D. Jones, and D. Ross. 1990. *The Machine That Changed the World.* New York: Rawson Associates.

Women Bank Into Stelco Committee. 1980. *Press Release,* 26 March. Hamilton: USWA Local 1005.

Wood, Harold. 1987. 'The Emergence of the Modern City: Hamilton, 1891–1950.' Pp. 119–37 in M.J. Dear, J.J. Drake, and L.G. Reeds (eds.), *Steel City: Hamilton and Region.* Toronto: University of Toronto Press.

Wood, S., (ed.). 1989. *The Transformation of Work?* London: Unwin Hyman.

Woods, Gordon, and Co. 1977. *Hamilton-Wentworth Steel and Related Industries.* Toronto: Woods, Gordon.

Wright, Erik Olin. 1997. *Class Counts: Comparative Studies in Class Analysis.* Cambridge: University of Cambridge Press.

Yalnizyan, Armine. 1998. *The Growing Gap: A Report on Growing Inequality between the Rich and poor in Canada.* Toronto: Centre for Social Justice.

Index